Friends in High Places

WE WON'T HAVE HOME RULE

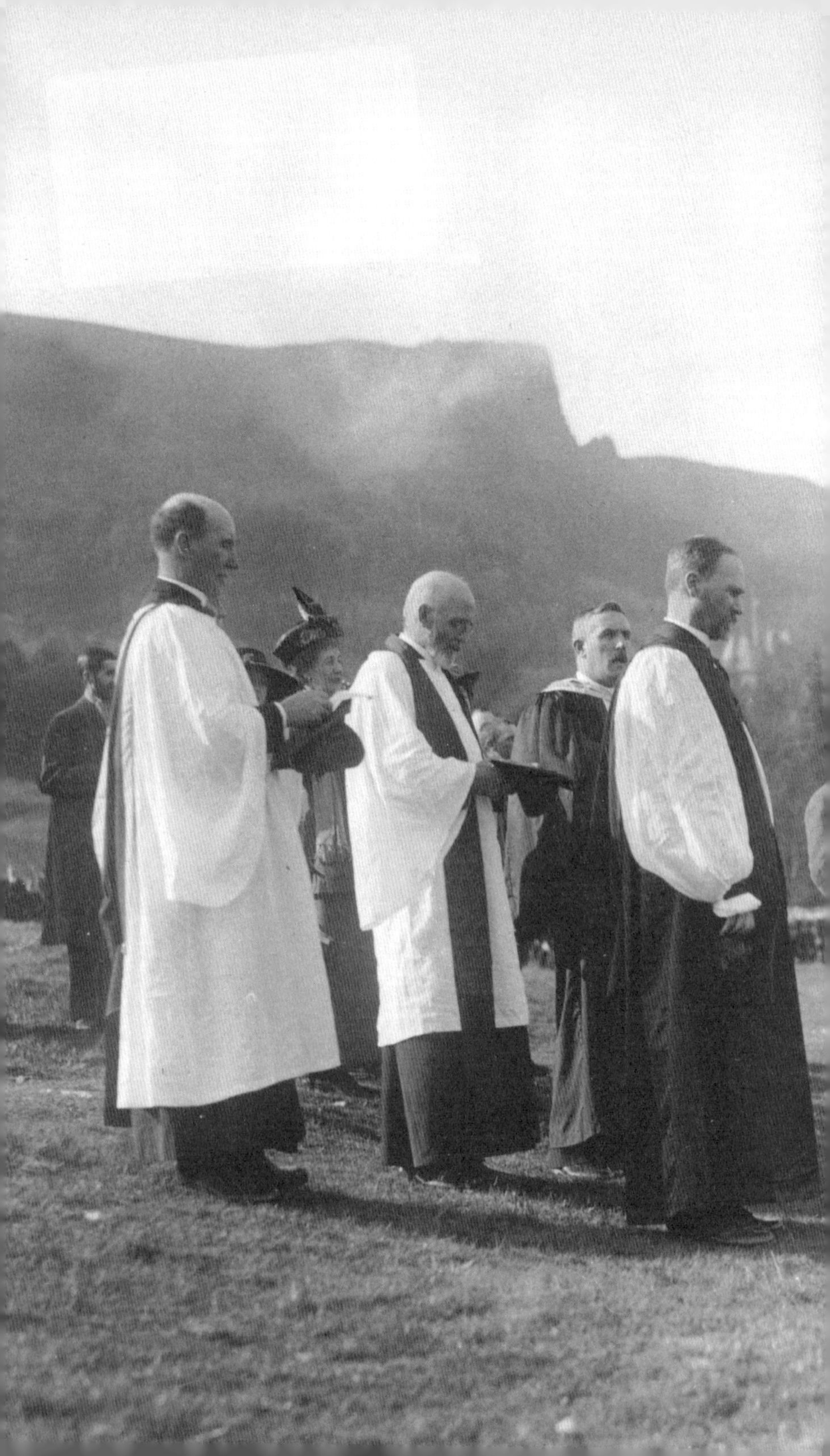

Friends in High Places

Ulster's resistance to Irish Home Rule,
1912–14

ALAN F. PARKINSON

ULSTER HISTORICAL FOUNDATION

This book has received financial support from the Northern Ireland Community Relations Council which aims to promote a pluralist society characterised by equity, respect for diversity and recognition of interdependence. The views expressed do not necessarily reflect those of the Council.

First published 2012
Ulster Historical Foundation
49 Malone Road, Belfast BT9 6RY

Except as otherwise permitted under the Copyright, Designs and Patents Act 1988, this publication may only be reproduced, stored or transmitted in any form or by any means with the prior permission in writing of the publisher or, in the case of reprographic reproduction, in accordance with the terms of a licence issued by The Copyright Licensing Agency. Enquiries concerning reproduction outside those terms should be sent to the publisher.

© Ulster Historical Foundation, 2012
ISBN 978-1-908448-52-1

Printed by Berforts Group Ltd
Design by Dunbar Design

Contents

List of illustrations	vi
Acknowledgements	vii
Foreword	ix
1 Prologue	1
2 Danger looms	9
3 Community resistance	68
4 Friends in high places	152
5 The tide turns	232
6 Epilogue	293
Appendix 1	313
Appendix 2	316
Notes	320
Index	331

List of illustrations

FRONTISPIECE: Blessing the colours of the Volunteers, Belfast Castle, April 1914

1	Edward Carson addresses a loyalist rally	1
2	Bonar Law arrives at Balmoral, April 1912	9
3	Crowds gather outside Belfast City Hall on Covenant Day, September 1912	68
4	Parading at Narrow Water Castle, County Down, 1913	152
5	Sir Edward Carson inspecting UVF ranks	232
6	The UVF march past Belfast's City Hall, May 1915	293

Picture section

1. Propaganda poster: 'We won't have Home Rule'
2. Sir Edward Carson briefing news reporters at Craigavon, September 1912
3. Carson alongside Colonel Wallace, on their way to a Covenant meeting, September 1912
4. Covenant Day scene, Belfast, September 1912
5. Arrival of the leaders at the City Hall, September 1912
6. Text of the Covenant
7. Edward Carson signing the Covenant, September 1912
8. Donegall Place, Belfast under Home Rule, postcard
9. 'Ulster's Prayer – Don't Let Go!', postcard
10. 'There's many a slip ...', *Punch* cartoon, 1 April 1914
11. 'No Home Rule!' propaganda postcard
12. 'The Ulster king-at-arms', *Punch*, 6 May 1914
13. Inspection by the leader
14. Drilling members of the UVF, County Tyrone, July 1913
15. Edward Carson addressing the massed ranks of the UVF at Balmoral, September 1913
16. UVF lining up for parade at Fortwilliam, north Belfast, September 1913
17. Unloading the guns at Donaghadee, postcard, April 1914
18. UVF gun-running, Bangor, postcard, April 1914
19. Inspection of UVF nursing staff, 1914
20. Ulster Volunteers on the march
21. Edward Carson addressing Orangemen, 1914
22. Edward Carson inspecting UVF personnel at the Ulster Hall, Belfast, July 1914

Acknowledgements

I would like to express my gratitude to representatives of a number of organisations and to several individuals who assisted me during a three-year period of research for this book. Staff at the various libraries I visited in Northern Ireland and Great Britain were courteous and helpful. In Belfast, I found the Northern Ireland Political Collection (pre-1960 section) at the Linen Hall Library invaluable and would like to thank staff there for their support (especially John Killen for his advice on the political cartoons of this period). Further help was given at the Belfast Central Library (particularly its newspaper section) and at the Public Record Office of Northern Ireland.

In England, I visited the Imperial War Museum (where Sir Henry Wilson's papers are housed), the House of Lords Record Office (where I consulted the Bonar Law and Willoughby de Broke papers), the British Newspaper Library at Colindale in London and the Bodleian Library in Oxford (where I gained access to the Milner papers). Funding for my travel and accommodation was provided by Northern Ireland's Department of Culture, Arts and Leisure, and I would like to give thanks to Nelson McCausland and Paul Sweeney for their assistance. Additional funding for my travel in England and for the purchase of reproduction rights for most of the images in this book was provided by the Taoiseach's Office in Dublin, and I would like to thank John Kennedy and Eimear Healy for their help. Thanks also must go to Ray Mullan and his colleagues from the Northern Ireland Community Relations Council for their promotion of this book (through the Decade of Anniversaries lecture series) and for financial assistance provided to aid publication. PRONI were especially helpful, granting me access to important textual material and illustrations (especially from the Ulster Unionist Council archives) and providing advice on copyright and reproduction of several of these. I would like to acknowledge the help of Aileen McLintock, David Huddleston,

Stephen Scarth and Ian Montgomery and I am grateful to the deputy keeper of records and the various depositors for allowing me to quote from some of these sources.

The bulk of the illustrations in this book are photographs from the *Belfast Telegraph*'s archives and I am obliged to that paper for facilitating their reproduction here (especially to Paul Carson, the *Telegraph*'s ever-helpful librarian). Two further illustrations have been used and I would like to thank *Punch* magazine for forwarding these cartoons and for granting me permission to reproduce them.

I have also received assistance and support from many individuals. Academics who have helped me include Professor D.G. Boyce, Professor Graham Walker and Dr Éamon Phoenix. Éamon has been particularly generous with his time and effort. I would like to thank Fintan Mullan, William Roulston, and Tim Smyth of the Ulster Historical Foundation; the designer Wendy Dunbar of Dunbar Design; and the copyeditor Alicia McAuley, for their professionalism during the editing and design stage of this work.

Finally, I would like to express my thanks to my family for their moral and practical support over the last three years. This book is dedicated to Janet, Nick, Katherine and Tom.

Foreword

Éamon Phoenix

This is a meticulously researched and cogent analysis, which places the Ulster unionist struggle against the Third Home Rule Bill in its wider British context. It takes as its start-point A.T.Q. Stewart's brilliant, if uncritical, 1967 classic, *The Ulster crisis*,[1] but pushes the boundaries out to highlight the centrality of the 'Ulster question' to the British Conservative Party's political ambitions in a period when Protestant sentiment and imperial pride were still strong in Britain.

Dr Parkinson's book promises to catch the tide of interest in the centenary of Ulster's Solemn League and Covenant and the rise of the Ulster Volunteer Force during 1913–14 and will be a viewed as a new and major study of a key moment in Irish and British history. Drawing on (often untapped) primary sources, the author assesses the range and strength of unionism's British backers, from the Tory establishment and its political leader, Andrew Bonar Law, to the military élite associated with Sir Henry Wilson, the Conservative press and the 'salon diplomacy' of Lady Londonderry. In addition, the significant parts played by King George V – notably in the 1914 Buckingham Palace conference – the imperialist Lord Milner, Geoffrey Robinson of *The Times* and others are fully explored.

The author also assesses the Ulster unionist propaganda campaign in Great Britain and analyses the nature of Edward Carson's 'tours' of major British towns and cities in 1912 and 1913.

New light is shed on the critical role played in the mobilisation of Ulster Protestant and British resistance to the Third Home Rule Bill by Edward Carson and his astute Belfast ally, James Craig. Carson was an archetypal Irish unionist with deep roots among the Dublin Protestant upper-middle classes and the Cromwellian gentry of County Galway. His original aim was to use the north-east with its Protestant strength and industrial might to 'kill Home Rule stone dead'. For the Dublin lawyer, Ulster was a weapon, never a cause, and it was with a sense of reluctant resignation in 1913 that he bowed to the inevitability of partition as the only means of averting Dublin rule in the north. Yet this 'lawyer with a Dublin accent' was haunted to his dying day by his failure to save his 'own people' – the 'abandoned' Protestants of the Irish Free State after 1922.

Carson's bitterness welled up during the debate on the Anglo-Irish Treaty in the House of Lords in 1921, when he denounced his former Conservative allies:

> What a fool I was. I was only a puppet, and so was Ulster, and so was Ireland in the political game that was to get the Conservative Party into power.[2]

For Carson's Ulster-based deputy, James Craig – a product both of Belfast's nineteenth-century industrial revolution and of the Orange revival after 1886 – the concept of a separate Ulster 'homeland' outside the nationalist 'Pale' had always exerted a powerful appeal. As early as 1905, Craig, along with his brother Charles and other middle-class unionists, had wrenched northern unionism from the dead hand of landlordism and set up the more broad-based – and implicitly partitionist – Ulster Unionist Council. It would be a short step from this amalgam of unionism's component parts to the provisional government of 1913 and the Northern Ireland parliament of 1921.[3]

Yet there can be no doubt that it was Carson, with his immense political and legal standing, rather than the signally uncharismatic Craig, who gave the anti-Home Rule cause a stature and status within Britain that it was never to enjoy again after 1914.

This is an account of a period in the recent history of the north of Ireland that has acquired an iconic, almost mythical status in the Ulster Protestant tradition. As such, it provides new insights into the communal mindset, sense of identity and alarm of the northern Irish unionist community when they were faced with the looming reality of a Roman Catholic and nationalist-dominated Irish parliament and government.

For high Tories like F.E. Smith (Lord Birkenhead), Home Rule not only threatened to place Irish Protestants under the thraldom of their 'hereditary enemies', but also heralded the disintegration of the empire. As the historian David Dutton has argued, the 'drastic' policy pursed by the Tories under Bonar Law during 1912–14 was to strain the bonds of the British constitution to the limit.[4]

Within Ireland, north and south, the great mass of nationalists under the moderate leadership of John Redmond and his Belfast lieutenant, 'Wee Joe' Devlin, had confidently expected the Liberal alliance of 1910 to deliver Home Rule for a 32-county Ireland. At Home Rule meetings throughout Ireland the Union Jack flew routinely alongside the green flag emblazoned with the harp.

Redmond, to a much greater extent than most of his party colleagues, was firmly committed to both self-government and 'imperial strength'. A parliamentarian *par excellence*, as his biographer Denis Gwynn asserts, Redmond was shocked by the militant response of Ulster unionism and its Conservative allies. 'There are things stronger than parliamentary majorities,' Bonar Law intoned darkly at a unionist rally at Blenheim in 1912.

At first, the Ulster Volunteer Force (UVF) were dismissed by the Home Rulers as 'Carson's comic circus', while the nationalist *Irish News* ridiculed the claim of Craig's provisional government to have 'conquered Ulster', a feat which 'that valiant warrior' John de Courcy had failed to achieve in Anglo-Norman times. Devlin, the astute populist MP for west Belfast and the Irish Nationalist Party's northern expert, assured Redmond and Liberal ministers that the danger of civil war was 'grotesquely exaggerated' and regarded by northern Home Rulers 'with absolute contempt'.[5] He alleged the existence of a large, silent body of Protestant Home Rulers in the north. However, although several hundred prominent Protestant Liberals (including the outspoken Presbyterian divine Rev. J.B. Armour of Ballymoney and Lord Pirrie, managing director of the Belfast shipyard) proclaimed their support for a Dublin parliament, they represented only a miniscule section of Ulster Protestantism. Nonetheless, they devised their own counter-covenant in favour of Home Rule. In boldly ecumenical terms and quasi-religious language not dissimilar to the mainstream unionist document, they declared:

> We, the undersigned, Ulster Protestant men and women ... hereby repudiate the claim of Sir Edward Carson to represent the united Protestant opinion of Ulster, reject the doctrine of armed resistance and declare our abhorrence of the attempt to revive ancient hatreds and dying habits in Ulster.
>
> We desire to live upon terms of friendship and equality with our Roman Catholic fellow-countrymen and in the event of the present measure for the Better Government of Ireland becoming law, we are prepared to take our part with them in working for the good of our common country.[6]

In October 1913, Armour, Sir Roger Casement (then still a constitutional nationalist) and other Irish Protestants held a meeting in Ballymoney Town Hall in favour of Irish self-government. This was to be the last Ulster Protestant protest against the proposal to partition Ireland.

While Herbert Asquith and the Liberal Party forced the nationalists to acquiesce to some form of exclusion 'as the price of peace' by 1914, Carson's methods, his formation of the illegal UVF and the subsequent Larne gun-running had a catastrophic impact on Irish nationalism. As the historian Michael Laffan has noted, in rejecting the right of the British parliament to impose a Dublin assembly on the north-east, Carson effectively, if unwittingly, 'rekindled the Fenian flame' of revolutionary nationalism.[7]

Eoin MacNeill, Antrim glensman, cultural nationalist and founder of the National Volunteers, welcomed the UVF in 'The North Began', an influential 1913 article in the Gaelic League journal *An Claidheamh Soluis*. He even called for 'three cheers for Carson' at a rally in Cork. (Admittedly, his risky injunction to the assembled Home Rulers provoked not three cheers but three chairs hurled at the platform!) The result of Carson's example was the launch of the 'defensive' National Volunteers 'to assert Ireland's rights' in November of the same year.

The militarisation of Ulster unionism in these years drew admiration from the shadowy world of the Irish Republican

Brotherhood (IRB), which had undergone a revival after 1904 by a group of northern 'young Turks' – among them Bulmer Hobson, Denis McCullough and Ernest Blythe and the veteran Ulster Fenian, Thomas J. Clarke. For the Belfast-born Quaker and IRB leader Bulmer Hobson, Carson had opened a revolutionary door to a republican insurrection when 'England's difficulty' might once again – as in 1798 – afford 'Ireland's opportunity'.

By 1914, Carson's rejection of the Asquithian compromise of 'county option' signalled a lurch into anarchy that was only arrested by the onset of the First World War in August 1914. The UVF gun-running of April 1914, together with the Curragh 'incident', exposed the intrinsic weakness of the Liberal government and led to a radical change in the balance of power in Ireland. Military supremacy now lay with the UVF, while the growth of the IRB-influenced National Volunteers under MacNeill meant that any collision between these rival forces might result in civil war.

By the eve of the Great War, the National Volunteers – now under Redmond's nominal control – had mushroomed to 170,000 men, a quarter of them concentrated in Ulster. The mood of the nationalist majorities west of the Bann in the midst of the crisis was captured by the Royal Irish Constabulary county inspector for Tyrone who reported in March 1914: 'The nationalists are disquieted by recent events and think they must have an army of their own.'[8]

In a final effort to break the impasse, King George V convened the abortive Buckingham Palace conference of 21–24 July 1914. This involved John Redmond and John Dillon in protracted negotiations with Herbert Asquith and David Lloyd George, representing the government, Andrew Bonar Law and Lord Lansdowne, representing the Conservatives, and Edward Carson and James Craig, representing the Ulster unionists. In the event, discussion focused on the 'acreage' question; the more critical issue of 'temporary v permanent exclusion' was never addressed. While Redmond insisted on the 'county option' – effectively a four-county partition – Carson revealed his 'irreducible minimum': the proposition that a six-county bloc (the present territory of

Northern Ireland) should be permanently excluded from the remit of the Home Rule Act. Though repudiated by the Home Rule leaders, this would prove a portentous development in the evolution of partition. By June 1916, in the changed circumstances following the Easter Rising, Redmond and Devlin would persuade a stunned conference of northern nationalists to vote for the (allegedly 'temporary') exclusion of six counties from Home Rule. The consequences for northern nationalism and the Home Rule party were ultimately calamitous.

The failure of the Buckingham Palace negotiations was at once overtaken by the outbreak of the Great War, an event marked by what the police called 'a mutual cessation of political strife' in Ireland as both Redmond and Carson pledged unequivocal support for Britain's war effort. The Irish leader's success in forcing a reluctant prime minister to place the Home Rule Act on the statute book was to prove a hollow victory, however. Not only was its operation suspended for the duration of the war, but Asquith also made it clear that any final settlement must include partition.

As Carson's Volunteers enlisted in the Thirty-Sixth Ulster Division and hastened to the battlefields of Europe, Redmond – ever the imperialist – made his great mistake in September 1914 by urging nationalists to enlist in the British Army. Many nationalists deeply mistrusted the British government over its failure to implement Home Rule and the show of force against the Howth gun-runners that July. As a direct result of Redmond's speech, the National Volunteers split. While the bulk joined the rush to the colours, a small anti-war section broke away under MacNeill. This element – 11,000 strong – now passed under the control of the IRB, who were to use it as the strike-force of the rising they were determined to bring about before the global conflict had ended.

The war was accompanied by a 'party truce'. Some 200,000 Irishmen from both traditions would serve in the conflict. Of these, some 49,000 from north and south would make the supreme sacrifice. In Ulster the bulk of the Catholic population remained loyal to constitutional nationalism right up to partition and beyond. Republican activism was very much a minority and highly localised pursuit in the north. Thus, while 130 pro-republican Volunteers mustered at Coalisland, County Tyrone at Easter 1916 in an ill-starred mobilisation, some 3,000 west-Belfast Catholics joined the Connaught Rangers in the First World War at the behest of their MP, Joe Devlin, head of the 120,000-strong Ancient Order of Hibernians.[9]

An early casualty of the war was Dr Hugh McNally, a Falls Road doctor and commander of the Redmondite National Volunteers, who perished on the HMS *Hampshire* along with Lord Kitchener in 1916.

Whatever the future held for Home Rule and unionism, the course of Irish history was irreparably changed by the 1916 Easter Rising and the crop of martyrs it produced. In the words of Lady Fingall, an aristocratic Irish woman, the executions of Pearse, Connolly, the Belfast-based socialist, and their comrades had the same effect on nationalist opinion as 'a stream of blood coming from beneath a closed door'.[10]

The result of British policy, coupled with the collapse of the Lloyd George partition scheme of May–July 1916, was the rapid eclipse of the Irish Nationalist Party over most of nationalist Ireland by a new republican Sinn Féin movement and its allies in the revived Irish Volunteers. The 1918 election marked not only the victory of Sinn Féin outside north-east Ulster, but also a shift in the balance of power at Westminster. The Liberal–Nationalist alliance of 1912 was replaced by the Tory-dominated Lloyd George coalition and its Ulster unionist allies.

As Sinn Féin moved to establish the first Dáil and the war between the IRA and the British state began, the government introduced the 1920 Government of Ireland Act. This was less a sincere attempt to solve the Irish question than an attempt to solve the 'Ulster question' on terms acceptable to Ulster unionism.

In the words of James Craig's brother, Captain Charles Craig, MP, the 1920 act placed unionism 'in a position of absolute security for the future'.[11] For the nationalist minority, one third of the population in the new Northern Ireland, it represented permanent partition and permanent minority status without any political or cultural safeguards.

In the treaty negotiations of October–December 1921, Michael Collins and Arthur Griffith tried but failed to undermine the partition settlement and were forced in the end to settle for dominion status for the south and the establishment of the fatally ambiguous Boundary Commission to revise the 1920 border. By 1925, the Boundary Commission had collapsed, leaving a more deeply entrenched border between north and south. Some 500 people died violently in the bloody birth-pangs of the new northern state.

This book is a compelling and balanced account of a pivotal moment in recent history. Its timing is especially significant as it marks the opening of the 'Decade of Centenaries' connected with the Irish Revolution of 1912–22. These will include the signing of Ulster's Solemn League and Covenant in 1912, the rise of the rival UVF and National Volunteers in 1913, the emergence of partition (1912–20), the republican 'blood-sacrifice' of 1916 and the Ulster unionist 'blood-sacrifice' at the Somme, the Anglo-Irish War/War of Independence, partition itself, the Anglo-Irish Treaty and the Irish Civil War. The same decade witnessed the struggle of women for the vote in Ireland and the first stirrings of the Irish Labour movement of James Connolly, James Larkin and William Walker.

It seems clear that there is little cross-community consensus on these controversial events and the iconic personalities behind them. Yet for those who wish to see the consolidation of the peace process in Ireland, north and south, and the promotion of mutual understanding in a divided society, the 'Decade of Centenaries' offers an opportunity as well as a challenge. The eminent Derry-born historian F.S.L. Lyons (1923–83) once observed, 'To understand the past is to cease to live in it.' In 2012 both the Government of Ireland and the Northern Ireland Executive committed themselves to promote a balanced, informed and inclusive approach towards 1912, 1914, 1916 and the rest.

In the spring of 2012 the Northern Ireland Community Relations Council (CRC) and Heritage Lottery Fund sponsored a ground-breaking series of public lectures in Belfast under the thoughtful title 'Remembering the Future'. The aim of the series –

which was a notable success – was to assemble a diverse and distinguished panel of historians who would seek to place these pivotal events in their proper context while promoting a constructive dialogue around them. The complex tapestry of events between the Covenant and partition was scrutinised from varying perspectives. Newly available primary sources were harnessed in an attempt to assess such issues as the impact of 'Carson's army' on Irish nationalism, the impact of the Great War on both traditions, the complex origins of the Easter Rising, the emergence of partition, the contribution of the Suffragists and Suffragettes in Ireland and the savage intensity of the violence of the 1919–23 period. Special emphasis was placed on those communities 'trapped by the border' and the experience of the northern nationalists and southern unionists after 1922.

The lecture series was jointly launched in the Ulster Museum by Carál Ní Chuilín, MLA, Minister for Culture, Arts and Leisure in the Stormont Executive, and Jimmy Deenihan, TD, Minister for Arts, Heritage and the Gaeltacht in the Irish government. The lectures marked the publication of a series of guiding principles on ethical commemoration by the CRC/Heritage Lottery Fund, which have been adopted by museums and public bodies throughout Northern Ireland.

For its part, the Irish government launched its own series of commemorations with a keynote lecture in March 2012 in Iveagh House – the former setting of a historic meeting between Carson, as MP for Trinity College, and southern unionists in 1913 – by Peter Robinson, First Minister of Northern Ireland. At the same time Taoiseach Enda Kenny, TD appointed an expert group of historians under the chairmanship of Dr Maurice Manning to advise the government on the issue of commemoration.

In August, Belfast City Council opened a series of commemorative events with an exhibition in Belfast City Hall aptly entitled 'Shared History – Different Allegiances'. The same approach has characterised events and exhibitions organised by councils, libraries, churches and community groups, north and south.

Alan Parkinson's book makes a significant contribution to a more informed understanding of this critical period and, more specifically, of the Home Rule crisis of 1912–14. Central to his thesis is the idea of the besiegement and isolation of a people. This sense of Ulster Protestant beleaguerment was matched by the isolation of the northern nationalists in the same decade and their fear of being marooned in a 'Protestant state'.

A century on, in a more settled constitutional framework within this island and with the normalisation of Anglo-Irish relations, it seems essential not only to promote a proper understanding of our recent history, but also to prevent any similar sense of alienation afflicting any section of the community in post-conflict Northern Ireland.

Dr Éamon Phoenix is principal lecturer and head of lifelong learning at Stranmillis University College (QUB). His books include *Northern nationalism* (1994) and *Conflicts in the north of Ireland 1900–2000*, co-edited with Alan F. Parkinson (Four Courts Press, 2010). A well-known broadcaster, he is a member of the Irish Government's Expert Group on Commemoration and the National Famine Commemoration Committee. He chaired 'Remembering the Future', a series of public lectures hosted by the Northern Ireland Community Relations Council and Heritage Lottery Fund in 2012.

1 A.T.Q. Stewart, *The Ulster crisis* (London, 1967).
2 G. Lewis, *Carson: the man who divided Ireland* (London, 2005), p. 231.
3 A. Jackson, 'Irish unionism' in P. Collins (ed.), *Nationalism and unionism: conflict in Ireland, 1885–1921* (Belfast, 1994), pp. 41–6.
4 D. Dutton, *'His majesty's loyal opposition': the Unionist Party in opposition, 1900–1915* (Liverpool, 1992), p. 203.
5 *Irish News*, 25 September 1913; É. Phoenix, *Northern nationalism: nationalist politics, partition and the Catholic minority in Northern Ireland 1890–1940* (Belfast, 1994), pp. 9–11.
6 Pro-Home Rule Declaration, 1913 (Queen's University, Belfast, R.M. Henry collection).
7 M. Laffan, *The partition of Ireland, 1911–25* (Dundalk, 1983), p. 32.
8 Phoenix, *Northern nationalism*, pp. 13–14.
9 6th Connaught Rangers Research Project, *The 6th Connaught Rangers: Belfast nationalists and the Great War* (Belfast, 2011).
10 Elizabeth, Countess of Fingall, *Seventy years young* (Dublin, 1991), p. 375.
11 Laffan, *Partition of Ireland*, p. 65.

Edward Carson addressing a loyalist rally

Prologue

1

One of my earliest memories is of a walk with my father in a tree-lined avenue in the south-Belfast suburb of Ormeau over half a century ago. As we approached the distinguished figure of an elderly gentleman walking slowly towards us, my father whispered, 'That's Sir Douglas Savory, one of Sir Edward's men!' After we had exchanged greetings and the old man had resumed his laborious journey, I tried to discover more about 'Sir Douglas' and 'Sir Edward'. However, it would be many years before I discovered much about Douglas Savory.

I was to find out a lot more about Sir Edward Carson during a history degree course over a decade later.[1] As part of that course, I took a module on Roman Britain. One of my tutors on this module was A.T.Q. Stewart, who had just published a major work on the Ulster crisis of 1912–14. His seminal work stirred my interest in this fascinating episode in Irish history and, many years later, I completed an MA dissertation at a London university, investigating the success of the Ulster unionist propaganda campaign of these years. Written in the late 1980s, at a stage in the modern northern-Irish conflict when sympathy for Ulster loyalists in the British media and among the public was in short supply, I found the contrast with the situation that had prevailed between 1912 and 1914 intriguing.

I mention the above to explain my long-standing personal interest in this subject. I have returned to it some half a century after my encounter with one of the 'Covenant men' to attempt to discover the true significance of a movement that has gained an almost iconic status amongst modern-day loyalists. Certainly it would be wrong to underestimate the historical importance of Sir Edward Carson's anti-Home Rule movement. The period between the introduction of the Third Home Rule Bill (April 1912) and the start of the Great War (August 1914) was one of unprecedented political and community uncertainty and tension in the north of Ireland. Ulster unionists felt increasingly pressurised and concerned about the increasing likelihood of Irish Home Rule, especially since the powers of the House of Lords had recently been diminished and the successful passage of the proposed Home Rule legislation seemed inevitable. The next two years witnessed the consolidation of the Protestant community in Ulster and its stubborn resistance to Home Rule. This found expression in a variety of ways, including political opposition (both parliamentary and extra-parliamentary), a propaganda campaign that made use of the most modern and effective strategies, and paramilitary resistance.

This unionist movement was very different from anything

that had preceded it and its rationale, especially in regard to eliciting the approval of the British public, contrasted starkly with that of loyalists during the modern Northern Ireland conflict. Claiming the moral high ground as the oppressed Irish minority community (in striking similarity to the Catholic community in Northern Ireland during the late 1960s), Ulster Protestants appealed directly for sympathy and political support from the wider British population. This meant that they canvassed support from within Britain's political elite, in particular from the strongly placed Conservative opposition and the vast majority of sympathetic peers in the House of Lords. Ulster unionists also conducted a major publicity campaign in Great Britain and further afield, which included 'monster' rallies and street protests across Ulster and in Britain. They also canvassed large sections of the British electorate, especially at by-elections, and they had the ear of several influential newspaper editors and press barons. Other friends in high places included army officers and leaders of legal, ecclesiastical and academic communities, all of whom expressed fulsome support for the Ulster cause.

This relatively short period – less than two and a half years – witnessed a number of key events in Ulster and Great Britain, which should be seen in the context of the wider national and international calendar of this period. As Britain and Europe slid inextricably towards international war, a minority Liberal administration in London faced the prospect of mass disorder on British streets, emanating from an unlikely combination of syndicalists, suffragettes and Ulster loyalists. The landmark events in the Ulster crisis of 1912–14 include: the Balmoral demonstration in south Belfast (April 1912); the unrivalled expression of British support for the plight of Irish unionists at Blenheim Palace in Oxfordshire (July 1912); the events leading up to the signing of Ulster's Solemn League and Covenant in September 1912; the parliamentary and street protests of Ulster unionists in 1913 and early 1914; the so-called 'mutiny' by army officers at the Curragh camp outside Dublin in March 1914; the drilling of the recently established Ulster Volunteer Force (UVF) throughout 1913 and early 1914, followed by a large-scale arms importation in April 1914; and the intervention of the monarch, George V, as an arbiter between the two sides after political deadlock (July 1914). These events left Ireland, and particularly its north-eastern corner, on the cusp of civil war during the long, hot summer of 1914. However, such an unwelcome prospect was averted by the intervention of international war, which placed the Irish question on Britain's domestic back burner.

The historian is spoiled by the wealth of available material – both primary and secondary sources – on this subject. The leading work on the theme, A.T.Q. Stewart's *The Ulster crisis*, was published over 40 years ago and, although it remains a crucial read for those interested in this period of Irish history, a more modern analysis of an ever-widening range of accessible material is required. Indeed, the imminent centenary of many of the events associated with Carson's resistance movement provides an ideal opportunity for such a reassessment. My research has centred on the Ulster Unionist Council (UUC) archives and the papers of leading unionist figures like Edward Carson, James Craig and Fred Crawford, which are based at PRONI, and newspaper collections at Belfast Central Library and the British Newspaper Library at Colindale in London.[2] Invaluable evidence from the personal papers of influential sympathisers with Ulster unionism, including Andrew Bonar Law, Lord Willoughby de Broke, Lord Alfred Milner and Sir Henry Wilson, have been consulted in the House of Lords Record Office, the Bodleian Library in Oxford and the Imperial War Museum archives in London. A range of political pamphlets and other Irish Unionist Party material were accessed in the Linen Hall Library's (pre-1960) Northern Ireland Political Collection in Belfast and my own collection of *Punch* cartoons was also a useful source. Biographies of the key figures of this crisis – including works on the lives of Edward Carson, Andrew

Bonar Law, James Craig, Fred Crawford, Henry Wilson, Lady Theresa Londonderry, Alfred Harmsworth, J.L. Garvin and Rudyard Kipling – have been helpful in unravelling the motivation behind their personal involvement in events around this time. In addition, studies focusing on specific aspects of unionist resistance during this period, most notably Daniel Jackson's research into unionist demonstrations in Britain between 1911 and 1914, and Andrew Scholes's work on the role played by Irish Protestant churches during the late Edwardian years, proved to be of considerable assistance.

This book aims to cover the key events in both the north of Ireland and London during the period between April 1912 and September 1914, the lifespan of the Third Home Rule Bill. It endeavours to tell the story of Ulster's resistance, both political and paramilitary, to Irish Home Rule, and analyses the reasons for the relative success of the Ulster unionist campaign. It suggests that unionists' postwar acceptance of a new form of 'home rule', or regional devolution, was in fact largely negotiated before the onset of World War I, rather than being the brainchild of postwar diplomats. The rationale for devolution was accepted by many at the time, although the need to sell this previously unthinkable policy was acknowledged and acted upon after the introduction of the Better Government of Ireland legislation in 1920.

At the centre of this book is the study of the nature of the support for the Ulster case emanating from 'important' people in Great Britain. These sources of influential backing were to be found not only in the political and social establishment of the day, but also in the church, the army and the press. Illustrations of this type of backing, including some based on relatively unexplored primary-source material, are also provided. The high volume of support for Ulster within Great Britain is contrasted with the relative dearth of sympathy for Ulster's loyalists during the early years of the modern conflict.

This book does not restrict itself to outlining the key events of these action-packed years. It also attempts to depict the atmosphere at key moments in both town and countryside during this pivotal time in the region's modern history. In looking at the backdrop to such events, the book examines how rising public feeling in the northern Protestant community was reflected in the columns of the local press. The focus is on unionist journals, although some references are also made to perceptions of Carson's movement in the nationalist press. Therefore, detail is given to the preparations for key demonstrations against Home Rule and examples of press coverage and public responses to the exhortations of loyalist politicians are observed. Owing to a combination of their unquestionable significance and a strong personal interest in these research spheres, a particular focus of this book is the emphasis placed on sympathetic newspaper coverage – reflected in supportive leading articles, sympathetic reporting of unionists' speeches and loyalist demonstrations, and condemnatory cartoons lampooning the enemies of unionism – both in Belfast and on the propaganda trail in Great Britain. I endeavour to assess the significance of the political statements and interventions of unionist leaders like Edward Carson, James Craig and Andrew Bonar Law and, in particular, assess the impact of loyalist lecture tours, political canvassing in Great Britain and propaganda postcards.

The book is set within the wider context of Irish history, specifically the period covering the Third Home Rule Bill. Although its central focus is the loyalist resistance campaign against this proposed measure, it also looks at the main nationalist and Liberal personalities and their aspirations, in particular observing how the interactions between the two communities in the north of Ireland were so strained that many were convinced that civil war was just around the corner by the summer of 1914. Though a broad chronological pattern is adopted in most chapters, occasionally certain events are placed in more appropriate, thematically linked sections of the book. In the first chapter, I recap on previous attempts to introduce

Home Rule and summarise the position of key radical and nationalist politicians. Key loyalist demonstrations before the bill's introduction at Westminster, such as those at Craigavon and Balmoral, are described and their significance is considered. Major stages in the measure's early parliamentary journey in both houses of parliament, including the amendments proposed by Thomas Agar-Robartes and Edward Carson in June 1912 and January 1913 respectively, are outlined, and the chapter concludes with descriptions of the pro-Ulster rally at Blenheim Palace and accounts of increasing sectarian tension in Ulster during the summer of 1912.

The second chapter focuses on developments within unionism in the province and explains the reasons behind the cohesion of the loyalist community. In this section, I look at the parts played by the various Protestant churches, the unionist clubs, the Orange Order and industrialists in maintaining such unity and investigate the nature of unionist propaganda material. In the second part of this chapter I present a case study on the resistance of Ulster unionists in 1912. This concentrates on the two-week-long Covenant campaign of September 1912 and explores the text of the Covenant and the rationale behind adopting such a tactic, before describing the frenetic atmosphere in unionist areas across Ulster on Covenant Day.

The third chapter, 'Friends in high places', deals with the increasing levels of support for the unionist cause in Great Britain. I explore the background to this sympathy for Ulster unionists amongst high officials within the Conservative Party and the House of Lords, and provide examples of right-wing press treatment of events in Ireland. In the penultimate chapter, 'The tide turns', the improving fortunes of Ulster unionists are outlined, including events at the Curragh military camp and the importation of arms by Carson's Volunteer movement along the Down and Antrim coasts in the spring of 1914. The bill's ultimate parliamentary stage, including the government's move towards possible Ulster exclusion, is also described.

The final chapter looks at the cruel and ironic fate that befell many Ulster Volunteers in 1916 and political changes affecting Ireland in the postwar world. A brief synopsis of events in the new state of Northern Ireland is provided and an attempt is made to explain the extent to which unionists maximised their friendships with influential people in the Edwardian era. I then contrast this success with the very different fortunes of Ulster loyalists some 60 years later.

I hope that this book, which is scheduled to be published on the eve of the centenary of Ulster's Solemn League and Covenant, will appeal to those especially interested in the modern history of Ireland and also to the general reader. The style adopted attempts to accommodate both audiences. I endeavour to answer some vital questions raised by this investigation of a vital two-year period in the history of the north of Ireland. What were the reasons behind the considerable sympathy exhibited by the British establishment for the Ulster cause? How genuine was this support? Without such help, how would the Ulster unionist campaign have fared? In particular, without the backing of aristocrats, press moguls and senior British politicians, what direction would Carson's UVF have taken? To what degree was Edward Carson in control of events, and indeed of his own movement, during this period? And what impact did all this political turmoil have on the lives of ordinary unionists in towns and villages across Ulster in these years before the start of the war?

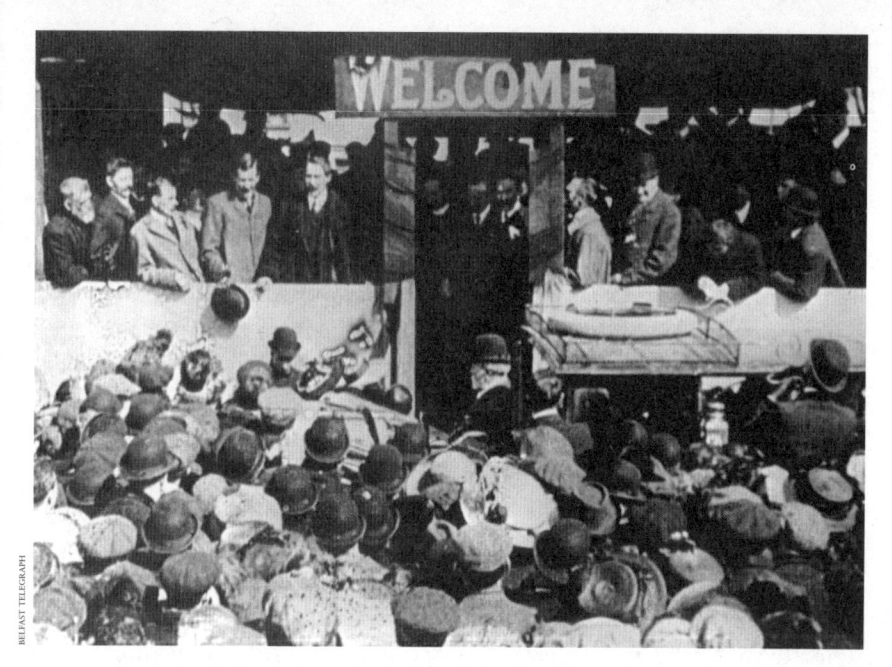

Bonar Law being welcomed at Balmoral, April 1912

Danger looms

2

Introduction

For many years, political and communal tension in Ulster had subsisted at a low level. This was to change, especially from the early part of 1912, on account of increasing nationalist pressure and the imminent introduction of Home Rule at Westminster, which many believed threatened the political unity of the United Kingdom.

During a period of nearly three years, the north of Ireland was an increasingly divided society, far from being at ease with itself or its future. The large Protestant majority in the province's industrial and political power base, Belfast and the Lagan Valley, felt endangered by political developments. Emboldened by the size of their numbers, the strength of their cause and the growing evidence of sympathy for their position in Great Britain, they started to organise a movement of defiance in Ulster that would be unprecedented in its scale and intensity. The main focus of this work is on the loyalist and predominantly Protestant resistance campaign and space forbids detailed coverage of the northern nationalist community at this time. Suffice it to say that the considerably smaller Catholic population in greater Belfast also felt vulnerable, though for very different reasons. Buoyed as they had been by the increasing momentum of the march towards Irish Home Rule, northern Catholics nevertheless felt like an isolated group enclosed within hostile territory.

From these respective feelings of insecurity and vulnerability, the scope for realistic political compromise appeared limited and civil war seemed like a very real prospect. This chapter will look at the key personalities leading the Liberal and Irish Nationalist Party march towards Home Rule and investigate the motives of the Liberal administration during this period. It will also explore the impact of these major political advances upon the consciousness of a rejuvenated northern Protestant community, specifically expressed at major political demonstrations such as Craigavon and Balmoral, and the introduction of Home Rule legislation. This will be followed by an account of the Third Home Rule Bill's parliamentary progress between April 1912 and the defeat of Sir Edward Carson's amendment the following January, an analysis of the pro-Ulster meeting at Blenheim Palace in Oxfordshire, and illustrations of growing sectarian tension in the province.

The Radical and Nationalist threat

Ever since Ireland's political integration within the United

Kingdom at the start of the nineteenth century, there had been a growing desire within its predominantly Catholic population to acquire some measure of self-government. This desire and determination had endured after the political emancipation of the island's Catholics in 1829 and Daniel O'Connell's subsequent campaign to repeal the Act of Union of 1800. (Indeed, some of O'Connell's strategies, including his 'monster' meetings and his wider extra-parliamentary campaign against the Act of Union, bear an interesting resemblance to the strategies Ulster unionists would use against Home Rule between 1912 and 1914.) A renewed constitutional campaign for an Irish parliament emerged in the late 1870s and early 1880s, led by charismatic Irish nationalist leader and Wicklow Protestant, Charles Stewart Parnell.

Following in the wake of this renewed nationalist aspiration of the last quarter of the nineteenth century was the stirring of unionist resistance to Irish Home Rule. What awakened the Protestant population in north-eastern Ireland was not just the perceived religious threat posed by their nationalist opponents, but also a considerably increased awareness of their economic difference from the rest of Ireland. This had been a consequence of the relatively late industrial revolution experienced in the Lagan Valley. On the eve of the introduction of the Second Home Rule Bill, Belfast exported 35,000 tons of linen and over six million gallons of whiskey. Inside 20 years over 40,000 were employed in the linen industry, 20,000 in ship-building, 5,000 in a number of engineering industries and around 6,000 in the manufacture of tobacco.[1] Belfast had quadrupled in size between 1830 and 1881 and had gained municipal status in 1888. This commercial and demographic transformation constituted an economic miracle, especially when one considers Belfast's geographical remoteness from its potential markets, its poor port facilities (at least for the first half of the nineteenth century) and its dearth of raw materials.

Although the timing and scale of the Lagan Valley's economic development did not coincide or correspond with that of most other British cities, what really set it apart from them was the effect such commercial success had on moulding the political and national allegiances of its citizens. The fact that Belfast's industrial might contrasted sharply with the lack of industry in other Irish urban centres proved to be a crucial factor in subsequent unionist resistance to a Dublin-based administration. The Lagan Valley was the only area in Ireland to have undergone a genuine industrial revolution and this was to sharpen Ulster Protestants' sense of a separate identity. An English visitor to the city in 1843 had commented that Belfast's 'bustling appearance' was 'decidedly unnational' and surmised that it was 'in Ireland but not of it'.[2] The great irony was that Belfast's economic success in the late nineteenth and early twentieth centuries, and the wealth it generated, actually increased political differences between the region and the rest of Ireland. The new city's economic boom and the emergence of large work units in mills, factories and shipyards solidified unionist resistance at a time of crisis and helped increase entrenchment within both communities. At a time when social reform and class compromise were beginning to be recognised at national level, the community divisions in Belfast, structured as they were on sectarian rather than class lines, were widening.[3]

On the eve of the general election in June 1885, the Liberal Party leader – and, at this stage, two-time premier – William Gladstone, had announced his desire to implement Home Rule in Ireland. Gladstone endeavoured to capture the moral high ground over the question of Ireland's political future, placing this latest policy within his long-standing 'mission to pacify Ireland'. However, political pragmatism was arguably behind this conversion to Home Rule. If so, it was well placed, as the result of the 1885 election was a hung parliament in which Irish nationalists held the balance of power. The Liberals won 335 seats to the Tories' total of 249, with Parnell's party gaining 86 seats, 17 of them in Ulster.

Gladstone introduced the First Home Rule Bill in April 1886. Although it recognised the desire of Irish nationalists for a parliament in Dublin, limited devolved powers were central to the proposed legislation. The Dublin parliament was to have no say in imperial, foreign, fiscal, security and a range of other key policy matters. The bill, which ministers acknowledged was unlikely to become legislation given the powers held by the House of Lords at this time, came as 'a huge shock' to Protestants across the island. Indeed, as one historian has noted, it appeared 'as if Gladstone had touched Irish Protestants with an electric cattle prod'.[4] Yet the British premier was aware of the special position of Ulster Protestants. He acknowledged that 'there should be reasonable safeguards for the Protestant minority, especially in the province of Ulster', but proceeded to argue that 'a Protestant minority in Ulster or elsewhere [should not] rule the question at large for Ireland, when five-sixths of its chosen representatives are on one mind on the matter'.[5]

Unionists across Ireland were not slow to respond to the prospect of Home Rule legislation. The Irish Unionist Party (IUP) had been founded at Westminster in 1886, with Colonel Edward Saunderson as party leader, and in Ulster the Loyalist Anti-Repeal Union was established. They too would soon find political friends across the Irish Sea. In an act of undoubted political expediency, former Tory minister Lord Randolph Churchill declared his true intentions regarding Ulster's resistance to the proposed legislation. In a letter to a friend, written in February 1886, Churchill admitted that he had previously decided that 'if Gladstone went for Home Rule, the Orange card would be the one to play' and prayed that it 'may turn out to be the ace of trumps and not the two'.[6] Making use of the fervent atmosphere prevailing in Ulster at the time, Churchill stirred the partisan emotions of the Protestant population and sowed the seeds of a local defence movement. In his passionate 'Ulster will fight and Ulster will be right' address delivered in the Ulster Hall on 22 February 1886,

Randolph Churchill declared that Ulster would 'emerge from the struggle victorious' because it possessed 'the sympathy and support of an enormous section of our British community'.[7]

Gladstone's bill deeply divided his party both in Britain and Ireland. The party was virtually decimated in Ireland, most notably in Ulster, a former stronghold. With the defection of 93 Liberal members, the bill was defeated in June 1886 by 341 votes to 311. What was significant about this bill was its legacy for the political scene both in Britain and in Ulster. In the north of Ireland, the political landscape altered almost overnight, as the majority of Ulster Protestants (especially those from strong Nonconformist backgrounds) had previously voted for the Liberal Party. Ulster unionists, who had been wooed by the opportunism of the likes of Lord Randolph Churchill, were to cement their alliance with their friends in Britain, whilst the alliance forged between their political enemies, the Irish nationalists and the Liberal Party, would endure until the Easter Rising of 1916. The fallout from the doomed legislation was evident upon the streets of Belfast (mainly its western quarter) during the summer of 1886. Close to 50 people lost their lives during a three-month bout of communal violence and there were hundreds of officially recorded injuries and arrests. Over £90,000 of damage was done to commercial properties, 190 Catholics were expelled from the shipyards and over 30 pubs were looted.

Unionist fears over Home Rule subsided when the Conservatives gained office in 1886. However, they were to re-emerge in the second half of 1892, when Gladstone was returned to power for the third time with a working majority of 40. His Second Home Rule Bill, introduced in the House of Commons early in 1893, touched a raw nerve in the unionist ranks and convinced their leaders of the need to organise. At local level, quasi-military groups joined the new unionist clubs and across the province there was a surge in membership of the Orange Order.

During the summer of 1892, a major loyalist convention was held in Belfast. Around 12,000 democratically elected delegates representing various unionist clubs and Orange lodges attended the convention in a specially constructed hall in the Botanic Gardens, south of the city centre, on 17 June.[8] *The Times* noted that 'these were men to be reckoned with'.[9] Ulster loyalism at this time did not possess a charismatic orator of the calibre of Edward Carson and it was left to men like the duke of Abercorn (who organised the event) and Thomas Sinclair (who would draft Ulster's Solemn League and Covenant 20 years later) to attempt to arouse the emotions of their huge audience. Abercorn and other platform speakers drew large cheers from the assembled hordes by insisting that the 'men of the north' would resist Home Rule at any cost, even pledging to 'shed blood to maintain the strength and salvation of the country'.[10]

The Second Home Rule Bill, though slightly different in its detail, offered similarly limited, devolved provisions as the 1886 measure had. Two key differences were the proposed reductions in Irish representation at Westminster (to 80 MPs) and the suggestion that the new Dublin parliament should consist of a bicameral legislature, with the upper-house representatives being elected only by voters with high property qualifications. This bill had a longer parliamentary journey than its 1886 predecessor, though it experienced a similar fate. Introduced by Gladstone in February 1893, the measure was passed by the House of Commons (by 307 votes to 206) but comprehensively rejected by the House of Lords in September (by 419 votes to 41). Perhaps on account of its inevitable rejection by the House of Lords, and also because of its tedious parliamentary passage – individual clauses had been endlessly debated – the measure's demise was not greatly mourned. Even the bill's leading advocate, William Gladstone, would describe it as 'that confounded Bill'.[11]

After over a decade in the political wilderness, the Liberals were returned to power with a huge majority in 1906.

Two years later, Herbert Asquith replaced Henry Campbell Bannerman as Liberal leader and prime minister.[12] Asquith and his dynamic team of front-bench colleagues, who included David Lloyd George and Winston Churchill, had as their main focus an extensive programme of social reform (referred to as 'New Liberalism') and Irish Home Rule was on the back burner during Asquith's early years in office (just as it had been during Campbell Bannerman's brief administration).

Two dramatically close elections contested at either point of 1910 illustrate the paper-thin divisions in support for the two main political parties in Britain at this time, and the peripheral position the Irish question held in both election campaigns of that year. As noted, the results of both elections were remarkably close. In January the Liberals gained 274 seats compared to the Conservatives' total of 272. The Labour Party, barely a decade in existence, gained 40 seats and the Irish Nationalist Party 82. By December, the number of seats held by the Tories was the same but the Liberals had dropped to 271, with Labour and the Irish Nationalist Party gaining two seats each.

Both elections resulted in 'hung' parliaments, with the Irish Nationalist Party holding the balance of power. An election-weary British public longed for some degree of political stability, and the only way that Asquith could satisfy this desire was to make an unofficial pact with the Irish Nationalists. Inevitably, Irish politics would command a sudden increase in attention in the new parliament, which was in sharp contrast to its low-key position in both electoral contests. Conservatives drew more attention to the perceived threat posed by Home Rule. Tory candidates were twice as likely to raise the Irish question as their Radical opponents and five per cent of Conservative candidates believed Home Rule to be the single most important topic in the December election. Overall, however, over a third of parliamentary candidates failed to mention the subject at all during the campaigns and only one per cent thought it constituted the most important issue during the first campaign.[13] The next six months were dominated by the debate concerning the powers of the House of Lords. The 'peers versus the people' issue would soon have massive ramifications for Irish Home Rule. The Parliament Act of 1911 meant that the upper chamber could no longer prevent the passage of any bill that had passed three successive sessions in the House of Commons.

Herbert Asquith was far from being the most vociferous proponent of Irish legislative autonomy before reaching Downing Street, and it is likely that political expediency rather than devotion to principle was the main impetus behind the determination of his Irish policy. This partly explains his party's downplaying of Home Rule during the two election campaigns of 1910 and his subsequent willingness to articulate the Irish 'one-nation' argument on a Dublin platform. Indeed, there is an element of irony in the fact that Asquith and John Redmond, the leader of the Irish Nationalist Party, effectively switched their previously held stances. As one historian has noted, Redmond had maintained back in 1894–5 that nationalists 'had to win support in Britain by conciliating Unionists', whilst Herbert Asquith had warned in 1901 about 'a Liberal Government becoming dependent upon the Irish Party'.[14] Perhaps aware of shifting political clouds at the end of 1909, Asquith declared that the Irish problem could only be solved by 'a policy which, while explicitly safeguarding the supremacy and indefectible authority of the Imperial Parliament, will set up in Ireland a system of full self-government in regard to purely Irish affairs'.[15] Tom Wilson has astutely observed how the predominant 'high moral tone' adopted by the Liberals over Home Rule was 'somewhat out of place'. Noting that the previous Liberal administration had 'not been much interested in Home Rule', Wilson questions their portrayal of Ulster loyalists as 'irresponsible anarchists'. He claims that 'to Ulster nostrils, there was a Pecksniffian odour about all this' that was 'somewhat disagreeable'.[16]

Liberals were prone to ignoring the demands of Ulster unionists or dismissing their resistance as 'bluff' until relatively late in the Home Rule campaign. On one level it was surprising that the Liberal Party, with its power base in Nonconformist regions, should line up opposing people of similar spiritual beliefs in the north of Ireland. As George Boyce has pointed out, there was a contradictory feel to the stance the Liberal administration was taking. Boyce maintains that New Liberalism 'hardly sat easily with the policy of coercing Ulster Protestants for the benefit of Irish Roman Catholics' and argues that Liberal principles made it 'difficult to contemplate using military force to subdue a minor influence'.[17] From their own perspective, Ulster loyalists were dismissive of what they regarded as the hypocrisy of the Liberal regime. They pointed out divisions in the party, both in the past and present, over the question of Home Rule, and also a perceived lack of passion regarding the measure, especially when compared to the party's social-reform programme. Like many other previous (and indeed subsequent) British premiers, Herbert Asquith's knowledge of the particular nuances of Ulster loyalism was – especially in the early phase of the campaign – limited. On meeting a delegation of commercial leaders from Belfast's Chamber of Commerce at Westminster in July 1912, Asquith commented that 'nothing is lost by our meeting face to face with one another and talking matters over freely'. The senior businessmen, united to a man in their opposition to Home Rule, considered that their important host was 'not his own master'.[18] A sympathetic London newspaper suggested that the prime minister's responses to the group showed that he was 'utterly unable to meet the strong case presented by the deputation'.[19]

However, the main flaw in Herbert Asquith's Irish policy lay less in his knowledge and understanding of the depth of the Ulstermen's conviction, rather more in his tendency to give in to political pressure from both Irish parties, and most of all in his failure to dissipate Ulster venom by incorporating a 'get-out clause' for Ulster (or part of it) in his bill. To some degree, this was not a surprise. Asquith, the quintessential parliamentarian, believed that political disputes should be settled within the framework of the constitution and through normal parliamentary protocol, whereby the minority would eventually accept the will of the majority. Yet an exclusion clause within the bill might well have defused unionist opposition and possibly paved the way for the successful delivery of Home Rule. It is debatable whether such a concession would have completely satisfied unionist sceptics, especially in Ulster. But, as Alvin Jackson has noted, in April 1912 such a deal would 'almost certainly have undermined the dangerous growth in Ulster Unionist militancy'.[20]

There were other influences on government policy on Ireland from within the cabinet and, indeed, divergent opinions led on occasion to impasse in governmental discussion. In theory, the most influential and informative colleague should have been the prime minister's experienced chief secretary for Ireland, Augustine Birrell.[21] However, the latter had two major failings. The unionist perception of Birrell was that he was too close to nationalists to be considered an even-handed Irish secretary. Even more importantly, he was unable to present himself to cabinet colleagues as informed and influential, partly on account of a lack of personal authority but also because of a shortfall in support from on-the-ground police agencies. One critic has suggested that 'no serious effort was made by the Irish authorities ever to make a systematic appraisal of the opposition's strength, let alone to spy on or penetrate its leadership' and that Dublin Castle was left 'in the hands of a worn-out, dispirited minister whose only ambition was to quit'.[22] Although, rather incredibly, Birrell remained in post as Irish secretary for nearly a decade, he was peripheral to decision making in Ireland, which was dominated by Asquith and his two charismatic lieutenants, David Lloyd George and Winston Churchill.

The most prominent member of Herbert Asquith's cabinet was his chancellor, David Lloyd George.[23] In public, Lloyd George could speak scathingly about unionist leaders like Bonar Law and Edward Carson and dismissively about Ulster loyalists' objections to Home Rule. Perhaps Lloyd George's most significant public utterance on Ulster unionists at this time was at Denmark Hill in south London on 20 June 1914, when he queried 'the nature of their protest'. Reminding his audience that they represented 'only 60% of the inhabitants of one corner of an island where 90% of the inhabitants supported the bill', Lloyd George eloquently reproached Ulster unionists for digging in their heels and asked his audience how Liberals would react if asked to 'submit to a government which we loathe and abhor'. He went on:

> We will take it philosophically; we will not arm; we will not drill; we will not organise ourselves into battalions; we will not salute; we will not gun-run; we will not have generals and colonels and captains – not even gallopers. What we will do is bide our time and vote them down when we get the chance. That is the very essence of democracy.[24]

Despite the occasional belligerence of his public and parliamentary speeches, Lloyd George believed that compromise was needed in Ireland and that exclusion for Ulster, or at least part of it, would be an essential feature of any final settlement. Indeed, these experiences of Ulster's resistance to Home Rule before 1914 eventually resulted in his postwar Government of Ireland Bill, which would produce partition and create the state of Northern Ireland.

Another Ulster unionist hate figure at this time was Winston Churchill.[25] The son of a legendary Tory supporter of Ulster during a previous Home Rule crisis, Churchill was also prone to venomous attacks on unionism. Before the crisis deepened, Churchill had joined in with Radical denunciation of the threats of his unionist opponents. In a lively speech in his Dundee constituency in 1911, Churchill argued that no importance should be attached to 'these frothings of Sir Edward Carson' and forecast that eventually 'civil war [would] evaporate in uncivil words'.[26] Like Lloyd George, Churchill combined a publicly aggressive approach to Carson and the Ulster Volunteers with an acknowledgement, often in private, of special treatment for Ulster. Thus, he would long be associated, at least by unionists, with his controversial speech in west Belfast in February 1912 and for condemning their 'violent' methods in Bradford during March 1914. In this latter speech, Winston Churchill challenged Ulstermen directly to denounce violence. He suggested that 'if all the loose, wanton and reckless chatter is in the end to disclose a sinister and revolutionary purpose, then put these grave matters to the proof'.[27]

Yet he could not be accused of failing to devise alternative political solutions for the accommodation of Ulster. Churchill had dabbled with notions of federalism in 1911 and, from an early stage in the crisis, advised his nationalist colleagues to consider adopting a conciliatory and non-coercive approach to Ulster. Writing to John Redmond, Winston Churchill suggested that 'something should be done to afford the characteristically Protestant and Orange counties the option of a moratorium of several years before acceding to the Irish Parliament'.[28]

When news came that the son of Ulster's great defender, Randolph Churchill, had been asked to address a Home Rule meeting in Belfast, many loyalists felt offended. An invitation for Winston Churchill to speak at an Ulster Liberal Association meeting in Belfast in February 1912 sparked a fury of protest and controversy, which was to last for some time. Lord Pirrie, shipyard owner and Protestant Home Ruler, acting on behalf of the Ulster Liberal Association, invited the first lord of the admiralty to address this group at what was regarded as the 'citadel of unionism', the Ulster Hall, on 8 February. Inevitably, the invitation provoked widespread objections from Ulster unionists, including interventions from Edward Carson and the unionist press. A colleague of Lord Pirrie, Rev. J.B. Armour, described the hostile loyalist reaction as 'lunacy in the ascendant' and, writing to a friend on the eve of the planned visit, argued that the Ulster Unionist Council (UUC) was 'threatening to raise a riot and commit murder if Winston dares to speak in the Ulster Hall'. Condemning this as 'an attack on the right of free speech', Armour noted that there were 'all sorts of rumours about the Ulster Hall being filled the night before with Orangemen who will refuse to leave', as well as an intimidating crowd in the streets outside.[29] On the opposite side of the political perspective, the *Saturday Review* defended the recent decision forbidding Churchill from speaking at the Ulster Hall, which they described as 'sacred ground'. The *Review* went on:

> to the mind of any calm outsider, there is something both imprudent and impious in the proposal that this temple of Unionism should be profaned by the son of the man who assisted at its consecration.[30]

Rumours and fears of outbreaks of sectarian street trouble abounded in Belfast and wider afield as Winston Churchill, accompanied by his wife Clementine, stepped off a boat in Larne in freezing, wet weather on 8 February. The Irish secretary and his officials had authorised the deployment of two squadrons of cavalry and five battalions of infantry to Belfast to offset the real threat of loyalist disturbance. However, Churchill's visit would gain notoriety less on account of its precipitating open sectarian warfare in the city – the huge police and military presence meant that this was a most unlikely outcome – and more because of the potentially fatal attack on the first lord by a mob of agitated loyalists in Belfast city centre before the meeting. The Churchills had been in the process of leaving the city's premier hotel, the Grand Central in Royal Avenue, when they were confronted by a hostile crowd, which booed and jostled the Liberal cabinet minister as he tried to board a car with his wife. Through a combination of alert policing and sheer good fortune, the couple and Liberal Association officials narrowly avoided the serious injuries that would undoubtedly have occurred if their vehicle had been overturned. An eyewitness described the incident as follows:

> As the Churchills appeared, the crowd surged forward with an angry growl. For a moment, it seemed the car would be thrown bodily over on top of the Liberal leader and his wife. The police, who were trying to humour the crowd up till now, realised the imminent danger and drove into the mob with fists and sticks, holding them off long enough to give the driver sufficient time to start the engine.[31]

The driver sped away down a side street and made his way over a mile to Celtic Park, a football ground off the main nationalist area, the Falls Road, to where the meeting had been moved. The contrast between the reception afforded to Churchill outside his hotel and his entrance into the rainswept soccer stadium could not have been starker. A correspondent writing for *The Times* observed that 'at the boundary line between the two nations the booing ceased and the cheering began' and concluded that 'the shock of the sudden transition from scowls to smiles helped to explain the Irish problem better than a hundred treatises'.[32] (That same day, Edward Carson and Lord Londonderry were greeted with cheering and the rendition of loyal tunes as they appeared at the windows of the Reform Club, just after Churchill's hurried departure from the city centre.)

When Winston Churchill arrived at Celtic Park he was ushered into a large marquee, where an audience consisting mostly of nationalists and Ulster Liberals, although fewer in number than expected (because of the threat of sectarian violence and the heavy rainfall that day), enthusiastically received his speech. This carefully crafted oration praised in turn the moral integrity of Ireland's claim to self-determination, the vitality of Britain's relationship with Ireland and a rebuke to Ulster's loyal population. Acknowledging that Ireland's claim to have a parliament of its own had 'never been fairly treated by the statesmen of Great Britain', Churchill asked, '[Why] should not her venerable nationhood enjoy a recognised and respected existence?'[33] Moving on to the question of the future relationship between the two countries, Churchill claimed that their separation was 'absolutely impossible' and that the two nations would be 'bound together till the end of time'.[34] Mischievously employing the phrase so memorably coined by his father over a quarter of a century before, Winston Churchill admonished Ulster loyalists, who, he pleaded, should 'fight for the spread of charity, tolerance and enlightenment among men'. Churchill concluded, 'then indeed, gentlemen, Ulster will fight and Ulster will be right'.[35]

After his speech and brief exchanges of pleasantries with nationalist and Ulster Liberal leaders, Churchill left the muddy soccer ground flanked by members of the Royal Irish Constabulary (RIC). In an attempt to confuse those hostile opponents awaiting his arrival back at the Grand Central Hotel, his party was taken by a special train back to Larne, leading to the accusation that he had escaped like a fugitive into the night. Unionist newspapers suggested that, although unnerving at the time, Churchill's experiences in Belfast would improve his understanding of the situation there, claiming that he had 'discovered in the course of his brief visit the existence of the two Irish nations' and trusting that he might 'perhaps communicate the discovery to his colleagues of the Cabinet'.[36]

John Redmond, an ex-follower of Charles Stewart Parnell, had assumed the latter's mantle when he accepted the leadership of the Irish Nationalist Party in 1900.[37] Yet his style of leadership was more muted and less charismatic than that of the 'uncrowned king of Ireland'. Although he shared his former leader's reluctance to compromise and was adamant, initially at least, in his insistence that Ulster should be included in the terms of any Home Rule legislation, Redmond's political beliefs were radically different from those of the men who, within a few years, would replace him at the forefront of anti-British agitation. John Redmond was not a hater of England or the British Empire. He combined a strong desire that a measure of devolved government be granted to the Irish people with a middle-class Victorian's rather vague allegiance to some form of imperialist identity. This manifested itself in a genuine loyalty to the British war effort, in which his brother and fellow Irish Nationalist Party MP, Willie, lost his life at the Somme in 1916. On the question of all-Ireland unity, Redmond was unequivocal. Speaking at Limerick in October 1913, he proclaimed that Ireland was 'a unit' and that the 'two-nation theory' was 'an abomination and a blasphemy'.[38] Yet Redmond was also a pragmatist and, to a degree, a political opportunist. He showed flexibility in his approach towards the moves to exempt Ulster from the measure and in his own responses to his supporters' changing reactions to increasing militancy within Ulster.

Even before the elections in 1910, John Redmond was aware of the unique political opportunity that might be afforded to Irish nationalists in the wake of an indecisive result at the hustings. Writing to the Liberal peer Lord Morley a few weeks before the first election in 1910, Redmond warned:

> unless an official declaration on the question of Home Rule can be made, not only will it be impossible for us to support Liberal candidates in England, but we will most unquestionably have to ask our friends to vote against them.[39]

The subsequent hung parliaments in 1910 led to an unofficial alliance between the two parties, as outlined above. Whilst electoral uncertainty in Britain had placed his party in an enviable, power-broking position, Redmond was frustrated by Asquith's indecision and back-tracking in the face of unionist pressure and the unsuccessful placatory promises of the government frequently delivered by the ineffectual Augustine Birrell. However, as we will observe from his response in parliament during the introduction of the Third Home Rule Bill, John Redmond, like many of his colleagues, was genuinely delighted by its proposed terms. Indeed, it is difficult not to agree with Roy Hattersley's perception that the proposed legislation constituted 'the Irish Nationalists' reward for supporting the government during the constitutional crisis which ended with the Parliament Bill and the reduction of the House of Lords' powers'.[40] It was this, along with the promise of the Irish Nationalist Party's continued support during an inevitably difficult parliament for a harassed government, that underpinned the Liberal–Nationalist alliance of 1912–14 and that proved a considerable rock in the path of Ulster unionists.

Redmond was also to experience problems from within his own party, especially from Joe Devlin, the west-Belfast MP and unofficial spokesman for Northern Catholics.[41] 'Wee Joe', a respected nationalist representative, had been instrumental in the development of an influential Catholic pressure group, the Ancient Order of Hibernians, which had a membership in excess of 60,000 by 1911. He was concerned by the lack of urgency given to the plight of northern Catholics by his party's leadership. The relative isolation of Catholics in Belfast (they were mostly congregated in the city's western district) explains Devlin's natural concern that they would be abandoned by the Irish Nationalist Party for the greater prize of a Dublin parliament. Although publicly dismissive of the claims of Ulster unionists – he had described them as 'a dying faction' in 1911 and frequently referred to his opponents' campaign as a 'comic circus' – Devlin's knowledge of the growing tension on the streets of Belfast meant that he was more conscious than most of his colleagues of the growing desperation and resolve of Ulster unionists.

A rare voice of moderation in Redmond's uncompromising parliamentary group was William O'Brien, the veteran Cork

MP, who had played an active role in the land-reform movement many years earlier. O'Brien foresaw a fusion of classes and religious groups in a new Ireland and was prepared to make concessions to his unionist opponents. O'Brien had frequent correspondence with newspapers like *The Times* and meetings with the prime minister and chief secretary for Ireland, in which he put the case for 'Home Rule all round' and even a trial period of Home Rule. He thereby proved to be a thorn in the flesh of his party leader, who was, especially in 1912 and 1913, reluctant to take Ulster opposition to the measure seriously.

Relatively recent history had, therefore, taught Ulster unionists to be wary of the intentions of their Liberal and Irish Nationalist opponents. New circumstances, including the passing of the Parliament Act, the existence of a hung parliament at Westminster and a determined parliamentary push by the Irish Nationalist Party, persuaded them to prepare for, from their perspective, the worst-case scenario. Two massive demonstrations expressing Ulster's opposition to such a fundamental change in the way it was governed would take place in Belfast within a period of six months.

'The dark eleventh hour'

Following the passing of the Parliament Act in the summer of 1911 and the real spectre of an unassailable Home Rule bill being introduced early in the next parliament, the new leader of the Irish Unionist Party, Sir Edward Carson, realised that it was necessary both to test the resolve of his own supporters and to step up the campaign of resistance. Carson requested reassurance from his Ulster colleagues over the extent of loyalist resolve and James Craig's reply came in the form of a mass meeting two months later. Craig offered the grounds of his spacious home and was the chief organiser of a loyalist demonstration there on Saturday, 23 September. Well over 50,000 unionists from all over Ulster, mostly belonging to Lord Templetown's unionist clubs and the Orange Order, assembled in Belfast city centre and marched four abreast to Craigavon, less than three miles to the east. Considerable planning went into the staging of this event, which was used as a model for even larger and more significant occasions during the months and years ahead. This 'multi-layered message of defiance, solidarity and aggression' would be repeated later at rallies, both in Ulster and in Great Britain.[42]

Special trains brought demonstrators into the city from the four corners of the province and marshals, rather than RIC personnel, ensured that the thousands of participants would be orderly and disciplined. A platform was erected on a hill in the grounds of Craig's home, overlooking Belfast Lough, and from there Edward Carson addressed his expectant audience. For most of them this was their first glimpse of their relatively new political leader and his first wife, Annette, who made her only visit to Ulster for this meeting. One eyewitness recalled how the multitude had gathered, 'intent and silent, to see what sort of man it really was that had come to lead them'. They were intrigued by 'what sort of practical scheme he had to offer for their acceptance'; they were firmly convinced that 'the day of words was drawing to its bitter close, and in the gathering gloom they felt that the hour to strike was at hand'.[43] Sir Edward Carson asked them to join him in a 'compact', which, he maintained, was essential, and declared that 'with the help of God, you and I joined together ... will yet defeat the most nefarious conspiracy that has ever been hatched against a free people'.[44]

Central to Carson's first address at a mass meeting in Ulster was the argument that voters' objections to Home Rule would be bypassed by an administration that had refused to declare its intentions at recent elections. This meant, the unionist leader stressed, that Ulster loyalists would have to be self-reliant and proactive in their resistance tactics:

> We must be prepared in the event of a Home Rule Bill passing, with such measures as will carry on for ourselves

the government of those districts of which we have control. We must be prepared ... the morning Home Rule passes, ourselves to become responsible for the government of the Protestant Province of Ulster.[45]

Within days, a committee was established to formulate procedure for such an emergency, 'provisional' government.

Ulster loyalists were greatly impressed both by the mass demonstration at Craigavon and by the performance of a relatively untested leader who, although an outsider, was instantly welcomed. The memories of this occasion would fortify Ulster unionists over the next few months, as Asquith's intentions on the future government of Ireland became clearer.

In the meantime, Ulster unionists were in a self-congratulatory mood. The meeting at Craigavon was 'one of the largest ever held in the open air in the vicinity of Belfast' and the enthusiasm displayed at Sydenham was 'unabounded' [sic]. It also provided 'striking evidence of the solidarity as well as the strength of Unionist opinion' and claimed that 'no one could witness it without recognising the power and reality of a cause that could claim such stalwart adherents'.[46]

However, a few months after this impressive demonstration in the grounds of James Craig's home, the fears expressed there had assumed an even more ominous tone. When the Liberal administration announced in a speech from the throne that it intended to introduce Irish Home Rule legislation, the UUC and other unionist groups in Ulster decided that it would be appropriate to stage a meeting that would amply illustrate the region's overwhelming opposition to the proposed measure. Initially, organisers in Belfast had been keen to hire the spacious grounds of Ormeau Park in south Belfast (which would go on to be the venue for other massive loyalist demonstrations, including a Vanguard protest meeting against direct rule in 1972 and a rearranged Orange Order meeting in July 1999). However, they eventually decided to stage the mass meeting three miles away, in the agricultural showgrounds at Balmoral.

The UUC agreed a fee of £75, plus an acknowledgement that it would pick up any bills for damage caused on the day. UUC plans for the demonstration, to be staged on Easter Tuesday, 9 April 1912, also indicate that a covered platform was hired to provide accommodation for 300 special guests, railway sleepers were laid down to withstand the marching feet of many thousands of men, and a schedule that involved the suspension of city tram services was drawn up. The sale of alcohol was to be forbidden at the site.[47]

There was significant newspaper speculation about the Balmoral meeting on Easter Tuesday and the parliamentary introduction of the Third Home Rule Bill two days later. *The Times* contextualised the imminent meeting in Belfast, which it described as a 'historic protest against the forcing of the measure upon the country', and its correspondent speculated on the likely degree of support that would be displayed at Balmoral the following day. Noting that membership of the unionist clubs had risen by nearly 50 per cent inside a year, with an estimated 150,000 members divided into 280 groups, the writer for *The Times* predicted that the likely 'muster' at the meeting would constitute 'the largest gathering of Irishmen ever brought together'.[48] The following day's leader in the same paper warned against cynical interpretations of unionists' motives and levels of determination. Suggesting that the real Ulster question was whether 'Englishmen and Scotchmen [were] prepared to fasten it [Home Rule] upon them by military force', *The Times* argued:

> Enlightened Liberalism may smile at the beliefs and passions of the Ulster Protestants, but it was those same beliefs and passions, in the forefathers of the men who will gather in Belfast today, which served Ireland for the British Crown, and freed the cause of civil and religious liberties in these islands from its last dangerous foes.[49]

In the same edition, readers were reminded that, although national attention had recently been centred on the coal strike,

Ulster was about to enter a momentous and history-making period, with the Balmoral demonstration promising to be 'the most remarkable ever seen in Ireland'. The on-the-spot reporter believed that the community in the north of Ireland was 'preparing for a great crisis in its history' and was 'determined that the issue shall not be against it through any failure on its own part of energy, zeal or resolution'.[50]

In a frenzy of press build-up to the Easter Tuesday event, loyalist papers in Ulster focused upon the imminent arrival of 'eminent noblemen bestowing names honoured in the history of the Empire'. These would join with 'merchant princes and country gentlemen esteemed and respected by their fellow citizens' and the more numerous ranks of 'sturdy artisans' and 'respectable farmers', to forge an atmosphere of 'fellowship and harmony for one purpose'.[51] In a reference to a recent pro-Home Rule demonstration in Dublin addressed by John Redmond and Joe Devlin, the *Northern Whig* haughtily suggested that there would be at Balmoral 'no evidence of the corner-boy and loafer element which so largely makes up the usual Nationalist assemblage'.[52]

Ulster loyalists would have followed the unfolding details of Herbert Asquith's plans for Ireland meticulously, with increasing anxiety and growing gloom. They ravenously devoured hundreds of column inches of press speculation about the forthcoming bill and reaction to the deepening political crisis. Many would have participated in hushed conversations in the shipyard, church vestry, football changing room and Orange hall. Despite these forebodings about the imminent introduction and ultimate passage of the Third Home Rule Bill, Ulster unionists were confident about the moral righteousness of their case and the vulnerability of the minority Liberal government that was promoting the legislation. They would also have been buoyed by the volume of support emanating from figures of influence in Great Britain. The local loyalist press carried details of the 'army' of peers and parliamentary representatives preparing to visit Belfast to lend their support to Ulster's cause, and most loyalists were determined to extend a hospitable welcome to these visitors and also to ensure that these important political allies, especially the relatively new Conservative Party leader, Andrew Bonar Law, would be impressed by their dignified, orderly and resolute resistance to the proposed legislation.[53]

Photographs of the scheduled speakers and platform figures were included in editions of the *Belfast Telegraph* on 5 and 6 April, and the mood of anticipation in Ulster reached a crescendo with Bonar Law's arrival on Easter Monday. His imminent appearance was warmly welcomed by papers like the *Northern Whig*, which pointed out that this political leader, unlike Winston Churchill a few weeks before, had required neither 'soldiers with fixed bayonets' nor 'police with drawn batons' to protect him.[54] The Conservative Party leader, who had travelled overnight to Scotland on the London train, encountered a stormy passage from Stranraer to the port of Larne, on the Antrim coast. Arriving mid-morning, Bonar Law was greeted by local dignitaries before boarding a train bound for Belfast. This stopped in several staunchly loyal Antrim towns and villages (including Carrickfergus and Greenisland), providing local people with the opportunity of welcoming Bonar Law, regarded by many as their saviour from imminent danger.

A more formal ceremony was provided at the Northern Counties Station in Belfast's York Road, where a large, flag-waving crowd and the familiar figure of Law's friend, Sir Edward Carson, awaited them. The two leaders and their entourages were taken in motor vehicles along crowded streets to the Reform Club in Belfast's Royal Avenue. Here, in the centre of the city, the crowds were thickest. In front of the club, with its pro-union banners (including one at the entrance proclaiming 'We stand firm for Ulster'), Andrew Bonar Law delivered a short address. He promised his admirers, 'though the brunt of the battle will be yours, there will not be help wanting'.[55] After a short reception in the club, the two men made their way to Mount Stewart, stopping briefly in the loyalist north-Down towns of Comber and Newtownards.

On the morning of the big parade in Belfast, a copy of Rudyard Kipling's specially commissioned poem, 'Ulster 1912', was printed in the *Morning Post*. Kipling, a renowned author of stories and novels about the British Empire, was a keen supporter of the unionist cause in Ireland, and a generous contributor to Carson's Ulster Fund. Like most contemporary imperialists, Kipling fully appreciated the value of Ulster's predicament in harnessing support for the greater imperial cause. Playing on emotive terms and images, he portrayed an intimidated and threatened loyal minority, who were being coerced and bullied by a larger neighbour and insufficiently protected by an indifferent 'mother' parliament. Kipling's poem was a call to both imperialists and Ulster loyalists to continue the fight against Home Rule. In the first stanza, the celebrated writer depicted the plight of Ulster unionists in their 'dark eleventh hour', having been 'sold to every evil Power' by 'England's act and deed'. In the last verse of his poem, Kipling exhorted Ulster loyalists to stand firm:

> What answer from the North?
> One Law, One Land, One Throne.
> If England drive us forth
> We shall not fall alone![56]

The atmosphere in Belfast on the morning of 9 April was one of vibrancy and expectation. The city was hardly a stranger to scenes of unionist protest, and memories of the Craigavon demonstration the previous year were fresh in the memories of many. The weather, so unpredictable in Ireland in spring, appeared to look kindly on the organisers. The demonstration had been planned for Easter Tuesday, which was a recognised holiday for most industrial and commercial workers. Whilst most Protestant Ulstermen would have ruminated about the political occasion scheduled for the south of the city that day, others – especially the many thousands of shipyard workers who had built her – would have cast their minds towards the *Titanic*, which was due to leave Southampton on its maiden voyage to New York the following day. The twin pride of many Belfast men was their industrial muscle, embodied by the achievement of building the *Titanic*, and their enduring political opposition to Irish unity. Both would soon be subjects for considerable distress. Within a few days the unthinkable would happen – the great ship would sink in the Atlantic Ocean, and a parliamentary bill proposing an all-Ireland administration would be introduced in the House of Commons. (When the *Titanic* did sink, on 14 April, claiming the lives of over 1,500 passengers and crew, news of the Irish Home Rule Bill and further reactions to the Balmoral meeting were kept off the front pages of many newspapers for several days.)

Organisers had been methodical in their preparations for the Balmoral event. Over 70 special trains had been booked to transport people from all corners of Ulster to Belfast. An estimated 80,000–100,000 members of unionist clubs and Orange lodges lined up to march in columns of four, mainly from the city centre, but also from Dunmurry, along the Lisburn Road, to the meeting point at Balmoral. The city was 'early astir' as its loyalist citizens prepared to participate in the event. One reporter observed that 'even a visitor from another planet would have known that something important was afoot'.[57]

Marchers had started to gather at the city's Orange halls and unionist-club premises before nine o'clock to get ready for the march from the city centre an hour or so later. There were several assembly points for demonstrators that morning. Orangemen and unionist-club members met in Templemore Avenue in the east of the city, at Clifton Park Avenue in the north and at various points south of the city centre, including Donegall Pass and Ballynafeigh. Even larger crowds lined the streets in the city centre and on the main approach roads to

Balmoral. There were many early arrivals, seeking good vantage points along the route of the march, which was expected to take close to three hours. Vocal encouragement was given to the demonstrators and bandsmen as they marched over two miles to the showgrounds. A news report described the scene on the Lisburn Road, about a mile from Balmoral:

> every house had one or more flags floating from the roof or fluttering from the windows, and the vivid note of colour was accentuated by the small Union Jacks carried by the spectators … At the Samaritan Hospital, there was a fine display of flags, and the outside of St Thomas's Parochial Hall was gaily embellished with Union Jacks and flowers, daffodils being conspicuous in the decorative scheme.[58]

The crowd at the venue were sober and well behaved and the police presence was low key throughout the city. When they entered the grounds at Balmoral, the marchers, symbolically headed by a contingent of Apprentice Boys, paraded past four platforms containing a host of dignitaries. These included an estimated 70–80 British MPs, most of the Irish Unionist Party and a large number of peers from both sides of the Irish Sea. As they were awaiting the arrival of all the contingents, spectators would have cast admiring glances at the figures on the platforms, many of whose faces would have been recognisable from recent press exposure. In particular, they would have strained their necks to spot the leader of the Conservative Party. External observers were particularly impressed by the orderly behaviour of the loyalist gathering and also by their cross-class nature. The correspondent from *The Times* noted that not only had contingents arrived at Balmoral from all parts of Ireland – including 'even distant Kerry and rebellious Cork and Clare' – but also that the majority of the marchers were men of 'serviceable age'. In a description illustrating the degree of class consciousness at the time, the reporter concluded that 'in spite of the mixture of classes, it was a remarkably well-dressed crowd', with working-class groups like the Belfast shipwrights 'looking specially well turned out'.[59] These visitors were also impressed by the size of the crowd and the sheer scale of the event. Many writers referred to the 'ocean' of faces encountered by the platform speakers and remarked how this degree of opposition to the planned legislation was not fully appreciated in Great Britain. One journalist wrote that 'if one-tenth of the electors could only see this it would be the end of Home Rule'.[60]

Balmoral provided further indication of Ulster unionists' growing awareness of the media and a developing understanding of how to utilise new propaganda techniques. Observers commented on how Union Jacks appeared to be everywhere at the venue; certainly, the organisers had an eye for spectacular detail. This included 'the largest Union Jack ever unfurled', which dominated the main platform. This enormous flag, on a 90-foot flagstaff and measuring 48 feet by 25, lent the occasion a potent symbolism. R. Dawson Bates, James Craig and their colleagues were conscious of the presence of so many national journalists and photographers and endeavoured to provide them with up-to-date statements from the main speakers, opportunities to photograph them and state-of-the-art media facilities. Thus, visiting and local newspapermen were given access to telegraph facilities. It was reported that a special observation platform had been erected for 'an army of photographers and cinematograph operators' to enable 'action' shots of marchers and key platform speakers.[61]

The atmosphere at the Balmoral Showgrounds was quite different from that experienced at Craigavon in 1911 and set the tone for other major demonstrations in the city later that year. Religious observance rather than raucous political campaigning set the mood for the day, as the meeting commenced with a rendition of Psalm 90. Platform speakers included Walter Long, James Craig and Lord Londonderry and keynote addresses were given by Sir Edward Carson and Andrew Bonar Law. Senior Irish Unionist Party member Walter Long had the task of warming up the crowd and introducing the main speakers. Addressing a mass of faces, Long spoke on behalf of the many thousands present, informing the Conservative Party leader and Carson that 'we are behind you' and that the giant audience assembled in front of them would 'follow and we shall win'.[62] Sir Edward Carson congratulated the marchers, bandsmen and spectators for their enthusiasm, their dignified bearing and resolute opposition to Irish Home Rule. Reminding them of the spirit shown by their forefathers at the Boyne over three centuries previously, he went on:

> I expected that this would be a great gathering, but the reality has far exceeded my expectations. It is not your numbers – great and imposing though they are – which seem to me so impressive. If ever the demeanour of men could be taken as an index of their inner spirit then what I have seen today convinces me ... that you are animated by a unity of purpose and a fixity of resolution which nothing can shake, and which must prove irresistible.[63]

Warning Asquith and his colleagues that 'as you have treated us with fraud, if necessary we will treat you with force', Carson vehemently dismissed his opponents' prevailing view that Ireland was a nation. An interrogation of the veracity of nationalist and Liberal claims was at the centre of his address. He maintained:

> Men do not constitute a nation because they happen to live in the same island. Ireland is not and never has been a nation. There are two peoples in Ireland separated from each other by a gulf of religion, of race, and above all, of prejudice far deeper than that which separates Ireland as a whole from the rest of the United Kingdom.[64]

The distinguished figure of Andrew Bonar Law was introduced to the multitude and received a resounding welcome. For Ulster loyalists, this was the moment they had long awaited. The leader of Britain's Conservative Party – and a man they fervently hoped was prime minister in waiting – was about to pledge himself wholeheartedly and without reservation to their cause. A complete hush spread around the huge arena. In his light Scottish Lowlands burr, Bonar Law condemned his political opponents for unhatching such a 'tremendous conspiracy' as the Home Rule Bill and argued that the case of Ulster was an imperial issue rather than just a local one. Although he did not attempt to conceal the 'very grave peril' facing his audience, the Conservative Party leader pointed out that they possessed several crucial advantages, including a 'fixity of resolve', the lack of a historical precedent for compelling a portion of the British population to 'secede' their citizenship, and the 'moral power' of Ulster's resistance. In the first part of his speech, Bonar Law stressed the point that Herbert Asquith was unlikely to succeed in his quest to force through Home Rule:

> It will be difficult – I think it will be impossible – to overcome your opposition. You make no claim except that you should not be deprived of your birthright, that you should not be driven out of the Empire which your fathers have done so much to create and to sustain. There is no instance in history where force has been used by any nation to drive out their fellow citizens. Is it conceivable that the British people would use force to compel you to secede?[65]

In the climax to his address, the Tory leader drew parallels with previous historical crises. Emphasising loyalists' sense of besiegement, he reassured them that they were far from being alone in their predicament. Over a background of huge cheering, Bonar Law told his emotional audience:

> Once again you hold the pass for the Empire. You are a besieged city. Does not the picture of the past, the glorious past with which you are so familiar, rise again before your eyes? The timid have left you – the Lundys have betrayed you. But you have closed your gates. The Government by

their Parliament Act have created a boom against you, a boom to cut you off from the help of the British people. You will burst that boom. The help will come, and when the crisis is over men will say of you in words not unlike those once used by Pitt: 'You have saved yourselves by your exertions and you will save the Empire by your example.'[66]

Undoubtedly, there was something striking in the contrast between the extreme language and exhortations made by the leader of a major national party and his mild-mannered personality and image. Edward Pearce has written that Andrew Bonar Law spoke 'like an Afrikaner politician invoking Blood River and the Voortrekkers'.[67] Yet Andrew Bonar Law, with his close family ties and intimate knowledge of Ulster, instinctively spoke its language, and he clearly realised the true significance of the Balmoral meeting. Moving and passionate as the speeches undoubtedly were, it was the symbolic unification of the two political parties involved in the afternoon's proceedings that provided the most memorable moment for most of those present. Obviously stage managed, but nonetheless effective, Edward Carson's warm handshake with Andrew Bonar Law at the end of the meeting prompted the loudest cheer of the day. As Tony Stewart wrote, this single moment represented 'the wedding of Protestant Ulster with the Conservative Party'.[68]

Press interest in the Balmoral demonstration was considerable and the event filled many column inches in most national papers, especially those that reflected opinion on the right of the political spectrum. Several focused on Ulster's Protestant community and not just on their leaders' political arguments, with *The Times* describing it as 'more than a political meeting'. According to that paper, it instead represented 'the assemblage of a nation to defend its existence, to plead against an attempt to suppress its identity, to plead and also to warn'.[69] Hyperbole was deemed to be the order of the day. The *Daily Telegraph* suggested that the events in south Belfast the previous day had constituted 'one of the greatest manifestos of the faith and determination of a people that the world has ever seen'.[70]

Several reports called attention to loyalist unity, class cohesion and self-sacrifice. The *Morning Post* informed its readers that the demonstration was a province-wide event and not simply one attended by the Belfast populace. Loyalists had, the *Post* pointed out, 'marched by night or travelled long distances in trains, tramped over mountains and rowed over loughs to reach a railway station in order to be present'.[71] *The Times* noted that 'patrician and plebeian, clergy and laity [and] masters and men' mingled freely together in a parade devoid, it maintained, of the class distinction so prevalent at the time.[72]

Another major theme of British press coverage was imperialistic and jingoistic rhetoric. The *Pall Mall Gazette* – which had led its editions on headlines such as 'Ulster's greatest day', 'Great demonstration of loyalty' and 'A stern resolve' – compared the plight of Ulster's loyalists to that of African empire builders. The *Gazette* likened Ulster's frustration to the resentment of white imperialists in Africa, claiming that in the north of Ireland 'the heirs of a higher civilisation repudiate the rule and rapine of a system marked by some of the worst passions and impediments of the Dark Ages'.[73] Arnold White, writing in the *Daily Express* the following day, even suggested that if England remained 'obdurate on Ulster's appeal to remain part of the United Kingdom, it must leave England!'[74]

The Times also emphasised the impact the Ulster unionist show of loyalty and political defiance had made upon the influential contingent from Great Britain, most of whom made their homeward journey that evening. Describing the Balmoral meeting in an editorial entitled 'The Ulster demonstration' as 'one of the very greatest, if not the very greatest that has ever been held in that Kingdom', the leader suggested that the occasion would have a dampening effect upon Home Rule legislation and would force its architects to rethink their proposals.[75] The paper argued that British politicians should consider alternatives to Home Rule:

Yesterday's demonstration will open the eyes, we trust, of many British Liberals to these truths, and lead them, before it is too late, to put their veto upon a project which is manifestly fraught with very awful possibilities ... The danger to the Union – and it is a real danger – does not lie in any fondness of the British voters for Home Rule, but in their weariness of the whole Irish question and in the indifference that weariness begets.[76]

The tone of Ulster press coverage was mostly self-congratulatory and almost reverent in its awareness of the 'special' and 'historic' nature of the occasion. Reporting the 'triumphal progress' and 'enthusiastic reception' afforded to the Conservative Party leader, the *Belfast News-Letter* claimed that there had 'never been such a march of civilians in the history of Ireland, [let alone] the United Kingdom', which had been 'so perfect in [its] orderly discipline'.[77] The following day, the *Northern Whig* attempted to step back from the heady emotion generated by the occasion to assess its real impact. It insisted that 'at last the Radical fiction about Ulster having been reconciled to Home Rule has been exploded' and, insisting there could be 'no compromise and no shrinking from stern action', the *Whig*'s editorial maintained, rather darkly, that 'in the nature of things it must be war to the death'.[78]

Meanwhile, left-leaning papers, whilst pouring scorn on the unionist position, did concede the impressive scale of the Balmoral meeting. The *Manchester Guardian* described as an 'impressive and imposing affair'.[79] Nationalist newspapers dismissed Bonar Law's visit, with the *Irish News* stressing his 'ignorance of Ireland and everything relating to it'.[80]

The events at Balmoral were perhaps most remarkable for their impact upon the respective leaders of the campaign against Home Rule. Andrew Bonar Law was almost overwhelmed by the size and enthusiasm of the crowds lining Belfast's central streets, as well as moved by the discipline and determination of the marching ranks of unionist-club members and Orangemen at Balmoral Showgrounds. Doubtless he shared this depth of feeling with Edward Carson as they proceeded by car through the dense, exuberant crowds back to the Ulster Club for dinner, before travelling by train to Larne later that evening.

When he arrived in London the following day, just in time to make his final preparations for the introduction of the Home Rule Bill in the House of Commons, Andrew Bonar Law told a journalist how deeply moved he had been by the 'unalterable resolve' of the Belfast people. He claimed that 'no one before in our generation and in this country has seen a whole city so moved'.[81] Sir Edward Carson had also been deeply impressed by the Belfast gathering, though he had undergone a range of emotions. Writing a few days later to his confidante, Lady Londonderry, he observed:

> The whole proceedings at Balmoral seem like a dream – it was the most thrilling experience I ever had or will have. But it has a demoralising effect in making me think of the criminal folly of decadent England in tampering with such a splendid people for the sake of throwing a sop to her implacable foes.[82]

With hindsight, it is difficult not to overestimate the significance of the events at the Balmoral Showgrounds in April 1912. The demonstration, happening as it did on the eve of the introduction of the Home Rule Bill, served as the first marker of the unionist resistance campaign. As A.T.Q. Stewart pointed out, the extra-parliamentary nature of Balmoral and the dubious legality implicit in the promises of the Conservative Party leader were developments of major significance, evidence of Bonar Law having 'committed his party to an extreme course'.[83] Balmoral also brought the two parties closer together on the question of Ireland's political future. Crucially, the meeting marked the beginning of a shared voyage from which neither traveller would find it easy to disembark.

'An unnecessary bill'

It was on 11 April 1912, less than 48 hours after the massive unionist demonstration in Belfast, amidst this increasingly tense and expectant atmosphere, that parliament reassembled following the Easter recess and Herbert Asquith introduced the Third Home Rule Bill in the House of Commons. The actual terms of the bill were comparatively modest. Like the 1893 bill, it made provision for a bicameral legislature in Dublin, which would be able to govern most aspects of domestic policy. There would be 164 members elected to the proposed House of Commons in Dublin and representatives would be nominated for the Senate. Significant local powers would be invested in this legislative creation but, as George Dangerfield pointed out many years ago, the bill was 'built on the old Gladstonian formula of transforming purely Irish matters to the Irish Parliament', and key governmental powers still lay within the grasp of the imperial parliament at Westminster.[84] Therefore, the London parliament had ultimate responsibility for defence, foreign policy, the imposition and direct collection of taxation, and 'reserved services'. These included newly created benefits such as pensions and national-insurance payments, tax collection and, for an initial period of six years, the RIC. Also, as was the case with the 1893 measure, the Irish electorate would still be permitted to send representatives to Westminster.

In other words, although the number of MPs would be halved (to 42), Westminster's sovereignty over the Irish parliament would be unambiguous. There had been, at this stage, no serious demand for independence. Therefore, Ireland's imperial status was not tampered with. Section three of the bill was indirectly aimed at Ulster Protestants. This prohibited the introduction of legislation in a Dublin parliament that would discriminate in any form against any religious group or individual. Undoubtedly influenced by the relatively recent furore over the *Ne temere* papal decree of 1908 and the McCann case in Belfast (both of which involved what unionists saw as undue interference from the Catholic Church in the institution of marriage), the bill prevented such a parliament legislating to make 'any religious belief or religious ceremony a condition of the validity of any marriage'.[85]

However, no direct reference to or consideration of the unionist cause was contained within the detail of the bill. Patricia Jalland has argued that Asquith missed an opportunity for nipping Ulster resistance to Home Rule in the bud.[86] She and others have maintained that if Asquith had built in provision for the exclusion of Ulster (or a significant part of it) from Home Rule, loyalists within Ulster and across the rest of Ireland – and, more crucially, unionists in the Conservative Party – would have been divided over such an offer. However, although a forward-looking and proactive intervention like this might have resulted in small-scale internal division, it is probable that the number of loyalist dissidents would have been relatively low and their resistance to the broader measure of Home Rule is not likely to have been fundamentally different.

Herbert Asquith, not normally the most impassioned of politicians, gave a lengthy and sometimes emotional defence of his proposed measure during the House of Commons debate. Stressing the one-nation idea of Irish society, he showed little willingness to compromise on any aspect of his legislation, especially on Ulster. Although Winston Churchill, speaking later that month, would be slightly more conciliatory in his tone, admitting that 'the perfectly genuine apprehension of the majority of people of North East Ulster constitutes the most serious obstacle to a thoroughly satisfactory settlement',[87] Asquith reminded his political opponents sitting opposite that Ulster loyalists represented only a minority, both in terms of their population and in their parliamentary representation. He argued that 'we cannot admit, and we will not admit the right of a minority of the people, and relatively a small minority, when every care is taken to safeguard their interests ... to veto the verdict of the vast body of their country men'.[88]

Predictably, the Liberal premier got an enthusiastic response from Irish Nationalist Party leader John Redmond, who described the bill as 'a great measure', before proceeding to 'thank God that I have lived to see this day'.[89] Believing it to be a historic day, Redmond claimed that Ireland had 'almost entirely, I believe, cast aside her suspicions and her rancour towards this country', whilst England was 'more willing than ever she was in her past history to admit Ireland on terms of equality, liberty and loyalty into that great sisterhood of nations that make up the British Empire'.[90]

Although Redmond's opponent Sir Edward Carson agreed with him on the futility of legislative autonomy without genuine financial independence, their perceptions of the proposed measure were radically different. Quoting an earlier opponent of Irish Home Rule, Lord Derby, Carson reminded John Redmond and the House of Commons that there was 'no mid course possible' between the unity of Britain and the freedom of Ireland. He demanded to be told of a historical precedent for 'any such action' as 'a parliament turning out a community which are satisfied to stay under its rule'. The unionist leader explained:

> We believe it to be an unnecessary Bill and we believe it to be a fatal Bill for our own country and an equally fatal Bill for yours, and above all things, we believe it to be involved in the greatest series of dishonest transactions that has ever disgraced any country.[91]

The most memorable pro-union speech during this debate came a few days later, not from Carson but from Andrew Bonar Law. He castigated his opposite number for his reluctance to call an election on this issue and also for his failure to recognise the scale of Ulster's resistance to the bill. Bonar Law declared that he would 'not carry this Bill without submitting it to the people of this country'. He warned Asquith, 'if you make the attempt, you will succeed only in breaking our Parliamentary machinery'.[92] Fresh from his experience in the emotional cauldron of Balmoral, Bonar Law suggested that the prime minister had not sufficiently reflected upon the possible repercussions of his actions, asking him bluntly how he was going 'to overcome that resistance'. Declaring that the case for 'a separate treatment of Ulster' was 'far stronger' than that for nationalist Ireland, Bonar Law ended his speech with the House of Commons in uproar. He painted a picture of a near future in which the British Army, with fixed bayonets, would find themselves directly facing thousands of Ulstermen singing the national anthem. Looking Herbert Asquith in the eye, Bonar Law maintained that his bill was doomed, and that forcing Ulster Protestants to accept Home Rule was impossible:

> All your talk about details, the union of hearts and the rest of it is a sham. This is a reality. It is a rock, and on that rock this Bill or any Bill like it will inevitably make shipwreck.[93]

The unionist press was predictably hostile to Herbert Asquith's bill. The *Daily Mail* criticised its 'makeshift' and 'provisional' nature, before going on to maintain that it 'solves no difficulty and creates a fresh and grave complication in the Ulster question'. It concluded that the Third Home Rule Bill 'contains in almost every clause the germs of perpetual strife and friction'.[94] Its sister paper, *The Times*, suggested that the bill would 'disappoint the hopes of Nationalist Ireland' and would not 'allay the fears of Unionist Ireland'.[95] A leading provincial paper, the *Glasgow Herald*, concentrated on the measure's economic ramifications. They asked the question, 'In all of this, where does Great Britain and the Empire come in?' Their answer was concise. 'For Great Britain it is all pay, pay, pay.'[96] The *Spectator* concentrated on what they believed was the government's indecision about Ulster, 'pretending that it does not exist'.[97]

Loyalist papers in Ulster instantly cast Asquith as the villain of the piece. The *Northern Whig* claimed that his heart was 'not in the work' of introducing Home Rule and suggested he was the 'bond slave of the Nationalist Party'. Claiming that the prime minister's treatment of Ulster was 'more like that of a pettifogging attorney than a statesman', the *Whig* argued that 'to place the Loyalists of Ulster under the heel of the avowed enemies of the Empire would be an act of betrayal, which would bring everlasting disgrace upon the British people'.[98]

The nationalist and Radical press were ebullient about the bill's introduction and gave it copious coverage. The *Daily News* (12 April) forecast that the measure would make 'entirely favourable' impressions on the electorate and provide Ireland with 'a substantial fulfilment of her demands',[99] whilst the *Irish News* lauded the proposed legislation as being 'the best of three Home Rule Bills'.[100]

Asquith's introduction of his bill was to set in motion a parliamentary campaign which, 'though bitterly – even violently – conducted, had about it an air of unreality'.[101] As a result of the main political parties in Great Britain becoming 'prisoners of their Irish allies', the traditional parliamentary sense of compromise was sorely tested, as external political and religious pressures extenuated the crisis. Arguably the turmoil experienced during the spring of 1914 and the drift towards civil war might have been avoided if an alternative deal, accommodating unionist concerns, had been struck. This would have been 'much less of an affront than the humiliations that Redmond had to endure while Asquith made policy on the hoof in February and March 1914'.[102] Yet, even with a more incisive and forward-thinking statesman at the helm that spring, the political campaign *outside* parliament would have tested the resolve both of parliament and a stronger, less vulnerable administration than that led by Herbert Asquith.

'Orange bitters and Irish whiskey will not mix'

The furore over the Third Home Rule Bill's introduction in April 1912 set the tone for its eventful passage over the next two years. Much against the wishes of the government, the political future of Ireland dominated the British political agenda more and more. Yet the bill's first reading in April and May received a relatively low-key and apathetic response from many non-Irish members, and dismal attendance coupled with poor quality of debate were noticeable in parliament. Herbert Asquith had promised his opponents that the government would not use its majority to invoke a parliamentary 'guillotine' on limiting sufficient debate on the bill's numerous clauses. Initially, at least, he kept his promise and the measure made slow progress over its first few months, passing its second reading in the House of Commons on 9 June. As the bill proceeded into its committee stage, many unionists feared that the Home Rule bandwagon was rumbling on regardless of the protests of Edward Carson and Andrew Bonar Law.

However, a young Liberal MP, Thomas Agar-Robartes, sparked off lively discussion by introducing a controversial amendment on 11 June. Agar-Robartes represented the Cornish constituency of St Austell and was fully cognizant of the doubts many of his Nonconformist constituents had about Home Rule. His amendment threw both the government and opposition parties into a quandary and led to considerable unionist reassessment of their political strategy. Although it would be defeated by a majority of 69 after a lively three days of debate, the discussion of an 'exclusion' option would prove to have long-term ramifications both for key politicians and their respective parties. Agar-Robartes argued that the four Ulster counties where Protestants constituted a majority of the population – Antrim, Down, Armagh and Londonderry – should be permanently excluded from the terms of the bill. Pointing out to his parliamentary audience that 'Orange bitters and Irish whiskey will not mix', Agar-Robartes maintained:

> You will not reconcile the two nations by putting one at the mercy of the other. By the adoption of this amendment

Parliament might be able to satisfy to a greater extent the demands of Irish Nationalists and in a large measure to quieten the anxiety and legitimate fear of the majority of the Protestants in Ireland.[103]

John Redmond was quick to reject such a proposal outright, asking why Ireland was to be 'the only country in the world where religious animosities are to be so permanently established'.[104] However, and despite their concerns for the predicament of unionists in Ireland's other three provinces, Sir Edward Carson's parliamentary group and Andrew Bonar Law's Tory members agreed to back the amendment for tactical reasons. They gambled that a successful amendment would result in the bill being brought down. It did not signify, they maintained, that leading unionist figures were abandoning loyalists in the rest of Ireland, nor did it mean that they were opting for Ulster exclusion as their first choice (although exclusion would be high on the Irish Unionist Party's agenda the following year).

The political stalemate produced by the amendment resulted in considerable soul-searching by senior members of the cabinet. It was in its wake that Winston Churchill started deliberating about offering Ulster a moratorium lasting several years before being required to join an Irish parliament. The stalemate was a factor in Liberal by-election defeats at South Manchester, Crewe and Midlothian during the early summer.

Ulster's loyalist press reassured its readers that the strategy of supporting such an amendment was 'simply and solely for the purpose of killing the Home Rule Bill' and suggested that the recent parliamentary debates had illustrated that Ulster was 'an impregnable barrier in the way of Home Rule'.[105] The *Northern Whig* confidently proclaimed that the measure would not survive the exclusion. The paper reminded its readers that 'as Parnell once put it, Ireland without Ulster would be Ireland robbed of the plums'.[106]

Edward Carson and Andrew Bonar Law were furious at

Herbert Asquith's failure to seriously consider the exclusion option, and also by the fact that the parliamentary front bench was ridiculing the opposition for deserting Protestants elsewhere in Ireland. Carson and Bonar Law expressed their outrage both in parliament and at a large protest meeting in the Royal Albert Hall on 14 June. The theme for this protest meeting was 'England's duty in the crisis'. At it, a resolution condemning the Home Rule legislation was carried unanimously. Carson told the large audience that Asquith's dismissal of the exclusion compromise could be regarded as 'a declaration of war'. Making full use of the melodramatic air he had honed during many years of practice in the highest courts of the land, the Irish Unionist Party leader hinted at an imminent departure from his party's current policy:

> We will accept the declaration of war. We are not altogether unprepared. I think it is time we should take a step forward in our campaign and I will recommend that to be done.[107]

On 18 June, the amendment was defeated by an overall majority of 69, but not before Bonar Law had launched another attack on the government for its 'irresponsibility' in dismissing Agar-Robartes's amendment. Referring to the Liberals' condemnation of the 'incendiary language' of their opponents, Bonar Law suggested that what the government was actually doing was 'inviting the people of Ulster to show not by language but by acts that they are in earnest'.[108]

With the long summer parliamentary recess looming, the attention of those following the Home Rule crisis switched from the debating chambers of the House of Commons to public halls and open-air venues in both Ulster and Great Britain. Tories and Irish Unionist Party members would again join forces in major pro-union occasions at Blenheim Palace in late July and for the signing of Ulster's Solemn League and Covenant towards the end of September. When parliament met again in mid-October, the events in Ulster and on Merseyside and Clydeside a few weeks previously had renewed interest in the Irish question and

MPs expectantly awaited the responses of their respective leaders. To unionist horror, Herbert Asquith reneged on an earlier promise and the parliamentary 'guillotine' was recalled to hasten the bill's first passage through the Commons. As ever, Winston Churchill found the appropriate phrase to irritate his parliamentary opponents. The first lord of the admiralty told unionists that 'those who talk of revolution ought to be prepared for the guillotine'.[109]

Unquestionably, proper discussion of the bill's 51 remaining clauses was restricted during committee stage in the run-up to Christmas. Only 6 clauses were fully debated and 27 others were partly considered, which meant that whole swathes of the proposed measure were not discussed at all. A major theme of the unionist press's coverage of the debates was the paucity of parliamentary time afforded to discussing the bill. Claiming that only 212 of its lines had been discussed during the recent committee stage (with 1,434 lines being ignored), the *Belfast News-Letter* claimed that the government was 'degrading the institution of Parliament', and was also culpable of 'filching from the people their inherent right to [be] the determining voice in the passage of legislation'.[110]

Meanwhile, the opposition was further dismayed when the government refused to accept any amendments they made. This growing resentment boiled over during a debate on 13 November, when pro-Ulster Tory MP and suspected arms smuggler Sir William Bull called the prime minister a 'traitor'. Refusing to withdraw his remark, the MP for Hammersmith left the house as the opposition benches chanted, 'Resign! Resign!' and 'Civil war! Civil war!' The speaker adjourned proceedings for an hour in a bid to allow tempers to subside. When the chamber reassembled, however, there was further disorder, which this time saw the government front benches deciding to leave the chamber. Winston Churchill exacerbated the situation by provocatively waving his handkerchief at his opponents, and one back bencher, Ronald McNeill, threw the day's order paper at the minister, striking him on the forehead. Both Churchill and the Kent MP had to be restrained. Following an apology from McNeill the next day, the atmosphere in the Commons thawed a little.[111]

Sir Edward Carson had been contemplating the option of exclusion throughout most of 1912 and was especially interested in extending the provisions Thomas Agar-Robartes had suggested in his defeated June amendment. What was radically different about Carson's thinking at this stage was the fact that he privately accepted the need for a new amendment that had the potential to be turned into an Ulster-only policy later. The bill's rapid progress in the House of Commons and the restricted powers of delay now at the disposal of the House of Lords, combined with Asquith's stubborn refusal to compromise, had convinced Carson that his only remaining option centred on some form of exclusion for Ulster. Shortly before Christmas, he had managed to persuade the UUC to support an amendment he was planning to present to parliament at the beginning of 1913. In this he would propose the exemption of all nine of Ulster's counties (not just the four identified by Agar-Robartes) from the terms of the bill.

On the eve of the introduction of Carson's amendment, the *Belfast News-Letter* tried to assuage the fears of its loyalist readership by denying that such a measure represented a shift in policy by their leader. Refuting the 'likely' charge from their opponents that the Irish Unionist Party was 'deserting the scattered Unionists in the other provinces', the morning paper's editorial remained hopeful that loyalists would 'understand the tactics underlying the decision to put his amendment forward'.[112]

At a time of personal as well as political crisis (his first wife Annette's health had started to decline; she eventually died in April), Sir Edward Carson introduced his amendment to the Third Home Rule Bill in the House of Commons on New Year's Day. This was regarded as one of Carson's finest speeches. It was acknowledged by Herbert Asquith as 'very powerful and moving' and by John Redmond as 'serious and solemn'.[113] In the introduction to his amendment, Carson returned to familiar economic arguments against Home Rule. He said that it was 'intolerable' that 'the great and expanding industries of the north of Ireland' should now be 'at the mercy of 400,000 small farmers ... in the south and west'. He reminded parliamentary colleagues of the fears of Belfast's merchants and businessmen, who had informed him of their 'dread' at the imminent 'shock to credit which would happen in Belfast if this Bill were passed'.[114] He also stressed the grave dangers involved in critics ridiculing unionist objections to the measure. In addition, Edward Carson maintained there was a need to revise the extent of the territory likely to be involved in any exclusion. He declared that 'when you are excluding a portion of Ireland I think you ought to exclude at least a province'.[115]

Though praising Carson for a statesmanlike speech, Herbert Asquith and John Redmond were dismissive of their opponent's claims and new proposal. Redmond derided the notion of Ulster's exclusion by insisting 'the idea of our agreement to the partition of our nation is unthinkable'.[116] The prime minister pointed out that 'no Government could allow so undemocratic a claim as that put forward by Ulster to veto Home Rule'.[117] However, this public display of support for the Irish nationalists camouflaged Asquith's private attitudes to such a move to solve the Irish problem. He and some other leading ministers, including Winston Churchill and David Lloyd George, were interested in the possibility of exploring such a strategy, but they were deterred by the reticence of a majority of the cabinet and, of course, by the need to satisfy the interests of their Irish nationalist allies.

The refusal of Herbert Asquith's government to accept Edward Carson's amendment – it was defeated by 97 votes – was roundly condemned in the loyalist press, with the *Northern Whig* suggesting that the government had committed 'a great crime last night when it refused to accept an amendment which would have prevented the shedding of blood in Ulster'. Comparing their predicament with that of the citizens of Derry in 1688, the paper reminded its readers:

> from this day forward the duty of every Protestant in Ulster is to go on making preparations in grim earnest, so that when the day of battle comes it will be possible to strike a blow that will surprise Mr Asquith's docile followers and render worthless any attempt on the part of an Irish Parliament to rule over Ulster.[118]

There was considerable excitement, both at Westminster and in Ulster, over the next fortnight as the bill's anticipated successful passage edged ever closer. Belfast loyalists expressed their anger and concern at a meeting in the Shankill Orange Hall on 8 January and details of a protest demonstration in the streets outside Westminster after the measure had been passed in the House of Commons were also announced. The *Northern Whig* reported 'circulating rumours' of 'possible disorder in the neighbourhood of the House of Commons' the following evening after the declaration of the final vote on the bill in the house.[119] James Craig and F.E. Smith were scheduled to lead a counter-demonstration to that organised by nationalists hoping to celebrate the bill's progression.

That evening, Thursday, 16 January, the third reading of the Home Rule Bill was approved by a majority of 110 in the House of Commons. In the streets outside, serious clashes between jubilant Irish nationalists and protesting Ulster loyalists were avoided, though scuffles were reported as hundreds of unionists gathered at the Constitutional Club, some 200 yards away in Whitehall. Emotions in Belfast that evening were mixed, as news of events at Westminster filtered back to residents of the Falls and Shankill Roads. In the former district, and in other nationalist areas such as the Short Strand, the Markets and North Queen Street, there was parading on the streets and bonfires were lit, whilst in loyalist areas for the next two evenings there was 'orderly' protest, during which copies of the bill were unceremoniously set alight.

'A reckless rodomontade'

The bond between the Conservative Party and the Irish Unionist Party, which had been formally acknowledged at Balmoral in the spring, was further strengthened at an extraordinary mass demonstration against Home Rule staged in rural Oxfordshire three months later. Buoyed by the success of recent 'monster' meetings in Belfast, and increasingly concerned by the rapid progress of Asquith's legislation, a range of unionist groups – including the Primrose League, unionist women's clubs and other organisations within both the Conservative and Irish Unionist Parties – joined together to organise this demonstration in late July 1912. Women took a very active role in organising this meeting, although the vast majority of participants that day were men. Its purpose was to demonstrate the scale of opposition to the proposed measure within Great Britain, as well as to cement the bond between the two parties. Such a demonstration, along with the forthcoming pledges of support from the leader of the opposition, were timely. The prime minister had visited Ireland the previous week and had defended his decision to introduce Home Rule. The unambiguous response from Andrew Bonar Law would be articulated at Blenheim Palace (ironically, the ancestral home of Winston Churchill) a few days later.

The mass outdoor meeting was held in the spacious grounds of Blenheim Palace on Saturday, 27 July. Warm, sunny weather greeted an estimated 3,000 delegates from the Conservative and Irish Unionist Parties, with at least another 10,000 members of the public streaming on to the palace's lawns and quadrangles. Attended by many luminaries of British society, ranging from some 40 peers (including the duke of Marlborough, who was hosting the event, the duke of Norfolk, a Catholic peer, Lord Lansdowne and Lord Londonderry) and dozens of Conservative and Irish Unionist Party MPs, to a vast 'assembly of picked men' from across Britain and Ireland, the Blenheim Palace meeting represented the pinnacle of unionist extra-parliamentary protest in Britain.

Special trains had ferried delegates from across the country to the sleepy Oxfordshire station of Woodstock. Once they had arrived, they had the opportunity of taking a stroll around the large estate of the duke of Marlborough and examining the treasures in his stately home. Some would have taken a boat trip on Blenheim's lake, whilst others would have enjoyed choral recitals and music served up by the military section of the London Philharmonic Orchestra. A mouth-watering luncheon, prepared by chefs hired for the occasion from the finest London clubs and houses, was served up to guests by an army of waiters in a large marquee, some 300 feet by 100.

Despite the relaxed setting – photos of the occasion show a large proportion of the large audience dressed in light summer jackets and wearing boaters – and the casual start to the day, it was not to be 'a mere holiday picnic', as the *Standard*'s reporter pointed out, but rather a meeting with 'a stern and earnest purpose'.[120] Serious proceedings started shortly after lunch, when the invited guests marched in procession to the ornate courtyard of the palace. There they were joined by various dignitaries and by members of the public, who were then admitted for the formal part of the Blenheim proceedings. *The Times* commented on the 'splendid organisation' of the event, which had been 'framed in an incomparable setting' and which had also been 'representative of the fighting strength of the Party throughout the length and breadth of the land'.[121] Lord Northcliffe's other London paper, the *Daily Mail*, also provided detailed descriptions of the pageantry and pomp of the Blenheim spectacle, unfolding in the grounds of a palace that resembled 'a peerless pearl of beauty set in a typical English landscape'. Its reporter stressed the resolute determination of unionists and also the wide, representative nature of involvement in the day's proceedings. He informed his readers:

> There was not an unrepresented county or city. Here were men from industrial centres such as Liverpool and Leeds fraternising with agriculturalists from Kent and Yorkshire; there Scotsmen holding out their hand to Ulstermen and Welshmen conversing with men from overseas. The same spirit imbued them – the spirit of the fight.[122]

A platform had been constructed in front of the palace courtyard and the vast crowd congregated close to this, listening in rapture to the speeches of many senior Conservative figures. F.E. Smith repeated his promise of practical help for Ulster loyalists, though not quite in the forthright language he had used in Belfast a fortnight before.[123] The Birkenhead MP advised his Ulster colleague:

> Should it happen that Ulster is threatened with a violent attempt to incorporate her in an Irish Parliament with no appeal to the English electors, I say to Sir Edward Carson, appeal to the young men of England![124]

Carson's own speech was also warmly received by an audience curious to hear at first hand the arguments of an Irish politician about whom they had read a lot in recent months. The Ulster leader's message was one of certainty of purpose and a refusal to compromise. Denying that he was advocating treason, Edward Carson maintained that Ulstermen would 'shortly challenge the Government to interfere with us if they dare', declaring that they would 'with equanimity await the result'.[125]

Although Edward Carson might well have been the speaker whom the majority of this predominantly English audience had gathered to hear, the most notable speech of the day came from the Conservative leader, Andrew Bonar Law. In many ways, it was his most significant utterance on Ulster, and it provoked a storm of protest, both in parliament and in the Liberal press. Initially the Tory leader, mindful that most of his audience had pressing political concerns apart from Ulster, talked about Conservative land and wages policies and tariff reform, but soon reminded the huge gathering that there were 'things stronger than parliamentary majorities'. Reversing a criticism frequently levelled at Ulster unionists, the leader of the opposition suggested that the government's tough talk on Ulster was mere bluster and that they would be reluctant to use force to implement Home Rule. He proceeded to argue:

> No nation will ever take up arms to compel loyal subjects to leave their community. I do not believe for a moment that any government would ever dare to make the attempt ... They would succeed only in lighting fires of civil war which would shatter the Empire to its foundations ... Does anyone imagine that British troops will be used to shoot down men who demand no privilege which is not enjoyed by you?[126]

In a wide-ranging speech, the Tory leader outlined the essence of Ulster loyalists' objections to Home Rule and how their ability to protect their civil and religious liberties would be impossible 'under a Parliament dominated by men who control the Ancient Order of Hibernians'. He also challenged Asquith on his assertion that Ireland constituted one nation. Reminding his audience that, in demographic terms, Ulster Protestants formed a larger population than the Dutch Boers who had come close to defeating British military forces in South Africa a decade previously, he suggested that in Ireland there were 'two nations arrayed against each other in hostile camps'.[127]

It was the last part of Bonar Law's speech that would prove to be the most controversial. Using virulent language described by opponents as that of 'insurrection', the Tory leader went further than any British party leader in history and appeared to sanction the breaking of the law by his friends in Ulster. What made it worse, at least in his opponents' eyes, was that he recognised the seriousness of his pledge. It ended with a reassurance to Ulster unionists:

> I say to them now, with a full sense of the responsibility which attaches to my position, that if any attempt were made to deprive these men of their birthright – as part of a corrupt parliamentary bargain – they would be justified in resisting such an attempt by all means in their power, including force ... I can imagine no length of resistance to which Ulster can go in which I would not be prepared to support them.[128]

Although most newspapers covered the Oxfordshire events in their Monday editions, reports commanded second or even third billing on the front page, or were even placed on the inside pages. In papers like *The Times* and the *Daily Mail*, for example, recent Tory by-election successes made bigger headlines than the Blenheim meeting. This relative lack of publicity also reflects the fact that the extent of Ulster resistance to Home Rule – and the potential for civil war if the bill became law – were not fully appreciated at this stage of the Ulster unionist campaign. There was also a definite, if somewhat understated, belief that Tory politicians and journalists should be doing more to restrain their hot-headed colleagues in Britain, as well as activists across in Ulster, and it is likely that many Tories were privately concerned by the aggression and venom evident in the Oxfordshire speeches. Lord Northcliffe himself was one who voiced disquiet at his editors' leading articles and general coverage of Blenheim and, indeed, at the Conservative leader's choice of words.

However, though coverage was not detailed, there was enthusiastic support for Ulster's cause in the British press. Attention in Tory newspapers was drawn to the 'magnificent' success of the Blenheim Palace spectacle and to the unified spirit of the crowd. The *Morning Post* picked up on Bonar Law's 'two nations' theme in its editorial, condemning Asquith for asking

Ulstermen to 'exchange the position of free citizenship in the British Empire for that of the trodden worm in Ireland', warning that 'in this case the worm will turn'.[129] Other headlines referred to Bonar Law's 'fine fighting speech' and his 'justification of force', though much of the coverage focused on the occasion rather than the implications of the Tory leader's rhetoric.

This was less the case in the Radical press and with Bonar Law's Liberal opponents in parliament a few weeks later. Within days the *Nation* dismissed the 'unremarkable' nature of Bonar Law's speech, but also attacked him for giving 'the clearest incitement to lawlessness yet given by a British parliamentary leader'.[130] When parliament resumed in October, Herbert Asquith soon returned to the inflammatory speeches of that summer's day, describing the Blenheim meeting as a 'reckless rodomontade' that had 'furnished for the future a complete grammar of anarchy'. He also suggested that 'a more deadly blow has never been dealt in our time by any body of responsible politicians at the very foundations on which democratic government rests'.[131]

How important, then, was this first major demonstration of support for Ulster in Great Britain? Clearly, it provided an undeniable illustration of the degree of political support for Ulster unionists and, as Daniel Jackson has suggested, it also constituted a 'powerful alliance of political oratory and political spectacle'.[132] To Ulstermen, the Oxfordshire meeting and the outpouring of sympathy for their plight, evident in both the speeches and enthusiasm of the delegates, symbolised their growing bond with British Conservatives. Also, the fact that Bonar Law had delivered this speech in the heart of England, rather than in the emotional crucible of a Belfast showground, epitomised the genuine nature of English resolve regarding their cause. Indeed, for many Ulster loyalists reading a summary of Bonar Law's speech two days later, the biggest surprise would have been that the most passionate denunciation of Asquith's legislation had come from the leader of the Conservative Party rather than from their own leader, Edward Carson. To describe Bonar Law's choice of words at the Blenheim meeting as intemperate and ill advised is an understatement. For the leader of a political party – indeed, one that espoused the sanctity of law and order – to use the language of sedition, especially in a period of political conformity, was truly remarkable. Geoffrey Lewis believes that 'nothing like it had been heard in England from a political leader since the republicans of the 17th century had turned the world upside down'.[133]

Why, then, did Bonar Law choose to make such irrational and illegal promises of support to Ulstermen at Blenheim? It is possible that the opposition leader, buoyed by recent electoral successes and believing that the Home Rule issue – and in particular the public's association of the Conservative Party with the 'threatened minority' in Ulster – would resonate positively with the British electorate on what he believed to be the eve of a general election, went further than he had intended, particularly in the latter stages of his speech. Indeed, although Andrew Bonar Law would affirm his Blenheim Palace promise in 1913 and 1914 and would remain closely aligned with Carson and his Ulster campaign, he was conscious of unease within the ranks of his own party and modified his language in future public speeches.

'A highly inflammable population'

Sectarian tensions manifested themselves in different ways in Ulster during the summer of 1912. The first major instance of increasingly bitter internecine feeling occurred at Castledawson on Sunday, 29 June. Many school and Sunday-school groups had chosen that end-of-term weekend for a summer excursion to the seaside or the country – a treat for city children. One such group was a large party (estimated at close to 500) of Sunday-school children from Whitehouse, to the north of Belfast. Accompanied by church leaders, parents and a band, the County Antrim group had chosen the rural location of

Castledawson, some 50 miles away in County Londonderry, for their summer outing. The large group, many of whom were carrying loyalist colours, clashed with a group of nationalists as they prepared to commence their return rail journey from Castledawson Station. A local Ancient Order of Hibernians party had been making its way to a political demonstration in Maghera and, following some name-calling, members of this group had attacked the Sunday-school party. In the chaotic scenes that followed, some children suffered serious injuries, whilst many others fled in hysterics. Local Protestants joined in the confrontation until the arrival of the police.

The incident provoked hostile reaction across Ulster and even resulted in questions being asked in the House of Commons a few days later. Unionist papers fumed at the 'discreditable and cowardly' actions of nationalists in County Londonderry and also castigated Chief Secretary Augustine Birrell for attempting to 'whitewash those who had broken the peace when returning home from a Home Rule meeting addressed by prominent members and officials of the Ulster Liberal Association'.[134]

The repercussions of this relatively minor incident in the depths of County Londonderry were far reaching. With feelings running high in the loyalist community, revenge for the attacks on the Sunday-school party was enacted many miles away in the Belfast shipyards. Just as they would be in 1920, young unskilled labourers were largely responsible for this intimidation of Catholic workers. Inside 72 hours of the incidents in Castledawson, sectarian trouble erupted in Belfast's shipyards and in the areas surrounding them. These were to endure sporadically for nearly a month, covering the period of the Twelfth of July fortnight. During July an estimated 80 workers had to receive hospital treatment following assaults both in the city's shipyards and in other industrial centres, mainly in the east of Belfast, or in the districts close to them. Of over 80 injuries suffered by Catholics, 55 of these were sustained outside the workplace. Of those injured, 5 were seriously hurt, and Joe

Devlin estimated that up to 2,500 Catholics had to take temporary, unpaid leave of absence from their work.[135]

Responses to the intimidation and assault of Catholic workers were forthright in their nature, but naturally differed in apportioning blame. The loyalist press, whilst acknowledging the reasons for the increased levels in sectarian bitterness and ill feeling, refused to accept that these excused the descent into communal violence. In a leader deploring the outbreak of disturbances in the city the previous evening, the *Belfast Telegraph* maintained that 'to engage in it [violence] is to commit the very thing that has been condemned in the Hibernians, and it brings those who do it down to the same level'.[136] In London, *The Times* chose to focus on those who they felt had allowed the tense situation to fester, condemning the government's decision to play 'a political game' with what they described as 'a highly inflammable population'. The editorial in *The Times* proceeded to condemn Asquith's administration for 'blindly persisting in a course which can only be described as a danger to the state', warning that 'if an explosion should result the people of this country will hold them responsible'.[137]

As further assaults on Catholic workers occurred a few days later, Catholic clergy in the north of Ireland condemned what they regarded as police 'inactivity' in Belfast, demanding a more proactive response, preferably from the military. The authorities were to prevaricate for nearly three weeks and only deployed troops as tension mounted in the city on the eve of the return to work after the Twelfth of July holidays. Opinion over whether a troop presence was needed was predictably split along political lines. The *Belfast Telegraph*, reporting a request by priests for greater protection for Catholic workers shortly before the start of the holiday fortnight, made a comparison between violence in Belfast's shipyards and similar disturbances in the Port of London, where there had been recent intimidation of workers refusing to participate in strike action in London's Docks.

Pointing out that over a three-month period there had been 'more violence and intimidation exercised against men who want to work in the Port of London than there has been in Belfast for the last 50 years', the *Belfast Telegraph* upbraided the Radical press in Britain for 'lecturing' Belfast workers.[138] A week after the chief secretary for Ireland had ordered troops into Belfast to protect Catholic workers, the *Belfast Telegraph* again attacked him for his 'wonderful alacrity in yielding to the demand of Nationalists that troops should be sent to Belfast to cope with the Belfast disorder'.[139] This contrasted sharply with the *Daily Chronicle*, which condemned the 'alarming' number of cases of nationalist workmen who had been 'brutally assaulted, in some cases almost to death, by those very Orangemen who helped to swell the cheers which greeted the lawless speeches of the Tory leaders'.[140] The presence of a military detachment had a calming effect on Belfast's industrial workforce and the army were able to withdraw from the shipyards in the middle of August.

It was evident that the Castledawson incident and the shipyard disturbances, along with the perennial political anxiety perpetuated by the ongoing Home Rule crisis, would be reflected in the atmosphere surrounding the Twelfth of July celebrations. The *Daily Mail* attempted to enlighten its readers on the true significance of Orangemen's Day in Ulster and also discussed the chances of communal violence breaking out in Ulster later that day. Accepting that its mainly English readership could not 'comprehend the state of nervous tension existing at the present moment throughout Ulster', the paper's correspondent, without ruling out the possibility of 'localised outbursts' of violence, maintained that the Boyne celebrations would again prove to be 'a popular emblem of the struggle for the Union and against Home Rule'.[141]

The gigantic Belfast parade was at Cloughfern, just outside the city. Despite heavy rain, which kept some spectators off the streets, the procession was described as 'a magnificent demonstration', full of 'inspirational scenes and speeches'. In an emotive report, 'Enthusiasm in the rain', the *Belfast Telegraph* described the 'grave determination and sturdy self-reliance' of the marchers as they proceeded to their meeting point.[142]

The most awaited and hard-hitting Twelfth of July speech came from F.E. Smith, who castigated the government for its Home Rule legislation. In the early part of his address, Smith stressed the minimal nature of unionist demands. Contrasting their behaviour and position with their nationalist opponents, Smith referred to recent events in the province, reminding his audience that they had 'maimed no dumb animal, shot no woman [and] stabbed no Sunday School child'. He went on:

> You only ask to be allowed to sit, as heretofore, in a Parliament which, amid all the vicissitudes of party politics, has not failed to retain your confidence. You only ask that you may be permitted still to enjoy the same rights, and still be bound by the same obligations, which are possessed and discharged by every citizen of these islands ... History records no instance of a state which has drawn the sword to extrude from its polity, a loyal, an industrious, and a wealthy population.[143]

In the second part of his speech, Smith dealt with Asquith's likely policy in regard to ongoing Ulster resistance and the likelihood of increased support from England. Postulating that the Liberal prime minister would 'drift, and still drift, till the rapids are reached, till the wrong, and it may be the tragedy, are consummated', Smith suggested that this would contrast with the 'clear' course of Ulster unionists. He reassured his large audience that if the 'dark hour' of 'trial' should come, they could expect backing from Great Britain:

> you will not lack the active support of thousands in England, who realise that your liberties are being subverted by revolutionary means, and that those who acquiesce in the consequences of revolution to others will in their turn become the victims of revolution.[144]

In response, the *Irish News* castigated Smith for 'donning an Orange sash' and for his 'incendiary words and notions branded on the foolish brains of his reckless dupes'.[145]

The next location for sectarian tension was a sporting one in west Belfast. In a period when there was an all-Ireland soccer league and a leading Catholic team was situated in the west of the city, derby matches between Belfast Celtic and their Protestant rivals from south-west Belfast, Linfield, were always tense affairs. On 14 September, the teams were involved in an early season league fixture at Celtic Park, close to the Falls Road. A large crowd, estimated at 20,000, was packed into the compact football ground and a large police force struggled to contain the rival groups. The trouble occurred during the half-time interval. Opposing groups of supporters waved their respective scarves and flags and scuffles broke out as home fans, housed at the Falls Broadway end, proceeded to the Donegall Road end of the ground, where the Linfield supporters stood. The police were unable to contain the large numbers of impassioned supporters. Jostling and fist-fighting were followed by stone-throwing and 'a fusillade of revolver shots'. A pitched battle commenced on the terraces, resulting in many supporters invading the field.

Most of the fans rushed out of the ground, but further disturbances occurred close to the Donegall Road, where new tramway lines were being constructed. Angry supporters helped themselves to building materials and debris and used these as weapons. Police found it necessary to baton charge the away supporters and forced them back onto the Donegall Road. The game, which Linfield had been winning 1–0, was abandoned and the authorities counted the human cost of the 'unprecedented scenes' at Celtic Park. Some 60 people had to receive medical treatment, including five for gunshot injuries.[146]

The apparent media indulgence of this outpouring of loyalist frustration and anger at a football match is significant. The *Pall Mall Gazette* focused on the inevitability of such trouble, pointing out that 'the community which feels itself upon the brink of engulfment in a regime of tyranny and misgovernment may be all too liable to explode upon trivial provocation'.[147]

The *Daily Telegraph* suggested that the authors of the Home Rule legislation 'must take upon their shoulders the blame for what has already occurred, and what in all human probability is only too likely to occur hereafter'.[148]

These instances of marked sectarian tension, both in Belfast and in the Ulster countryside, added to the prevailing mood of uncertainty that had been evident in parliament and at major demonstrations in Ulster and Great Britain. Loyalists in the north of Ireland had been vigilant in their anticipation of such drama and would continue to be flexible and creative in stepping up their resistance campaign.

Crowds gather outside Belfast City Hall on Covenant Day, September 1912

Community resistance

3

Introduction

The danger directly facing Ulster's loyalist population in 1912 was stark, but the community was fully prepared to counter the threat. This chapter looks at how it united in its endeavours to defeat those advocating a Home Rule parliament in Dublin.

The central theme is the cohesion of that section of the population in the north of Ireland. This permeated across the various Protestant churches, social classes and different economic groups (encompassing the owners of industry and commerce as well as their employees) and was reflected in a professional, efficient and ultimately united political response from the party representing loyalist opposition to the proposed measure. The political philosophy and sense of identity of Ulster unionists will be examined, as will the roles of the Ulster Unionist Council, the unionist clubs and the Orange Order, and the individual contributions of leaders like Edward Carson and James Craig during this campaign. The nature of Ulster unionist political propaganda and its impact on large sections of the Great British public will be examined in greater depth, as will the rationale behind the Protestant community's religious objections to the proposed legislation and the unity of response by the Anglican, Presbyterian and Nonconformist churches across Ulster. The clarity of purpose and underlying conviction of the loyalist population was embodied by the Ulster Covenant campaign and the signing of that document in September 1912, and the second part of this chapter presents a detailed analysis of this key event.

'I am not for a mere game of bluff ...'

As outlined below, less than three years before the start of the Great War, unionism in Ulster would present itself to the world as an invigorated organisation and the structures of a modern resistance movement would be in place. What drove so many Ulster Protestants into unequivocally supporting a movement that incorporated extreme parliamentary tactics and large-scale street protest, and that seriously threatened the preservation of order both in Britain and Ireland? How aware were they of the extent of this danger? And what was their understanding of their own identity as part of this movement? As far as the latter was concerned, this differed somewhat from the region's loyalist community during the early 1970s, when disillusionment with British politicians and public alike resulted in their open espousal of an 'Ulster' rather than a 'British' sense of identity. In Edwardian Britain, Ulster unionists were more likely to talk of an 'Irish' rather than a 'British' identity. In an essay of the time, Ulster-born imperialist and polemical writer W.F. Monypenny reminded his readers that Ulster unionists were not interested in any psychological or physical partitioning of the island. He wrote, 'Unionists are Irishmen too. We love our country and work for its good. We do not wish to be separated from our fellow countrymen.'[1]

Until the crisis deepened and discussion about Ulster's exclusion grew significantly louder, unionists in the province resisted the temptation to ask for special treatment. This was not to deny that they believed they were somehow different from the rest of Ireland. Indeed, the idea that they were different would be a central element in their economic and religious reasons for denouncing the proposed legislative change. Their sense of Britishness largely centred on a basic loyalty towards the institutions of monarchy and empire. Although some have argued that the religious nature of their opposition to a Dublin-based parliament (illustrated by the religious fervour displayed during the Ulster Covenant campaign) exhibited a desire for self-determination, this was not as clearly defined as in the demands of Irish nationalists for a new Dublin-based legislature.[2] Ulster Protestants' loyalty to Britain was, and indeed remains, a complicated phenomenon. As David Miller pointed out in his classic 1970s analysis, it was, in its very essence, a reciprocal arrangement, based upon notions of contract, with dual responsibilities and entitlements. Miller argued:

> The dilemma of the Ulster Protestant community derived from their conception of both their political obligation and their rights of citizenship in contractual terms. Lacking a genuine feeling of co-nationality with the British people, they could not entrust their fate to 'safeguards' which depended on the willingness of that people to intervene in Irish affairs to rectify abuses.[3]

Thus, despite the initial emphasis on all-Ireland unionism, the objections of Ulster Protestants to Home Rule were governed by their loyalty to their own community and regional unit, Ulster. It is worth mentioning that declarations of 'loyalty' and 'community' contained few references to the predicament of the region's Catholic minority, or any provision that might be made for such a religious minority within any emergency or provisional government to be established in the north of Ireland.

What was more transparent and convincing about Ulster unionists' exposition of their political and cultural identity was their understanding of the past and how to use this to their advantage. They were also aware of the extent of danger facing them between 1912 and 1914 and were circumspect in ensuring that they had constructed a sound organisation prior to the introduction of Home Rule. They were also conscious of the potential consequences of stifling the natural evolution of their movement and responded positively to its utilisation of street protest, modern propaganda techniques and the paramilitary dimension.

Even before a genuine threat to Ulster's constitutional status had emerged, many unionists (most prominently a new group of wealthy Ulster businessmen and Westminster representatives, including James and Charles Craig, J.B. Lonsdale and William Moore) were aware of the need to modernise the party's internal organisation and to broaden the appeal of unionism. The UUC had been formally established in March 1905 as a democratically structured body. It was to be a representative, centralised policy-making group with a permanent executive committee and would contribute to devising and disseminating political literature. The new organisation, which initially consisted of 200 members, comprised all Irish Unionist Party MPs, peers and representatives of unionist clubs and associations throughout Ulster, as well as leading officials from the Orange Order (a quarter of the group's total composition). The delegates were appointed according to polling districts and were drawn from across the social classes. The size of the body had risen to 370 by 1911 and to 500 by the end of 1913. The group's standing committee, under the stewardship of its secretary, R. Dawson Bates, supervised the everyday organisation of Ulster unionism. There were various other committees – including, rather blatantly, one for arms importation – and a special committee would be established later with the purpose of drafting a constitution for a provisional government, which was to take over if Home Rule were confirmed. (This group contained a disproportionate number of landed gentry – about a third – in 1910.)

The organisation was at pains to emphasise its professional approach and its pan-unionist appeal. Denying it was simply a vehicle for the Orange Order (as claimed by its opponents), a report issued by the standing committee in February 1912 pointed out that the UUC was 'representative of every shade of Unionist opinion and includes not only the Orange Society but every other Unionist organisation in Ulster'. They claimed also to possess 'the support of large numbers of men of strong Radical views on general politics' and affirmed that 'all sections of Unionist opinion in Ulster' were 'resolutely determined to work together to defeat the disastrous policy of the Government'.[4]

The records of the UUC for this period (especially the annual reports covering the period of the Home Rule crisis) provide evidence of the scale of the work executed by the organisation and its various committees, and also indicate the nature of unionist opinion on major recent events. For instance, the 1914 UUC yearbook (covering 1913) reported on the debate at the Irish Unionist Party's annual conference at the Ulster Hall on 31 January 1913. It dismissed the financial arguments of their opponents, who hoped that setting up an Irish parliament would cut the losses incurred by British electors and also 'rid them of the Irish question'. It went on:

> The presence at Westminster of 42 representatives from Ireland, increased to 72 on certain financial matters, would

be sufficient guarantee that Irish grievances would continue to be brought forward and their discussion insisted upon. The extraordinary anomaly would thus exist that Irish representatives would still have in their hands the making and unmaking of British Ministers, whilst representatives of Great Britain would have no power to interfere with the proceedings of the Irish Parliament.[5]

Plans for an alternative administration to govern Ulster if Home Rule were passed at Westminster were unveiled within days of the first 'pro-Ulster' mass meeting at Craigavon in September 1911. A commission of five men (one of whom was James Craig) was entrusted with the task of framing a constitution that would come into operation once Home Rule was passed. Two years later, the precise detail of the constitution was confirmed at a UUC meeting in Belfast. The new administration's 77 appointed members would take over the authority previously held by the UUC as well as responsibility for administering the province. The Irish Unionist Party leader, Sir Edward Carson, was appointed chair of the executive of this central authority. Delegation of power was crucial to the architects of such an administration, with responsibility for running specific spheres of government policy being distributed to a number of committees, including business and finance, education, law, transport, health, customs and excise and 'military affairs'.

The lengthy deliberation that had clearly preceded the establishment of such a body was not indicative of a knee-jerk, idle threat sanctioned by a small group of increasingly desperate men. Rather, it showed the raw determination and resourcefulness of unionism's political leaders and their awareness of the need to plan for any eventuality. Though not a sign of desperation, there was some evidence that the creators of such a constitution and administration believed it would only be required for a restricted period of time. One article in the constitution – published in July 1914 – proclaimed that the administration would take over 'in trust for the constitution of the United Kingdom' and that 'upon the restoration of direct Imperial Government, the Provincial Government would cease to exist'.[6] The executive of the provisional government was formally established by the UUC in July 1914 and, with the passing of Home Rule legislation imminent, it was given permission to assume power at short notice.

Opponents of unionism lambasted such talk of constitutions and provisional governments. In a fiery speech in Bradford on 14 March 1914 (which fuelled tension that would erupt at the Curragh military camp within days), Winston Churchill dismissed the proposed provisional government in Ulster as 'a self-elected body, composed of persons who, to put it mildly, are engaged in a treasonable conspiracy'.[7] Yet despite the unconventional and illegal nature of such an administration, David Fitzpatrick reminds us that, in the light of the statements and unambiguous position adopted by the unionist leadership in Ulster, this was not an irrational strategy. He writes:

> Despite nationalist sneers that Ulster's militancy was mere sabre-rattling, there is little reason to doubt the willingness, readiness, and in some cases eagerness of Ulster loyalists to assert control over 'their' Province. The logic of 'conditional loyalty' made it perfectly appropriate for Ulstermen to seize local power if betrayed by the government and ultimately, through the granting of royal assent, the monarch.[8]

The significance of gaining the universal support of the loyalist industrial and agricultural workforce – especially during an era of increasing Radical and syndicalist agitation (Belfast had experienced a major dock strike, led by Dublin trade unionist James Larkin, in 1907) – was fully appreciated by the unionist leadership. This was ensured by the unanimous support of members of the Orange Order, unionist clubs and vociferous opposition to Home Rule from trade unionists (often at shop-steward rather than at official union level), especially in the

Greater Belfast area. This latter group periodically condemned what they regarded as the misrepresentation of their cause by the pro-Home Rule Belfast Trades Council and the Labour Party. At one meeting in the spring of 1914, a large audience of trade unionists meeting in Belfast's Ulster Hall expressed the reasons behind their opposition to a Dublin-based administration. Denying they were the 'dupes' and 'catspaws' of an aristocratic plot, their 'manifesto' declared that the unity of Ulster employers and employees was due to their shared recognition that 'the whole social and individual fabric of Belfast and, indeed, all Ireland' was threatened by the Home Rule Bill. In 'beseeching' the support of British trade unionists, the men representing 'the democracy of Ulster' acknowledged that 'the privileges won for the workers by trade unionism are in danger, and that the loss of these privileges mean the degradation of labour in Ireland'.[9]

One way of channelling the more active and enthusiastic participation of younger, fitter men into the unionist movement was through the unionist clubs, which would prove to be the Ulster Volunteer Force (UVF) in an embryonic form. These clubs, which consisted of local groups of male loyalists, had been founded by Lord Templetown in 1893 during a previous period of Home Rule crisis. Once this threat had subsided, the clubs were suspended, only to be revived by Templetown in late 1910 when the threat of Irish unification again became real. These clubs, even more than the Orange lodges, were very much the face and voice of unionism at local level. They contributed to a plethora of tasks, including stewarding at many key demonstrations, protecting key loyalist personalities, writing letters supporting the Ulster case to national newspapers, canvassing for several by-election campaigns in England and Scotland and providing hospitality for sympathetic political visitors to demonstrations and on 'study tours' of Ulster. Their main contribution, however, was their implicit physical role, whether in the form of drilling, arms training or keeping a controlling eye on their younger, more aggressive members. They certainly proved to be popular and by May 1913 there were a reported 61,000 members in 315 clubs across Ulster.[10] When the Ulster Volunteers were formed later in 1913, there was a seamless transition for many unionist-club members into the more overtly militaristic ranks of Richardson's new force, but it is important to bear in mind that the unionist-club members had also been serious in their intentions.

The celebrated journalist Charles E. Hands penned a report on the activities of unionist-club personnel in August 1912. Hands pointed out that double the number of clubs had been formed in the previous six months than in the seven years before this, and he described how young men received small-arms training at shooting ranges. Hands stressed the spontaneous aspect of club membership:

> Nobody orders these things, as nobody orders the young men to practise marksmanship. They are spontaneous manifestations of the present mood and inclination of the people.[11]

A constant influence upon anti-Home Rule campaigns was the Orange Order, which tended to revive during prolonged spells of sectarian tension. Just as it was revitalised in 1886 and in 1892–3, so its membership rose dramatically in the first decade of the twentieth century. The Orange Order doubled in size in Belfast to just under 19,000 between 1908 and 1913. The appeal of Orangeism, with its unique combination of unequivocal religious beliefs and historical symbolism, was genuine for a community fully aware of the promise of ultimate deliverance from potential disaster. Membership of the Orange Order and of unionist clubs (and later, of course, the Ulster Volunteers) frequently overlapped, with many men opting for the convenience of joining both an Orange lodge and a unionist club (which often shared premises) in their own districts. However, the increased physical demands of drilling, physical training and arms use would have deterred many older men from joining the clubs and, certainly, the Volunteers.

The respect afforded to leaders of the Orange Order within the wider community earned many of them a place on political platforms at many of the big unionist occasions during these years. One of the leading Orange figures was Colonel R.H. Wallace, head of the Grand Lodge of Belfast, who was frequently pictured sharing carriages or political platforms with Sir Edward Carson (this was especially so during the Ulster Covenant campaign). Yet, as noted above, Wallace and other leading figures in the Orange Order were at pains to point out that the political organisation at the centre of the drive against Home Rule, the UUC, was far from being a purely Orange body.

The Orange Order was also growing in size in Great Britain, especially on Merseyside and in other parts of northern England. There were close relationships between the Irish Unionist Party and the Orange Order within the Liverpool area, with the former group active in organising several large political meetings in north-west England. Strong underlying sectarian feelings were prevalent in Liverpool at the time, with fanatical street preachers like George Wise stoking up passions at a time when there were street disturbances in the city. As Frank Neal has observed:

> [The Orange Order,] with its large meetings, anniversaries, ceremonies, benefit clubs, parades and political activities, provided the *raison d'être* for a large section of Liverpool's unskilled Protestant working class, who, under the guise of patriotism, could indulge their hostility to the Irish invaders.[12]

Despite the enthusiastic reception granted to Edward Carson and other unionist speakers at meetings elsewhere in the north of England, the influence of Orangeism on other parts of the region was substantially less than on Merseyside. The Orange Order, especially in parts of north-east England, was 'only one of a number of overlapping constituencies of potential voters whom a successful Tory candidate would need to woo', and the 'dangers of an overly close allegiance' with an organisation prone to 'habitually raucous displays of sectarian prejudice' meant there was never more than 'a loose affiliation between Toryism and Orangeism in northern England'.[13]

The Orange Order would also periodically play a prominent role in anti-Home Rule protest meetings elsewhere in England. At a conference of Protestants opposed to Home Rule at London's Caxton Hall on 3 June 1914, the deputy grand master of the Loyal Orange Institution of England, J.W. Hesse, supported the use of arms by his co-religionists in Ulster.

The loyalist campaign received a huge boost from the general, though not universal, support forthcoming from Ulster's leading businessmen and industrialists. With the notable exception of Liberal Party member and Home Rule supporter, Lord Pirrie, owner of Harland and Wolff, leading factory, shipyard and business owners were unequivocal in their support of the anti-Home Rule campaign. Among them were R.M. Liddell, Milne Barbour, George S. Clark and, of course, James Craig (a director of Dunville's Whiskey Company). This was reflected in their platform presence at key loyalist meetings and their generous contributions to Carson's Ulster Defence Fund, as well as their support during the gun-running in 1914. They also tolerated the widespread expulsion of Catholics from Belfast's industrial centres during the summer of 1912. For instance, whilst Lord Pirrie was threatening to lay off his entire workforce if the intimidation of Catholic workers continued, the staunchly loyalist George Clark (a former Irish Unionist Party MP for north Belfast), who was the managing director of the smaller Belfast shipyard, Workman, Clark & Co., refrained from guaranteeing Catholic workers a safe return to work. Indeed, Clark was a frequent propagandist for the Ulster unionist cause. In an article published in the *Daily Mail* in 1912, he pointed out that Belfast 'contains several of the largest industries of their kind to be found in the whole world' and argued that there was 'no more absurd assertion than that the resources of Ireland are incapable of developing except under Home Rule'.[14] He would later offer berthing facilities at his yard to the UVF during the landing of guns in 1914.

The business and commercial sector in Ulster had several unambiguous financial objections to Home Rule. They maintained that 'capital would be deflected from Ireland' and that 'business credit would be granted only on more onerous terms'. They argued that any loans sanctioned by the new Dublin administration would be 'impossible except at high rates' and that there would be an inevitable rise in rates because banks would have to impose higher rates of interest.[15]

Invaluable help from the business and commercial community came in a variety of ways. These included periodic expressions of support for Edward Carson's political fight against Home Rule, organised in the main by the Belfast Chamber of Commerce, generous contributions by individual employers and industrialists to Carson's Ulster Defence Fund (this was established early in 1912), expert financial and business advice provided for the provisional government, and a general enthusiasm for the Ulster cause that certainly had an immeasurable effect upon their employees. Representatives from the Belfast Chamber of Commerce also pressurised Herbert Asquith at Westminster, and businessmen and industrialists even considered withholding tax payments to the exchequer in 1913.

Undoubtedly many of the province's leading employers had to balance the future of their commercial concerns with their personal consciences. Fearing a potential loss of trade and custom if they were personally associated with contributing to Edward Carson's Defence Fund, many demanded anonymity. Linen manufacturer R.M. Liddell wrote to Carson about the need for secrecy for many subscribers, informing him that there were 'several men, representing large industries like whiskey, who fear their trade would suffer if their names were made public'.[16]

The massive strides in the organisation of Ulster unionism

during the first decade of the twentieth century clearly placed the anti-Home Rule movement on a sound footing. An efficient central organisation was in place and backing was forthcoming from all sections of the Protestant community. However, one vital element was missing – namely efficient, charismatic leadership. This would be rectified when Sir Edward Carson was appointed new leader of the Irish Unionist Party on 27 February 1910. Carson, who replaced Walter Long in this role, was not the most obvious candidate to lead a movement that would inevitably focus mainly on the question of Ulster's opposition to Home Rule. He had made his reputation and fortune in the legal field and had entered parliament as MP for Dublin University in 1892. He was a good public speaker and could move an audience more easily than some of his colleagues, including Andrew Bonar Law and James Craig. However, he was relatively unfamiliar with Ulster and the particular nuances of its politics. A Dubliner from an upper-middle-class background, Carson's first visit to Belfast as party leader was in December 1910. He also presided over the UUC's annual conference the following month. Edward Carson was more used to moving in the very different circles of London and Dublin gentlemen's clubs and legal societies and, although aware of the sectarian undertones associated with northern unionism, he did not at this stage possess a detailed or expert knowledge of Ulster or its people. Nor was he totally convinced about their likely degree of commitment to the pro-union cause. His lack of awareness of the depth of resolve of Ulster unionists during this early phase of his leadership perhaps contributed to the concern evident in a letter he sent to James Craig on the eve of the Craigavon meeting in September 1911. He wrote:

> What I am very anxious about is to satisfy myself that the people over there really mean to resist. I am not for a mere game of bluff and unless men are prepared to make sacrifices they clearly understand, the talk of resistance is no use.[17]

Despite his introduction to a society with a reputation for being suspicious of outsiders, Edward Carson would soon gain acceptance and genuine affection. In an interesting comparison, Russell Rees has suggested that Carson was 'strangely similar' to another great southern Irish Protestant leader, Charles Stewart Parnell. He argued that 'both were outsiders leading followers very different from themselves, and both men used the same tactic of militant constitutionalism to achieve their objectives'.[18] Carson's physical appearance and platform persona were a godsend for the cartoonists of the day, but, more importantly, he personified the nature of the political movement whose leadership he had assumed. His lantern-jawed, stern expression and strident gesticulations suggested that this was not a man who would be easily intimidated. Indeed, despite the fact that they publicly mocked the IUP leader, his opponents admired his ability and wished that he had been on their side. Republican leader James Connolly wrote in the *Irish Worker* (August 1914) that it 'would be to Ireland's advantage if Sir Edward Carson would fight for Ireland as successfully and courageously as he has fought against her'.[19]

In many ways, Edward Carson was a complex and at times contradictory character. Although continually fretting about his health, he pushed himself relentlessly through tight parliamentary schedules and speaking tours and coped with the loss of his first wife, Annette, at the height of the Home Rule crisis. As his opponents ceaselessly taunted him, there was a stark contrast between Carson the leading criminal lawyer of his day, and Carson the Irish Unionist Party leader, whose spoken threats and unspoken menace bordered on the illegal. He also combined an unusual mixture of high political principle and pragmatism. Accepting the IUP job in February 1910 and declining to stand for the leadership of the Conservative Party the following year, Edward Carson displayed genuine political courage and integrity. Opting to take a position that promised little personal gain but rather extreme personal pressure and danger, at the expense of seizing an opportunity to lead the British Conservative Party, Carson showed that he was not a politician on the make. Yet, on a number of occasions during the Home Rule crisis, and most notably in his reluctant acceptance of the Government of Ireland Act in 1920, he also displayed a political realism that ultimately took precedence over his principles. Despite these strengths and an ability to harness a considerable degree of influential support for Ulster in Britain, Sir Edward Carson's political legacy – a diluted form of Home Rule for most of the province of Ulster – represented the antithesis of what had motivated him to accept his leadership of the party in 1910. Although he had 'saved' six counties of Ulster by his slick campaign of 1912–14, the IUP leader (like his nationalist counterpart Parnell over 20 years before) had been unsuccessful in his prime political objective.

What, then, were Edward Carson's perceptions of Ulster in 1911? He was a traditional Irish unionist and fervently believed that, by exploiting the high levels of resistance in Ulster, he would succeed in derailing Home Rule legislation for the whole of Ireland. Like most unionists of his generation, he would not have seen or thought of Ulster in a separate, partitionist mindset. By championing the cause of Ulster, he also intended to articulate the voice of unionist Ireland. This would prove to be a far from easy task, as the strident voice of Ulster resistance to Home Rule tended to drown the equally genuine objections of southern unionists, and ultimately it was a political failure on Carson's part to reconcile the two perspectives. Whilst he shared Ulster loyalists' religious objections to a Dublin-based parliament, the political, economic and imperial arguments against the proposed legislation were probably higher on his personal agenda. As will be observed at various points in this book, Edward Carson would modify his own position in response to his opponents' actions – especially over the issue of Ulster exclusion – becoming in the process more of a leader of unionists in Ulster than of unionists across Ireland. However, this was borne out of necessity and was certainly not something he had desired or, indeed, something of which he was proud. Much of the debate over Ulster's resistance to Home Rule revolved around notions of rights and the nature of citizenship, especially the relationship between the citizen and the state. As a leading lawyer, Edward Carson was well positioned to comprehend Ulster unionist fears about the receding nature of their citizenship and would have sympathised with their perception of the contractual nature of their Britishness.[20]

Edward Carson knew he was inheriting a strong, well-organised movement at local level, which simply required an input of clear political direction articulated by a leader of genuine national standing. It was also essential for the IUP leader to have able backup support from a major, Ulster-born, political figure. Carson, and indeed Ulster unionism, were fortunate in having such an individual in Captain James Craig.[21] The latter was the consummate political organiser. He was much happier chairing meetings of local unionists in east Belfast or masterminding such striking exhibitions of loyalist opposition to Home Rule as those in the grounds of his home (Craigavon) in September 1911 or at Balmoral in April 1912 than delivering a speech on a political platform or from the floor of the House of Commons. There was good personal chemistry between Craig and Carson and, with Craig also a Westminster MP, the channels of communication between them were normally clear. Carson undoubtedly leaned on Craig, particularly during the early phase of his leadership, sounding him out on the mood within the loyalist heartlands. Despite the Dubliner's 'instinctive ability to tap the deepest feelings and memories of a people of whom he knew nothing', he would also gain confidence from James Craig's counsel, especially during the first two years of his leadership.[22] Though also ostensibly committed to saving all of Ireland for the union, Craig's main priority was keeping Ulster, or as much of it as possible, within the United Kingdom. Even more than his leader, James Craig was frequently the butt of Radical ridicule and disdain. One contemporary description of him read:

> This tall, broad-shouldered, florid-faced stonewaller is at once the delight and despair of the House of Commons ... Scores of motions in the Captain's name were down on the [order] paper ... Taunts are flung at him across the gangway by the Nationalists. No matter. The brogue-tongued Captain plods along, snapping Ministerial time and patience by the dreary drip of words.[23]

Sir Edward Carson's involvement in every aspect of Ulster's resistance campaign was undoubted. Although there was some inevitable delegation of tasks during moments of illness or bereavement, there were few decisions – including those relating to propaganda strategies and gun-running expeditions – that would not have been personally affirmed by Carson. The two full years of the Home Rule crisis would have been an exhausting time, both physically and emotionally, for the IUP leader. Leading opposition debates on the bill in parliament, speaking at political meetings and on tours across Great Britain and Ulster, Edward Carson was very much the face and voice of Ulster unionist resistance. He was even at the centre of fundraising.

The Ulster Defence Fund was set up in Carson's name and contributions poured in from across Ireland and from wealthy supporters and benefactors in England. One example came from W.E. Horne, the Conservative MP for Guildford, who presented Edward Carson with a cheque for £433.[24] Much of the money collected in Carson's Ulster Defence Fund was used to subsidise political literature and to underpin the costs of expensive political occasions such as the Balmoral demonstration and the Covenant fortnight. The appeal for subscriptions increased in intensity across Ulster as the crisis deepened. It was reported from Irish Unionist Party headquarters towards the end of 1913 that 'every Unionist will be approached in the next few months for a subscription to this fund'. R.M. Liddell, the secretary of the fund, wrote to branch organisers asking them to chase up members' fund-collecting cards, reminding potential subscribers that they were 'in more urgent need of funds than ever'. Liddell went on:

> If we are to continue our canvassing and speaking in the United Kingdom, on the same lines as before, and if we are to make adequate preparations for our Provisional Government and for due protection of Ulster interests in case of the iniquitous Home Rule Bill becoming law, we must have financial support. For this object it is absolutely essential that every Unionist, and every signer of the Covenant or Women's Declaration, should contribute his or her quota, however small.[25]

A large part of Edward Carson's role during the crisis was to speak directly to his followers in Ulster. Consequently, he spoke at numerous political meetings and rallies, both indoor and outdoor, in towns across Ulster's nine counties, between the end of 1911 and the summer of 1914. The tenor of these platform speeches varied according to the political temperature of the day. Thus, his early speeches were constructed with the aim of getting to know his new supporters (and his new supporters getting to know him) as well as warning them of the dangers of Asquith's imminent legislation. The main feature of his later visits to rural towns was to reassure the Volunteers about his expectations for their disciplined behaviour.[26] The following is a short illustration of the arduous, exacting nature of such political street and public-hall encounters. In the autumn of 1913, Edward Carson conducted a three-week-long visit to Ulster, during which he addressed close to 20 meetings, including the first anniversary of the signing of the Ulster Covenant at a large UVF demonstration at Balmoral. The denunciation of political opponents was, of course, a perennial characteristic of such meetings. For example, at a meeting in

Cookstown, Carson rubbished John Redmond's promise to meet him in a 'conference' if he accepted the principle of Home Rule and publicly thanked his nationalist counterpart for 'nothing'.[27] These personal appearances in small towns were regarded by local unionists as rewards for their own endeavours in their own areas. Therefore, in the County Tyrone town, Sir Edward's visit was 'anticipated with the liveliest interest'. It was expected that 'a huge crowd from the surrounding country' would 'welcome the Unionist leader'.[28] At Cookstown and other venues, Sir Edward Carson would meet local dignitaries, representatives of the Orange Order and Irish Unionist Party, and then inspect the ranks of local battalions of the UVF, encouraging them to 'go full speed ahead'.[29] Carson made a point of visiting more challenging towns and districts, often situated in the midst of politically hostile country. The following day he reviewed 1,500 UVF men at Raphoe in County Donegal. The *Northern Whig* described the enthusiasm and excitement surrounding his appearance:

> On arrival at the town, which was decorated with bunting and flags, they were accorded a most enthusiastic reception. The road to Oakfield House (where he was staying) was lined on both sides by Volunteers who came to the salute as the motors passed along. Great preparations had been made in Oakfield Demesne for the meeting. A large platform which was erected for the speakers was decorated in true Unionist style and bore the words in bold letters 'No Surrender!'[30]

Carson recognised the special effort unionists made in these areas and acknowledged this in his speech at Raphoe. He expressed his 'gratification at this splendid turnout' because he knew they were 'turning out in a county where, though in a great minority, nothing has ever for a moment inclined you to swerve from your allegiance to our King and the old flag'.[31]

Taking the message to Britain

As would be illustrated during World War I, political propaganda was a psychological tool most fully exploited during times of stress and ideological struggle. It was an appropriate strategy for Ulster unionists to employ during the Home Rule crisis, which coincided with a growth in the recognition of the potential of propaganda and with many developments within the mass-communications industry. The extension of the franchise in Britain and the broadening of its political base had meant that winning over public opinion was ever more important. Although the anti-Home Rule campaign took place before the age of radio and television, it did benefit from several developments in the communications field. For instance, newspaper circulation had increased dramatically, mainly because of the ready availability of cheap, popular newspapers such as the *Daily Mail* and the *Daily Express*, and events in Ulster featured in many of the newsreels shown in picturehouses up and down the country. Knowledge of specific propaganda techniques was also improving during the Edwardian period. The need to disseminate information with an unambiguous message (such as criticising the Liberals for 'treachery' in handing over loyalists to their nationalist opponents without a clear mandate) and to a targeted audience (Irish news stories with overtly sectarian undertones were generally well received on Merseyside and Clydeside) were fundamental considerations for unionist propagandists at this time. Additionally, they were to employ stereotypes in their depiction of the 'enemy': cartoons lampooned government ministers like Birrell, Churchill, Lloyd George and Asquith. Certainly, unionists were fully aware of the potential afforded by successful propaganda. The minutes of the inaugural meeting of the joint committee of the Unionist Associations of Ireland (UAI) in 1908 promised that 'no exertion will be spared to make the arguments against Home Rule, and any policy leading there to be known in every part of Great Britain'.[32]

Historians have, over a considerable period of time, concurred in their assessment of the quality and significance of unionist propaganda. Writing in 1967, James Beckett maintained that the 'persistent propaganda' and 'obvious determination' of Ulster unionists 'began to have some effect on liberal opinion, even when the home rule bill was being debated'.[33] More recently, David Fitzpatrick and Alvin Jackson have acknowledged the pivotal role of propaganda in the unionist campaign, stressing in particular its 'slickly professional' and 'relentlessly modern' nature.[34] Fitzpatrick and others have emphasised the sheer range of propaganda techniques adopted by unionist publicists. These included 'lecture campaigns using pre-circulated speech notes, mobilisation of sympathetic British academics and public figures, discreet canvassing of editors, and a barrage of picture postcards, leaflets, newsletters and treatises'.[35] Alvin Jackson has pointed out that unionists did not merely exploit the developing technologies and recent popularity of souvenirs such as chinaware, medals, badges, rosettes and portrait postcards, but succeeded in combining these new approaches with tried-and-tested strategies, such as the production of countless flyers and pamphlets. Jackson describes the halfpenny postcard as 'the Edwardian equivalent of the e-mail message' and 'the medium by which thousands of different unionist images were conveyed'.[36]

Some time before the introduction of the Home Rule Bill, Irish unionists had recognised the importance of maintaining Conservative support and winning over both opponents and neutrals to their cause. They realised that a sophisticated backup publicity service was required to support unionist politicians in their broader campaign. Indeed, such a group had been created in Dublin in December 1907, when a propaganda-orientated body, the Unionist Associations of Ireland (UAI), had been established.

The UAI was controlled by a joint committee – this 12-strong body consisted of equal numbers of Irish Unionist Alliance

(IUA) and Irish Unionist Party representatives – and the new organisation was not a policy-making one. Rather, its function was to coordinate the unionist propaganda campaign in Great Britain, where a new generation of electors was still uneducated on the Home Rule question. Apart from resolving to start a concerted propaganda push in March 1908, possible strategies were determined at the inaugural meeting. In calling for meetings in 'selected British Constituencies' to be addressed by speakers with 'knowledge of the condition of Ireland under the rule of the present Government', the UAI stressed the need to 'greatly extend the present circulation of Irish Unionist literature in Great Britain, for which there has been an increasing demand since the General Election'.[37]

The UAI had made timely refinements in its overall approach before the parliamentary introduction of the Third Home Rule Bill. Earlier campaigns had focused on protest meetings in the chief secretary for Ireland's Bristol constituency in 1908–09 and in the two elections in 1910, where propaganda concentrated on the financial perils of Home Rule. A huge volume of literature was handed out to British electors in 1910. In the January election, 3.783 million copies of 11 new or revised leaflets and posters were distributed and in December over 3 million copies of 18 new or revised publications were circulated.[38] Once it became clear that Home Rule was, on account of the abolition of the lords' veto and guaranteed Irish nationalist support, likely to become law, the campaign was stepped up, with much of its force, especially as the crisis deepened, coming from Ulster. The UAI campaign was four-pronged in its approach. Apart from producing and distributing a large amount of propaganda literature, the UAI orchestrated a series of anti-Home Rule meetings and demonstrations. It also canvassed activities, particularly in marginal seats during the course of by-elections, and was prepared to run an ancillary service, including the organisation of political tours of Ireland for British voters.

Not only did the nature of unionist propaganda vary from one region of Great Britain to another, or from one campaign incident to the next, but there was also a distinct difference in the emphasis adopted by northern and southern propagandists. Whilst Dublin-based workers were more concerned about the imperialist dimension and what they saw as the undemocratic nature of the Home Rule campaign, northern unionists laid more emphasis on religious objections to Home Rule. They were, therefore, not slow to spell out the 'injustice' of an Irish Catholic parliament, and these fears got a particularly sympathetic reception in areas within Great Britain where anti-Catholic feelings ran high (most notably in Glasgow and Liverpool). As early as December 1910, unionists were stressing the religious dimension in their literature and this was to increase as the campaign went on. R. Dawson Bates was quoted in a UAI report at the start of 1911 calling for 'the preparation and circulation of pamphlets suited to the Non-Conformists of Great Britain'.[39] Bates proceeded to argue that favourable election results in several constituencies had been mainly due to 'the distribution of leaflets dealing with the attitude of the Church of Rome towards the Protestant religion in Ireland, and to the influential advocacy of our Cause by Presbyterian and Methodist Ministers who represent us in these Constituencies'.[40]

The religious argument was also popular in those far-flung parts of the empire to where Protestant Ulstermen had emigrated. Like most exiles, this group was particularly susceptible to traditional religious fears and, not surprisingly, the Orange Order was swift to harness such support. Sympathy was especially forthcoming in Canada, where many regions had strong Orange representation (including Winnipeg, Saskatchewan, Alberta and Vancouver). Others were prepared to offer support of a more physical kind – the Orange Association of Manitoba was prepared to send a regiment of Volunteers to Ulster. Additionally, there were positive responses to the call from New Zealand and even nationalist-leaning

America, where contributions were generally of the financial kind. Although Australia also contained larger pockets of nationalist support, there was still a sizeable degree of sympathy for the Ulster cause, and some large contributions were received from wealthy individuals there. For example, Sir Samuel McCaughey, a wealthy Ulster exile and sheep-station millionaire in New South Wales, sent £25,000 to Carson's fund.[41]

Whilst the religious component of Ulster unionist propaganda was pronounced, it could be modified from time to time to cater for regional circumstances, and on its own would not have been sufficient to gain the support of large sections of British public opinion. Other approaches were needed. The large volume of sympathy for the anti-Home Rule movement, especially in influential social circles, was less for Ulster itself than for what it represented. The patriotism displayed by 'loyal' Ulster was, particularly to imperialist-minded Englishmen, invigorating. A geographical minority espousing their loyalty to the kingdom and empire, not only in the face of more numerous nationalist neighbours in Ireland, but also in the face of the 'undemocratic' plans of their own government, attracted the imagination and backing of jingoists in Britain. As Nicholas Mansergh aptly summarised it, 'The appeal for readiness and, if need be, resistance, was directed to Ulster but it was not for Ulster. It was for the integrity of the Empire that Ulster was to fight.'[42]

Apart from the keenness, dedication and adaptability displayed by unionist propagandists, the clarity of their message owed much to the successful way in which they employed a variety of propaganda techniques and tactics. For instance, unionist groups sponsored talks by 'Belfast working men' and other speakers in England. They realised the value of encouraging first-hand experience of the situation in Ireland and therefore the IUA organised tours there. Over 1,250 representatives from an estimated 116 British constituencies visited the province during the first half of 1914. Unionists claimed that many of these visitors were Liberal voters and encouraged working-class community or work groups to visit Ireland. Such a combination travelled there from Leicestershire early in June 1914. In their report on their fact-finding visit, the Loughborough Working Men's Group differentiated between Ulster and other parts of Ireland 'regarding industry, cleanliness and prosperity', before concluding that the deputation had been 'much impressed by the evident sincerity and earnestness of the people of Ulster, and their determination to resist the domination of an Irish Parliament'. They were convinced that the question of Home Rule was of 'great national importance' and that its introduction would be 'a grave injustice to Ulster'.[43] The *Belfast Telegraph* argued that government ministers should contemplate gaining first-hand experience of Ulster. It urged ministers who had 'sent their destroyers, their generals, their police armed with rifles' to Ulster to 'go themselves, bearing a message, if not of peace, at least of good will'.[44]

Unionist groups and the loyalist press believed that experiencing life in Ulster first hand had a cathartic effect upon many of these visitors. The UUC argued that many Radicals who had formerly believed 'the stories of unreasoning Protestant bigotry' were now cognizant of 'the stifling, throttling dominance of Roman Catholicism'.[45] One Radical group transformed by their experiences of the situation in Ulster was a deputation from west Staffordshire, who admitted that their views on Ireland had been 'completely revolutionised' after their visit. Writing a group letter to the *Belfast Telegraph*, they maintained:

> We have not the shadow of a doubt that if the Home Rule Bill becomes law in its present form it will be resisted to the bitter end by the Loyalists of Ireland. We are, therefore, unanimous of opinion that to force the Home Rule Bill on the Statute Book without an appeal to the electors of the United Kingdom by a General Election or by means of the referendum will bring about the great calamity of civil war.[46]

Inevitably, not all deputations experienced such Damascus-style conversions, especially in the cases of individuals with strong Radical principles or from Catholic backgrounds. A Catholic labourer, James Wilkinson, was a member of a Darlington trade-union delegation despatched to Ireland by a local Tory group in May 1914. His party visited southern cities like Dublin and Cork before making their way north. They visited factories in Belfast and met the city's lord mayor, who informed them that Home Rule was 'chiefly a question of religion'. Wilkinson's report, printed in the *Darlington Star* on 20 June, described how they had witnessed 'a good number of Ulster Volunteers mustering in the streets of west Belfast and afterwards saw them drilling on Black Mountain'. Although impressed by the sincerity of these Volunteers, his overall impression of Ulster had not altered:

> May I say that I left England a staunch Home Ruler and returned from Ireland the same, for I see no reason why the majority in Ireland should not be ruled by the minority and I, knowing the Catholic Church as I do, have no fear of the same interfering with the people's civic or political duties.[47]

Unionists were realistic enough to see the limited scope of such study tours. Their main thrust would take place in Great Britain, where they would concentrate on political canvassing, stage demonstrations and meetings, assist in collecting signatures for petitions and also distribute a vast amount of propaganda literature. However, the UAI were also aware that it was not enough simply to flood Great Britain with constituency agents, special speakers and purveyors of propaganda sheets and political postcards. Unionist leaders realised that it would be essential to prepare its workers properly for the inevitably contentious, impassioned debates that lay ahead of them in Great Britain. Therefore, in 1911, they prepared a pocket advice book for the use of unionist workers. In this small, 29-question booklet, enquiries by interested parties were in turn anticipated and answered. For instance, 'The majority in Ireland want Home Rule and being the majority, why should they not get it?' was perceived to be a question that would frequently be asked. In answering, unionist workers were advised not only to stress the existence of Ulster's anti-Home Rule majority, but also the opposition to the proposed measure in Britain:

> Shall the majority in Ulster and in England, Scotland and Wales be governed by the majority in the least industrial, the most disorderly and the worst educated parts of Ireland?[48]

Unionists also anticipated the nature of critical opposition within Liberal circles in Great Britain and were prepared to quote freely from opposition literature in defending their own political position. Quoting from the nationalist *Freeman's Journal*, for example, unionist publicists contended that, even in 1914, crime in southern Ireland was rampant.[49] Other questions tackled equally contentious issues such as possible accusations of religious bigotry within the unionist movement – described as measures of 'self defence against the priestly element in Nationalist circles' – and criticism of the Protestant Ascendancy.[50]

Unionists were aware that the main way of reaching the great mass of the British electorate was through their propaganda literature. Certainly, the scale of this campaign was impressive. Well over six million booklets, pamphlets and leaflets were distributed in Great Britain during the Home Rule period. Maximising their links with the Conservative Party, publicity handbills were designed by Irish Unionist Party workers in order to attract many thousands of sympathisers to over 5,000 meetings held in Britain during this two-year campaign.[51] Other forms of visual propaganda were also used. Anti-Home Rule postage stamps, frequently bearing the familiar craggy features of Edward Carson and a traditional slogan of Ulster's defiance, were produced to counteract the effects of similar pro-Home

Rule propaganda. Such stamps had neither monetary value nor legal status. Private agencies such as the Picture Stamp Company at Wellington Place in Belfast produced them and most were distributed by the UAI among sympathisers in Great Britain.

Another favoured propaganda device was the political pamphlet. Leading unionist politicians such as James Craig and former Conservative leader Arthur J. Balfour contributed cogently argued information summarising the reasons for Ulster's opposition to Home Rule. They were joined by clerics from a range of positions within the various Protestant churches. The appeal of political pamphlets was very different from that of political postcards and other visual material. Aimed at improving the political understanding of the outsider rather than appealing directly to individual emotions, pamphlets were successful in raising the level of political debate, especially amongst the committed. However, although vast numbers were printed and distributed, they are more likely to have influenced partisan than neutral voters, many of whom would have been deterred by their intellectual, polemical tone.

Many of these pamphlets were the work of Nonconformist ministers or leading figures within their churches, and some were aimed at specific parts of Great Britain. For example, Presbyterian cleric Rev. T.G. Houston, a teacher at Coleraine Academical Institution, spoke at a large meeting of co-religionists in Edinburgh towards the end of 1913, in which he asked them to support their brethren in Ulster. His rationale for denouncing Home Rule was articulated in a booklet distributed both at the meeting and afterwards. Warning the prime minister to 'look to the defences of his own country when he empties it of troops to slaughter the men of Ulster', Houston prophesied that the province would become 'the storm centre of the world'. He ended his emotive address by reminding his audience:

> here in this great city a cloud of witness encompasses you, a thousand hallowed memories call to you to stand by your

brethren in their hour of need – they bid you to aid us heart and soul in all our peaceful efforts to avoid this terrible danger, and if all such efforts fail, they bid you, when the trumpet sounds, to come over and help us.'[52]

Leading Methodist Sir William Whitla also had one of his key anti-Home Rule speeches – delivered to a large audience at the Ulster Hall on 14 March 1912 – reprinted in a booklet entitled 'Messages to English Nonconformists'. In this, he pointed out that although his audience, and indeed his church, were politically split over broader issues, they were 'solidly united as one man in the deliberate conviction that Home Rule means disaster and ruin to our native land, and irreparable injury to our church and to the civil and religious liberty which we and our fathers have enjoyed under the impartial freedom of the British flag'.[53]

Other pamphlets originated from UUC headquarters. Many of these adopted an unashamedly partisan approach to the religious dimension of Home Rule. In one such booklet, James Craig denounced the portrayal of Ulster Protestants as 'bigots' and concluded that the 'first and most natural attitude' of Ulster towards the proposed legislation was that 'she has nothing whatever to gain by the change and everything to lose'.[54] An Ulster unionist flyer from this period informed its readers that a Strabane priest had warned his congregation not to vote for the unionist candidate in a forthcoming by-election. He counselled that such an action would result in his becoming regarded as 'a recreant to his country' and that the offender would be 'held responsible at the day of judgement'. Further pamphlets stressed imperial and economic considerations in opposing a Dublin-based Irish legislature. An early UUC pamphlet, 'Ulster and home union: unionist policy', stressed the latter factor, reminding its readers that Ulster unionists had 'made their province a not unworthy constituency of the British Empire' and that their industries had achieved 'a world-wide fame'.[55]

Undoubtedly the most colourful technique employed by the UAI was that of political postcards. Such cards were published by commercial companies, both large and small, within Ulster as well as in England. Mainland-produced cards tended to focus on photographic and factual illustrations of major contemporary events. The situation in Ulster was frequently portrayed in the 'Historic events series' and firms such as the Corona Publishing Company in Blackpool, the art publishers Millar and Lang (London and Glasgow), and the Photocrom Company (London and Tunbridge Wells) all produced a variety of cards dealing sympathetically with the unionist campaign. Locally produced cards comprised most of this material and Ulster-based firms included John Adams, an 'artistic letter-press printer' based in Belfast's King Street, the larger firm of W. and G. Baird (later owners of the *Belfast Telegraph*) in the city's Royal Avenue, H.R. Cater of Waring Street and the Ulster Publishing Company, situated on the city's Shankill Road. These were more likely to have used satire against their opponents, as well as exhibiting their arguments for opposing Home Rule. They were not only distributed by the UAI in Great Britain, but also sent by loyalists to relatives and sympathisers across the globe.

As an art genre, the political picture postcard was popular in Edwardian Britain. A direct descendant of the political cartoon – many of the designers of the early cards were contributors to *Punch* and *Vanity Fair* – publishers used them to deal with topics as divergent as tariff reform, income tax and female suffrage. Unionists had a clear idea of the purposes of such material. Apart from being designed to counter the impression given by pro-Home Rule cards already in circulation, the fact that they showcased key events and personalities and satirised political opponents meant that they were a visual platform for the dissemination of loyalist objections to opposition to Home Rule. The fears, aspirations, attitudes and actions of individuals and groups involved in the Home Rule crisis provided ideas for illustrators in designing hundreds of cards. In terms both of quality and quantity, the political postcard was a vital component of the unionist propaganda campaign, especially in Great Britain and overseas.

One of the most constant messages emanating from these political postcards was the need to preserve the unity both of the United Kingdom and the British empire. Unionists exploited the strategy of depicting figures from each of the home countries in national costume, under the slogan 'No Home Rule – united we stand, divided we fall'. On this card, a shamrock-wielding 'Pat' was joined by a kilted 'Sandy' and a leek-carrying 'Taffy' and was drawn holding arms with the benevolent John Bull. The latter featured on numerous cards, often in a protective role, including one where he was defending the loyalists of 'prosperous' Ulster from the triple attack of 'poverty-ridden' Connacht, 'priestly' Leinster and 'rustic' Munster.[56]

This personification of the bulldog spirit was not confined to the English figure of John Bull, but was also effectively utilised in numerous cards depicting the profile of Sir Edward Carson. The tactic of using the leader's face for publicity material would later become a powerful propaganda weapon in Nazi Germany, and Carson's distinctive profile – hair combed back from a high forehead, eyes deep set and intense, lips set in a defiant scowl and chin jutting out aggressively – was ideal for epitomising the stubborn resistance of his followers. Edward Carson and other unionist leaders – especially James Craig who, as a Boer War veteran, was an ideal figure for combining the roles of politician and soldier – featured on many cards, usually alongside one of the more common slogans of Ulster resistance.

This was not confined to Irish leaders. In one card, entitled 'No thoroughfare', the authoritative figure of policeman Andrew Bonar Law (carrying the red hand of Ulster) halts the jaunting-car of Herbert Asquith, adorned in rural Irish attire, whose Home Rule package is precariously perched at the rear of the vehicle. The unambiguous use of images – Law as the fair-minded protector and Asquith the rustic intruder – shows the increasing sophistication of unionist propaganda.

Nor was the pugnacious face of resistance confined to politicians. Perhaps one of the most popular cards was that portraying a young boy squaring up to all comers, provocatively demanding, 'Who says we're to have Home Rule?' The reply, delivered in the unmistakable Belfast vernacular, is explicit – 'Come to Belfast and we'll shew them!'[57]

Unionist propagandists were fully aware of the importance of spreading the message that a loyal minority was being bullied by a larger neighbour. Adopting a tactic that would be widely used by both sides during the Great War, women were depicted to illustrate the helplessness of a little country threatened by larger nearby enemies and facing the prospect of being deserted by its friends. A colleen with a Union Jack behind her looks forlornly for help in one picture, but her message – 'I can stand alone' – symbolises the self-reliance of Ulster as the crisis neared its climax. The increase in references to weapons during the latter part of the campaign and the increasingly likely threat of physical action is exemplified on a card entitled 'Ulster 1914'. This bears the images of a billowing Union Jack flying alongside the joined emblems of the crown, Ulster's red hand and crossed rifles. As if in any doubt of the card's message, the reader was reminded of its meaning by the stanzas that accompanied it:

> Lo! The mighty heart of Ulster
> All too big to slumber more.
> Bursts in wrath and exultation
> Like a loud volcano's roar!
>
> There they stand, the lonely columns
> Underneath a darkening sky.
> In the hush of desperation
> There to conquer or to die![58]

Other cards used satire in their efforts to spell out the message that Home Rule would mean economic ruin for Belfast. One card depicted the destruction that would befall the recently built City Hall once Home Rule was implemented. Using racial stereotypes favoured by *Punch* decades previously, cards in this category depicted a crumbling City Hall, surrounded by derelict offices and cattle grazing in its grounds, with a full-scale fight in progress inside the once-grand municipal building.[59]

In conducting this propaganda campaign, the UAI and other loyalist groups encountered a number of difficulties, some of which they never really solved. Financing pro-Ulster publicity was a major problem (especially during the early part of the crisis), despite the hard work of unionist agencies in Ireland and the fund-raising efforts of the UAI, Union Defence League (UDL) and British League in Great Britain. Despite the eagerness of its British workers, the UAI never overcame the problem of providing adequately trained field workers, nor were relations between these workers and Tory agents as smooth as they might have been. Yet the UAI was successful in achieving its stated objective at the inaugural meeting. Unionist arguments against Home Rule were conveyed with vigour to large sections of the British public and the Ulster issue proved to be a significant factor in determining the outcome of several by-election contests. By the size and scope of its propaganda campaign and by the ingenuity displayed by those working in this sphere, loyalists regarded the campaign as hugely successful. Thus, James Craig enthused in a UUC statement in 1913:

> It [the campaign] far exceeded our best hopes. We could never have imagined ... the enthusiasm which was awakened for the cause of Irish Loyalists ... There was in those English and Scottish demonstrations in our support depth of understanding and a profound note of friendship which augurs well for the future.[60]

Irish nationalists were less impressed by the impact of unionist propaganda. John Redmond noted how loyalists had 'inundated every constituency with hostile literature and hostile speakers' but concluded that they had 'utterly failed to arouse even the faintest echo of the old antagonisms and prejudices'.[61]

It is always difficult to assess reaction to a political cause, especially one that dates back to the Edwardian period. Problems invariably arise, not only when deciding what to measure – the government's response to such material or its impact upon British public opinion – but also in how to interpret it. Patricia Jalland, a prominent sceptic of anti-Home Rule propaganda, contended that it made less impact on government policy before 1914 than it did after the end of the Great War. She maintained that British voters between 1910 and 1914 were apathetic and ignorant about Ireland and that Liberal voters' only real response to the issue of Home Rule was a negative one, frequently centring on criticism of their ministers' indecisive leadership.[62] Although Jalland was correct to point out that unionist pressure did not lead to Herbert Asquith withdrawing his bill, the persistence of Ulster opposition to the measure – largely the result of their propaganda and use of important friends – did result in a gradual shift in government policy, leading to the isolation of Ulster. This, in itself, laid the seeds of partition.

Whilst there were ups and downs in the public response to events affecting Ulster (including somewhat different reactions to the Curragh mutiny and the UVF gun-running), it is undoubtedly true that Liberal political and press opinion, which had initially derided the Orangemen with their wooden rifles and solemn religious fervour, had by the start of 1914 finally recognised that it had underestimated unionist determination and support in Great Britain. In this sense, by determining an eventual shift in Liberal opinion and policy over a period of time, the UAI and other loyalist agencies engaged in propaganda did manage to make an impact upon political attitudes and policy in Great Britain.

Blessing the colours of the Volunteers

An important element in the resistance of Ulster unionists was the vigorous support and unity exhibited by the various Protestant churches in Ireland. The religious factor in loyalist opposition was a significant one and it featured heavily in how Ulster unionists justified their opposition to Home Rule and in the propaganda material they designed for the British and overseas market (particularly in areas with large numbers of non-established church members). Protestants constituted approximately a quarter of Ireland's total population in 1911, with the Anglican Church retaining its place as the largest of the country's Protestant churches. The 1911 census reported that there were 576,000 members of the Church of Ireland, some 13 per cent of the island's population, 439,000 Presbyterians (10 per cent), and 68,000 Methodists (1.4 per cent). Barriers between Anglicans and other Protestant denominations had started to come down before the Home Rule crisis and the perilous predicament facing Irish Protestants would hasten their removal. This is not to deny that suspicions remained, most notably over Presbyterian resentment at the degree of aristocratic involvement in the loyalist campaign and Anglican suspicions over Presbyterians' natural sympathies with the social policies of a Radical government. However, as Alan Megahey noted, 'the things that united the Protestants were far more important than those which divided them'.[63] As previous campaigns against Home Rule had illustrated, resistance was genuine and not cosmetic and was built on 'a cultural bedrock of Protestant assumptions and values which were central to the emergence of a Protestant identity in Ulster'.[64] The power of evangelical religion was not restricted to the 'fringe' Protestant denominations. Most northern loyalists empathised with a movement that closely related the sustenance of prosperity and happiness in their present existence with earning salvation in a future spiritual life. Anglicans, Presbyterians and Methodists alike felt threatened by the bleak economic and constitutional future predicted by Ulster unionist leaders and also shared fear and disdain over the possible encroachment of the Catholic Church into the lives of northern Protestants in a post-Home Rule Ireland.

One feature of the Protestant clergy was the degree of support they were prepared to contribute to the political movement between 1912 and 1914. This contrasted sharply with church attitudes in subsequent decades. Although there had been several instances of pulpit rhetoric in previous anti-Home Rule campaigns, religious leaders of Ulster's Protestant community were open in their support – both for the extreme political strategy of the Ulster unionists and, more crucially, in their presence at military demonstrations of armed UVF members. This backing showed itself in ways ranging from the Presbyterian moderator describing the Volunteers as 'a great and noble army' to many clergymen at local level helping in practical ways (including supplying motor vehicles and storing weapons) during the gun-running operation of April 1914.[65] Indeed, the apparent sanctioning of armed revolt by church leaders was recognised as a bizarre and surreal feature of Ulster resistance, especially by foreign observers. One of these, an Austro-Hungarian diplomat based in London at the time, wrote about the 'state of feverish ferment' he discovered in Ulster during a visit in 1914. Baron von Franckenstein later recorded:

> Ulster's grim determination to offer armed resistance was brought home to me in Belfast, where I saw Protestant clergy in full canonicals bless the colours of the volunteers ... The extraordinary character which marked this whole crisis was especially emphasised on this occasion by the loud cheers for the King, against whose government the men of Ulster were arming.[66]

A long-standing northern Protestant fear was that the already vulnerable position of their co-religionists in the south and west of Ireland would be reflected in their own circumstances in the advent of major political and constitutional change. Loyalist opinion makers argued that the perceived intolerant stance of the Catholic hierarchy would manifest itself in similar cases of alleged religious prejudice against Protestants if Ulster was subject to a Dublin administration. Listing examples of communal intolerance precipitated by condemnatory or provocative clerical statements, the *Northern Whig* described how a Protestant minister in Connemara had been stoned for staging an outdoor temperance meeting, and how a Protestant woman who had held prayer meetings in her Roscommon home was ostracised by Catholic neighbours and former friends after being denounced from the pulpit (she later left the area).[67]

Perhaps the most controversial aspect of so-called encroachment upon Protestant liberties was in the sphere of mixed marriages. Prior to Pope Pius X's *Ne temere* decree in 1907, the Catholic Church's attitude to mixed marriages had been ambiguous. The papal intervention meant that mixed marriages would only be considered valid by the church if they had been conducted by a Catholic priest. Whilst such marriages were relatively rare at that time (and were also far from popular in Protestant communities), the Catholic Church's stance on the issue irritated Protestant sensitivities. Essentially, they felt aggrieved that Protestant interests in such marital unions appeared to be of peripheral significance. For much of 1908 and 1909, churches and other groups protested vehemently against the papal ruling. However, it was a test case involving the marriage of a Belfast couple, the McCanns, in November 1910, that was to propel the issue of mixed marriage into the forefront of Irish political debate, especially in the period preceding the introduction of Asquith's Third Home Rule Bill.

Agnes McCann had attended Townsend Presbyterian Church in west Belfast before marrying her Catholic-born husband, Alexander, in a non-religious ceremony. Advised by a priest that his marriage could not be, in the light of the decree, considered a proper one unless they remarried in a Catholic church, Alexander McCann attempted to persuade his wife to agree. When she was reluctant to do so, he left the marital home, taking their two young children with him. The exposure of the case in the press horrified Ulster Protestants. The resulting furore and recriminations in church pulpits across Ulster were unprecedented. There were protests in Belfast, Dublin and even at Westminster, where unionist representatives castigated the Catholic Church and the RIC for their 'connivance' in helping McCann to 'disappear' with the children. The Ulster Women's Unionist Council (UWUC) organised a petition condemning the decree and collected over 104,000 signatures from women across the province. The organisation noted the 'serious dangers' that would beset their 'social and domestic liberties' by entrusting legislative power to 'a body of which a large permanent majority would be under ecclesiastical control'.[68] Loyalist responses to the *Ne temere* decree and the resulting McCann case provided a model of action for the much larger political campaign that would be launched within two years. The petition tactic would be successfully adopted for Ulster's Solemn League and Covenant, and the evident cohesion of the various Protestant churches in the north 'foreshadowed their political unanimity a year later'.[69]

The Anglican Church in Ireland, disestablished over 40 years before, was still the largest and most influential of Ireland's Protestant churches. As Andrew Scholes has pointed out, the Church of Ireland played a more prominent role in Ulster's resistance to Home Rule than historians have previously acknowledged. Indeed, Scholes has suggested that the fortunes and unity of Irish unionism and the island's Anglican Church were inextricably intertwined.[70] The Church of Ireland increasingly became embroiled in the political quagmire surrounding Home Rule and, as it continued to offer apparently unequivocal backing for political and even paramilitary leaders, divisions within its support base at diocesan level widened.

Whilst it eschewed most of the loyalist arguments for opposing Home Rule, the Church of Ireland's most fundamental objections to the measure were religious ones. The Cavan-born Bishop of Down and Connor, Rev. Dr Charles Frederick D'Arcy, wrote in a church newspaper in August 1912:

> It is not sufficiently realised that behind Ulster's opposition to home rule there is an immensely strong conviction which is essentially religious. We contend for life, for civil liberty, for progress, for our rightful heritage of British citizenship. We also contend for faith and for the freedom of our souls.[71]

The ruling body of the church was also explicit in its rationale for vehemently opposing an Irish parliament. At a specially called meeting on 16 April 1912 (just a few days after the introduction of the Third Home Rule Bill in the House of Commons), the General Synod passed several resolutions 'reaffirming our constant allegiance to the Throne and to our unswerving attachment to legislative Union'.[72] These statements enlighten us on the thinking of church members on the question of Home Rule. Appealing to 'our co-religionists in Great Britain not to desert their brethren in Ireland', Irish members of the Anglican Church pledged their loyalty to the empire, but central to their thinking were economic and religious considerations. This was reflected in the wording of part of a resolution unanimously passed at the mass meeting:

> We cannot accept any assurances that either the prosperity of our Church, or our civil and religious liberty may safely be entrusted to a Parliament in which we should be outnumbered by men who are dominated by traditions and aspirations wholly different from our own.[73]

The religious leadership of the Anglican Church in Ireland maintained close links with the unionist movement's political leaders and also had a high-profile presence at several key loyalist events between the spring of 1912 and the summer of

1914. The two key figures were Dr John Baptist Crozier, primate of all Ireland, and Rev. Dr Charles Frederick D'Arcy. The latter had a more natural empathy with Ulster's loyalists and was a hard-working advocate of their cause, corresponding regularly with Sir Edward Carson and counselling important clerics in Britain (including the Archbishop of Canterbury) on the Irish question. Although more at ease with the prospect of *all* of Ulster being excluded from Home Rule (and not just a part) and conscious of the fears of more vulnerable Anglicans elsewhere in Ireland, Crozier managed to prevent a split between a group of southern bishops and their northern counterparts. The former were, in private at least, increasingly critical of what they believed to be an undue emphasis on the position of Ulster's Protestants, largely at the expense of the dire prospects facing Anglicans in the south and west. Bishop D'Arcy, on the other hand, was prominent in his support of Sir Edward Carson and the Ulster Covenant and in his justification of the armed presence of Ulster Volunteers. At a difficult stage in the bill's parliamentary passage, D'Arcy wrote to Carson:

> Will you let me say how much your speech in the House last night has stirred our hearts here, and how thankful and grateful we are for it and for the effect which it so obviously produced[?] A few days ago, the outlook was very black. There is a break in the clouds now.[74]

Bishop D'Arcy took a prominent role during the Covenant campaign of September 1912 and delivered the main address in St Anne's Cathedral on Covenant Day. Although the religious and historical symbolism of such an occasion was fundamentally Presbyterian, the Church of Ireland was fully committed to the proceedings, not only during Covenant Day itself, but also during the two-week campaign that preceded the signing. However, this cohesion in the north's Anglican community came at a cost. Andrew Scholes has written that, by its unequivocal backing for the Covenant and in the subsequent path towards some form of Ulster exclusion, the Anglican Church 'in parts of Ulster was poised to exclude their Anglican brethren in the rest of Ireland from the protection of the citadel'.[75]

At grass-roots level across Ulster, Church of Ireland ministers sustained a high degree of support for Carson and his movement long after Covenant Day. Rousing sermons praising the defiant stand of politicians and Volunteers ensured that Anglican Church attendances during these two years were well above average. Clergy opened up their church halls to enable Ulster Volunteers to practise their drill. They officiated at fund-raising events, joined auxiliary sections of the UVF and had their laudatory letters of support for political leaders and the UVF published in the local loyalist press. Some even lent their cars for the transportation of UVF weaponry or stored rifles in the grounds of their manses after April 1914. Other Anglican ministers spoke at conferences in Great Britain and wrote propaganda pamphlets, which were distributed to a wide cross-channel audience. These were frequently targeted at sympathetic co-religionists and usually the tone was one of unapologetic moral self-righteousness. The rector of Limavady Parish in County Londonderry, Rev. R.G.S. King, wrote a booklet entitled 'Ulster's protest', in which he outlined Ulster loyalists' objections to Home Rule. In his concluding remarks, he implored his readers to 'be true to us':

> We have mingled our blood with yours in the battlefields of our glorious Empire ... What verdict will history pass upon you if you try to consign the Loyalists of Ireland to the power of the bitterest foes of the Empire, to a prospect which they hate worse than death? ... We expect of you ... that you should unite your forces with those who are determined to prevent the establishment at the very heart of the Empire, of a great hostile power, fostering unreasoning hate, malicious prejudice, discord and division, criminal and cruel agitators?[76]

Compared with the enthusiastic support from several senior figures in British Nonconformist churches, there were few outpourings of public support for the Ulster cause emanating from the leaders of the Church of England. Anglican leaders in Britain did not appear on pro-Ulster political platforms, nor were there many letters or articles from vicars or bishops in support of Edward Carson's stance in the Tory press. Yet this reluctance to identify the institution of the church with one section of the Irish population did not imply a lack of interest in what was going on. At a time when religious participation in Britain was still relatively high, there was some substance in the claim that the Church of England 'represented the Tory Party at prayer'. Certainly, Andrew Bonar Law and other political leaders had briefings with senior clerics, including Randall Davidson, the Archbishop of Canterbury. It is likely that the leader of England's Protestant Church would have advised his political counterpart on the need for caution on Ireland, yet he would also have expressed his concern for the plight of religious minorities there, especially those affiliated to his own church. Archbishop Davidson appears to have played a backstage role on the Irish issue, meeting on occasions to discuss the situation with the troubled monarch, George V, and also acting as an intermediary between the various political leaders. For instance, he was engaged in meetings with senior Tories and Liberals in March 1913 after Herbert Asquith put forward strategies for the exclusion of Ulster from the provisions of Home Rule.

Considering the significant contribution made by members of the Presbyterian Church to the Ulster unionist cause during this period and the high volume of support declared by Presbyterians (especially during the Covenant preparations in 1912), it is ironic that the natural political instincts of Nonconformists were to remain distant from policies advocated by the Conservative Party. Yet Presbyterians, Methodists and Congregationalists were prepared to put aside their political differences in their determination to mount a unified campaign against the proposed legislation. Delegates at a Presbyterian convention organised by Thomas Sinclair in Belfast on 1 February 1912 were reminded of such irony in a resolution which would be unanimously agreed at the various meetings:

> In our opposition to Home Rule we are activated by no spirit of sectarian exclusiveness and we seek for no ascendancy, religious or otherwise. Many of us were active sharers in the struggle which, over 40 years ago, secured religious equality and initiated land reform in Ireland; and, if permitted, we are all of us ready to co-operate with Irishmen of every creed in the advancement of the social, moral and material prosperity of our common country.[77]

This irony, set alongside Presbyterian support for Edward Carson's movement, is even more incredible when one considers the efforts of Presbyterians in helping create a shared Ulster identity through the use of Presbyterian images, symbols and propaganda.[78] The 'unchangeable opposition' of the Presbyterian Church to Asquith's Home Rule proposals was voiced at the Presbyterian convention of February 1912. At this event, 11 meetings were arranged to facilitate the attendance and participation of some 40,000 Presbyterian delegates. At these meetings, fears of increasing interference by the Catholic Church and the negative impact of a Dublin administration on the region's unparalleled economic prosperity were clearly articulated. Reminders of the potential damage that might be the consequence of 'Romish rule' and comparisons with previous battles for the maintenance of civil and religious liberties (at places like the Boyne and Derry) formed part of the rhetoric delivered by current and former church moderators, as well as in parish pulpits across Ulster. In its essence, the objections of those present centred on 'a matter of elementary right and justice, the undisturbed continuance of our present place in the constitution under which our Church and our country have so signally prospered'.[79] One of the resolutions unanimously agreed at the meetings was a plea for support from co-religionists in Great Britain. Part of this stressed that there was 'an obligation upon our fellow citizens of the same faith to stand by us in securing the rejection of a policy so dangerous to our highest interests'.[80]

Whilst political, religious and social cohesion amongst the Protestant community at this time was not in doubt, it should not be assumed that all Protestants were against Home Rule. Although the numbers of Protestants publicly supporting the proposed political changes were very small, they did include several leading figures, including shipyard owner Lord Pirrie, Swift MacNeill, Douglas Hyde, George Birmingham and Fermanagh-born Jeremiah Jordan, MP for West Clare. Most people in this category supported Home Rule for ideological reasons but, as Jonathan Bardon has pointed out, a number of other Ulster Protestants were increasingly swayed towards accepting the prospect of a united Ireland on account of the extreme tactics adopted by Carson's movement.[81] The fear of bloodshed following a confrontation with either the British Army or Redmondite forces in a new Irish administration filled many with dread and, whilst undoubtedly reluctant to verbalise their fears in public, it is likely that a small proportion of the Protestant population would not have been fully committed to the loyalist cause as the crisis deepened during 1914.

A small number of Presbyterian and Methodist ministers spoke out in favour of Home Rule. Their statements had relatively little impact upon their congregations, who generally remained loyal to Edward Carson, the Irish Unionist Party and the Ulster Volunteer Force. However, the single-mindedness and personal bravery of Presbyterian dissidents, like Rev. James Brown Armour, in criticising the Ulster unionist leadership and openly supporting Home Rule cannot be in question. Armour, a minister in Ballymoney, County Antrim, was a Liberal Party activist and had been involved in the land campaign many years previously. Apart from his pulpit denunciations of the extreme course being taken by Ulster unionists, Armour also participated in counter-Covenant public meetings, including one in Ballymoney Town Hall, which was attended by Roger Casement. Armour was not afraid to tackle the leadership of Ulster unionism and once memorably described its leader as 'a sheer mountebank, the greatest enemy of Protestantism in my opinion existing, inciting men to violence'.[82]

The considerably smaller Wesleyan community in Ulster shared similar reservations about opposing a Radical government, but were equally determined in their resistance to Home Rule. Methodists also organised protest meetings on the eve of the introduction of Herbert Asquith's legislation. A Methodist convention met in Belfast on 14 March 1912 and ended with the unanimous acceptance of several pro-Ulster resolutions at five separate meetings. Methodists felt that Home Rule would 'open and prepare the way for further changes in the Constitution of very wide and far-reaching civic consequences, especially imperilling the best interests of education, temperance and Sabbath observance'.[83] The mood of Methodists had not altered two years later when, after a further convention, they resolved to 'stand by their fellow Protestants in offering it [Home Rule] continued and determined resistance'.[84]

Nonconformists were aware of the usefulness of the tactic of appealing directly to their co-religionists in specific regions of Great Britain, especially Wales, south-west England and Lowlands Scotland. A number of Nonconformist ministers were active in writing press articles and speaking on religious and political platforms at this time. Amongst the most active was Methodist minister Rev. Dr W.L. Watkinson, who wrote three articles inside a week in November 1912 for the *Morning Post*. Also at this time, Congregationalist minister Rev. J. Radford Thompson asked fellow Nonconformists if they were prepared 'to put down such resistance by force of arms and to impose upon their brethren the yoke of tyranny and bondage'.[85]

'Being convinced ...'

Political demonstrations involving endless ranks of marching men at places such as Craigavon and Balmoral had served the useful purpose of illustrating loyalist strength to the external audience, as well as bolstering the confidence of its supporters at home. However, Sir Edward Carson and his senior colleagues realised that a new approach, which would offer loyalists an outlet for exhibiting their opposition to Home Rule whilst helping to control the more volatile elements within their movement, was urgently required. Carson in particular was extremely perturbed about the repercussions of potential communal street disturbances fuelled by the high emotions unleashed by his political campaign and wanted to devise strategies that would act as safety valves in controlling such passions.

These fears were well founded. In a six-week period between July and early September 1912, there were disturbances in the shipyards and at a football match in west Belfast. With increased access to 'real' guns a likely prospect for a large-scale military movement soon to be drilled by former army officers, as well as a darkening political situation, a major new approach that would symbolise unionist principles and fears was urgently needed. It was decided that a mass petition, incorporating a pledge of loyalty and statement of underlying principles, would be drawn up and, following a campaign, presented to followers to be signed.

Mass petitions were, of course, not a new device for influencing parliamentary opinion. Both Daniel O'Connell and the Chartist movement had, with varying degrees of success, attempted such an approach in the mid-nineteenth century. Although rather gratuitously compared to famous biblical, legal and constitutional documents from the distant past, such as the Old Testament Covenant of the Israelites, the thirteenth-century Magna Carta and the eighteenth-century American Declaration of Independence, Ulster's Solemn League and Covenant was more closely modelled on the Scottish Covenant of 1638, which had denounced the discriminatory actions of King Charles I. With its powerful emotional appeal to a religiously devout population more concerned about keeping the laws of God than those of any parliament, the idea of a covenant centred on concepts of citizenship and fealty to a constitutional monarch was a masterstroke quickly adopted by Carson and his senior colleagues. It was believed to have been the idea of B.W.D. Montgomery, the secretary of Belfast's unionist club, who had come up with the notion during a conversation with James Craig. Once it was decided to pursue this idea, another Belfast businessman, Thomas Sinclair, worked on the short text and a Covenant committee, including R. Dawson Bates and James Craig, was established to monitor its progress and supervise its dissemination.

This new tactic was an instant success with Carson's numerous supporters. The Covenant 'combined solemnity, religiosity and military discipline'.[86] It provided loyalists with a clear opportunity to state their political perspective and, on a more personal level, invited unionists in town and country across the province to become involved in a mass movement aimed at defending their most vital interests. It was this combination of individual and community interests that formed the substance of the Covenant's appeal. The Covenant campaign was announced in the local press on 17 August 1912 and for the next month newspapers, propagandists and politicians debated the pledge's key clauses. Many of these concentrated on the reciprocal nature of their loyalty and their views on the essence of citizenship. The *Belfast News-Letter* maintained that Ulster's place within the UK was 'an inalienable right of their citizenship which no Government of any time has the right to deprive them of'.[87]

Ulster's reasons for resisting Home Rule and indeed a *précis* of their political philosophy are embodied in the one-paragraph text of Ulster's Solemn League and Covenant. The designers of the document realised that a lengthy treatise of constitutional complexities, emanating from the pen of an eminent constitutionalist like A.V. Dicey, would have been inappropriate for a pledge designed to attract mass support. Instead, they opted for the use of relatively simple and concise language, devoid of innuendo or possible confusion.

In the days and hours before they dutifully presented themselves at the signing stations across Ulster, many loyalists would have pondered over the pledge, which was printed in full in newspapers and on posters displayed in civic halls and street corners. Few would have disagreed with its content and it would have clarified the thinking of many on this fundamental issue. The order of the phrases and the request for unequivocal commitment to these pleas was certainly not accidental and was something that Craig, Bates and others had carefully considered. Yet the ordering of some of these objections to Home Rule appears a little surprising. For instance, the first key phrase – 'Being convinced in our consciences that Home Rule would be disastrous to the material well-being of Ulster as well as of the whole of Ireland ...' – reflects the significance of unionists' economic opposition to the measure.[88] Whilst the importance of this factor was acknowledged by politicians and propagandists alike, it was not the most attractive of pleas to an external audience, given its association with self-interest.

Yet unionists made no secret of their economic differences with the rest of Ireland. The relatively late industrial revolution experienced in the Lagan Valley and the resulting rapid increase in the area's population meant that Belfast's economic infrastructure was radically different from that of, for instance, the south and west of the island. Unionists feared that their industrial might and commercial prosperity would be seriously endangered if they were no longer an integral part of the British economy and instead faced the prospect of subsidising other, economically backward parts of the island.

Whilst the fundamental fear of self-preservation was reflected in its pivotal position in the document, other key objections to Home Rule received strategic prioritisation in the Covenant pledge. Thus, religious fears over the measure were clearly expressed, but in the context of a desire to preserve religious 'freedom' rather than in more contentious and overtly sectarian tones, employing direct references to Catholicism or the pope. Crucially, there are two references to citizenship and also an important plea for preserving the unity of the empire. Home Rule is described in the fourth and fifth lines of the Covenant as being potentially 'destructive of our citizenship and perilous to the unity of the Empire'; later in the pledge, the desire to defend 'our cherished position of equal citizenship in the United Kingdom' is stated.

Not surprisingly – given that recent constitutional changes had meant that the protection of parliament would evaporate on the ultimate passing of the proposed legislation – the Covenant did not seek parliamentary approval. Instead, the only 'superior' powers mentioned in the Covenant were the king – those signing are described as 'loyal subjects of His Gracious Majesty King George V' – and God, in whom they placed their 'sure confidence', as did their 'fathers in days of stress'. Inevitably, in what was designed as a document aimed at the Protestant population of Ulster, there are references to community cohesion and to previous struggles against inequity. The need to 'pledge ourselves in solemn Covenant throughout this our time of threatened calamity to stand by one another' and to protect 'our cherished position' within the UK, is articulated halfway down the paragraph.[89]

Although essentially a defensive enunciation of their position and principles, Ulster's Solemn League and Covenant did contain a mixture of aggression and obstinacy that promised to express itself in a refusal to cooperate in the eventuality of political defeat. Therefore, in the second half of the document – 'using all means which may be found necessary to defeat the present conspiracy to set up a Home Rule Parliament in Ireland'

– there is little doubt about the determination of signatories in resisting such legislation. This barely concealed threat of physical opposition to a successfully carried parliamentary bill was not immediately followed by a pledge to 'refuse to recognise its authority' if such a parliament was 'forced' upon them.[90] As mentioned above, there would be no direct plea to the Liberal government for clemency, nor would there be a more detailed exposition of their position. The pledge ended with a request for those signing to declare that they had not already signed the Covenant; the venue of the signing was clearly stated.

There is no doubt that the Covenant, with its clear tones of moral certainty, provided the unionist movement with a symbol of unity. It also gave them an opportunity to verbalise disapproval at what most of them regarded as a 'betrayal' by the Liberal administration and to put forward a clear, concise statement of their own political position. One historian has described the impact the Covenant had on its intended audience:

> In its simple but eloquent phrases Ulster men and women found the expression of their deepest convictions, their deepest loyalties and their most fervent hopes for their future and that of their children.[91]

Loyal ports of call

Loyalists had been looking forward to the Covenant campaign (which had been meticulously planned by Craig and his colleagues) since it had been announced in August. Excitement naturally increased with the arrival of the IUP leader in Ulster in the middle of September. Edward Carson arrived at Belfast docks in the early hours of Saturday, 14 September 1912, looking 'fresh and fit ... after an interval of holiday rest'.[92] His always suspect health was to be severely tested during the next energy-sapping fortnight. Apart from announcing the terms of the Covenant at Craigavon on 19 September and seeking approval for it at Belfast's Old Town Hall four days later, the

IUP leader was to make key speeches at six of the eleven meetings that the Covenant committee had scheduled to take place across the province over a ten-day period during the second half of September. At the start of the Covenant campaign, Carson explained and justified his mission. He told a group of journalists at Craigavon:

> If it be rebellion to stand against what is ridiculous in the sight of mankind, then indeed we are rebels. The Covenant will be signed in no spirit of challenge or truculence. It will be signed calmly and determinedly, and because it is the duty of Unionists to make plain to their countrymen where they stand and what is their final resolve.[93]

There was a mood of excited anticipation in the early afternoon of 17 September as Edward Carson was photographed leaning out of a railway carriage and waving his hat at photographers. He was on his way to Enniskillen at the start of his ten-day tour, described by a sympathetic paper as 'a great campaign of resistance'.[94] There was also an increased awareness of the serious mood of Ulster resistance in the British press on the eve of the Covenant campaign. A few days before it started in Enniskillen, the *Daily Mail* warned against any settlement of the Irish question that might involve 'sacrificing Ulster', which 'differs from the rest of Ireland in race, culture, religion, political ideals and economic development' and concluded that 'this fact gives tremendous force to her plea for different treatment'.[95] The scale of support for Carson's Covenant and its classless appeal was stressed in a leader in *The Times* at the outset of the campaign. This article commented that 'practically ... the whole Unionist or Protestant population of the province will before the end of the month take part in the movement for resistance to Home Rule'.[96] The *Morning Post* focused on the degree of support for Ulster's cause within Tory circles in Great Britain, claiming that 'no English Unionist' could 'withhold his hearty sympathy from the people of Ulster in the hour of their trial'.[97]

The 'island town' of Enniskillen, situated in the deep west of Ulster and an important part of Orange folklore, was a 'fitting' venue for the first of the major Covenant campaign meetings.[98] Many had travelled to the busy Fermanagh market town from across the county, from Tyrone and from places further afield, including Leitrim, Sligo, Monaghan and Donegal. Special trains transported some 15,000 loyalists and the streets of the market town were bustling by mid-morning of 18 September. Edward Carson had stayed overnight at the mansion of the earl of Erne, who would later open the meeting at Portora Hill, just outside the town. A popular meeting point for those attending the demonstration was the Portora Gate Hotel, where the diverse social range of Protestant opposition to Home Rule was fully illustrated by the mingling of aristocrats and country folk. The reporter from *The Times* described how the Portora Gate Hotel filled with 'clergymen, landlords and ladies, while outside these aristocratic precincts, sauntered bearded Protestant peasants of extraordinary age, as if they had always remained faithful to the memory of King William'.[99]

Carson, the earl of Erne and close colleagues were met at Enniskillen Station by a group of mounted yeomanry carrying lances and loyalist banners and wearing rosettes. A London reporter observed that 'these young Fermanagh men, bronzed, self-confident, with a look of colonials [and] riding the horses of their farms and wearing slouch hats and gaiters were in deadly earnest'.[100] At Portora Hill, up to 40,000 Orangemen and unionist-club members marched past the platform party in military formation. In an emotional speech, Carson reminded them of the seriousness of the threat facing Ulster and also of their rights and duties to oppose the measure of Home Rule. He declared 'in the most solemn way that if this unprovoked and wicked attack is allowed to go on and this Bill to become law, it is not only the right but a duty to prepare to resist it'.[101]

The unionist press were united in their positive assessment of this first major meeting in the Covenant 'roadshow'. The *Belfast*

Telegraph described the occasion as 'a striking success' and suggested that 'the assembling of such a vast multitude' dispelled the notion that opposition to Home Rule was 'confined to the north east portion of Ulster'. Its leading article, 'Ulster's resolve', stressed the 'No surrender!' message emanating from the demonstration and avowed that the gathering had been 'tremendously in earnest'.[102] Both the *Daily Telegraph* and *Daily Express* argued that the unity of response illustrated at Enniskillen belied the suggestion that Ulster unionists were 'bluffing' in their opposition to Home Rule. The *Telegraph* said such 'radicals' who made these claims should 'hide their diminished heads', whilst the *Express* maintained that it was 'impossible for the most bigoted partisan or for the most light-minded politician to mistake the meaning or underestimate the significance of Ulster's protest'.[103] *The Times* attempted to explain the rationale behind Ulster unionists' actions and why they were responding in such a back-to-the-wall manner. Noting that neither they nor the British electorate had been directly consulted on the issue in question and that they no longer enjoyed the constitutional protection previously provided by the House of Lords, the paper described loyalist fears that they would be 'sold into bondage'. The leader ended with a hugely positive assessment of the Enniskillen meeting and the wider campaign, which represented 'the expression of a determination which no words and no arguments can alter'.[104]

Radical and nationalist journalists, meanwhile, were dismissive of the Enniskillen meeting, with the *Irish News* describing it as 'a silly masquerade'[105] and the *Daily Chronicle* arguing it was 'plain to see that the less reputable elements in Ulster have been lashed into a state of fury'.[106]

The second port of call for Carson on his much-publicised campaign tour was the County Antrim linen town of Lisburn. As the reporter from *The Times* noted, the crowd contrasted quite sharply with 'the agricultural men of Enniskillen' the previous afternoon – Lisburn's 'mill and factory operatives appeared to be just the type of men to be seen at a great Labour demonstration in the North of England'.[107] Nevertheless, the evening meeting in the town's grain market attracted an audience of several thousand. Situated in an area with a large Protestant majority, Lisburn was brightly decorated, with loyalist arches stretching across the main street. Apart from the political meeting itself, there were march pasts by members of the unionist clubs (in military formation, but using wooden rifles) and several bands, including the Lisburn Temperance Silver Band, which entertained the large crowd before and after the meeting with a selection of popular loyalist tunes such as 'Boyne water' and 'Protestant boys'. The *Belfast Telegraph* was one unionist paper to be impressed by the loyalist fervour so evident in the town and its headlines the following day – 'East follows west: the loyalty of Lisnagarvey' – emphasised the pan-Ulster nature of support for the Covenant.[108] *The Times* report of the meeting commented upon the resolute mood of the people. The large crowd, it noted, seemed to be 'animated by a more desperate resolve, and as they carried the resolution with a roar of cheers, the multitude looked as dark and forbidding as the sea with a storm brooding over it'.[109]

One writer later described the scene facing Edward Carson as he rose to address the large crowd. He noted how 'the working-girls [were] sitting under him, the men beyond them, line upon line in the lights of the torches, until lost in the shadow beyond'.[110] The unionist leader, forever aware of the mood of his adopted people, had received another mounted escort to the town's meeting point; he and his colleagues were later to be given a 'torchlight' escort from the marketplace. In his address, Carson worked the crowd almost to fever pitch, reading directly from the text of the Covenant, stressing time and again its 'solemn' purpose and urging them to ponder it meticulously, with 'religious deliberation'. He told them that the Covenant represented 'the most solemn step that a God-fearing and a law-abiding people have ever been asked to take in defence of their civil and religious liberties'.[111]

The campaign trail led next from the east to the north-west of Ulster, with both Carson and F.E. Smith addressing large crowds of supporters in Derry on 20 September and in Coleraine the following day. The Maiden City, with its profound historical symbolism for Ulster Protestants, was an inevitable, if potentially dangerous, stop for Carson. However, with fears of street trouble in the city, security was raised for the leader's visit. When they arrived at Derry Railway Station, Carson, Smith and the duke of Abercorn were given a 100-strong bodyguard (in the form of unionist-club members) and taken in open carriages to the Guildhall, the venue for the evening's meeting. The city was bedecked with unionist and Orange bunting, and welcoming crowds extended from the city centre the whole way down Shipquay Street. Flute bands accompanied by the marching ranks of unionist clubs paraded through the city, gaining a warm welcome from the 'dense' crowd of 'strongly enthusiastic' observers. Carson and Smith seemed 'thoroughly gratified by their welcome to the Maiden City'.[112] In their addresses, both men played to the full the city's historic association with Orangeism and unionism, with F.E. Smith comparing their struggle with that of Derry's citizens in 1688 and Carson reminding them of the spectre of Lundy the traitor. (Hours after the demonstration ended, nationalists attacked police and bandsmen.)

The following day they travelled again by train to Coleraine, where they were met by a unionist-club guard and taken to the demonstration in the grounds of Manor House. The market town of Coleraine, with its largely Protestant population, was enthusiastic in its welcome and drew in loyalists from across the province, especially its northern and western counties. The theme of Coleraine's resistance to Home Rule was emphatically conveyed in a banner reading, 'No, never!', which stretched across the town's main street. Edward Carson's speech at Manor House was wide ranging in its nature and contained a mixture of conciliatory and controversial statements. Doubtless related to minor disturbances in nationalist areas of Derry the previous evening, he declared that unionists were not prepared to become embroiled in a sectarian fight and offered the 'hand of friendship' to nationalist opponents. However, referring to the likelihood of the Home Rule Bill passing through parliament, he also reiterated unionists' determination not to recognise its authority and, raising the tempo a notch, said he did 'not care tuppence whether it was treason or not'.[113] Describing it as 'the soul of a nation fighting against injustice', Carson argued that theirs was 'the protest of men that no gold can buy [but] the protest of men who will not allow themselves to be sold'.[114]

Over the next five days the Irish Unionist Party staged another seven meetings. The venues chosen for these special meetings included towns in Counties Down, Antrim, Armagh and Tyrone. Many of the features of loyalist resistance to Home Rule that had been so evident during the early meetings – central streets gaily decorated in loyal colours, marching bands, marching ranks of unionist-club members and Orangemen and leaders being cheered in torchlight processions – were repeated at the subsequent demonstrations. Some of these meetings – for instance, the ones in Crumlin on 25 September and outside Ballyroney Station in south Down the following day – were relatively low key, but by taking the campaign into every corner of the province, including areas where there was significant opposition (such as Derry and Ballyroney), Ulster unionists showed their determination and unwillingness to bend under pressure from opponents. On the evening of 24 September, Lord Willoughby de Broke addressed a meeting in Dromore, County Tyrone, and assured his audience that Ulster unionists were not alone in their fight. He explained:

> The Unionists of England are going to help Unionists over here, not only by making speeches. Peaceable methods will be tried first, but if the last resort is forced upon them by the Radical government, the latter would find that they had not only Orangemen against them, but that every white man in

the British Empire would be giving support, either moral or active, to one of the most loyal populations that ever fought under the Union Jack.[115]

The following day, the 'triumphal progress' of Sir Edward Carson's campaign continued as a large force of men paraded through County Armagh's most prominent citadel of unionism, Portadown.[116] This demonstration, like most of the others during that fortnight, took place in beautiful autumnal weather, as 'volunteer soldiers' with wooden rifles paraded alongside women dressed as 'volunteer nurses' in what appeared to outsiders to constitute a slightly unreal atmosphere. On this demonstration, Edward Pearce has written, 'The menace was clear enough – menace attended by ceremonial Presbyterian theatre.'[117]

A mere three days before the climax of the Covenant campaign in Belfast, British press interest in Ulster's resistance to Home Rule increased significantly. The *Daily Express* noted how Ulster unionists had received support from politicians in both houses of parliament, from the armed services, from churches and from the worlds of medicine, academia and exploration. The paper's editorial proclaimed its full support for Ulster's cause and declared that it was 'a flame in defence of civil and religious liberties'. It went on:

> Unionists in this country share all the apprehensions which have nerved Ulster to a desperate mood and understand that their honour and interests are equally involved ... We hope that every unionist will hang out his banner and show his colour.[118]

On the evening of Monday, 23 September, the UUC met in Belfast's Old Town Hall to ratify the Covenant. After dinner at the Exhibition Hall in Botanic Gardens, delegates representing local branches across the province met with the joint objectives of ratifying the Covenant and justifying the case for adopting the document. It had already received the formal approval of the leadership of the Protestant churches. The meeting, presided over by Lord Londonderry and boasting a platform party of numerous Conservative and Irish Unionist Party notables (they included F.E. Smith, James Craig, Ronald McNeill, Lord Hugh Cecil, Admiral Lord Charles Beresford and Lord Castlereagh), was addressed by Edward Carson, who outlined the case for backing the Covenant.

Making full use of his considerable legal skills, which had been honed in the leading courts of London, the IUP leader, standing in front of another enormous Union Jack (this one measured 48 feet by 25), told the delegates that he had mulled for many hours over the wording and potential consequences of adopting such a document and political position, and informed them it was 'the gravest matter in all the grave matters in the various offices I have held that I have ever had to consider'. Promising them that he was 'prepared to go to the end' in pursuit of the demands made in the Covenant, his enthusiastic audience cheered wildly, promising, 'We will back you!'[119] It was no great surprise that a resolution was passed proclaiming the supreme right of a people to oppose legislation that would deny them their fundamental rights and freedom. The central passage of this resolution read:

> Inasmuch as we, the duly elected delegates and members of the Ulster Unionist Council, representing all parts of Ulster, are firmly persuaded that by no law can the right to govern those whom we represent be battered away without their consent; that, although the present Government ... may drive us forth from a constitution which we have ever loyally upheld, they may not deliver us bound into the hands of our enemies.[120]

In the three days leading up to Covenant Day itself, there was considerable feverish activity at the UUC's headquarters in Belfast's Old Town Hall, as the UUC's organising committee put the finishing touches to their preparations. This committee was led by R. Dawson Bates and comprised key figures in the unionist movement including Frank Hall and T.V.P. McCammon. They organised the production and despatch of thousands of circulars and posters to local Covenant Day committees across Ulster, as well as the distribution of 700 large cardboard boxes containing copies of the Covenant and signature forms on 25 September. Photographs of UUC staff packing the 'Covenant boxes' were featured in that day's edition of the *Belfast Telegraph*. Bates and his colleagues were fully aware of the need for the efficient and orderly distribution of boxes and collection of signatures, both at the main event in Belfast and also at the smaller signing venues across the province. Mindful of the need to ward off possible allegations that the boxes had been tampered with and signatures forged, emphasis was placed on the secure handling of these boxes before and after the signings, and unionist-club members were briefed on how to cope with excited crowds on the big day.

The final stage of the Covenant trail took place in Belfast's Ulster Hall on the eve of Covenant Day. Although everyday business in the city carried on as normal, a unique atmosphere prevailed in Belfast throughout the day. The city was bedecked in Union Jacks, which seemed to personify 'the spirit that was in possession of the people'.[121] An overflowing hall was in sober and circumspect mood, setting the tone for the major event the following day. Supporters turned up at the meeting, attired in their Sunday best, two to three hours before its start and whiled away the time by leafing through the special souvenir programme, 'Ulster demonstration against Home Rule', with its photo portraits of Edward Carson and several other leading unionist personalities. The excited gathering lustily rendered patriotic songs and roared in anticipation of the appearance onstage of Sir Edward Carson and Lord Londonderry. Proceedings started with prayers and there were constant exhortations for God's protection. Messages of support were conveyed from leading British politicians including Arthur J. Balfour and Bonar Law, and Carson and Londonderry delivered rousing speeches. Although feeling fatigue after his long Covenant campaign, during which he had given six major speeches, Carson gave an effective speech in the Ulster Hall. He stressed the underlying principles of his movement, those of defence and unity of purpose, and received rapturous applause at its conclusion. The IUP leader argued:

> We will take deliberately a step forward, not in defiance but in defence, and the Covenant which we will most willingly sign tomorrow will be a great step forward, in no spirit of aggression, in no spirit of ascendancy, but with a full knowledge that, if necessary, you and I – you trusting me, and I trusting you – will follow out everything that this Covenant means to the very end, whatever the consequences.[122]

Realising that there would be many disappointed supporters who would be unable to gain access to the main Ulster Hall meeting, the Covenant committee organised a post-event demonstration outside the hall in Bedford Street, where an estimated 25,000 had gathered. A platform had been erected over the glass porch of the main entrance to the hall and on this, 'flamed in electric lights', a small group of unionist dignitaries – including Carson and Colonel Wallace, head of the Belfast Orange Order – presented themselves to the cheering crowds.[123] Above the platform, the unionist slogan 'We will not have Home Rule' was displayed on a large banner and below the platform a poster stood, blaring out another loyalist battle-cry – 'Ulster will fight'.

Reputedly on James Craig's orders, it had been planned that a striking visual demonstration of loyalist intent and unity rather than another lengthy speech (which wouldn't have been heard by many in Bedford Street or adjoining streets) would be offered to the patient multitude. In an unashamed piece of choreographed street theatre, Colonel Wallace presented Carson with a faded yellow silk banner bearing the cross of St George in one of its corners. The banner, it was claimed, had been presented to William III at the battle of the Boyne. Lord Beresford had borrowed it from a friend in Hampton Court, whose distant relative had fought at the Boyne. Before he waved the flag, literally to bring the curtain down on the build-up to Covenant day, Carson proclaimed to the delirious crowd, 'May this flag ever float over a people that can boast of civil and religious liberties.'[124]

Unionist papers described 'most moving scenes' both inside and outside the hall, in what they claimed had been 'the biggest gathering of the campaign',[125] while journals with different political perspectives were cynical in their interpretation of events in Belfast that Friday evening. The *Irish News* suggested, with more than a hint of irony, that 'if that flag ever saw the Battle of the Boyne, all we can say is the man who manufactured it deserves undying fame for the strength and durability of the material'.[126]

'Not the sound of a hammer'

For those who managed to sleep that night, the early morning of Saturday, 28 September proved to be no disappointment. A crisp yet sunny autumn day, devoid of showery rain or dark clouds, beckoned. The new day would see 'a magnificent morning of fine and durable weather that made the hills around the city look blue in the sunlight'.[127] In an era when Saturday-morning work was commonplace, Belfast's industrial workers had been granted an additional half day's leave and all major industrial and commercial firms closed their gates. The atmosphere in one of Britain's busiest industrial cities was almost surreal – silence befell Belfast's factories and shipyards. A *Belfast News-Letter* reporter described the 'sabbatical appearance' of the city's streets in the early morning, when 'the clang of the hammer' and the 'throbbing of machinery' were noticeably absent.[128] The city's industrial workforce – or at least its predominantly Protestant element, concentrated largely in the shipyards, the linen and cigarette factories, the ropeworks and the engineering works – were united in swapping industrial labour for what they saw as an even more noble enterprise that Saturday. As a London journalist observed in his Belfast despatch, the sweat-stained endeavours of the 25,000-strong shipyard workforce the previous day contrasted sharply with that Saturday morning, when there was 'not the sound of a hammer' and the atmosphere was 'as silent as the grave'.[129]

Although all industrial centres had closed for the day, Protestant households across the city, and indeed the province, would have experienced a mixture of devout contemplation and practical preparations for a special day. Those who had the time or inclination would have glanced at the fiercely partisan headlines of the local morning newspapers. The *Belfast News-Letter* highlighted the significance of the signing of the Covenant and also the support Ulster unionists were receiving from their friends in Britain. Referring to Andrew Bonar Law's assurance that Ulster did 'not stand alone, but can rely upon the support of the whole Unionist Party', the *News-Letter* urged its readers to 'go forward with fresh confidence and courage'.[130] The paper published a poem, 'Ulster Day, 28 September 1912' by Samuel K. Cowan, who urged 'prosperous, loyal, Protestant Ulster' to 'sign your Covenant solemnly'. He informed them that their pens that day would 'replace the swords used by [their] forefathers'.[131]

For the man who had quickly managed to symbolise Ulster resistance to Home Rule, there was probably an early start to the most important day in his political career. Staying overnight at his colleague James Craig's substantial property just outside Belfast, Carson would have mulled over the likely impact of the forthcoming events a few miles away in the city centre. As he took an early morning constitutional in the gardens of Craig's Sydenham mansion, Edward Carson would have been quietly satisfied with the smooth running of the Covenant campaign and the crystal-clear unity of response from Ulster's majority community. Yet the forever broody and agitated politician would have retained concern about the chances of a sectarian skirmish that might remove the shine from what had been a highly impressive campaign. As he joined James Craig in the limousine that took them into central Belfast and the Ulster Hall in Bedford Street, Carson would have smoked a cigarette to calm his nerves and looked out of the car window for any distant dark clouds.

His devoted supporters in their little terraced homes on Belfast's Shankill Road were more likely to have engaged in mundane, practical tasks. Unionist-club members and Orange brethren would have been up early, leaving aside their labouring clothes and instead donning Sunday suits, Orange sashes and other regalia, whilst their wives prepared sandwiches for the long day ahead before also changing into their Sunday finest. Many, aware of the day's significance, would have taken time to read from the scriptures or say a prayer for the province.

A few streets away, on the Falls Road, there would have been no such frenetic activity. Those Catholics released from their labours that day would have appreciated the extra lie-in and additional time with their families in their own districts. Of course, this would have been offset by the threat of sectarian invasion by over-excited loyalists and, more particularly, by the likely long-term impact of the unionist action and associated paramilitary build-up.

The serious nature of their mission had clearly dominated how the vast majority of Protestants thought about the day's events. In contrast with the pageantry associated with the Orange celebrations in July, the mood of the loyalist community on that autumn Saturday was one of 'solemn observation', calmness and dignity, which also illustrated the unity and determination on this issue of the separate Protestant churches.[132] One reporter noted how 'artisans, dressed in their best attire, joined their employers' at the various services, where prayer would be offered for divine intervention to 'avert the very grave and real danger that threatens the country'.[133] As Carson again took his place on the platform at a special 'Ulster Day' service at the Ulster Hall, similar services took place at St Anne's Cathedral and the Presbyterian Assembly Hall. In the grounds of the City Hall there was a short service for the Ulster Day stewards and lower-key services were taking place in 500 other venues across Ulster. One of Ulster's most prominent writers noted how, that day, Belfast had 'suspended all its labours and become like a place of prayer' and how 'very solemnly, the people went to church to prepare their minds for their responsibility, as postulants prepare themselves for consecrations'.[134] The *Standard*'s reporter, on a similar theme, observed how the 'splendid craftsmen who build the largest ships in the world have donned their Sunday clothes and, with Unionist buttons on the lapels of their coats, or Orange sashes on their shoulders, are about to engage in what to them is an even more important task'.[135]

Service and prayer sheets from that day illustrate the commonality and unity of theme. The prayers request God's 'protection' and 'deliverance' at 'this time of national danger', as well as asking God to grant to 'the people of our community such patience and self-control that no occasion of bitterness may have power to move them'.[136] For the text of his sermon, the former Presbyterian moderator, Rev. Dr William McKean, had selected 1 Timothy 6:20, 'Keep that which is committed to thy trust.' Though it was not to the forefront of the actual Covenant, the cleric stressed the religious dimension in Ulster's opposition to Irish Home Rule. Dr McKean argued that the bill was 'at bottom a war against Ulster Protestantism; it is an attempt to begin the disintegration of the Empire by securing a second parliament in Dublin'.[137]

At the Ulster Hall and, indeed, in most services across Ulster, solemn-faced Protestants from different churches joined in hearty renditions of 'O God our help in ages past'. This hymn of Protestant unification, with its emphasis on placing trust in oneself, in the cause of the community and in one's God, was an appropriate one. Although it would be the images of Ulster's political leaders signing the Covenant at the City Hall less than an hour later that would dominate the considerable press coverage of the day's events, the significance of these religious ceremonies should not be underestimated. Indeed, this religious reassurance would set the tone for the rest of the day. The Anglican Bishop of Down and Connor, Charles D'Arcy, described the day as 'wonderful'. He would later write:

> Never have I felt such a sense of solemn and unwavering determination as that which filled the hearts of the vast multitude which thronged all the approaches to the great central building of the city. We did not doubt the outcome – such faith in the righteousness of the cause animated us – but we felt that whatever happened we were sharing in a most noble endeavour and that it was good to be alive.[138]

Buoyed by the display of unity and spiritual sustenance produced by the emotional atmosphere in the Ulster Hall, Carson and senior Irish Unionist Party figures proceeded on foot along Bedford Street towards the relatively new municipal headquarters for Belfast. For this short walk he was accompanied by a guard party from the unionist clubs, with the Boyne flag, unveiled at the Ulster Hall the previous evening, to the fore. As the Ulster leader walked briskly and purposefully towards the venue staging the day's main proceedings, the atmosphere of the crowd changed from one of respectful silence or muted applause to one filled with loud cheering. The *Northern Whig* described the scene from the front of the City Hall:

> A faint faraway noise of cheering announced that the great moment of a great day was at hand. Sir Edward Carson was marching from the Ulster Hall and a thrill ran through to

waiting crowds as round the corner of Donegall Square there came into sight King William's flag, with the red cross and star. While the religious services were in progress only a thin fringe of spectators lined the footpaths. Now all the approaches were black with sightseers and the trams could hardly force a passage through the dense masses clustered in Donegall Place.[139]

Crowds had been gathering for a couple of hours at the City Hall before Edward Carson's arrival soon after midday. By the time Carson got there, the crowds were thick in Donegall Place and the streets surrounding the City Hall. Flags flew from shops and commercial buildings around Donegall Square and most of the way down Royal Avenue and the other parallel thoroughfares. The threat to public order, despite the massed crowds on the city's central streets, was not considered to be a major one, as the minimal police presence in the immediate vicinity of the City Hall indicated. In effect, the protection of leaders, the maintenance of order and the overall organisation of the event lay in the hands of unionist-club marshals. An army of marshals, estimated at around 2,500 and led by Major Fred Crawford, was in position inside and outside the grounds of the municipal building hours before Carson's arrival. Hundreds of marshals guarded the perimeter of the large building, ensuring that the grounds, 'bright with masses of autumn flowers, lay bare and empty in the sunshine'.[140]

Party officials and City Hall personnel had been rigorous in their practical preparations for the signing ceremony. Desks were laid out in many of the City Hall corridors and organisers anticipated that up to 540 people would be able to sign the Covenant simultaneously. The building would remain open until 11 o'clock that evening, when over 80,000 would have signed the Covenant. Apart from hundreds of Covenant booklets (each sheet accommodated places for ten signatures and addresses), dozens of pens and inkpots, Bates and his organisational committee had been shrewd enough to remember the issuing of personal rewards for the tens of thousands who had waited patiently to sign the Covenant. Every signatory was presented with a souvenir copy of the historic document printed on parchment.

When Carson arrived at the City Hall he was greeted by the lord mayor of the city, Sir William McMordie, MP, and a host of members of the City Corporation, Poor Law Guardians, Water Board officials and Harbour Commissioners. Small talk between them would have been kept to a minimum as Carson was motioned to the circular table draped with a large Union Jack, below the staircase and beside the building's main entrance. Ulster's man of the moment was undoubtedly surrounded by men of distinction within the local community. Industrialists, politicians, ministers and bishops, merchants and leading businessmen, lawyers, surgeons and academics were positioned in a semi-circle behind Carson as he was formally presented with a silver pen. In a moment of high drama, as photographers and newsreel film-makers feverishly scrambled to record the moment for posterity, Edward Carson deliberately paused, looked up at the cameras and then signed the largest political petition in Britain since the Chartist documents over 60 years before. He was followed by Lord Londonderry, leading representatives of the Protestant churches, and James Craig. Photographs of the event record the seriousness of purpose shown by Carson and the besuited, largely mustachioed group of men (many of whom were sporting carnations or unionist emblems in their lapels).

Perhaps the most evocative description of the signing of the Covenant came from Ronald McNeill (later Lord Cushendun). Describing the 'thrill' of the moment when Carson signed the Covenant, he went on:

> The sunshine sending a beam through the stained-glass window on the stairway threw warm tints of colour on the marbles of the column and the tessellated floor of the Hall, sparkled on the Lord Mayor's chain, lent a rich glow to the

scarlet gowns of the City fathers and lit up the red and blue and white of the imperial flag, which was the symbol of so much that they revered to those who stood looking on ... whilst behind them, through the open door could be seen a vast forest of human heads, endless as far as eye could reach, everyone of whom was in eager accord with the work in hand and whose blended voices, while they waited to perform their own part in the great transaction, were carried to the ears of those in the Hall, like the inarticulate noise of moving waters.[141]

As Carson and his colleagues left the City Hall, they would have been aware of the long lines of people waiting to sign the Covenant. They would continue to be patient for many hours. Indeed, people were still queuing to sign as Edward Carson and his entourage prepared to leave for the docks. Folklore has it that many of these tough Belfast working men had actually signed the document in their own blood (this was claimed by Fred Crawford in his account of the day), though for most this was probably an exaggeration. However, the determination of the people to sign this pledge of support for Edward Carson and Ulster could not be doubted. The crowds outside the City Hall were at their most dense just before Carson's arrival. Photographs taken of the scene outside the City Hall – with the Robinson and Cleaver department-store clock providing the necessary evidence – suggest that the crowds thinned a little as many sought refreshments in city restaurants, cafés and bars, but by mid-afternoon many had returned to the municipal building either to sign the Covenant themselves or to watch and listen to the bands and marching Orangemen and unionist-club members. J.L. Garvin managed to observe the spectacle from an outside gallery in the dome of the City Hall and noted how 'the square below and the streets striking away from it were black with people'.[142]

The raw emotions engendered by the sober nature of the occasion and the iconic images of Carson signing the Covenant would live long in the memories of those who had witnessed them. A rare example of the impact the day had on working-class women was noted in a unionist paper the following week. A woman had forwarded a copy of a letter she had written to her sister at the end of Covenant Day. Part of it read:

> I shall never forget it if I were to live another 50 years. I went out thinking to get to the City Hall, but I could not get near it. I got wedged in a crowd in front of the Reform Club and I just had to stay there. Everywhere I looked there were seas of faces and Union Jacks. But I was well repaid for the crush. For about 4 o'clock Sir Edward Carson, followed by other gentlemen, came out on the balcony and spoke to the crowds who were assembled ... I looked on the old Orange flag that went before King William at the Boyne. I could not help crying I was so overcome with emotion.[143]

Across the province of Ulster and in other British and Irish cities, enthusiastic canvassing for and collection of signatures was also carried out. Whilst most ordinary people in the countryside would not have enjoyed the up-to-date information services we take for granted in today's society, they would have been *au fait* with the scale of unionist opposition to Home Rule and the Covenant campaign. The unionist press, especially the *Belfast Telegraph*, *Northern Whig* and *Belfast News-Letter*, could be accessed with relative ease by a readership right across the region, and rural loyalists would have followed the news of the campaign on a daily basis, just as closely as their urban counterparts. It is likely that, given the cross-provincial nature of the Covenant campaign, many of them would have been able to attend a large Covenant demonstration close to their locality, which would have provided them with the opportunity of seeing the movement's leaders in the flesh and made them feel more closely involved with the wider political movement.

Certainly, rural loyalists responded with equal determination and enthusiasm to the exhortations of the leadership to support the cause on Covenant Day. Agricultural workers and village shopkeepers either abandoned their tasks for the whole day or severely curtailed them, instead changing into their best clothes, before heading off to church services and to sign the Covenant. For farm workers, considerable sacrifices and changes to routines – in particular involving the feeding of livestock and essential harvest preparations (the Covenant campaign had clashed with harvest season) – were required. The journeys of those living in the countryside, especially to the signing centres, would have been more complicated than for those living in towns and cities, but people used ingenuity to overcome such difficulties. They travelled to church and signing centre by horse, bicycle, hired car and, probably in most cases, on foot.

Market towns and villages were, like those centres of larger population, bedecked with loyalist colours. Union Jacks, Orange bunting and posters reminding people to sign the Covenant would have been everywhere. These towns and villages, although lacking the density and electric atmosphere of Belfast's central streets, would have been busy and alive with the sense of a major occasion. Here, people also headed to their little churches to pray for Ulster. They would have prayed for God's help and sung the Ulster Covenanters' hymn with gusto, asking God to grant:

> The faith that does not shrink;
> And of the cup our fathers drank
> Give us the strength to drink.[144]

In larger towns, unionist-club personnel and Orangemen would have paraded from the church service to the centre for the signing of the Covenant (more often than not, the town hall). Photographs of Covenant Day outside Belfast indicate that there was considerable enthusiasm and support in large provincial towns such as Enniskillen. There, 2,000 Orangemen and Volunteers (many of whom would doubtless have been involved in the initial meeting of Carson's Covenant trail) heard the bishop of Clogher address the congregation in the parish church before marching in formation to the town hall. There were few reported instances of disturbances or clashes with nationalists, although these were obviously more likely in areas well away from Belfast with more mixed populations and in some outlying areas – for example, in County Monaghan – there were cases of intimidation and assault on loyalist families.

Although the true force behind Ulster unionism now came from the burgeoning ranks of the Protestant middle class, the owners of Ulster's Big Houses still played a major role in their own areas, especially during the period of the Covenant campaign. Whether it was hosting the Irish Unionist Party's leadership as they toured the province or having a platform presence during the various Covenant meetings, or hosting social occasions and parties, the north's aristocracy held an influence, both symbolic and practical, that far exceeded its numbers.

Many British peers (including Willoughby de Broke, Lord Salisbury, Lord Beresford and Hugh Cecil) visited Ulster during the Covenant fortnight, but it was the contributions of locally based aristocrats during this time that impacted more at local level. For instance, the ageing and infirm duke of Abercorn, who had chaired the UUC convention in Belfast during a previous Home Rule threat some 20 years before, was able to sign the Covenant under an old oak tree at his County Tyrone estate of Baronscourt, whilst Lord Templetown, so closely connected with the unionist clubs, signed the document on an old drum of the Templepatrick Infantry at his demesne, Castle Upton in County Antrim. In many ways, this role during the Covenant campaign constituted the political swansong for this small but significant group of Ulster-based aristocrats, and represented 'the last great occasion in which they could truly feel that they occupied their rightful place as the leaders of their people'.[145] Despite the combination of factors that proved unfavourable to their position within a changing society – the gradual breakup of their large northern estates and the political sidelining of aristocrats both within British society and in the control of Irish unionism – the owners of the Big Houses in the north of Ireland still managed to 'preside over the enactment of this great historical event in the demesnes and villages and towns where generations of their family had held sway'.[146]

The women of these aristocratic families were also active in organising social events, which also helped to bind the local community. One such event took place at Lord Kilmorey's estate in south Down on 28 September. A reporter's description of the afternoon illustrates both the prestige afforded to the social gathering and the way in which it bonded the local community:

> The beautiful seat of the Earl of Kilmorey, situated in the valley of the Mourne Mountains, was the scene of one of the biggest social functions of the Ulster Campaign ... The Countess of Kilmorey ... received the guests on the garden terrace. She was accompanied by the Earl of Kilmorey and her son, Viscount Newry and Mourne. All Unionist Members of Parliament and their speakers were invited, and the residents of the County Down immediate neighbourhood. Refreshments were served in a large marquee and on small tables beneath the trees, while a band played selections during the afternoon.[147]

The fear that a privileged position within local society was under threat united the very different social groups within Ulster's Protestant community. James Beckett wrote in 1967 that 'what Protestants of all ranks were prepared to fight for' was 'the threatened Protestant ascendancy in Ireland'.[148] Middle-class unionists were especially fearful of the impact that Home Rule would have on commerce and industry and many working-class loyalists would have shared concerns about the religious consequences of Home Rule. However, for these aristocrats, the sense of potential personal loss was much greater, given the extent of the privileges they currently enjoyed. Their perhaps understated but crucially important role in supporting the Covenant campaign helped to shape a movement that united industrial and agricultural workers, rich and poor, aristocrat and commoner.

Back in Belfast, Edward Carson and his closest colleagues moved later in the afternoon from the Reform Club to the Ulster Club in Castle Place, where they enjoyed dinner with the lord mayor and his lieutenants. Doubtless they shared their satisfaction and pride in the scale and dignity of their protest. After this there were further balcony speeches from the unionist leader and F.E. Smith, who had played such a prominent part during the Covenant fortnight. Smith, a parliamentary representative for Liverpool, promised the crowd below that their campaign would be taken next to that city where, with some justification, he assured them that they would find 'another Belfast'. He maintained that there was 'hardly a centre of population where I could not get a crowd like this to sign'. His legal and political friend, Sir Edward Carson, chose to focus on the likely repercussions of such a show of unionist solidarity upon the tactics of their opponents, doubtless a topic of pre-dinner conversation at the club. He argued:

> One thing I feel particularly confident [about] is that today we have taken a step which has put our enemies into such a state of difficulty that they are wondering what on earth they are going to do.[149]

Around 8.30 p.m. that day, one of the bands outside the Ulster Club in Castle Place struck up a number of patriotic tunes including 'See the conquering hero comes' as Carson and his select group made their way to the docks. Gunfire as well as prolonged cheering by many thousands of people accompanied the leader as his man-drawn wagonette slowly made its way to the dockside (its progress was frequently interrupted as over-excited loyalists insisted on trying to shake the hand of their 'chief', and the journey took most of an hour). Garvin wrote in the *Pall Mall Gazette* about the 'roaring hurricane of cheers punctuated on every side by the steady rattle of revolver shots' that had 'swept this whole city in motion with a tumult that was mad'.[150] Carson was greeted by maritime officials on arrival at the docks and escorted on board the steamship *Patriotic*, which was to take him to Merseyside and the next stage of his campaign trail. An estimated 100,000 people lined the streets on the way to the docks and at the quayside, where a band played loyal tunes, including 'Come back to Erin' and the national anthem. In his final act of defiance during this Ulster leg of the Covenant campaign, Edward Carson delivered a few appropriate final soundbites for his devoted followers, who implored him not to leave. Speaking from the top deck of the steamer, Carson begged his audience to 'keep the old flag flying' in Belfast and to remember the Orange watchwords, 'No surrender!' Further shots and rockets were fired as the *Patriotic* set off for Liverpool.

Their leader might have left Ulster soil but he and his cause were still very much on the minds of his followers. Queues of people still desiring to sign the Covenant snaked around the corners of Donegall Square and exuberant loyalists lit a host of bonfires in central Belfast, on Cave Hill and along Belfast Lough, to give their leader a regal send-off. As the boat made its way into the lough and on towards the Irish Sea, Edward Carson and his lieutenants would have reflected with pleasure upon both the day's events and the fortnight of Covenant events. Equally satisfied, back on shore, were the Covenant's organising team. Even the city's police force would have been content with the day's proceedings. That Saturday had proved to have one of the lowest instances of drunkenness and rowdiness in the city's recent history. Though there had been some clashes between rival groups of supporters after a football match in west Belfast between Distillery and Belfast Celtic, the crowds in Belfast's main thoroughfares had been on their best behaviour.

There was little opportunity for most people to enjoy a lie-in the day after the Covenant ceremony. Services of thanksgiving were held across the province as thousands of Protestants worshipped in their different churches. Pride in the scale and smooth running of the Belfast event and the obvious determination of signatories across Ulster, as well as relief that street violence had been averted, would have mingled with thoughts of uncertainty over the region's constitutional future. These church services were not restricted to the north of Ireland. Ulster Day was 'not forgotten' in far-off Nova Scotia, where Sunday, 29 September was designated a 'special day of intercession on behalf of the sister Protestant churches in Ireland'. An Ulster exile, Rev. Herbert Lindsay, prayed:

> May our Protestant fellow-countrymen learn the grand lesson God would have them now learn, and may their present brave stand be crowned with lasting success.[151]

Industry and commerce in Ulster returned to normal the following day, but that evening loyalists ensured they would keep the political pendulum swinging in their direction by staging another major political event in the Ulster Hall. This meeting was designed for an exclusively female audience, consisting of UWUC members and delegates. Chaired by Lady Dufferin, the meeting concentrated less on the political aspect of Home Rule – deemed by the conventions of the day to be a matter for men – and instead focused on the other catastrophic influences of a potential Dublin parliament. Described as an 'inspiring' occasion and 'one of the most notable events ever held in Belfast', the hall, packed with delegates two hours before its scheduled start, was buzzing in anticipation of a frank discussion of issues which related directly to 'a matter of their religion, their homes and their children'.[152]

The onerous task of counting the Covenant signatures started at Belfast's Old Town Hall the following day. After the count it was announced that 218,206 men had signed the Covenant in Ulster and even more women (228,941) had put their names to a similar 'female pledge'. These figures illustrate that a considerable majority of Protestants signed the Covenant, but they also suggest that up to a third of adult Protestants did not, for a number of reasons. These likely included apathy, an unwillingness to become involved in overtly political matters, an opposition to Carson's extreme approach or an outright rejection of the Covenant's principles.

Unionists had been able to sign the Covenant at selected venues in Great Britain and in Dublin, where over 2,000 men signed. Close to 25,000 people (over 19,000 of these were men) pledged their support for Ulster in Great Britain, including many big cities like London, Glasgow, Liverpool, Manchester, Edinburgh, Bristol and York. There was considerable support for the anti-Home Rule movement in areas of the empire where Ulstermen had settled, especially Canada. Over the next few weeks and months, following the distribution of Covenant Day postcards and news reports, signatures were collected and posted to unionist headquarters in Belfast. Impromptu signings of the Covenant were even arranged for people crossing the Atlantic. On one steamer, SS *Lake Champlain*, a large number of second- and third-class passengers were reported to have signed the Covenant pledge. One resourceful *émigré*, Thomas McKee, collected over 50 signatures, mainly from fellow Ulster exiles, in Winnipeg City. McKee posted these to R. Dawson Bates, joint secretary of the UAI, in March 1913, promising to start 'a good unionist club' in the city, as there was 'plenty of material here'.[153]

As the *Patriotic* made its way up the Mersey during the early hours of Sunday, 29 September, Edward Carson and F.E. Smith were cheered by large crowds lining the quayside at Princes Dock and also thronged the streets leading to Liverpool's city centre. The turnout was estimated at 100,000. Smith, a local parliamentary representative, would not have been surprised by such Merseyside fervour. The crowd at the quayside had been, on account of it being the Sabbath, relatively restrained, singing

'O God, our help in ages past', rather than the more rousing loyalist anthems. Liverpool, of course, shared political and religious links with the Lagan Valley. Both were major industrial centres, with ship-building dominating the respective economies of the two regions; Liverpool was also a staunchly unionist city with a population divided along religious lines. As England's leading port, Liverpool had been the arrival point for many Irish migrants during the period of famine in the mid-nineteenth century and there had been instances of sectarian strife in the city for nearly a century.[154]

Although the unionist leaders refrained from making political speeches that day, they did receive a rousing welcome to the city from leading Merseyside unionist Archibald Salvidge, who had been responsible for organising the Liverpool Working Men's Association. Salvidge, a local brewer, had utilised the help of both this organisation and that offered by the city's Orange lodges (of which there were nearly 200) in preparing a major political event which would promote the cause of Ulster loyalism. Extra trams and trains conveyed the large numbers of unionist supporters to the dockside at this early hour, and details of these transport arrangements were published in the local press. Archibald Salvidge's formal welcome to the unionist leaders was warm and sincere. He assured Carson, 'We Unionists of the Port which is connected with Belfast in so many ways, stand by Ulster in this great struggle for political justice, Imperial unity and religious liberty.'[155] The local paper was fulsome in its praise of the reception afforded to the Irish Unionist Party leader, suggesting that 'no reception was ever so unique in its character, so touching in its cordiality as that which awaited the gallant unionist leaders'.[156]

Salvidge and Liverpool's other unionist-club and Orange leaders had worked diligently on making the pro-Ulster demonstration at Sheil Park in the north of the city the following evening a resounding success. Special trains had been arranged to take many thousands of people – including many dockers straight from their day's labours – to the venue, where they were entertained by several bands and a fireworks display. Endless ranks of Orangemen and unionist-club members marched four deep from three entry points, taking nearly an hour to enter the park. Unlike Ulster, where women did not normally join their men at political meetings, there were many women present at this demonstration, which was fully lit. Salvidge and his colleagues had realised the dramatic impact of using arc lights, which covered 'a wide area, stretching from the platform', though the sheer density of the crowd meant that it was 'impossible for the eye to see those at the extreme limits'.[157]

The stage management of this and subsequent loyalist meetings, both on Merseyside and further afield in Great Britain, was professional and ahead of its time. Adopting propaganda methods later refined by fascist regimes in Europe, Salvidge and his fellow organisers had designed a slick schedule that ensured that demonstrators would have easy access to transport to convey them to and from the venue, and that they would be entertained during the long wait before the speeches. Also, the instalment of electric lighting managed to capture the full drama of the occasion and the speakers' orations, as well as the post-meeting scenes, especially a torchlight parade, which reached a climactic crescendo as the leaders were escorted back, along crowded streets, into the city. Despite some scuffles between loyalists and nationalists in the area around Lime Street Station, major street violence was averted. Daniel Jackson has stated that these loyalist street marches and demonstrations in Great Britain during the years leading up to the Great War represented perhaps the best example of working-class street protest. He writes:

> The aesthetic created by Orangemen and women on parade was unrivalled by any other proletarian organisation; their disciplined marching, their gaudy banners and their martial music were very attractive and effective, symbolising both muscle and gravitas.[158]

Before the meeting, an estimated 150,000 crammed into Sheil Park and enjoyed singing patriotic tunes. At other times during the long wait before the proceedings officially started, they would have strained their necks to glimpse the arrival of even minor political and religious personalities, including local rabble-rouser Pastor George Wise and King William lookalikes. However, the real excitement started with the arrival of the platform party shortly before nine o'clock. Edward Carson was joined on stage by F.E. Smith, Salvidge, Lord Londonderry and Viscount Templetown, and another gigantic Union Jack was unfurled. The Ulster leader received an overwhelming response from this massive audience but it was the outspoken, maverick local politician, F.E. Smith, who made the next day's headlines, promising to give Carson and his supporters three ships and 10,000 young fighting men from Merseyside.

The next day, Edward Carson and his colleagues moved to the third and final point on the north-west-British industrial triangle, Glasgow. Carson had not been present at a massive anti-Home Rule rally at Coatbridge, near Glasgow, two months previously and this would be the first time he had made a political speech there. Glasgow had different political dynamics from Liverpool. Dominated by the Liberal Party and with a tradition of radical political culture, the city's working class were less likely to have been attracted by appeals to national and imperial unity. Yet there was strong and traditional support, closely related to religious and ethnic allegiances, in a city where industry was also dominated by ship-building. Carson spoke to nearly 7,000 at two indoor meetings in the city on the evening of 1 October. The experienced Ulster leader was visibly moved by the warm reception he received from the audience and told a journalist that 'our action has made a profound impression throughout the United Kingdom'.[159] The *Belfast News-Letter* reported the following day, 'Glasgow supports Ulster – stirring scenes of enthusiasm'.[160] Edward Carson's lengthy political roadshow came to an end and he wearily returned to his Kent home the following evening. Yet even here he did not avoid crowds and fuss, as the villagers in Rottingdean honoured their most illustrious resident with a torchlight procession to his home.

'The work of orderly, prosperous, and deeply religious men'

The unionist press were unable to control their use of superlatives in describing the climax to the Covenant ceremonies. Even the political judgement of experienced journalists was clouded by the heady emotionalism engendered by Covenant Day. J.L. Garvin was one who was somewhat over-optimistic in his assessment of the Covenant campaign. Reminding his readers that 'the spirit of Ulster has been made plain the past week', the *Observer*'s editor, an eyewitness to events in Belfast, claimed that Home Rule was 'dead, killed by the resistance of Sir Edward Carson and his followers'.[161] The *Pall Mall Gazette*, which had Garvin and other journalists on the scene in Belfast, had a distinct advantage over its rivals. Scenes of 'great enthusiasm' were described in that same evening's edition:

> The streets wore the calm of a Sunday; some shops were open, but most business places were closed. The city would have seemed dull and lifeless were it not for the bright bits of colour that broke out over the house fronts of every street except those in the Nationalist quarter of west Belfast.[162]

Several papers insisted that the unity and resoluteness of the unionist multitude in Ulster had dealt a fatal blow to their opponents' argument that they were 'bluffing' in their refusal to countenance Home Rule. *The Times*, in its leader, 'The significance of the Ulster protest', argued that such a suggestion was 'absurd', whilst the *Daily Express* condemned the 'most obtuse and the least sincere' critics of Ulster loyalism for their misrepresentation of Ulster's mood.[163] The *Express* maintained that to call Ulster's resistance to Home Rule 'bluff, or to deny the desperate earnestness which inspires it is quite impossible' and concluded, 'Ulster will not have Home Rule and all the world now knows it.'[164] Some writers tried to deride the criticism that the unionist stance – parading 'armies' of Volunteers with wooden rifles, led by a prominent lawyer pledging loyalty to the constitution – was irrational. In an article, *The Times* denied that Edward Carson was leading a movement of 'loyal rebels', claiming that this interpretation that Ulster loyalism was working towards a 'forcible' or 'revolutionary' climax was 'a wilful misunderstanding of their whole position'. Indeed, it went on, 'so long as the Constitution of the United Kingdom is maintained they have no more occasion to rebel than the inhabitants of Sussex'. The writer added that Ulster's resistance was 'the rock upon which the [Home Rule] Bill must make shipwreck in the end'.[165] The same paper had, shortly after the Covenant campaign had been announced the previous month, focused upon the unique community-based nature of the Covenant protest. *The Times* wrote:

> We remember no precedent in our domestic history since the Revolution of 1688 for a movement among citizens, law-abiding by temperament and habit, which resembles the present movement of the Ulster Protestants. It is no rabble who have undertaken it. It is the work of orderly, prosperous and deeply religious men.[166]

Today, some writers recognise the potent religious and communal symbolism of the Covenant strategy and appreciate that it had significant repercussions for British politics in the Edwardian era. Marcus Tanner has described the Covenant tactic as 'a brilliant stroke', as the word 'covenant' instantly reminded Ulster Protestants of previous dangers against their liberty, reaffirming their ultimate belief in 'the higher law of God'. Tanner argues that the Covenant 'captured the imagination of almost all the Protestant population and rallied an instinctively cautious and law-abiding people to the idea of armed resistance to the British Government'.[167] Graham Walker has also noted the powerful religious language and symbolism within the text of the Covenant and how this closely resonated with the province's large Presbyterian population, many of whom were of Scottish ancestry. Walker stresses the populist and radical nature of both the Covenant and Carson's movement, and concluded that the former helped 'in the shaping of an ethnic consciousness around notions of contracts and rights, and entitlements to separate treatment'.[168] In his biography of Edward Carson, Geoffrey Lewis has maintained that it was during this Covenant fortnight that Carson truly won over the Ulster people and how this occasion – one in which he 'attained an extraordinary ascendancy over the Protestants of Ulster' – produced considerable personal success for the Ulster Unionist leader.[169] Richard Grayson has stressed the national significance of Carson's Covenant campaign and also claimed that it had a profound role in 'dramatically shifting the political debate' surrounding Ulster in the period after September 1912. He argues that there has 'never been any such example of mass public support for a political campaign in any part of the United Kingdom before or since' and that the propaganda impact of the Covenant demonstrations resulted in debates 'revolving around whether Ulster might be excluded from the Home Rule settlement'.[170]

What, then, was the true significance of the Covenant campaign of September 1912? Edward Carson's own assessment was that it represented 'a huge and magnificent success'.[171] But he was also clearly concerned that the heady emotions provoked by the Covenant campaign might result in the situation spiralling out of his party's control. In a congratulatory letter to R. Dawson Bates, Carson hoped that his supporters would maintain self-discipline. He wrote that 'we are now bound in a solemn covenant each to the other' and therefore expected each man to be 'a worthy covenanter'.[172]

Certainly, the impact of the Covenant campaign upon the local Protestant community was immediate and lasting. The Covenant fortnight had resulted in a very visual unification of the loyalist community, binding them together in their opposition to the Home Rule legislation progressing through parliament. Both for Irish unionists and the external audience, the events at places like Enniskillen's Portora Hill, Lisburn's grain market and especially Belfast's City Hall provided an instant and memorable symbol of their resolute determination to resist Irish Home Rule. As with earlier significant events, such as the Craigavon and Balmoral demonstrations, the Covenant campaign proved to be an undisputed organisational success, in which unionists gained their key goals of dissipating loyalist frustration and anger and channelling it into a noble cause. These trouble-free meetings, they hoped, would be interpreted as indicative of an orderly, dignified and articulate movement of community resistance to Home Rule.

Politically, the Covenant fortnight of September 1912 was probably the clearest illustration of how Ulster loyalists were setting the political agenda for an Irish political settlement. Armed insurrection in Dublin in 1916 and more widespread paramilitary action between 1919 and 1921, followed by civil war between co-religionists the following year, would result in the different political circumstances that existed in Ulster being relegated to Westminster's back burner. As far as their main objective was concerned, the Covenant trail across Ulster did not result in the immediate ditching of the offending legislation – the Liberals contemptuously dismissed its significance when parliament reassembled – but it did prompt some of unionism's opponents to start considering compromise proposals, involving the province opting out of such a proposed political unit. Therefore it did constitute a turning point in unionist fortunes.

Paradoxically, the political and propaganda success of the Covenant fortnight had a negative effect on the fortunes of their co-religionists elsewhere in Ireland. Their minority status in the other Irish provinces contrasted sharply with their large numbers and the apparently uniform nature of unionist resistance in Ulster. Ideas of differences between Ulster and the other Irish provinces started to germinate from this period, much to the detriment of the position of Irish unionists across the island. Another political repercussion of the Covenant demonstrations and signings in Ulster was that many in Great Britain started to appreciate the intricacies of the Ulster situation. This galvanised English and Scottish supporters into establishing a parallel political and propaganda campaign, centred on a British version of the Covenant. Finally, the Covenant campaign in Ulster during September 1912 provided later generations of Ulster unionists with an iconic moment of a halcyon period for their cause, when charismatic unionist leaders, supported by leading British politicians, pledged their followers to resist the creation of a Dublin-based Parliament, at the same time succeeding in grabbing the moral high ground as an imperilled religious minority in Ireland.

Parading at Narrow Water Castle, County Down, 1913

Friends in high places

4

Introduction

The response of Ulster's loyalist community to what they perceived as impending danger was immediate, resolute and well organised. However, although community solidarity was an essential prerequisite for Ulster's campaign against Home Rule, another vital ingredient for any potentially successful resolution of the crisis was required.

Not only was fulsome and widespread support forthcoming from the British public, but the unequivocal backing of leading figures in British society would also be a key bonus for northern unionists. This emanated from a range of personalities in aristocratic, press and political spheres. Additionally, Ulster unionists could rely on regal concern and the open sympathy of many army officers.[1] The warmth and embracing welcome afforded to Carson's movement by the Conservative Party and the higher ranks of society, as well as the willingness of several press barons and influential editors to facilitate sympathetic coverage of Irish issues – in leading articles, reports penned by special on-the-spot correspondents, cartoons mocking their political opponents and supportive correspondence in their letters' pages – all combined to strengthen the arm of unionist opposition to Home Rule and to reassure Irish loyalists that they were not alone in their struggle.

Bonar Law's friends in need

Political isolationism during this period of crisis would undoubtedly have proved to be the death-knell for Ulster unionists. Instead, they were able (like their nationalist opponents and their Liberal allies) to enjoy a mutually beneficial relationship with the Conservative Party. As we will observe, this unprecedented degree of support for Ulster's Protestants, which was unrestrained in some sections of the party, was surprising given that such a close relationship blatantly entwined the 'party of law and order' with a movement seriously threatening the wishes of parliament and the maintenance of order in Ireland. This was due, in the main, to the party's desire for power and to the Irish Unionist Party's need for political support at Westminster.

Such backing was, however, not universally enthusiastic or unqualified, and there were different factions within the wider Tory movement urging restraint or promoting the case for further consideration of unionist interests in other parts of Ireland. In this section I will investigate the factors that motivated Andrew Bonar Law to endorse Ulster's protest and assess both his stewardship of his party's Irish policy and the contributions made by other individuals and elements within Conservatism. The political impact made at British by-elections by Ulster unionist activists with their persuasive propaganda techniques, and the phenomenal success of the unionist roadshows of 1911–14, to which the Conservative Party made a major contribution, will also be investigated.

Following two election defeats in 1910 under the leadership of Arthur James Balfour, the Conservative Party was divided and demoralised. There was no obvious successor to Balfour. The favourites to succeed him had been Austen Chamberlain and former leader of the Irish Unionist Party, Walter Long, with the Scot Andrew Bonar Law regarded as an outsider for the post. Bonar Law, a relative latecomer to the political stage and lacking in ministerial experience, was regarded as a compromise candidate, however, and was duly elected as Conservative Party leader in November 1911. Essentially a politician of two issues – Ireland and tariff reform – Bonar Law set about tightening his precarious grip on the party, soon realising that the best way to achieve party unity was on the emotive question of Ulster.

The personal background of the Conservative Party's new leader was crucial in terms of its impact on his attitudes to Ulster and his broader Irish policy. Andrew Bonar Law's father came from Ulster and his Presbyterian upbringing in New Brunswick, Canada and later in Glasgow ensured a natural empathy with the religious beliefs and fears of Ulstermen. His knowledge of the north of Ireland was detailed and he had a brother practising medicine in Coleraine, County Londonderry. Hard working and methodical in his approach, rather than exuding natural charisma, the pipe-smoking, bridge-playing father of six had been widowed barely two years before assuming his party's leadership.

Despite his intimate knowledge of Ulster society and politics, Bonar Law had made relatively few parliamentary pronouncements on Ireland. This was to change within a few months, as the time for the introduction of Asquith's Home Rule Bill drew closer. Influenced by party splits and ambiguities in policy, and suffering the legacy of two recent electoral defeats, Bonar Law chose a fresh approach on which to launch the party's new campaign against the proposed measure. Avoiding the condescending approach to Ireland that Tory leaders had shown during previous periods of Home Rule crisis – centred on the assumption that the Irish were not fit to govern themselves – Andrew Bonar Law chose a direction that exhibited a sense of moral self-righteousness. Also, from the earliest of his public utterances on Ulster, Bonar Law stressed the principle that the electorate had to sanction such a radical constitutional change as Home Rule. Addressing a large, flag-waving audience at London's Albert Hall in January 1912, the recently elected Conservative Party leader pledged his support to the 'loyal minority' in Ulster, reminding his listeners that 'we support them not because we are intolerant but because their claims are just'.[2] Speaking in Bootle on Merseyside a few weeks before, Andrew Bonar Law had made clear the extent of his personal opposition to Home Rule:

> My Irish policy is to treat Ireland precisely as I treat England, Scotland and Wales ... We have treated Ireland far more generously than we treated any other part of the Kingdom ... What Ireland needs and what we have given her is less politics and more industries. What our opponents, led by Mr Redmond and his band, are promising to Ireland is more politics and less industry ... When the time comes there will be no shrinking from strong action. There will be no shrinking from any action which we think necessary to defeat one of the most ignoble conspiracies which has ever been formed against the liberties of free-born men.[3]

What then, motivated Andrew Bonar Law in his Irish policy and how should historians assess his legacy to Ireland? As mentioned above, the constant factor that underpinned his opposition to Home Rule was the principle of the consent of the electorate in sanctioning major constitutional change – he believed that this had been violated in this instance. This suggests that national rather than regional (Ulster) interests really motivated him in constructing his policy on Ireland. Not surprisingly, his main concern as a new party leader was to stop the drift and decline within the Conservative Party, and he considered that the best way to achieve this was to maximise the emotional appeal attached to Protestants' perilous predicament in Ulster. Andrew Bonar Law believed that this issue would pressurise Herbert Asquith and his party into conceding an election – which, he was convinced, would result in the Tories returning to power.

Yet his commitment to Ulster is considered by his most recent biographer to have been 'undeniable and his language ... remained unabashedly combative'.[4] Certainly, Bonar Law was unusually generous in the time he allocated to supporting Ulster unionists. He did so on a consistent and regular basis and not, like other twentieth-century British political leaders, spasmodically at moments of crisis. Despite a cooling in the relationship in the early 1920s, when Carson felt aggrieved at Bonar Law's support for the Anglo-Irish Treaty, Andrew Bonar Law's friendship with Edward Carson was genuine and the men respected each other. Bonar Law spoke forcefully on behalf of Ulster loyalists in parliament, addressed mass meetings (often in the company of Carson or other Irish Unionist Party leaders), endured lengthy, tiring political tours, maintained regular contact with Carson and other politicians, churchmen and opinion makers, and even found time to review the ranks of the UVF at the height of the crisis in 1914.

Bonar Law's advocates contend that his 'hard-man' image was designed both to unsettle Asquith from what they regarded as his natural smugness and also to reassure northern Protestants, and that he was more circumspect in private, especially with regard to becoming over-involved in Ulster. He was aware of other Irish Unionist Party considerations and motives, most notably the arguments of some for a federalist or devolutionary approach, and also listened to those voices of concern or disapproval (such as Walter Long or Lord Lansdowne) about a 'one-province' emphasis, at the expense of southern unionists. In the end, however, the interests of Ulster unionists, rather than Irish unionists as a whole, would predominate and result in Bonar Law's eventual acceptance and championing of an exclusion policy for part of Ulster.

Although his biographers maintain that his commitment to Ulster was clear and he attempted to steer a responsible course under difficult circumstances, there are many critics of Andrew Bonar Law's policy.[5] Castigated by Nicholas Mansergh for 'allowing a great English party to follow a small Irish faction', Bonar Law has been admonished by many historians for encouraging Ulster unionists to conduct unconstitutional and illegal activity, bringing the province to the precipice of civil war.[6] Bonar Law was also criticised for his restricted view of unionism, which resulted in 'the transmuting [of] United Kingdom Unionism into Ulster Unionism'.[7] The same authors point to the 'sudden switch' in Tory policy from 'defenders of the union to defence of Ulster'.[8] An interesting observation on Andrew Bonar Law's Irish strategy – and one that contrasted sharply with his seemingly sober, methodical character – is that he played mind games with his Liberal counterpart over Home Rule. John Ramsden has suggested that Bonar Law believed he was in 'an eyeball-to-eyeball face-off with Asquith' and that he was convinced 'his nerve would hold out longer'.[9] It can not be denied that Bonar Law conducted a high-risk strategy on Ulster, and there is also some truth in Ramsden's assertion that his 'absolutist political campaign' had 'led the Irish Unionists ... into such an intransigent state of mind that they would not accept any negotiated deal'.[10]

In drawing conclusions on the ramifications of Andrew Bonar Law's Irish policy, one has to balance claims that he was playing a game of risk with the fortunes of his own party and the danger of inciting civil war in Ulster with suggestions that he was genuinely committed to Ulster's cause. Certainly, Bonar Law was not drawn involuntarily into the Irish imbroglio and he did not make a habit of retracting his more extreme statements on Ulster. This indicates a clarity and resolve of purpose as well as approach. It is likely he was motivated by what he considered best for his party and by what he also considered to be Ireland's best interests. What is, perhaps, of more importance than his exact motivation on Ulster is the impact of his contribution to the anti-Home Rule campaign. Without the support of the leader of opposition, both in parliament and at numerous political meetings across Britain and Ireland, Edward Carson and his colleagues would have been increasingly marginalised and isolated during a time of extreme political crisis. It is likely that, instead of the resulting political stalemate, communal tension would have erupted on the streets of Belfast.

Although Andrew Bonar Law's all-consuming passion for the Irish question tended to dominate his party's thinking on the issue, there were several noteworthy contributions from a range of other Tory luminaries. His predecessor as leader of the Conservative Party, Arthur James Balfour, was a unionist of the old school, whose adherence to the principle of national unity was intertwined with his passion for imperial unity. Whilst Balfour was uncomfortable with the ever-more-likely prospect of communal violence in Belfast, he was attracted to the promotion of the province in Tory propaganda, as he believed it would prove to be Asquith's major stumbling block. At a meeting in Nottingham towards the end of November 1913, Arthur J. Balfour contested Ireland's claims to genuine nationhood:

> Ireland never had an organic political past as a single great community and when an Irishman asks us to restore to Ireland Irish institutions ... you will always find it is an English institution ... it is a fact that there are no Irish

laws, there is nothing in existence at this moment that could possibly be restored to Ireland which is of itself of pure national origin.[11]

On the same theme, another ageing Tory icon, Joseph Chamberlain, suggested that Ulster unionists were criticised simply because they 'clung to the traditions and history of the United Kingdom, which is just as much their possession and heritage as it is ours'.[12]

The most flamboyant and charismatic of front-line campaigners for Ulster was the Conservative Party's rising star, F.E. Smith. Smith, a future lord chancellor and peer (Lord Birkenhead) was an intelligent and witty, though hard-line, Tory, who became a favourite butt of Liberal parliamentary jibes following his outspoken utterances on Ulster (including his suggestions of raising an 'army' on Merseyside). As noted, Smith made a special contribution to the Covenant campaign in September 1912, when he addressed five meetings in Ulster, before welcoming Edward Carson back onto English soil at a mass meeting in Liverpool in early October.

Smith was not the only Tory to be accused of reckless oratory on Ulster. Another Tory MP, Lieutenant-Colonel P. Newman, was even more careless with his choice of words. Warning that the employment of British troops in imposing Home Rule on Ulster would result in bloodshed, he suggested that 'any man would be justified in shooting Mr Asquith in the streets of London'.[13]

Other unionist voices who competed for the attention of their not-always-receptive leader were those who propounded a federalist solution to Ireland's political problems and those (frequently peers) who reminded Bonar Law of the precarious plight of Protestants in the south and west of Ireland. Although proposed in detail later by Liberals like Winston Churchill, unionists had suggested a devolved system of government as early as 1910. Journalist F.S. Oliver, using the pen name

'Pacificus', had published a number of letters on the theme in *The Times* that October, but the notion of 'Home Rule all round', as it was called, was not high on Bonar Law's political agenda. Critics of such schemes – based on the imperial parliament at Westminster overseeing separate parliaments for each of the four countries in the United Kingdom – argued that it would signal the start of the breakup of a genuinely united country and also herald the erosion of imperial unity. Further figures on the right, including J.L. Garvin, flirted with the idea some time later.

Andrew Bonar Law and more traditional Tories were more sympathetic to the pleas of colleagues not to desert the smaller minority of Protestants in other parts of Ireland. Peers like Curzon and Lansdowne, as well as other senior Tory figures like Walter Long, who had family property in southern Ireland, constantly reminded their party leader that their opposition to Home Rule was not restricted to a mere endorsement of Ulster's admittedly strong claim for exclusion from its effects. Whilst their concerns and disagreements with the policy of their party leader – in particular, his focus on Ulster's opposition to the proposed measure – did not spill over into rebellion, they remained wary of the direction in which he was taking the party over Ulster. Walter Long was the unofficial spokesman for these vexed unionists in the south and west of Ireland. Concerned by the threat posed by Carson's Volunteers and by the activities of Willoughby de Broke's British League, Long was particularly cautious of parliamentary strategies that would weaken unionist cohesion across Ireland. Writing to Bonar Law in June 1912, he expressed his hopes that Ulster loyalists would 'not be caught by the very open trap set for them' by Liberal MP Thomas Agar-Robartes's recent Commons amendment. He maintained that if they went along with this option, 'for the first time in the history of the Home Rule question our Party will be divided'. Asserting his opposition to Home Rule 'in any form', Walter Long refused to 'sacrifice' his friends in Leinster and Munster for a policy

(Ulster exclusion) which he regarded as 'a clumsy expediency at the best'.[14]

Magic-lantern shows

Realising the mutual benefit to be gained from a close relationship, the bond between the Conservative Party and the Ulster unionists grew closer during these two years. Ulster delegates were frequent and welcome visitors at Conservative annual conferences, especially during the years of Home Rule crisis. A UUC report noted the success of Ulster delegates to the Conservative conference at Leeds in November 1912 and observed that their speeches were 'received with the greatest enthusiasm'.[15] Their constant criticism of the bill's 'undemocratic' nature – a pillar of Tory policy on Ireland – was well received at the 1913 conference in Norwich. At this event, Edward Carson, who had received 'a most cordial welcome' from the delegates, moved a resolution declaring Asquith's Home Rule policy to be 'both disastrous to Ireland and a danger to the Empire', and condemned the proposed measure which 'has never been, and is not, if the Government can prevent it, to be submitted to the electors'.[16]

Support for the Ulster unionist cause did not stop at party conferences or on the Tory front bench at Westminster. As we will observe, leading unionist figures manned numerous party platforms at protest meetings across Britain, especially as the crisis neared a climax. Over 5,000 meetings pertaining to Home Rule were organised by Ulster unionists and Conservatives in England during the period between September 1911 and July 1914. Unionist speakers, including Viscount Templetown, Lord Chamberlain, Lord Lansdowne, Walter Long, Arthur James Balfour, Lord Milner, Rudyard Kipling and Sir Edward Carson, were particularly active in April and May 1914. They appeared in towns and cities including Ipswich, Coventry, Wolverhampton, Tunbridge Wells, Oxford and London.

With the help of local unionist associations, close to one

and a quarter million 'doubtful' voters were canvassed in over 200 constituencies. The numbers of meetings staged in Scotland over a similar period was also high (3,843) but, owing to demographic and geographical differences, the number of voters canvassed (205,654 in 50 constituencies) was somewhat lower.[17] Irish Unionist Party officials knew it would not be enough to preach merely to the converted. The organisation of political meetings and canvassing activities, accompanied by the distribution of large quantities of political literature, were orchestrated by the UAI, and were key strategies at by-elections, especially in marginal seats. The UAI were active at 33 fiercely contested by-elections during the period of intense debate over Home Rule.

The UAI oversaw the work of a plethora of unionist groups operating in Great Britain, including the IUA, the UUC, the UDL, Lord Willoughby de Broke's British League for the Support of Ulster and the Union (BLSUU) and Lord Milner's British Covenant movement. The UDL, founded by Walter Long in 1907, shared London premises with the UAI and cooperated in fund-raising, organising petitions and canvassing at by-elections (including manning anti-Home Rule vans) and assisted in organising key political meetings. The various unionist groups had gained useful experience in developing canvassing techniques and, by the end of 1911, the UAI had largely succeeded in promoting greater efficiency as well as providing opportunities for local initiative. Though two standing committees in Dublin and Belfast formed its administrative base, the day-to-day running of their political propaganda campaign was executed by regional agents (five in England and two in Scotland). These agents, working alongside local Conservative agents, controlled the distribution of literature, made canvassing arrangements and called public meetings. They were allocated up to six speakers, several of whom were on a speakers' panel brought over from Ireland, as well as canvassers, mainly recruited in Ulster and paid ten shillings each per day.

The UAI's propaganda weapons could also be original. For the by-election campaigns they brought onto the road anti-Home Rule vans, fitted with magic lanterns, and their slide shows proved popular with audiences. These vans, or 'motor car tours' as described in Ulster unionist literature, were busy during by-elections across the country in the first half of 1914. In March alone, vans were reported to have visited the constituencies of South Hackney ('a cold and wet night', explaining the poor turnout of under 150), Northamptonshire (only 30 attended here because there was 'no publicity available in the village'), South Somerset (over 100 turned up here) and Ilford in Essex, where 500 were attracted by the van. Some of the earliest motor tours had taken place in western England and in Ayrshire, Scotland during May 1913. Although impressed by their success, a UAI committee member, R.R. Smylie, had recommended that some of the speakers needed to update their material and to focus more on the 'disloyalty' of their opponents. By this time, however, Smylie was happier with the speakers' performance:

> At each of the meetings I attended, the lecture was listened to with much interest and attention of the crowd, the pictures were 'put on' in much the same order, the lecture followed on precisely the same lines and indeed in each case the lecturer might well be complimented for delivering a connected address illustrated by these pictures and not merely explaining a series of pictures. Certainly I thought the lecturers most conscientious in the discharge of their duty.[18]

Although Ulster unionists regarded their English by-election campaign as having had less impact than their efforts in Scotland, they still managed to assist Conservative candidates in 23 by-elections between 1911 and the summer of 1914. They were particularly active during the first two months of 1914, when they enjoyed successes in South Buckinghamshire, Poplar and South-West Bethnal Green. The London agent, Vernon

Wilkins, was especially stretched at this time, but decided to employ most of his available resources in Bethnal Green and in Buckinghamshire, where hopes of electoral success were high. Over 30 Irish workers assisted in the return of the unionist candidate in South Buckinghamshire and were actively engaged in C.F.G. Masterman's narrow defeat in Bethnal Green, but their single-issue canvassing cut little ice with the mainly working-class electorate (many of whom were of Irish Catholic origin).

Effective pooling of resources in the northern regions produced another success in the North-East Derbyshire by-election of May 1914. Making the most of favourable local political quirks, the UAI moved in eight speakers, made the most of their magic-lantern vans (these featured at five meetings, drawing an average audience of 300) and brought in many canvassers, including 'a body of Belfast working men ... seeking quietly to convince their fellow Trade Unionists of the justice of Ulster's opposition to Home Rule'.[19] The previous MP had been a Labour representative, sitting on account of a Liberal–Labour pact, but there were now separate candidates for these parties and a split in the vote was anticipated. The Tory candidate, Major H. Bowden, was returned with a majority of 300. The local Tory agent, A.P. Blackburn, wrote to the unionist agents in the area to thank the UAI for their assistance in the by-election and the subsequent Tory success, which he maintained was due in no small way to the prominence of the Ulster issue. Praising the Ulster workers' 'quiet determination' and 'gentlemanly manner', Blackburn concluded that if the election was won, 'no small portion of the credit will be due to you and your gallant band, and the least I can do is to tell you so'.[20]

The religious aspect of the unionist campaign was particularly important in electoral contests in Scotland. However, on occasion, this focus on religious objections to Home Rule could backfire on Ulster unionists. This appears to have been the case in the Wick Burghs by-election of December 1913. Despite distributing a huge volume of political literature, staging seventy meetings, bringing in four guest speakers and canvassing for a five-week period, the relevance of the Ulster question was obscured as the victorious Liberal candidate (a Mr Munro) focused on key local issues (in particular, the demand for a grant to develop Wick Harbour). Yet, merely two months later, the unionists would celebrate their greatest by-election success of this period. The Tories had not won Leith Burghs in Midlothian since 1832, but the UAI's campaign in this constituency stretched over a 15-month period and had involved 19 canvassers and 6 speakers. The tightness of the UAI propaganda campaign, the increasing tension within Ulster, its greater prominence in the British press as the crisis deepened and an absence of controversial local issues help explain the Tory success. *The Times* argued that the Leith Burghs electors were 'deeply stirred by the Ulster question' and acknowledged that it was the key factor in G.W. Currie's narrow election victory.[21]

Even in defeat, considerable inroads could be made into previously safe Liberal constituencies in Scotland. The narrowly defeated Conservative candidate in the West Lothian by-election of November 1913, James Kidd, thanked the Irish Unionist Party for their help during this unsuccessful campaign. He believed that making Home Rule the 'main plank in my platform' had resulted in an 'enormous reduction' in the Radical majority, constituting 'a moral victory' for his party. He went on to suggest that 'the most prominent Radicals here frankly admit the Election damns Home Rule, as far as this County is concerned, while others freely admit that this County has illuminated the position for Scotland in such a way that a General Election on Home Rule will see an overwhelming change in this County'.[22]

Unionist strategists adapted their tactics and topics for discussion to suit the demands and interests of particular regions. Therefore, from the autumn of 1913 onwards (when compromise talks between Herbert Asquith and Andrew Bonar Law had commenced), more emphasis was given to demonstrations and meetings, with canvassing taking a back seat. The UAI were also flexible in using resources in the Scottish region. They were realistic enough to advocate a shift of emphasis in their scheduled target constituencies if support for their cause started to wane. In a report emanating from their Belfast office, for example, the UAI 'strongly recommended ... the advisability of dropping Hawick Burghs and Dumfries Burghs from our list of selected constituencies in the East and North of Scotland'.[23] Having 'completely canvassed' and staged public meetings in these constituencies, the report's authors noted that workers complained of 'bad local organisation and a decided want of sympathy and a marked degree of apathy in the Unionist agents and electors'.[24] Further deployment of unionist manpower was evident when the UAI, anticipating the large-scale exodus of Central Lowland workers to the seaside resorts in the summers of 1913 and 1914, prepared accordingly. UAI workers covered a large number of resorts (several of which were also popular with Ulster holidaymakers). Meetings were held in places like Rothesay, Millport, Troon, Largs, Ardrossan and Ayr.[25]

The Ulster roadshow

Campaigning at widely publicised by-elections in Great Britain certainly brought the Ulster question to the attention of many, but a more direct presentation of its key issues needed to be made to the British public. This was particularly the case given the bill's inevitable parliamentary success and the comparative complexities and intricacies of Irish politics. Indeed, the importance of making a major impact on public opinion in Great Britain was constantly trumpeted in Ulster's loyalist press. A leader in the *Northern Whig* in May 1912 showed this increasing awareness of the significant role to be played by the British public, as distinct from their political representatives, and reminded the former of their responsibilities to Ulster loyalists:

When the British people come to consider this question they have got to ask themselves who are their real friends in Ireland ... [Ulster loyalists] have never betrayed their trust. Is it going to be said of the British people that they are about to requite that service by handing over their staunch friends to their bitter enemies? We have too much faith in the good sense, in the honour and in the loyalty of the people of Great Britain to believe for one moment that they would be guilty of such a base act. We never for a moment entertain the idea that the British people would desert us in a crisis.[26]

Despite the optimism of loyalist opinion makers, British knowledge of Irish affairs – apart from the partisan views held on Clydeside and Merseyside – was limited by the very different nature of Irish politics and also by geographical barriers. Besides this failure to comprehend the gravity and complexity of the Home Rule issue, the levels of interest in what was going on in Ireland were seemingly rather low. There was undoubtedly a considerable degree of apathy on the Irish question, especially in isolated, rural areas of Britain during the early stage of the crisis. Indeed, this lack of interest was acknowledged in various Conservative newspapers. A leading article in the *Standard* in March 1914 expressed its concern that that people were more interested in their 'ordinary affairs and interests' than in the 'appalling peril' facing Ireland, of which they were 'barely conscious'. In high moralistic tones, the paper lambasted the British public for its perceived apathy to Ulster: 'it buys and sells and does its work; it continues occasionally to read a book; it swarms into picture palaces and music halls and theatres, especially theatres which provide their judicious patrons with bedroom scenes'.[27] Yet it is also true that these levels of apathy had dropped rather dramatically by the summer of 1914. Certainly, the degree of British indifference to Ireland was nowhere near as high between 1912 and 1914 as it turned out to be during the 1970s and 1980s, when the constancy of negative news stories deterred British public sympathy for loyalists in Northern Ireland.[28] Daniel Jackson, in his fascinating study of British-based, extra-parliamentary opposition to Home Rule during this 1912–14 period, has contested the degree of apathy. He has maintained that the increased interest in events in Ulster and its higher profile in the British press (especially between late 1913 and the early summer of 1914), the vital relationship between the Ulster question and by-election successes for the Tories in places like Leith, North-East Derbyshire and Bethnal Green around this time and, most especially, the degree of support for 'political street theatre' in the cause of Ulster, suggests that a sizeable section of British public opinion was won over. Jackson has compared the success of unionist rallies in Great Britain – 'certainly the most impressive of any of the Edwardian political movements' – with the subdued, lacklustre nature of Radical meetings on the Irish issue. Describing Herbert Asquith's appearance at a by-election in Fife in April 1914, Jackson has written:

> Although the Prime Minister had mustered some enthusiasm among his supporters, it paled in comparison with the contemporaneous unionist Mardi Gras in London and elsewhere.[29]

Political tours had been mainly associated with the electoral campaigns of important individuals during the Victorian period (most notably William Gladstone), rather than with whole political parties on a periodic basis over a period of two and a half years. These popular demonstrations – held in streets, in market places, in public halls, in fields and on ice rinks between the end of 1911 and the early summer of 1914 – probably constituted the last of these street meetings on a national scale. Although such gatherings on Ulster's opposition to Home Rule were staged up and down the country throughout this period, at least four major tours – involving Edward Carson, James Craig and, during the summer of 1913, the whole of the Irish Unionist Party parliamentary group and Bonar Law – were organised in the winter of 1911–12, June 1913, the autumn of 1913 and the winter of 1913–14. Over the course of these tours, Carson visited virtually every city in Great Britain and spoke to sympathetic audiences in places like Liverpool, Newcastle, Birmingham and Glasgow, as well as entering enemy territory when he visited Radical-sympathising cities such as Manchester and Leeds. Like William Gladstone in his Midlothian campaign over 25 years before, Edward Carson spoke to enthusiastic audiences gathered at key railway stations *en route* to his speaking engagements in major cities in north and west England and also in Scotland. These meetings, much publicised in national and local newspapers, were theatrical occasions. Bands entertained crowds gathering outside the venues where unionist figures like Edward Carson, James Craig and Walter Long were scheduled to speak, and accompanied attendees in singing numerous patriotic songs. Torchlight processions were used after the meetings to guide the main speakers to their hotels or to the local Conservative club. Months before the Third Home Rule Bill had been introduced in the House of Commons, unionist leaders had covered over 20 towns and cities, mostly in England, with Edward Carson speaking in Liverpool and Manchester, James Craig at various venues across the west country and Walter Long appearing at meetings in Leeds, Newcastle and Salisbury. *The Times* informed its readers that 'the keenest interest was taken in the campaign'.[30]

The need to step up the tempo of such tours was recognised after the Home Rule Bill had been introduced in parliament and the inevitability of its success was gradually accepted. In mid-June 1913, at the start of the parliamentary recess, all 18 IUP representatives set off on an 'unparalleled' tour of Scotland and England. As they made their way to Scotland and the first of their 18 meetings, their train came to a halt at several major railway junctions where local Conservatives had gathered to wish them well on their journey north. Sir Edward Carson made impromptu speeches to his supporters, including one at Rugby, where he promised them: 'We are going to appeal on behalf of our democracy in Ireland to the democracy in Great Britain.'[31] Unionists back in Ulster were under no misapprehension about the relevance of such a campaign. UUC records described such a tour as 'the real campaign for the Union', reminding loyalists that 'the real attack has to be made in the country, not in Parliament'. Describing the tour as 'an astonishing success', the UUC analysed its significance and likely impact as follows:

> It is a moving spectacle, that of a whole party leaving Parliament behind them to appeal to the people, who are the masters of Parliament. It is an event unique in our Constitutional history. It is so understood by the people, it has fired their imagination as nothing else could do … Not only have they heard the solemn menace of internal strife, but they have seen, for the first time, what is the true foundation and excuse for the menace. The people have begun to realise that Ulster is not only fighting for her own land, that she is not only standing for all Ireland against this disastrous Bill, but that she is also standing for all the political liberties of the whole nation.[32]

Although the speakers encountered some opposition and heckling in places, they were warmly received at most venues, especially at meetings in Glasgow, Norwich and Bristol. A huge audience welcomed Sir Edward Carson and his parliamentary colleagues onto a platform adorned by a gigantic Union Jack in Glasgow's St Andrew's Hall, where 'unrestrained cheering' endured unabated until the gathering was 'brought to silence by the solemn tones of the great organ'. The report in *The Times* also tells us that the IUP leader was carried shoulder high into the Glasgow Conservative Club at the end of the meeting.[33] Even in places where there was significant opposition to their cause, the IUP delegation received 'enthusiastic welcomes'. Such an occasion was in Leeds centre, where 'people lined the streets along the route and loudly cheered Sir Edward Carson and the other Irish members'.[34]

This tour ended in the west of England, where, shortly after being welcomed by a cheering crowd at Temple Meads Station, Edward Carson addressed a 5,000-strong audience in Bristol's Colston Hall. The programme for this 'Great west of England' demonstration on 20 June had on its front page a photo of a stern Carson, arms resolutely folded, surrounded by Union Jacks and messages of support including 'We stand for a United Empire' and 'We Stand for a United Kingdom'. Before the political speeches began, the audience was treated to an organ recital and sang patriotic songs, including 'Rule Britannia', 'Heart of oak', 'O God our help in ages past' and the national anthem.[35]

Whilst considered not to have been as successful as the summer tour of 1913, further series of political meetings were held that autumn and winter. The most talked-about gathering in Carson's north of England tour in the autumn was at Wallsend Ice Rink on 29 October. Organised by the National Unionist Association and featuring representatives of north-east England's Orange Order, the rally was stewarded by nearly 500 men and an estimated 12,000 were in attendance. Union Jacks 'flew from every girder', the stage was lit by 16 arc lamps and bands entertained the enormous crowd for nearly two hours before the arrival of Andrew Bonar Law and Edward Carson. After the meeting, the leaders were driven in an open motor landau around Wallsend in a mile-long procession.

Further demonstrations were held during the last two months of 1913. These included meetings in Liberal strongholds such as Manchester and Sheffield (where Carson was heckled), although warmer receptions were granted in Scotland and in the west of England. The *Northern Whig* argued that the recent meetings in towns like Inverness, Aberdeen, Perth and Dundee would 'bring home to the public that while Scotland is Liberal, she is not Home Rule'.[36] Ulster loyalists particularly appreciated the warm reception they had in the far south-west of England. Described as 'the greatest meeting of the tour', the demonstration at Plymouth's Drill Hall on 8 December gave the Ulster leader an enthusiastic welcome and dominated local press coverage. A couple of days later, Carson spoke in the Anglican city of Truro in Cornwall. The Cornish capital's strong currents of anti-Catholicism ensured huge interest in the meeting, which was attended by what was regarded as the largest ever crowd for a political event in the county. Special trains had been chartered and motorbuses transported ticket holders from places like the remote Lizard and St Keverne to Truro's Market Hall.[37] The long winter tour certainly took its toll on the representatives of the Irish Unionist Party parliamentary group who had accompanied Edward Carson and the *Northern Whig* reminded its readers that it had been 'no pleasure picnic, but a stern and strenuous task' for all involved.[38]

As the crisis gathered pace in the first half of 1914, lengthy tours were replaced by one-off rallies or small series of demonstrations, including a spectacular loyalist rally held in London's Hyde Park in April and meetings in Glasgow, Inverness, Leeds and Eastbourne in June. Edward Carson also visited Lancashire around this time, addressing 10,000 in a Blackburn field overlooking the corporation tram sheds. He also spoke at neighbouring Bolton, where he paid tribute to the support he and his colleagues had encountered during their numerous meetings across Britain. Carson concluded:

> If I gather anything from the spirit of the meetings that I have addressed throughout Great Britain, if they entered on this Civil War in Ulster, the Civil War would not be confined to Ulster.[39]

There is little question that the presentational success of unionism's extra-parliamentary campaign during the late Edwardian period would have resonated deeply on large sections of British public opinion. It is difficult to assess its precise impact, especially in terms of its success in converting political sceptics or neutrals to Ulster's cause. However, it cannot be disputed that in terms of the breadth of its appeal – posing the stark choice of standing by or deserting a minority pledging its loyalty to king and empire during a time of political and constitutional crisis – and in Edwardian unionists' use of street theatre, the political tours of Irish unionists resulted in large sections of the British public empathising with the predicament of Ulster loyalists.[40] As Daniel Jackson has pointed out, unionists were certainly able to draw greater crowds onto British streets than other mass movements of the time, including trade unionists and suffragettes. He has argued:

> [The union issue] dominated politics in the last two years before the Great War and mobilised the most supporters. Did the campaign against national insurance bring legions of torch-bearers on to the streets? Could even the suffragettes have mustered similar numbers of supporters in demonstrations from Inverness to Truro?[41]

How then, do we assess the true impact of the Irish policies and strategies of Bonar Law's Conservative Party during the latter part of the Edwardian period? The party has been variously described as the 'prisoner' of its Irish unionist allies (just as the Liberals were reliant on the parliamentary backing of John Redmond's Irish Nationalist Party), conducting itself in a negative, sectional and opportunistic manner and with no apparent alternative strategy to the Liberals' policy of Home Rule. There is considerable truth in each of these descriptions, though it would be wrong to ignore the genuine sympathy felt by many ordinary Conservative voters across the country for the predicament of Ulster Protestants. The most damning indictment of the Tories was given by George Dangerfield in his classic critique of Liberal England. Pointing to the self-interest of Ulster's loyalists, Dangerfield argued:

> It is not to be supposed that English Conservatives had any feelings of bosom friendship for Ulster ... the Conservative

Party did not love it; but, looking around for a weapon with which to replace the Lords' veto, its eye lit upon ... Ulster's bigotry. With Ulster's bigotry it could break the Liberal Party.[42]

Other writers have suggested that it was sectional interests rather than national ones that prompted the Tories to seize a rare opportunity to patch together their bitterly divided party between 1911 and 1914. The Ulster question was a godsend for a party that desired to be re-elected on a patriotic ticket, and this included 'pro-British' concerns like tariff reform, the empire, protecting and expanding the navy, and fighting Home Rule.[43]

Although described as 'prisoners' of their Irish allies, it must not be forgotten that Conservatives actually chose to align themselves with a precarious cause and, in the words of one writer, arguably 'manufactured' the crisis in Ulster.[44] Irish Home Rule provided the party with a chance to unite behind a single issue and they swiftly grasped the opportunity to back a genuine grievance, which they would exploit electorally. Perhaps the most honest appraisal of Tory motivation was given by Conservative politician Leo Amery at the height of the crisis. Writing to Neville Chamberlain in July 1914, he admitted:

> We only drifted into it really, if we are to be honest with ourselves, because Ulster was the easiest thing to talk about when public opinion was apathetic and because, on the face of it, it seemed a moderate and reasonable attitude.[45]

In his detailed analysis of Conservative motivation on the issue, Jeremy Smith does not attempt to minimise the self-serving nature of Conservative endeavours to save their party from electoral extinction. Ulster, he argues, was of secondary importance. However, as Smith has crucially reminded us, this was a successful policy, which 'undoubtedly maintained the unity of the Conservative Party in a way that Arthur Balfour's leadership surely would never have done'.[46] Thus, Andrew Bonar Law's particular approach and emphasis on Ulster was

Propaganda poster: 'We won't have Home Rule'

Sir Edward Carson briefing news reporters at Craigavon, September 1912

Carson alongside Colonel Wallace, on their way to a Covenant meeting, September 1912

Covenant Day scene, Belfast, September 1912

Arrival of the leaders at the City Hall, September 1912

Ulster's Solemn League and Covenant.

Being convinced in our consciences that Home Rule would be disastrous to the material well-being of Ulster as well as of the whole of Ireland, subversive of our civil and religious freedom, destructive of our citizenship and perilous to the unity of the Empire, we, whose names are underwritten, men of Ulster, loyal subjects of His Gracious Majesty King George V., humbly relying on the God whom our fathers in days of stress and trial confidently trusted, do hereby pledge ourselves in solemn Covenant throughout this our time of threatened calamity to stand by one another in defending for ourselves and our children our cherished position of equal citizenship in the United Kingdom and in using all means which may be found necessary to defeat the present conspiracy to set up a Home Rule Parliament in Ireland. ¶ And in the event of such a Parliament being forced upon us we further solemnly and mutually pledge ourselves to refuse to recognise its authority. In sure confidence that God will defend the right we hereto subscribe our names. ¶ And further, we individually declare that we have not already signed this Covenant.

The above was signed by me at _____
"Ulster Day," Saturday, 28th September, 1912.

Edward Carson

God Save the King.

Text of the Covenant

Edward Carson signing the Covenant, September 1912

Donegall Place, Belfast under Home Rule, postcard

'Ulster's Prayer – don't let go!', postcard

'There's many a slip …',
Punch cartoon,
1 April 1914

"THERE'S MANY A SLIP …"

'No Home Rule!' propaganda postcard

'The Ulster king-at-arms', *Punch*, 6 May 1914

Inspection by the leader

Drilling members of the UVF, County Tyrone, July 1913

Edward Carson addressing the massed ranks of the UVF at Balmoral, September 1913

UVF lining up for parade at Fortwilliam, north Belfast, September 1913

Unloading the guns at Donaghadee, postcard, April 1914

UVF gun-running, Bangor, postcard, April 1914

Inspection of UVF nursing staff, 1914

Ulster Volunteers on the march

Edward Carson addressing Orangemen, 1914

Edward Carson inspecting UVF personnel at the Ulster Hall, Belfast, July 1914

successful in uniting the party and in making it increasingly confident about its chances of being returned to power. In moral terms, it is less clear whether the Tories were fully frank about what was driving them – electoral success in itself or the single dominant issue of the party's opposition to Home Rule. Yet this confusion should not detract from Conservatives' genuine emotional attachment to Ireland's loyalist minority, nor should it obscure the fact that Ulster unionists were far from guiltless in manipulating the situation for their own ends. As Smith has pointed out, both parties 'clasped each other in a shot-gun marriage of mutual concern'.[47]

Peer influences

Ulster unionists during the Edwardian period were fortunate enough to enjoy considerable support from the aristocracy, both in Ulster and in Great Britain. At a time when aristocratic involvement in politics and class deference remained high, the correlation between aristocratic support for Ulster's resistance to Home Rule and the movement's general success in Great Britain and Ulster was significant, and will be analysed in this section. More attention will be paid to the nature of support provided by aristocrats in Britain, and the contributions and role performed by members of high society who were not ennobled will be observed. In addition, the contribution of women to the Ulster unionist movement – in the context of the leadership provided by Ulster-based aristocratic women – will also be considered.

Many aristocratic families retained their considerable influence both in Ulster and across Ireland in the early years of the twentieth century. The nature of that influence, especially in the political sphere, had altered since previous Home Rule campaigns of the late nineteenth century, when many Anglo-Irish families had enjoyed a more secure financial position, which had also boosted their political influence. A consequence of new economic constraints was that only the wealthiest of these families could continue to devote financial resources to electoral campaigns. Another major change to the position of Anglo-Irish aristocrats was their weakening grasp on the political reins of the House of Commons. Even before the 1911 Parliament Act, the landed gentry had experienced a considerable decline in its membership of the House of Commons. Less than a third of Commons representatives in 1900 were from aristocratic backgrounds, compared with over half some 15 years previously. With the shift in national political power to the middle classes came other changes in the base of class politics, including the emergence of the Labour Party in 1900. In Ulster, the relatively late industrialisation of the Lagan Valley had given rise to a new group of wealthy men from middle-class backgrounds, such as James Craig, J.B. Lonsdale and William Moore, who were elected Westminster MPs and constituted a major group within the IUP.

Nonetheless, as Olwen Purdue has observed, the landed gentry still 'continued to play an important role in the unionist movement, albeit an increasingly emblematic one'.[48] On account of the high levels of class deference in a conservative society such as Edwardian Ulster, the presence of aristocrats on political platforms, or the drilling of Volunteers on their huge estates, lent 'an air of legitimacy and tradition' to proceedings, sometimes queried by other, more hostile voices. These Ulster-based aristocrats, unlike many of their southern counterparts, were not deterred by the intemperate language of unionist politicians or the drilling of Volunteers. They contributed to the anti-Home Rule campaign in a variety of ways. Although most peers were not directly involved in the day-to-day organisation of resistance, many did speak at, or chair, important meetings and demonstrations. Others made their grounds available for UVF drilling and training exercises or hosted political leaders visiting their districts for major meetings. In addition, many of their wives were heavily involved in the work of the UUC and, later on, the UVF.

The marquis of Londonderry had a high profile at many demonstrations, both in Ulster and in Great Britain, often sharing a platform with his close friend Sir Edward Carson. Other peers who spoke at major loyalist political gatherings in places like Craigavon, Balmoral, Blenheim and during the Covenant campaign included the earl of Erne, Viscount Templetown, Viscount Castlereagh, the duke of Abercorn and the earl of Kilmorey. Templetown, who had been instrumental in the revival of the unionist clubs, was also engaged in advocating Ulster's resistance to Home Rule at a series of meetings in Great Britain. After one of these trips, he reported back to the Unionist Clubs Council (UCC) that 'the deepest interest is taken in our organisation and it is understood as representing the existence of the fixed determination of loyalists in Ireland never to submit to Home Rule'.[49] Their contributions to the campaign, although not crucial, were certainly significant and their presence on numerous political platforms and 'warm words' of support to Volunteers drilling or on training manoeuvres at their grounds would certainly have been noted and approved by loyalist diehards. It would be the 'new' Ulster unionist leadership rather than the 'old' that would dominate Covenant Day, but the contribution of Ulster's aristocracy to the campaign – and, indeed, its historical significance – should not be underestimated. Olwen Purdue has reminded us that 'the signing of the Covenant across the North took place against the backdrop of the big house'. She writes that, on that day, the representatives of the north's landed families 'returned home to their estates to enact what was perhaps their last great symbolic gesture of political leadership'.[50]

A major contribution by the aristocracy to the Ulster cause was in the preparation and drilling of the Ulster Volunteers. Members of many northern landed families had traditionally served in the British Army and several of these, now retired, organised and trained this civilian militia. Some of the leading aristocratic figures in the UVF included: Captain Roger Hall, who owned Narrow Water Castle and was commanding officer of the Second Battalion South Down UVF; Viscount Newry, who was in charge of the force's Kilkeel battalion; and Colonel Pakenham of Longford Lodge, who was in charge of the South Antrim UVF.

Drilling and military training took place at estates like Killyleagh Castle, Clandeboye, Dean's Hall in County Armagh, Crom Castle in County Fermanagh, the duke of Abercorn's estate at Baronscourt and Templetown's mansion at Castle Upton in County Antrim. Photographs of UVF personnel training at Baronscourt appeared on a regular basis in the loyalist press. They indicated the cross-class nature of UVF membership in the area. The caption below one photo of a UVF squad informed the reader that it included 'two Presbyterian clergymen, a barrister-at-law, an engineer, a Church of Ireland clergyman (who was in charge of the squad), a solicitor, a merchant, a farmer, a motor engineer, a carpenter and an auctioneer'.[51]

Inspection of the ranks by Ulster unionist leaders, including Edward Carson and James Craig, frequently took place in the grounds of stately houses and several of these aristocrats directly supported the gun-running operation of April 1914, either by receiving rifles at their estates hours after they had been unloaded along the Antrim and Down coasts or by offering their estates as depots for the motor vehicles that would be used to collect and transport the arms across the province. These included Shane's Castle and the Templetown estate in County Antrim and Springhill in County Tyrone.

In some ways, however, the most effective contribution of the landed aristocracy to the UVF movement was a symbolic one. As Olwen Purdue has pointed out, the 'very prominent involvement' of landowners in the drilling and arming of Volunteers was 'crucial' for the UVF's success, in the sense that their presence and patronage of what was effectively a paramilitary movement was 'vital in allaying any misgivings' the Volunteers held.[52]

The contributions of three aristocratic ladies to the anti-Home Rule campaign are especially worth considering here. Theresa, the sixth marchioness of Londonderry, was a supportive wife to a husband very much to the fore in Ulster's political resistance. However, she would also in her own right play an effective role in 'salon diplomacy' and help to create and lead the largest female political association in Irish history. Theresa Londonderry, like her great-grandmother, was renowned for her qualities as a political hostess and confidante, and Londonderry House (her London home) was used for many political receptions. These occasions won her a substantial reputation on London's social scene. Though events at Londonderry House were not reserved solely for Irish Unionist and Conservative guests, Theresa barred Radicals like Lloyd George and Churchill from attending. She was close to newspaper editors like H.A. Gwynne and Geoffrey Robinson (both of whom had visited the family's home at Mount Stewart in County Down) and was a frequent letter writer to several newspapers, particularly the *Morning Post*. She was also on good terms with leading politicians on the right, including F.E. Smith, Walter Long and especially Sir Edward Carson, to whom she was a great source of comfort after his first wife died. The IUP leader wrote to Theresa on a regular basis (often three or four times a week), and frequently stayed at the Londonderrys' country homes at Mount Stewart and in County Durham. Many regarded that Theresa provided an ear to Carson, and some would in turn have confided in her, appreciating that any interesting bits of conversation would probably have been relayed to Ulster's leader.

Yet, as Diane Urquhart has pointed out, there were 'obvious limits' to Lady Londonderry's influence on Edward Carson and IUP policy.[53] She failed to persuade Edward Carson to stand for the Conservative leadership in 1911, for example, and was ignorant of the imminent gun-running off the Ulster coast in April 1914. Rather, it was in her salon diplomacy, her patronage of the UWUC and her simple but effective speeches at meetings both in Ulster and Great Britain, where she made her greatest contribution to the loyalist campaign. Speaking to an anti-Home Rule audience in Stockton-upon-Tees in north-east England in November 1913, Lady Londonderry told her mainly English audience that the mothers and wives of Ulster Volunteers were 'firm and unflinching' in their support of their male relatives, believing that they were doing 'their women's part in endeavouring [to] save the Province they love so well from being saved for the Empire'. She also asked her audience if they were prepared to allow British soldiers to fire upon loyal men who ... seek to stay with you', and concluded that she 'as an Ulster woman appeal to you [to] uphold our principles [of] liberty, patriotism and citizenship'.[54]

Theresa Londonderry was very much to the fore in establishing and helping to mould the Ulster Women's Unionist Council. Her network of relationships with the key players in Ulster's resistance to Home Rule meant she was supremely suitable for attracting leading speakers and seeking the approval and advice of the leadership regarding the council's activities. Theresa, who had established an association of unionist women in London in 1912, became president of the UWUC in April 1913 at a crucial point in its history. In previous anti-Home Rule campaigns, the meaningful involvement of women had been considered frivolous, but the UWUC was an auxiliary movement to the UUC, led by aristocrats like Lady Londonderry but managing to attract all classes. It was seen as another vital step in consolidating loyalist resistance to Irish unity. The organisation grew rapidly, with over 80,000 members on the rolls inside a year. As many as 94 UWUC meetings had been held in 27 associations across the province and over 5,000 letters or propaganda pamphlets were sent weekly to Britain. As Diane Urquhart has noted, 'the sheer size of the council, its multiple class membership and the extent of its political work broke many boundaries for Ulster women in the early 20th century'.[55]

Although the role of women within the wider unionist movement tended to be low key, it certainly extended beyond merely making tea. Members of local unionist women's associations across Ulster were involved in a plethora of relatively mundane but necessary tasks, such as updating electoral registers, fund-raising, distributing propaganda material and assisting in electioneering. Loyalist women were also engaged in other activities, including participating in the recently revived women's section of the Orange Order, organising a petition against the *Ne temere* decree, signing the Women's Covenant in September and, from the second half of 1913, assisting in the work of the Ulster Volunteers. After a lengthy protest against the *Ne temere* decree, a petition containing over 104,000 signatures was presented to parliament in June 1912. As observed in the previous chapter, more women actually signed the Ulster Covenant than men. Middle- and upper-class women were to the fore in propaganda activism, with one of the most resourceful campaigners appearing to be a Mrs Sinclair of Strabane. This lady campaigned in Cambridgeshire during the winter of 1911–12, utilising the services of a conjuror and magician to attract the attention of the working classes.[56] Up to 5,000 women were involved in assisting the UVF. Their tasks ranged from helping as signallers and despatch riders to driving ambulances and working as nurses. Finally, upper-class women took the lead in the UWUC and also at local level, chairing meetings and addressing these gatherings. They included Lady Dunleath, Lady Erne, Lady Stronge, Lady Kilmorey and Lady O'Neill, as well as Theresa Londonderry.

This contribution of women to the unionist cause was recognised both in public and private by Ulster unionist leaders. Addressing a County Armagh Women's Unionist Association meeting on the eve of the Covenant demonstrations in 1912, James Craig described the UWUC as 'the motherhood of Ulster' and warned his female audience that Home Rule threatened the fundamental quality of domestic life in Ulster. He argued that the home was a woman's 'first consideration' and that, if Home Rule was passed, 'the sanctity and happiness of home life in Ulster' would be 'permanently destroyed'.[57] A private letter from the secretary of the UUC, R. Dawson Bates, to his counterpart within the UWUC in September 1913, pledging that an Ulster provincial government would enfranchise women, was subsequently dismissed by the party leader, who did not support female suffrage. Although there was some suffragette activity in Ireland, it was never going to be, given the conservative nature of that society, a breeding ground for suffragettes. The traditional roles and expectations of women were stressed by Ulster unionist leaders and personified in Lady Londonderry's personal contributions. For her and many other aristocratic women, their personal duty and responsibility towards their husbands blended with a wider sense of duty to the province, the United Kingdom and the British Empire. Addressing a UWUC meeting in July 1914, Lady Londonderry admitted that the prospect of bloodshed was 'an unspeakable horror' but reminded her audience of the 'righteousness' of their cause, which actually transcended any talk of violence:

> we women of Ulster are resolved not to be a hindrance but a help to the men who are prepared to risk everything for that cause ... we must give them our sympathy, our encouragement, our approval, [and] our admiration in the noble stand they have made ... While there is life there is hope, I do not altogether despair of yet seeing the happy day when the poisonous Home Rule reptile shall have to be driven beyond the borders of our province, if not our island.[58]

Although increasingly depressed by the threat of civil war in the early summer of 1914, Theresa Londonderry busied herself by promoting the Ulster cause, including by organising of a series of political rallies in north-east England.

Other female members of the upper classes provided different, and even more practical, support for Ulster unionists. Lady Spender, the wife of UVF luminary Wilfrid Spender, participated in first-aid classes for women in the Carnmoney area (to the north of Belfast) and in the district's UVF Ambulance Corps. She also helped distribute propaganda material to Great Britain, especially to constituencies experiencing by-elections, and visited Sir Edward Carson during one of his frequent trips to Craigavon. She was fulsome in her praise of Ulster Volunteers, especially during one parade in the grounds of Belfast Castle:

> It was a perfect summer's day, cloudless sky, and no wind, and the Castle stands on the side of Cave Hill, with its fir-clad slopes as a background, and its wild perpendicular crags rising sheer above it, cut clear against the deep blue sky. In front, the ground drops to the Lough, which stretched calm, and misty blue, away to the open sea. No one who wasn't there can realise the feeling it gave one to see those thousands of men, with their heads bowed, while the prayers were offered up, to join in 'O God our help in ages past', and to see them marching past, old men and boys, rich men and poor men, side by side, all cheerfully ready to sacrifice themselves for the cause they hold so dear. I longed so to be marching with them.[59]

Edward Carson also received a considerable number of offers of help from aristocratic women in Britain, who were prepared to assist not only with political advocacy of Ulster's case and fund-raising, but also in organising social relief and medical assistance for the anticipated casualties of an Ulster conflict. The duchess of Somerset informed the IUP leader that she had 'undertaken to house 100 women and children from Ulster'. In assuring him of the large volume of support for his movement in England, she inferred that the complex and intricate nature of Irish politics and the Home Rule legislation was proving to be a difficult obstacle. She wrote that it was 'not for want of sympathy on this side the fight is so uphill at the moment, but from the fatigue of the people to comprehend more legislation'.[60]

Men of law and letters

There were many advocates of the legal and constitutional illegitimacy of the proposed Home Rule legislation. The most prominent were the veteran constitutionalist professor A.V. Dicey and the pro-Ulster peer the earl of Selborne. Dicey had made his reputation during the second half of the Victorian era, when he had been most vocal in his denunciation of Gladstone's proposed Home Rule legislation. Although an old man in 1912, he was still active in his opposition to Home Rule, publishing a critique, *A fool's paradise*, in 1913. Extracts of this, along with Dicey's analysis, were later serialised in *The Times*. Arguing that the bill would 'work great evil to England' and the rest of Britain, he maintained that it would 'fail to maintain the supremacy of the Imperial Parliament'. Interestingly, Dicey drew attention to the negative repercussions Home Rule would have on England, before he proceeded to support the plight of Ulster unionists in particular. Criticising Asquith and his colleagues – 'the dupes of credulous optimism' – he concluded that the legislation would 'not maintain in Ireland the true supremacy of the imperial parliament from the burden of considering Irish affairs' and that, further, it would 'not conciliate Ireland'.[61] Later in this booklet, Dicey turned to the Ulster unionists, who were protesting against the 'double injustice' of being deprived of their British citizenship and being forced to acknowledge a Dublin parliament 'to which they owed no allegiance'. Dicey suggested that, in placating Irish nationalists with their Home Rule promises, British politicians would later encounter even more pronounced difficulties from Irish Unionists at Westminster. He postulated:

The men of Ulster ask for nothing more than to enjoy, under the constitution of the United Kingdom, the full rights of citizenship. If this claim is denied them they may well turn into the most vigorous and the most bitter of Irish Nationalists. During the whole Home Rule controversy far too much has been said about Irish nature and far too little has been thought about human nature. Ulstermen, treated with gross injustice, will not be the allies of England which has wronged them. Assume, if you like, that Home Rule may, from one point of view, lighten for the Parliament at Westminster the burden of Irish affairs, though personally, I dispute the truth of the assumption. It will, from another point of view, stir the energy and increase the bitterness of Irish intrigue.[62]

As George Boyce has pointed out, for Dicey the 'moral, if not legal, check upon Westminster over-ruling an Irish Parliament was a significant invasion of British sovereignty'. Stressing the need for a general election on the Home Rule issue, and predicting a landslide verdict condemning the measure, Dicey maintained that such a mandate was necessary if 'constitutional authority' was to be restored.[63] Dicey was supremely confident that if the electorate was sufficiently informed about what was at stake – 'whether the UK is morally a nation, and whether as a nation it has a right to insist upon the supreme authority belonging to the majority of its citizens' – the outcome of such an election would inevitably be the clear rejection of Home Rule.

Yet A.V. Dicey did have reservations about Ulster's resistance to Home Rule and it posed for him a dilemma that he shared with many British constitutionalists and lawyers. This was that passive resistance to a Dublin parliament (such as refusing to pay taxes to such an institution) or such extra-parliamentary strategies as the Covenant would rapidly be replaced by resistance of a more physical, or rebellious, kind. He thus hesitated for a while before signing the British Covenant and was concerned by the deep threats posed by army mutiny and gun-running. Despite such dilemmas and confusion, the fact that Dicey, 'the foremost legal and constitutional expert of the day', was so perturbed that Ulster's attempts to 'save the Constitution might end up, if not destroying, then certainly undermining it, showed how far Unionists had advanced into a revolutionary situation'.[64]

Another influential figure highly motivated by the constitutional and legal detail of Irish Home Rule was Lord Salisbury's son-in-law, the second earl of Selborne.[65] Whilst sharing a similar imperialist background to men like Alfred Milner, Lord Selborne had a less emotive and more cerebral justification for his opposition to Home Rule and was reluctant to pursue the physical-force approach of so-called 'backwoodsmen' like Willoughby de Broke or Milner. This contrast between those peers more likely to contemplate a violent outcome in Ulster and those trying to avoid such a path was evident in a letter that Milner wrote to Selborne in February 1914. Criticising those who had dismissed the idea of 'a British Pledge' (the British Covenant), Milner maintained that such sceptics should 'suggest something better' which would produce more 'effective aid' for those at the front line in Ulster. He went on to denounce Selborne's reluctance to become involved in a civil-war scenario in Ulster:

> It is quite true, as you say, that many of us, with the best will in the world, may have no chance of doing anything. But it is also true that many chances will be missed, if people are not on the look out for them, and have not realised that it is their duty to try and find some work for the cause.[66]

Selborne's overriding objection to Home Rule was his belief that it was, without direct electoral endorsement, an unconstitutional measure. A strong supporter of the monarchy and the House of Lords (he organised the Halsbury Club, a Tory pressure group campaigning against 'single-chamber tyranny'),

Selborne had no doubt that the British electorate would repudiate such legislative and constitutional proposals. He was constant in his pleas in the Tory-leaning newspapers and in his correspondence with fellow peers, especially those on the government benches, for an election to be declared on the issue. Writing to the foreign secretary, Sir Edward Grey, in April 1914, Lord Selborne conceded that the government could 'crush Ulster with the Army and Fleet', but pointed out that it would be 'at the cost of thousands of lives'. He reminded Grey that, until an election had been conducted, 'no party really knows its final strength in this controversy or what force of opinion it represents', and that to proceed with the Home Rule legislation without such an election would lead to conflict in Ulster.[67] Selborne's strong opinions on 'our obligation of honour to Ulster' and an 'absorbing belief in the necessity for the federation of the Empire' were, however, held in check by an equally fundamental commitment to abide by the law. Reminding Thomas Comyn-Platt in September 1912 that it was 'always wrong to take up arms', Selborne suggested that civil war was 'the ultima ratio and the last party in the world that ought to turn to arms if it can possibly avoid it or go outside legal and constitutional forms is the Conservative and Unionist Party'.[68]

Although, like most Conservative politicians, Lord Selborne's views on Ulster's vulnerable position were generally sympathetic, he did become vehemently opposed to his party's subsequent acceptance of exclusion, either for Ulster as a whole or for part of it. Representative of many Tory peers who were concerned that, by focusing all their attention on Ulster, unionists in the rest of Ireland were in danger of being abandoned by their erstwhile supporters in Great Britain, Selborne expressed his concern at the stance adopted by his party leadership over Ulster exclusion in 1914. Writing to Austen Chamberlain that summer, Selborne confided:

I could never follow Bonar Law in accepting the present Government of Ireland Bill with the complete exclusion of the six Ulster counties as a final settlement of the Irish constitutional question (even if I thought it would work, which I don't), and I cannot conceive it possible that Redmond either should accept it as a final settlement.[69]

A federalist at heart, Selborne was keen for a revision of the British constitution. Though he started to doubt the degree to which a Conservative administration, in the event that they achieved an electoral mandate, might resist Home Rule, Selborne held on to his principle that they should continue to try to amend the pending legislation.

Cultural celebrities of the day, including Edward Elgar and Rudyard Kipling, were to the fore in championing Ulster's cause. Few men could have had greater claim to national, or indeed international, reknown than Rudyard Kipling.[70] Kipling was at the peak of his fame during the Edwardian era and had been fortunate enough to have amassed a fortune by an early stage of his writing career. A strong supporter of the Conservative Party and its leader, Bonar Law, Kipling had flirted with the notion of becoming a Tory MP and had turned down the offer of a safe Conservative seat. He was also friends with influential people and had the ear of many Fleet Street editors, especially H.A. Gwynne, in whose *Morning Post* Kipling's work often featured. His poem, published in the *Post* on Covenant Day in September 1912, won considerable praise from loyalists but provoked Joseph Martin, a Radical MP, to ask the attorney-general to prosecute the poet on grounds of sedition. In typically bullish fashion, Kipling invited Conservative MPs to quote lines or stanzas from the poem in order to disrupt the government's parliamentary business. Rudyard Kipling encouraged his friend Gwynne not to contemplate 'any compromise on any point' regarding Home Rule. To Kipling, the only choice was between civil war and the government dropping its bill – as otherwise 'we lose the game!' He explained:

If by any means the present Government can be visibly shown that Home Rule is more dangerous to its own hides and positions than leaving it alone would be, they will leave it alone ... It's a naked trial of strength that is forced on us and all the talking in the world won't make it anything else. For goodness sake stick to that line, old man. If we fight we may win. If we don't fight we MUST lose![71]

Kipling's position on Ulster was more akin to that of his old friend Alfred Milner than Bonar Law. He adopted a position of 'no compromise' on Home Rule in general, including a refusal to consider the option of exclusion, originally proposed by Carson. Kipling became increasingly obsessed with the Irish crisis, especially as it deepened during 1913 and the first half of 1914. He offered his support in a variety of ways. These included writing poems and articles for sympathetic newspapers like the *Morning Post* and for Milner's magazine, the *Covenanter*, seeking to counsel the key politicians involved in the crisis, speaking at political demonstrations and even offering generous donations to Ulster unionist organisations (Kipling, along with other wealthy supporters of Ulster – including Waldorf Astor, Lord Rothschild and the duke of Bedford – promised Milner a contribution of £30,000 in March 1914).

Kipling's attraction to Ulster emanated from his own strong advocacy of imperialism. Combining a natural disdain for nationalist Ireland – he dismissed John Redmond's movement as one associated with 'boycott, intimidation, outrage and murder' – with a dismissive view of the Liberal government, which for Kipling consisted of 'outlaws' and 'conspirators' and was generally 'corrupt', he considered that Ulster was a test case not only for Ireland but also for the security of the United Kingdom and, indeed, the British empire. Speaking on an anti-Home Rule platform in Tunbridge Wells in May 1914, he identified betrayal as being at the centre of Liberal motivation. He told an audience estimated at over 10,000:

> A province and a people of Great Britain are to be sold to their and our enemies. We are forbidden to have any voice in this sale of our own flesh and blood; we have no tribunal under Heaven to appeal to except the corrupt parties to that sale and their paid followers ... Civil war is inevitable unless our rulers can be brought to realise that, even now, they must submit these grave matters to the judgement of a free people. If they do not, all the history of our island shows that there is but one end – destruction from within or without.[72]

On the eve of war in Europe, Kipling seemed reconciled to the prospect of civil war in Ireland, and Carrie, his wife, was preparing clothing for anticipated Ulster refugees.

'I can ride and shoot'

The Ulster unionist cause attracted extremists and diehards, and none was more obvious than the quixotic Lord Willoughby de Broke.[73] He was a radical Tory and a symbol of reaction in that most reactionary of institutions in Edwardian Britain, the House of Lords. To the fore in denouncing the Parliament Bill, Willoughby de Broke was also keen to be heavily involved in what he regarded as a clear-cut, practical cause – the destruction of Asquith's Home Rule Bill – and was not interested in alternatives or hints of compromise, such as the federalist option or exclusion for Ulster. In an amusing description of the 'genial and sporting young peer', George Dangerfield recalled that de Broke's face 'bore a pleasing resemblance to the horse', and sardonically added that, in his trenchant views, which were non-negotiable, the peer was 'not more than 200 years behind his time'.[74]

Especially with regard to his interventions on Home Rule – his proposed House of Lords amendment to the Home Rule Bill, his provocative letters to Tory-leaning newspapers, his virulent speeches on public platforms in support of Ulster and his tireless organisation of the British League – Willoughby de Broke soon became a thorn in the flesh of the Tory leadership. Increasingly, Bonar Law and his colleagues became embarrassed by de Broke and gradually distanced themselves from him as the threat of splits within the Conservative Party over Ireland became more real. He was a frequent letter writer to his party leader and in September 1913 reminded Andrew Bonar Law that the party should 'focus public attention in England on the fact that Englishmen are as much concerned in the Repeal of [the] Union as are the Ulstermen, and that in the absence of the old Constitution, the only thing left is physical force'.[75]

Lord Willoughby de Broke's support for Ulster was unconditional. In a letter to the *Morning Post* he expressed many of his views on Ulster:

> On every count Ulster should be supported by British Unionists. But we of the rank and file must make ready to support her with something more strenuous than speech-making ... The Ulstermen have shown us that there are still things which neither money nor a majority can settle. They will never surrender ... a civil war is not going to be avoided by any weakening towards Ulster on the part of British Unionism ... For my own part I shall volunteer for active service in the event of his Majesty's Government deciding to coerce men and women whose only offence is that they wish to remain inside the British Constitution, and I have little doubt that many other Unionists will do the same.[76]

Worried about the possibility of a variety of 'backdoor deals' over the Home Rule Bill as it made rapid progress in the houses of parliament, Willoughby de Broke wrote to his fellow Conservative peers in January 1914, asking for their support in opposing a compromise solution to the Irish political problem before a general election was called.[77] Along with fellow peers Lords Arran, Ampthill and Stanhope, Willoughby de Broke's proposed amendment regretted the government's failure to obtain 'the sanction of the Nation before carrying into law grave changes in the Constitution'. They maintained that if unionist peers were to abandon Irish unionists before a general election was held, it would constitute 'an act of betrayal, the consequences of which would be felt for generations, and might indeed lead to the very conflict that we all of us desire to avoid'.[78]

In the fortnight before the amendment was discussed in the House of Lords, several unionist peers either voiced their support for Willoughby de Broke's tough stance or conceded their apprehension about Tory peers aligning themselves with armed Ulster Volunteers and therefore seeming to act rashly on the issue before the government had responded to the latest demands for an election, ahead of Sir Edward Carson's own proposals. For instance, Lord Northumberland wrote to de Broke on 7 February 1914 opposing the arming of Ulster Volunteers, and Lord Stanhope hesitated about backing civil war in the event of an international war breaking out.[79]

Some of de Broke's closest colleagues, like Lords Ampthill and Arran, were later to fall out with their fellow critic over the issue of exclusion.[80] In condemning the exclusion option as 'an outrageous suggestion that the Unionist Party should thus be invited to share responsibility for the consequences of passing the Home Rule Bill', this group of aristocratic Tory diehards were at odds with the leadership of the party and Edward Carson himself, who had by this stage accepted that the election option was the only card left in the loyalist pack.[81]

In his lengthy amendment proposal speech in the House of Lords on 10 February 1914, Willoughby de Broke criticised leading Liberal ministers like the foreign secretary, Sir Edward Grey, for a Commons speech that 'deliberately' sustained 'the present state of tension in the hope of inciting these men in Ulster to some act or other which might be construed as an act of insubordination or riot', which in turn would necessitate military intervention.[82] Willoughby de Broke's final onslaught against Grey was to suggest that 'if that is the kind of language and attitude he adopts [for] foreign nations, it is more by good luck than good management he has got through all the foreign difficulties we have had the last few years'.[83] Other parts of de Broke's long appeal to fellow peers criticised the proposed military engagement in Ulster and the suggested exclusion of Ulster from Home Rule. His reasoning was that 'if the electors have not agreed to this Bill, they certainly can not have agreed to what is virtually a totally new Bill for the exclusion of Ulster'. In conclusion, Willoughby de Broke demanded that electors should have the opportunity to ratify any legislation and summarised his own views on the bill and its proponents. Admitting that the Third Home Rule Bill campaign was 'nearer to success than any other', he pointed out that it had 'lesser men behind it' than previous campaigns, which had involved leaders like Parnell and Gladstone. He ended by saying that the bill had been 'supported by more dishonest methods, and is a baser political conspiracy than has ever been attempted to break up the unity of the United Kingdom'.[84]

Willoughby de Broke's extra-parliamentary contribution to the Ulster cause was even more forceful than his back-bench parliamentary interventions. He wanted to galvanise support in Britain against the proposed legislation and a new group which he chaired, the BLSUU, joined forces with other pro-union groups by vowing to combat apathy in Britain and to collect vital campaign revenue. In March 1913, a letter from de Broke appeared in the national press, announcing the formation of the British League, with its headquarters in Ryder Street near St James's Park. In this, he appealed to 'all British citizens who sympathise with Ulster and who value their own freedom to join the above League that has been formed to support the men of Ulster in the great struggle that lies before them'.[85] It quickly won the backing of close to 200 peers, including the duke of Bedford, Lord Castlereagh and Lord Charles Beresford, as well as some 120 MPs. Its ranks also contained many serving and retired army officers. Two parliamentarians served in influential positions within the league. A confidant of Sir Edward Carson's, Thomas Comyn-Platt, took on the role of secretary, whilst Colonel T.E. Hickman, an ex-army officer and Tory MP, served on the pressure group's executive committee. The league attracted the attention of disgruntled right-wingers and ex-military men, and inside nine months it claimed a membership of 10,000.

The BLSUU appealed to male Britons' sense of patriotism and their fundamental desire that national and imperial unity be maintained, rather than simply calling for support for Ulster. This patriotic appeal was reflected in songs composed by its members, including 'Ulster and the union' (sung to the tune of 'John Brown's body') and 'Men of Ulster'. As many as 400 agents were employed at local level across Britain, as the group focused on the double mission of organising pro-Ulster meetings up and down the country and collecting funds at local level. Many pro-Ulster rallies were organised by de Broke, Platt and their colleagues. Apart from the key meetings and speeches of leading political figures in key cities at this time, local BLSUU groups were not forgotten. By the early summer of 1914, there was at least one BLSUU rally a week in places like Oxford, Surbiton, Liverpool and Mountain Ash in south Wales. The new organisation stressed its classless nature. A reporter was told by league officials in west London that thousands of new members had enrolled, including men who 'represent all classes of the community' and funding was 'also doing well', with subscriptions ranging from '£500 to sixpence-worth of stamps'.[86]

Although the BLSUU was, at least initially, more concerned about 'spreading the word' about Ulster, they were soon openly supporting more 'practical' help. With the formation and drilling in Ulster of the Volunteers and open talk of gun-smuggling towards the end of 1913, Willoughby de Broke made a further plea in papers like *The Times* and *Morning Post* for 'men who have been trained to bear arms and who have been accustomed both to command and to obey' to join the league's ranks.[87] In his League 'manifesto', Willoughby de Broke reminded British people that Ulster's need for meaningful support was urgent as 'we are in sight of civil war'.[88] Over the next few months, many of the league's branches were actively involved in drilling and physical-fitness classes, and senior figures such as Hickman were advising the UVF in their appointments of senior officers and in their wider military preparations. Undoubtedly much of the money raised by the British League went towards financing the arms shipment brought in from Germany in early 1914. (Indeed, one senior BLSUU figure, Sir William Bull, was implicated in an earlier arms raid in west London.) Certainly, it was likely that most of the league's new recruits had not regarded the movement as a mere talking shop. A Birmingham agent for the league wrote to de Broke on the eve of Edward Carson's visit to the city's ambiguously titled New Street branch, the Ulster Athletic Club. W.H. Nightingale informed the peer that the branch had held its first public meeting the previous week, when the organisation's principles were endorsed with 'hearty unanimity' by those present and a local committee was formed. Drill was to commence under the direction of two military men. Nightingale ended his letter:

> I have long been of [the] opinion that nothing but a strong display of force in Great Britain will influence Mr Redmond in the least. We will show him that in this district we can raise in a few weeks 1,000 soldiers of civil and religious liberty. The time for mere talk is about over.[89]

The main protagonists within the British League needed little persuasion in adopting such an aggressive approach. At the height of the Curragh crisis, Willoughby de Broke wrote to General Richardson, the UVF's commanding officer, reminding him that he could 'ride and shoot' and would be prepared to 'serve in the ranks, or [do] any duty you wish'.[90] Two days later he received a reply from Richardson's aide, Captain Frank Hall. In this, the peer's offer of active support was gratefully acknowledged but it was made clear that Richardson favoured de Broke 'remaining at the head of the British League'. He told the peer, 'you can be of more assistance to us in England than over here at the present moment, where everything is working smoothly and well'.[91]

This reply from the Ulster Volunteer leadership points to the increasing strain between them and the BLSUU, who increasingly believed that their brothers in arms across the Irish Sea were not taking them seriously enough. Major Fred Crawford had, in face-to-face meetings with the league in England, rejected their offer of men rather than arms, at a time when they had greater need for the former. Relations between the BLSUU and the UVF cooled so much that de Broke's lieutenant, Comyn-Platt, wrote to UUC Secretary R.D. Bates asking him to 'put a brake' on Captain Hall and the UVF, despairing of their perception that 'all the idiots in the Universe are lodged at 25, Ryder Street' (the BLSUU's London headquarters).[92]

In a sense, the influence of the BLSUU on the Tory leadership more than its practical support for unionists in Ulster was that organisation's main legacy. Thomas Kennedy has maintained that it was de Broke's eccentricity and single-mindedness that helped make him such a central figure in the Conservative Party's struggle against Home Rule. De Broke 'would stand his ground and fight' a number of disparate forces. These included the 'coalition of radical wreckers, the Conservative Party leadership ... and if need be, against Ulster Protestants unwilling, in spirit or in arms, to sustain their struggle'. Kennedy also reminds us that the 'radical right's ironical and impossible rush to support a clash whose final objectives they staunchly repudiated' crystallised the chasm between the 'pragmatic if perilous' unionism of Bonar Law and the 'value-laden, absolutist, old Toryism of Willoughby de Broke'.[93] Yet Jeremy

Smith has been quick to point out that Lord Willoughby de Broke's BLSUU sent out 'a clear warning to their [Tory] leaders against compromise'. Smith maintains that, 'far from being a dangerous company of extremists', the BLSSU 'actually worked to control matters by channelling right wing frustration' into a structure and cause. In doing so, the league 'performed for the Tory right what the Covenant did for the wilder elements within the northern Protestant community'.[94]

British Covenanters

Viscount Alfred Milner, a former high commissioner for South Africa and a leading spokesman for imperial issues in the House of Lords, had been relatively muted in his support for Ulster's loyalists during the early stages of the anti-Home Rule campaign.[95] However, as he became increasingly convinced both that Ulster was the key to dismantling Asquith's bill and that its loyal proponents in Ulster had to be fully supported in the eventuality of civil war, his stance rapidly hardened. In October 1913 he confidently predicted that the 'diehard' opposition of Ulster unionists would bring about a political 'deadlock', which he believed would prove to be 'the one thing that can save us'.[96] Within weeks he had written to Edward Carson, requesting a meeting and confessing his utter frustration with the nihilism of British party politics. What he desired was an opportunity to galvanise widespread support for what he believed constituted a worthier, cross-party cause. Admitting he was 'completely in accord with [Carson] about Ulster', Alfred Milner argued that pro-union forces should combine to prevent an imminent Ulster 'rebellion', which he believed was inevitable 'inside the year'. Milner suggested that, if unionists could be organised and proactive in their interventions, they would be able to 'paralyse the arm which might be raised to strike'.[97] Lord Milner was certainly genuine in his offer of support, even suggesting he could be Carson's replacement in Britain if Carson was arrested while campaigning in Ireland.

Milner soon canvassed the support of existing pressure groups like the UDL and Willoughby de Broke's BLSUU. Supported by the capable South Birmingham Conservative MP, Leo Amery, Alfred Milner dedicated himself to the massive task of orchestrating a British mainland movement that would directly appeal to public opinion on the plight of Ulster. His hope was that an overwhelmingly positive public response would force Asquith into staging the general election demanded by all groups on the political right. He was soon active in gaining practical support from the UDL (a sub-committee was set up towards the end of February in order to liaise with Milner's organisation), the BLSUU, leading players and 'conduits' like Lady Londonderry, and guarded approval from party leader Andrew Bonar Law. Milner was concerned both about recruiting leading names in British society and reaching ordinary people at grassroots level.

Inspired by the success of Edward Carson's Covenant campaign in Ulster some 18 months before, Alfred Milner opted for a British equivalent: a pledge of support for Ulster. Writing to the earl of Selborne in January 1914, Alfred Milner expressed his conviction that such a pledge would transcend political alignments and appeal directly to the individual citizen's sense of fair play. Milner wrote:

> for when before, in our lifetime, have thousands upon thousands of sober, steady-going citizens deliberately contemplated resistance to an Act of Parliament, because they sincerely believed it was devoid of all moral sanction? There are a great many people who still fail entirely to realise what the strength of our feeling is on this subject.[98]

This was publicised in large sections of the British press at the start of March. Arguing that the successful passage of the Home Rule Bill would 'plunge this kingdom into civil turmoil without parallel in living memory', Milner and his associates in the new British Covenant movement argued that, as Home Rule violated the British constitution, its citizens would be justified in 'taking or supporting any action that may be effective to prevent it being put into operation, and more particularly to prevent the armed forces of the crown being used to deprive the people of Ulster of their rights as citizens of the United Kingdom'.[99]

Signatures for the British Covenant were harnessed by the various political groups, especially the UDL and the BLSUU, at designated times and meeting places publicised in sympathetic newspapers and, of course, at political demonstrations such as Milner's spectacular meeting in Hyde Park a few weeks later. The UDL were actively engaged in harnessing interested groups and individuals, moving to larger premises in London's Victoria Street. Although the British Covenant organisers emphasised the fact that the pledge had gained the support of many leading members of British society, it was more significant that it had cross-class appeal. The *Morning Post* noted 'the rush for forms to sign', and pointed out that 'the demand comes from men and women of all ranks and situations of life'.[100] An equivalent pledge for women was designed and the popularity of the petition was especially strong in the south of England (including London's financial quarter) and in Wales. Alfred Milner was conscious about the need to obtain the names of the leading lights of British society – aristocrats and politicians, leading businessmen, key figures from the world of arts, academia and the law, the City and leaders of the armed forces – as this would bring in considerable revenue, as well as encouraging people at local level to follow their lead.

Signatories to the Ulster pledge included General Roberts, Viscount Halifax, Sir E. Seymour (admiral of the fleet), Rudyard Kipling, Sir Edward Elgar, Waldorf Astor, Lord Rothschild and Professor A.V. Dicey. Many of these distinguished and wealthy men also provided generous financial backing for the British Covenant movement, some of which undoubtedly helped Major Crawford to procure thousands of German rifles in April.

Pledges of financial support were given by Astor and Kipling (both of these men offered in the region of £30,000, a vast sum in 1914) and by Lords Rothschild and Iveagh (both of whom offered around £10,000). Offers of help also came in from across the world. Different sorts of practical help were promised by Orangemen across Canada, with over a thousand of them pledging to help Ulster loyalists in the event of a civil war. In London, Constance Bloomfield planned to establish an ambulance corps for injured Volunteers and other likely conflict victims. By the end of July 1914, Milner and Amery were able to boast that their efforts had resulted in nearly two million signatures being received for the British pledge.

For Lord Milner, the Ulster 'crusade' would be put on hold when war was declared in the summer of 1914. Although it appears that he had underestimated the scale of his proposed enterprise – he admitted to Willoughby de Broke in March that 'this Covenant business is assuming enormous proportions' – he was plainly satisfied that the movement's efforts had 'given a good shake to the alleged apathy of the public'.[101] Indeed, at the height of the Buckingham Palace discussions in July, Milner wrote to Edward Carson, complaining about the 'eel' Asquith and his reluctance to 'take a definite stand'. Urging the 'Man at the Wheel' to 'stick out for the six counties as a minimum', Alfred Milner claimed that, on account of their failure to rely on the army and their reluctance to call an election, Asquith and his administration were in 'a weak position'. He reassured Carson by saying, 'If we stick our toes in the ground, I don't see what they can do but give way to us or else go blindly to destruction.'[102]

Milner recognised the need to create a magazine designed to inform and educate members and sympathisers of the British Covenant movement. Its first (and, to my knowledge, only) edition duly appeared on 20 May 1914. The *Covenanter*'s contents included a guide to forthcoming meetings and demonstrations against Home Rule, the first appearance in print of Rudyard Kipling's poem, 'The Covenant', a direct appeal by Edward Carson to British sympathisers to support his mission in Ulster, an article by Alfred Milner justifying the British Covenant, articles condemning the government's 'great conspiracy' over the Curragh incident (written by Leo Amery), a historical insight into Scotland's own covenant experience nearly 300 years previously (by leading Nonconformist minister Rev. W.L. Watkinson), photos of the recent Hyde Park rally and cartoons relating to the main events of the crisis.

A big task of the British Covenant leadership was to persuade more people who shared their broad political perspective to support their pro-Ulster campaign more actively. In his appeal in the *Covenanter* for mainland pledges of support for Ulster loyalists, Edward Carson reminded his readers that 'the cause for which they [Ulster unionists] stand is not theirs alone', but 'the cause of the whole Kingdom, as it was in 1690'.[103] As an aid for enticing such support, the *Covenanter* asked a series of prominent people, including knights of the realm, bishops and university professors, why they had signed the British Covenant.[104] One of these alumuni, Professor Stanley Lane-Poole, claimed that Ulster's 'mistrust' of the creation of an Irish administration was 'justified'. Lane-Poole condemned a situation where 'loyal subjects' were being asked to accept 'a rule which they resent'.[105] The *Covenanter* also appealed to British workers for 'a fair hearing to the arguments of Protestant trade-unionists in Ulster'. In an article entitled 'Labour's appeal to labour', the claims of the Radical and socialist press that Ulster's resistance to Home Rule was 'an aristocratic plot' were denounced and an appeal was made to British trade unionists 'not to desert us in the present crisis'.[106]

In his own article, 'The British Covenant', Alfred Milner set out his rationale for supporting Ulster. He started by dismissing notions that the British Covenant committed signatories into 'offer[ing] forcible resistance' to the implementation of the terms of the Home Rule Bill, and also maintained that it constituted 'much more than a mere protest against the Home Rule Bill or against the coercion of Ulster'.[107] Insisting that a Covenanter had to be 'an active propagandist in his daily life', Milner acknowledged the potential dilemma facing British supporters of Ulster, who simply wanted to know 'how they can effectively help their fellow citizens in Ireland whom they regard as the victims of tyranny'. Indeed, he stressed that British sympathisers to Ulster's position actually held pole position in a potentially pleasing (from the unionist perspective) solution to the crisis. Thus, Lord Milner concluded that 'the best that we can hope is that the rising tide of popular disapproval in Great Britain, which British Covenanters must continue to do all in their power to swell, will deter the Government from proceeding to extremes'.[108]

There had been plans to organise a pro-Ulster meeting in Liverpool, but increasing sectarian tension on Merseyside forced Alfred Milner, the UDL and their co-organisers, the BLSUU and the Primrose League, to stage a mass rally against Home Rule and the government's handling of the recent Curragh crisis in London's Hyde Park. The meeting took place on Saturday, 4 April and was considered by some to have been not only the most impressive exhibition of support for Ulster in Great Britain during this period, but also the largest demonstration of popular political protest for some 60 years. The short notice of the meeting and the already crowded diaries of Tory and Irish Unionist Party leaders resulted in a relative shortage of available top-rank speakers. However, some leading lights within unionism, including Edward Carson, Walter Long and Alfred Milner, did speak at this meeting. The organisers chose 22 convenient meeting points for demonstrators to commence their march to Cleopatra's Needle and Hyde Park. The anticipated opposition from suffragettes and Labour Party supporters was, despite a few minor skirmishes, muted and restricted to the fringes of the park. Though some wild estimates of the crowd in London were given – the *Belfast Telegraph* estimated this to have been close to half a million – it is likely that the number present in Hyde Park and its environs that afternoon was in the region of 100,000 to 150,000.

Milner's organisation of the Hyde Park proceedings was masterly. Fourteen platforms had been erected, forming a huge circle between the Serpentine and Bayswater Road. Bands accompanied the marchers, who came from across England and also from a range of social classes. City stockbrokers marched alongside dockers. Groups representing the BLSUU, the Primrose League and the British Covenant movement were to the fore; press accounts and photographs confirm that there were contingents from Kent (including 500 from Sevenoaks), Wiltshire, Sussex (including 300 from Eastbourne) and strong representation from London's boroughs (including deputations from Chelsea – featuring some Chelsea Pensioners – Walworth, Battersea, Hoxton and outer districts).

The large crowd of marchers and supporters were entertained by patriotic tunes played by the bands and the predominant image of the day was the hundreds of Union Jacks waving in the enormous crowd, many of whom were wearing red, white and blue badges appealing to bystanders to 'support loyal Ulster'. Speakers requested support for the Covenant petition and, although there were few memorable speeches that afternoon in Hyde Park, the *Belfast Telegraph* was not alone in estimating the demonstration to have been the equal of Covenant Day in Belfast, 18 months earlier.[109] Towards the end of the afternoon, resolutions were unanimously passed, including one directly protesting against the recent 'use of the navy and army to drive out by force of arms our fellow-subjects in Ireland from their full heritage in the Parliament of the United Kingdom'.[110] Another resolution demanded 'the subjection of this grave issue to the people'. A 'roar like that of breaking waves' accompanied the passing of these resolutions.[111] Reporters noted both the earnestness of most of the crowd and their shared sense of fun, despite the showers that scattered many spectators during the lengthy speeches. Writing in the

Daily Mail, Hamilton Fyfe declared that witnessing these events had resulted in 'a hallucination that I was in Ulster again' and that it had only been 'with effort' that he had 'recollected that these were Londoners'. Noting the presence of many 'non partisan folk' who did 'not care for the purely party speeches', Fyfe reported the constant calls from within the crowd for Carson to salute his English admirers.[112]

Unionist papers were unanimous in their assessment of the mood of the Hyde Park multitude. The *Morning Post* gushed that the event, in terms of the dignity of the participants and its sheer scale, proved 'beyond doubt or challenge, the reality of the sympathy kindled in the hearts of the people for Ulster's resistance to Home Rule'.[113] The *Belfast Telegraph* went even further in its euphoric analysis of events in London the previous weekend. Claiming that 'in all its history' London had 'never beheld a sight as that witnessed in Hyde Park', the paper's editorial proceeded to suggest that it had proved to be the 'hugest gathering of people that has ever assembled in London for a common purpose'.[114] It concluded by declaring that the capital of the British empire had 'in such striking and unmistakeable fashion told the world on Saturday that they detest and repudiate and will help to resist the attempt to dragoon Ulster into submission'.[115] There was less enthusiasm in Liberal tabloids, with the *Daily Chronicle* noting the 'strange absence' of London's workers. The paper maintained that the rally was mostly composed of 'society people' who had to 'run the gauntlet of the bus conductor's wit'.[116]

The Hyde Park rally afforded an opportunity to a much larger British audience than had appeared at Blenheim Palace nearly two years before of participating in a special ceremony that identified with an increasingly popular political cause in Edwardian Britain. It also provided the caucus of unionist groups like the UDL, the British Covenant movement and the BLSUU with a chance to illustrate their unity and cohesion at a climactic stage in the Ulster crisis.

In this section I have outlined the wide-ranging nature and the extent of high-society support for Ulster's unionists during the late Edwardian period. This was clearly evident in Great Britain within the debating chambers of the House of Lords, where the resistance of Ulster was sympathetically received, and by the publicity devoted to pressure groups like the British Covenant movement and Willoughby de Broke's BLSUU. Wealthy and influential aristocrats, a host of knighted gentlemen and leading academic, legal and cultural figures flocked to the cause of Ulster's 'beleagured and loyal' population, bringing a touch of glamour and panache to Carson's otherwise dour movement – a glamour that was certainly absent in subsequent loyal resistance campaigns. Back in Ireland, aristocrats and leading figures in society, although not as prominent in terms of political leadership as they had been during previous campaigns, were to play a major role in lending respectability to Carson's movement. In terms of political influence, this would prove to be the Anglo-Irish aristocracy's last hurrah in Ireland.

'The greatest figure who ever strode down Fleet Street'

In an age before television and instant and universal access to unfolding major events, the need for the press to inform the comparatively unaware British public about the growing crisis in Ulster was of paramount importance. Certainly, the political, economic and religious complexities of the Ulster question presented Fleet Street with increased scope for thumping out the issues of the day, many of which were to rise above the insularities of Irish politics. The nature of the Ulster problem was appropriate for the emerging tabloid press with their desire for 'human' news stories. Moreover, the links between national political parties and parties in Ireland – and, in turn, specific newspapers – meant that both main political strands of the press had a golden opportunity to drive home their party line, often at moments of crisis in Ulster. Above all, the situation in the province was, unlike the static nature of much of the more enduring modern conflict in Northern Ireland, an ongoing and flexible one, with numerous mass meetings, demonstrations and petition signings both in Great Britain and in Ireland. In addition, the increasingly militaristic nature of the Ulster unionist campaign was exemplified by the cloak-and-dagger atmosphere surrounding the gun-running incident in April 1914. By that stage, the whole situation appeared to be rolling towards an inevitably bloody climax, so it was hardly surprising that, whilst it was far from being the only news story to grip the attention of Edwardian Britain, events in Ireland managed to capture more than a fair share of media attention between 1912 and 1914.

The Ulster crisis occurred at a time when the British press was adapting to massive changes in newspaper style, content and circulation. Newspaper editors in Edwardian Britain endeavoured to present the key stories of the day in a more entertaining and less dry manner, but at the same time ensured that the journal's political perspective was unambiguously transmitted to the reader. This resistance to simply being used as a vehicle for the regurgitation of political leaders' speeches and party doggerel was generally reflected in press coverage of the Ulster crisis. Although individual papers' partisan political lines were evident, it also showed that the press was endeavouring to analyse events and political developments. Sympathetic unionist editors would further the cause of both the Conservative Party and the Irish Unionist Party by the hard-hitting tone of editorials, by lampooning government ministers and nationalist leaders in regular cartoons, by including regular photographic accounts of Ulster's resolute leaders and defiant Volunteers and by affording space for a wide range of unionist supporters to air their views in support of the endangered Ulster unionists.

Undoubtedly the Ulster unionist cause also benefited from the relative decline of the Radical press during the last quarter of the nineteenth century. The militaristic and dramatic nature of the ever-deepening Ulster crisis – with its overt imperialistic undertones – clearly resonated with a newspaper readership that had quadrupled between 1896 and 1914. Without question, this degree of press expansion made the Edwardians 'better informed and better entertained than any previous generation'.[117] In addition, the growing belief that warfare was 'fun', 'exciting' and a 'thrilling' experience for 'both participant and spectator' – a public response very much in evidence during the early phase of the Great War – may well have given an extra edge to the British public's reaction to paramilitarism amongst Ulster loyalists.[118] Standards of literacy had improved (thanks to the introduction of universal elementary education in 1870); a large increase had been seen in the readership and circulation of newspapers; working-class men were increasingly interested in the political process (a fact reflected by the presence of the vast majority of them on electoral registers); and newspapers were being presented in a more attractive way. This included the common usage of photography by 1912 (the *Daily Mirror* had been, in 1904, the first paper to use photos). These factors all combined to ensure that it would be obligatory for the leadership of a mass movement like the anti-Home Rule campaign to maximise the potential of 'sympathetic ears' in the national press. Thus, Edward Carson, Andrew Bonar Law and other leading Ulster unionist and Tory figures regularly met with sympathetic newspaper owners and editors. In this Edwardian era, politicians were obliged to ask favours of press magnates and editors, often confiding in them, fully aware that the views or news, if not the actual source, would be revealed.

The Edwardian era proved to be a halcyon period for newspaper proprietors and editors, whose increased assertiveness accompanied their greater independence. The names of these editors and owners (some men combined the two roles for decades) were often synonymous with their journals. Therefore, C.P. Scott ('Great Scott') was editor and owner of the *Manchester Guardian* for over 40 years; A. Gardiner was editor of the Radical paper *Daily News*; J.L. Garvin was editor of the Conservative *Observer* and, later, the *Pall Mall Gazette*; and, after the death of the campaigning journalist W.T. Stead on the *Titanic* in April 1912, H.A. Gwynne was editor of the *Morning Post*.

Undoubtedly, the most influential figure in Fleet Street at this time was Alfred Harmsworth, Lord Northcliffe.[119] Later described by Lord Beaverbrook as 'the greatest figure who ever strode down Fleet Street', Harmsworth was unique not only in that he owned the two most significant journals in the land (the *Daily Mail* for its circulation figures and *The Times* for its 'voice'), but also in that he distanced himself from the control of a political party.[120] The views of Harmsworth's papers, normally a mirror image of his own, were usually in agreement with the broad principles of the Conservative Party's Irish policy, but there were occasions when his papers attacked the virulence of unionist language and proposed actions. Although some critics of Harmsworth have suggested he dominated his editors, some could, from time to time, express more empathy with Ulster unionists, whilst their owner expressed his concern that they spent too much time 'leading with this gloomy Irish stuff'.[121] Harmsworth's significant contribution to the anti-Home Rule campaign was his broad, if conditional, support for Ulster's cause. Specifically, he was aware of the potential threat posed by Ulster's resistance to the Home Rule Bill from an early stage. The depth of coverage afforded to what he perceived to be the major domestic crisis during an era of crises was also significant.

Harmsworth was a useful asset to Ulster unionism because of his special position in British journalism and the manner in which he could command the attention of the most senior politicians, including the opponents of Sir Edward Carson's party. In a letter to Winston Churchill during the spring of 1914, in which he espoused the case for Ulster's permanent exclusion,

Harmsworth turned down Churchill's subsequent offer of lunch – 'these are not lunching times' – but instead curtly reminded the first lord of the admiralty of his 'misguided' Home Rule policy:

> Any attempt to overcome the Ulster Protestants will mean Civil War. A tragic aspect of the situation is that the South of Ireland does not particularly want Home Rule. I went into the matter minutely on my last visit, and was surprised at the apathy existing. Your position seems completely out of touch with the real views of the English as well as the Irish peoples.[122]

Whilst Harmsworth influence was pervasive, not everyone was enamoured by his power in the British press. An Irish landowner, writing in the letter page of the *Nation* in 1914, bemoaned that 'the triviality of London is mirrored in its mafficking press, which ... has ceased to be representative of Great Britain. With a few distinguished exceptions the London press is representative only of the income and opinions of Northcliffe.'[123]

A childhood of relative poverty in Dublin and a fortune later gained in London clearly moulded Harmsworth's underlying unionist principles. Yet it would be wrong to imply that he concurred with every Conservative Party reaction to the ongoing Ulster crisis or even with the leading articles of his editors. In particular, he was concerned that his papers were leaning too far towards politicians apparently advocating civil disobedience and law-breaking and that this would lead to civil unrest and the potential engagement of British military force. Harmsworth was especially concerned after Bonar Law's fiery speech in support of Carson at Blenheim in July 1912 and was believed to have had reservations about the threat posed by the Volunteers during the early part of 1914. For instance, *The Times* apparently backtracked on its own support for Bonar Law's stance on Ulster a fortnight before, when it warned that the use of physical force would 'only invalidate Ulster's cause'.[124] A pleased Harmsworth informed Geoffrey Robinson, that paper's editor, that he had 'liked the leader better this morning' and had 'not cared for the violent Ulster language of Bonar Law, Carson and others'.[125]

As political stalemate deepened and the threat of civil war intensified during the spring and early summer of 1914, Harmsworth and his papers continued to supply political backing to Carson and his followers. Indeed, Alfred Harmsworth nailed his colours to the mast by agreeing to write a pro-loyalist article for the *New York Times* in July 1914, clearly intended to 'educate' American readers on the Irish question. In this, Harmsworth contended that there was 'room for two happy, prosperous states in Ireland' and contrasted the 'shrewd and industrious Northern Irish', who were 'by nature better equipped for work than for talk', with their 'charming and poetical' but 'unpractical' southern Irish counterparts. He described the UVF as being 'the last word in military organisation' and a force 'already much larger than that which the South African Boers put into the field in 1899'. Basing his verdict on a recent trip to Ulster just before the outbreak of war in Europe, he went on:

> Apart altogether from their vast stores of ammunition, their night and day signalling system, their automobile transport and great stocks of gasoline, they are equipped with hospitals far ahead of those used by the Japanese in their [recent] war with Russia and their nursing and ambulance arrangements have met with the approval of interested experts from all over the world.[126]

Friends in Fleet Street

Months after the introduction of the Third Home Rule Bill, the new editor of *The Times*, Geoffrey Robinson, wanted to raise the profile of the Ulster question in his newspaper's coverage of

Irish events. In a letter to *Irish Times* editor John Healy in April 1913, Robinson had expressed his perception that the Ulster question was 'falling into the background in England' and that from this 'obscurity' he was 'anxious to rescue it'.[127] Initially, Robinson despatched a relatively inexperienced journalist, J.M. Hone, to Ireland, but felt that his reports during May 1913 lacked genuine authority. He then turned to a more substantial voice, former *Times of India* editor Lovat Fraser. The latter's brief was to sound out how serious Ulster unionists were in their resistance to Home Rule and to compile despatches that would update the paper's readership on the mood of Ulster's loyalists and to help interpret unfolding events. Fraser's output in a relatively short period (some four or five months) was considerable. Aside from his meetings with Irish correspondents, Lovat Fraser also drafted over 20 leading articles on the Irish question during the last quarter of 1913 and start of 1914, and his correspondence with Geoffrey Robinson, though not intended for the public domain, was regarded as providing essential background information for the editorial staff of *The Times* back in London.[128] Fraser regarded his letters to Robinson as a kind of journal, which would inform editorial comment. Relatively unaware of Irish affairs at the start of his tour, Fraser was encouraged by Healy, his Irish host, to conceal the real purpose of his trip. Indeed, he was often introduced, alongside his wife, as being on honeymoon.

An analysis of Fraser's correspondence with Robinson provides us with a fascinating insight into both Fraser's growing awareness of the Ulster situation and the impact of this recent knowledge on his paper's coverage of the Irish question. Shortly before he left for Ireland, Fraser admitted knowing 'nothing' about Ulster, but reassured his editor that he had met the 'mediocre' General Richardson (officer in charge of the newly created Ulster Volunteers) a couple of times during his spell in India. Though admitting 'hate' for the Home Rule proposals, Fraser doubted whether 'solid Englishmen' would 'back up serious rebellion in Ulster and comic opera touches will kill it anyway'.[129] Writing from the Grand Central Hotel in Belfast less than a fortnight later, Fraser informed Robinson that he had visited the Belfast shipyards and, 'masquerading as a tourist with a pair of field-glasses and a wife', observed a demonstration involving the Ulster Volunteers in Armagh, where the streets were 'thronged with marching battalions and swarms of onlookers'. Though he had some reservations about a small minority of the Volunteers, including the relative youth of some company leaders and the fear of Belfast chiefs that 'the present exemplary control may not continue in times of extreme tension', his overall assessment of the force was positive and supportive.[130] He informed Robinson that the 'dynamic force' behind the UVF was 'genuine and sincere' and suggested that the force would have been brought into existence even if 'Carson had never been born'. He went on:

> I don't believe they have even 25,000 rifles, and the total number of enrolled volunteers is admitted to be at present under 60,000; but if there are 1,000 men with the true ghazi spirit the position has got to be taken seriously. How far is it bluff? I think it is bluff to this extent, that they know they couldn't hold out against the forces of the crown and Dreadnoughts in Belfast Lough, but it is not bluff in that they mean to go as far as they are able.[131]

Dismissing Robinson's preference of provincial councils for the governance of Ireland, Fraser noted that 'everybody wants Home Rule of some sort or the other'. He believed that an inter-party conference would 'do no good at this juncture' and maintained that 'the only feasible course is to try to force a general election', which could 'only be legitimately done by arousing a greater depth of feeling in England about the Ulster question'.[132] Writing to Geoffrey Robinson three days later, following a meeting with the duke of Abercorn and watching Ulster Volunteers training in his grounds at Baronscourt in

County Tyrone, Fraser stressed to his editor that 'this is not a movement of aristocrats or landlords; it is a movement of the people, that is to say, the people who are the backbone of Ulster'.[133] After considerable touring throughout Ulster – he covered over 600 miles by road inside a few days – and indeed across Ireland, Fraser found himself continually reassessing political alternatives and possible solutions to the Irish political morass as his levels of knowledge constantly increased. Therefore, on 12 October, he found himself warming to the idea of four provincial councils (an idea he had dismissed the previous week). However, what did not change was his steadfast belief in the sincerity and resoluteness of the Ulster loyalist position. In another letter to his editor, he contrasted what he believed to have been the relative lack of conviction and the absence of a mood reflecting the 'joy of victory' at a Home Rule demonstration addressed by John Redmond that he had witnessed in Limerick earlier that day. Stating that 'the whole business' in Limerick was 'in strange contrast to the resolute determination of Ulster', Fraser concluded that whilst 'the bulk of the people in Ireland want Home Rule ... they don't want it with the determination visible in Ulster against it'.[134]

Although wary of the strong opinions on the Irish question held by the paper's owner and especially his reluctance to become too closely embroiled in a potential civil-war situation, Geoffrey Robinson and *The Times* sustained a surprisingly high degree of support for the Ulster cause throughout the course of the crisis. Several extracts from editorials from *The Times* are considered at relevant points of this study, and I will only highlight a few here. Three months before the Third Home Rule Bill was introduced at Westminster, the paper warned the Liberal administration to take into consideration the undoubted opposition of Ulster unionists. *The Times* pointed out that 'English Liberals may think that the attitude of this great community of Irishmen, composed of many churches and of different political schools, is unreasonable and unjustifiable, but no sane statesmanship can ignore it'.[135] Central to the paper's opposition to Home Rule, and indeed underpinning that of most Conservative opinion, was the conviction that a measure likely to precipitate major constitutional and not just political change had to be rubber stamped by the British electorate. This was clearly stated in an editorial halfway through the bill's passage:

> A free community cannot justify, or even constitutionally be deprived of its privileges or its position in the realm by any measure that is not stamped with the considered and unquestioned approach of the great body of electors in the UK. Any attempt so to deprive them is a fraud upon their fundamental rights, which they are justified in resisting, as an act of violence, by any means in their power. This is an elementary doctrine, borne out by the whole course of English history.[136]

Even at a time of apparent climax in the crisis, such as the gun-running incident in April 1914 — a moment when loyalists could quite easily have been sidelined by their friends in the British press — *The Times* opted to criticise the government for its apparent inability to understand the 'real gravity' of the Ulster situation, rather than to condemn Ulster unionists for the clear illegality of their planned actions. The paper's leading column pointed out that the importation of rifles was 'not new' and that the 'striking' solidarity of the Ulster unionists conveyed a 'warning to Asquith's administration, as 'a population so united and so determined cannot be dealt with by coercive measures'.[137]

A striking characteristic of Edwardian journalism was the vivid, empathetic and on-the-ground nature of the reporting of key incidents. This was as true for 'quality' papers like *The Times* as it was for its more sensational tabloid sister papers. Thus, *The Times* featured a report by its Dublin correspondent at the height of the Curragh crisis, describing the perceived mood inside the military camp. Its 'special Irish' correspondent noted that 'the army has been brought into one sole bond of brotherhood in its determination to refuse to coerce the loyalists of Ulster, and regiments which were indifferent to each other before are now sworn allies'.[138] Just over a week later, another journalist from *The Times* described the patriotic scene in the area around Hyde Park in central London as thousands of pro-Ulster British loyalists congregated for a rally, organised by Milner, in support of Ulster. Noting that the national flag 'hung from Piccadilly windows, omnibuses, cars, bicycles, barrows and even the dustcart of a road sweeper', he went on to describe the cross-class nature of support for the loyalist cause as 'Grosvenor Street rubbed shoulders with Whitechapel' and peers struggled for places near the platforms with dockers from the East End'.[139]

The Times, again, had its reporter on the spot the following month, this time in Belfast, reporting on the mood in Ulster as the Home Rule Bill entered its final parliamentary stage. In a report, 'The war cloud: ominous quiet of the Covenanters', readers of *The Times* were warned against mistaking the 'quiet' response of Ulster unionists for a weakening resolve, and rather stressed the 'depth' of their commitment to Carson's cause:

> Let no one suppose that because Ulster is quiet she has weakened in her resolve. The stillness which prevails is not indifference; it is the stillness of water which runs deep. Deep is Ulster's mistrust of the Ministry; deep her resentment against it; deep is the feeling of danger which has bound all classes together in defensive preparation; and deep the determination that the whole of Ulster shall be left outside Home Rule.[140]

Apart from the contributions of staff reporters and editorial teams, the opinion columns and letter pages of *The Times* reverberated to the strident and predominantly supportive noises emanating in the main from leading politicians (F.E. Smith and Milner were frequent contributors and even political opponents such as Lord Loreburn would use the letters page of *The Times* to help germinate new political ideas and directions), policy makers such as F.S. Oliver (a leading proponent of a federal solution to Ireland's political problems, believed to have written a series of letters under the psyeudonym 'Pacificus', published in *The Times* during October 1910) and leading writers. One English writer, S. Weyman, wrote to the paper describing his experiences during a 'fact-finding' trip to Ulster. He was 'moved' and 'appalled' by the 'fierce, unconquerable determination of the Ulster Protestant working classes in the shipyards, in the factories and in the streets'. Weyman added that such 'loyalty' or 'bigotry' remained 'the one outstanding fact of the situation'.[141]

William Flavelle Monypenny, a leading imperialist writer, who had established his reputation in South Africa, wrote a series of articles on a 'two Irish nation' theme. An Ulsterman by birth, Monypenny rejected the argument that Irish self-government based on the South African model would actually work, pointing out that dominion status for Ireland would fail to heal the ancient rift between its two peoples. He maintained that Home Rule could 'not be applied to Ireland without at the same time violating those very principles to which its advocates appeal' and that self-government for either of Ireland's two peoples 'in the violated Home Rule sense means subjection for the other'.[142]

Harmsworth's other leading national journal, appealing to a rather different but even more numerous audience, was the *Daily Mail*. Although its presentation, style and readership were very different from that of *The Times*, the *Mail*'s unremitting support for Ulster and its focus on big Irish news stories was similar to that of its more fashionable sister paper. The million-a-day-selling *Mail*, competitively priced at one halfpenny and enjoying a daily circulation five times greater than other, similarly priced papers, was starting to encompass many of the features of modern tabloid newspapers. Although relatively literary features articles were more common in the Edwardian *Mail* than today's, commercially motivated and 'human' story factors were very much to the fore. Therefore, for much of the second half of April 1912, the paper led on the *Titanic* disaster, updating readers on the fate of its passengers and crew. Also, full-page advertisements were devoted to a variety of products, including Bird's cream custards, weight-reduction aids, and creams guaranteeing 'a beautiful bust in 30 days'. Yet supporters of Harmsworth contended that, whilst he was clearly using commercial techniques to sell as many as of his papers as possible, he was not deliberately attempting to trivialise the news, nor indeed dominating his paper's position on various issues, including Ireland. Tom Clarke argued the case for Harmsworth to be considered as the *vox populi*, a compromising personality with a surprisingly liberal streak on many issues. In suggesting that Harmsworth was the main driving force behind a newspaper revolution, Clarke has argued that he battled all his life for 'the freedom of the printed word, not merely as a privilege of the press, but as the fundamental right of the people and as one of the safeguards against political misgovernment'.[143]

The *Daily Mail*, founded by Harmsworth in 1896, was therefore in the vanguard of British tabloid journalism. With its huge sales and circulation range, the paper was the most obvious example of the 'New Journalism in Britain'.[144] The *Mail* certainly gave widespread coverage to the anti-Home Rule campaign. Throughout the period between 1912 and 1914, news of political developments and crises, photographs of the leading personalities and many leading articles on the Ulster question appeared in many editions of the paper. Apart from well-written articles by leading journalists such as Charles E. Hands and H. Hamilton Fyfe, the paper would devote column inches and illustrations or photographs to controversial and sensational events. Its political line was constant in supporting the cause embodied by the resistance of Ulster unionists.

Although the *Mail* sometimes carried minimal coverage of events in Ulster for weeks on end, it quickly reverted to in-depth and, occasionally, saturation coverage when there were major developments in the crisis. Two examples of the *Mail*'s detailed reporting of key events during the crisis are the Curragh mutiny and the gun-running incident of March and April 1914.[145] For over a week the *Mail* kept its readers up to date with the 'sensational' developments at the Curragh camp near Dublin and the War Office in London. Sir Edward Carson was pictured leaving his home in London's fashionable Eaton Place at the height of the military crisis. Harmsworth had telegraphed editors of his papers from Paris, instructing them to expose the government's attempts to coerce Ulster. The *Mail* responded clearly to its owner's directive, claiming that the prime minister would be unable to 'bully the Ulster Unionists without the whole-hearted support of the Army'.[146] The paper's editorial demanded the dissolution of parliament. If it resulted in Asquith's defeat, this would mean that the king would have to 'enforce his constitutional right [to call on the leader of the Opposition Party to form a government] before Ulster was 'goaded into insurrection' or 'the discipline of the Army destroyed'.[147]

The sensational events of the gun-running along Ulster's coastline in April 1914 were tailor made for a newspaper like the *Mail*, which was, like its competitors (such as the *Express*), constantly looking for scoops. One of its main writers, H. Hamilton Fyfe, composed an article praising the 'discipline' of the Ulster Volunteers and 'the precision of the whole gun-running operation'.[148] The central theme of this evocative piece was the cohesive nature of Ulster's loyalist population, with whom Fyfe invited his readers to empathise. Detailing the normal, everyday lives of the Orangemen, Fyfe went on:

> I know perfectly well that the man who sells me collars was on picket duty. I know that the wealthy manufacturer who

sits yawning in his office had no sleep last night. I know that almost every man I speak to was in some capacity or other contributing to the success of the manoeuvre ... but they make no boast of it. It has become part of their life. They are going about their ordinary occupations today just as if they had never handled anything more lethal than a ledger or taken part in any action more warlike than a football match on a Saturday excursion to the sea.[149]

In the same edition of the *Mail*, an editorial mocked the prime minister's previous claim that he would take 'appropriate steps to vindicate the authority of the law' in Ulster by suggesting he was merely 'locking the stable door after the steed has been stolen'.[150]

During the early summer of 1914, as the crisis appeared to be heading towards a bloody conclusion, the *Mail* devoted significant sections of many editions to the deteriorating situation in Ireland. For instance, at a time when Harmsworth was himself 'observing' in Ulster, as many as 12 *Daily Mail* journalists were reporting Edward Carson's address to the massed ranks of Orangemen and Ulster Volunteers in Belfast during the Twelfth of July celebrations. One especially forceful leading article was entitled 'No surrender'.[151] One of this large team of journalists, however, had a rather different brief. The paper's travel correspondent, V.E. Ward, was there to assess the potential of the region as a tourist centre and for holidaymakers. In a bizarre invitation to readers to visit an area arguably on the brink of a civil war, Ward pointed out its 'scenic beauty' and 'excellent motoring, golf and angling facilities', adding that the region was 'at the present moment unique as a holiday ground for the student of politics'. Much of the rest of his article was on the 'situation' and the demeanour of the Ulster Volunteers. He claimed that the Volunteer movement provided 'many interesting spectacles for the visitor' and declared that 'during my tour, which embraced all the principal places of interest in the north of Ireland, I met with the greatest courtesy and kindness wherever I went'. Ward concluded his article by informing his readers that a 'friendly local' who had been approached for directions actually walked the visitor to the spot. The man, Ward noted, had been 'wearing in his coat the badge of the Ulster Volunteers'.[152]

Another major press figure and a constant friend of Ulster unionists was J.L. Garvin, editor of the *Observer* and *Pall Mall Gazette*.[153] A leading figure in a golden generation of Fleet Street scribes, Garvin had a highly successful 40-year career at the heart of British journalism. Forthright and fearless, he could be controversial and, by going further than most journalists in his support for Ulster unionists, he fell out with senior members of the Conservative Party over some of his Ulster rhetoric. Garvin was of fundamental importance for Edward Carson and his colleagues, not only on account of his unqualified support for their campaign, but also because of his willingness to directly target prevailing apathy over the Home Rule issue. Garvin, firmly to the right in his political philosophy, believed that the electorate was relatively unsophisticated and needed to have simple propaganda-style messages communicated to them in a straightforward but powerful manner. In some ways Garvin's *Observer* – the first 'quality' newspaper – outdistanced the Tory leadership in the steps it was prepared to take to help Ulster unionists, though this can be partially attributed to Garvin's poor relations with the new Tory leader, Bonar Law.

Garvin (like F.S. Oliver) had previously been an advocate of federalism but, as his influence on Conservative Party policy waned, his support for Ulster resistance hardened. A biographer has maintained that Garvin's objective from 1912 was to force the government into realising that unionists would not countenance the Third Home Rule Bill becoming law before an election took place on the issue – in other words, the basic position of the Tory hierarchy with whom Garvin was out of favour – but many of the *Observer*'s articles during this period gave more sustenance to the Ulster unionist leadership than to

Bonar Law.[154] In a leading article entitled 'The next step?' Garvin urged that 'public' meetings be organised on an unprecedented scale throughout Great Britain. In that same editorial, Garvin went on to suggest a possible route to which the Tory Party was reluctant to commit itself:

> The time is approaching, and in our view has almost arrived, when a great departure must be taken once and for all in the methods of Unionist resistance. Many respectable persons seem unwilling to contemplate ultimate bloodshed while deprecating any intermediate breach of the parliamentary conventions.[155]

J.L. Garvin wrote most of his paper's leaders on Ulster and visited the province to describe the mood of Carson's Volunteers. The most memorable of his despatches were those he penned for both the *Observer* and *Pall Mall Gazette* during the Covenant campaign of September 1912. Three issues of the *Observer* in late August and September were virtually devoted to Covenant proceedings. Garvin's justification for this was that apathy towards Irish Home Rule in Great Britain was superficial and what was needed was 'a great national awakening to the menace of the peril which draws slowly nearer'.[156] Garvin's report of events on Covenant Day in Belfast, penned from a precarious position in the dome of Belfast's City Hall, spoke of the 'concentrated will and courage' of Ulster's loyalists. His assessment of the impact of the Covenant proceedings was frank. He argued that Home Rule was 'dead, killed by the resistance of Sir Edward Carson and his followers' and concluded that it was for 'the British electorate to see that it has no resurrection'.[157]

Although Garvin maintained unswerving support for Ulster's cause, he was to radically assess his hopes for the future governance of the region. The events during the build-up to the signing of the Covenant made him realise that 'Ulster too needed a place of its own', and he started to consider devolutionary options for Ulster:

We may think the causes for which the Scottish Covenanters or the French revolutionaries bonded themselves right or wrong. But the results of the Solemn League and Covenant and the Oath of the Tennis Court are written across the pages of history in letters of blood.[158]

J.L. Garvin became editor of the *Pall Mall Gazette* in 1912. The *Gazette*, popular in London's club land, had a relatively small but influential readership. Being an evening paper, it had distinct advantages over other daily papers as far as breaking news stories were concerned. An audit of editions of the *Pall Mall Gazette* throughout September and October 1912 reveal the extent of coverage and the degree of support which Garvin and his newspaper devoted to the Ulster question. Inevitably, the paper did react to the peaks and troughs of the crisis, so there were relatively few Irish stories in issues of *Pall Mall Gazette* for the first half of September and October. However, for the other three weeks – corresponding to the period that included the build-up to the Covenant campaign, Covenant Day itself and its sequel, most notably Carson's visits to Liverpool and Glasgow – coverage of events in Ulster was detailed and sympathy for the Ulster unionist predicament clearly evident. Over this two-month period the *Gazette* carried Ulster stories on its front page for at least twelve issues. There were eight editorials on the subject, as well as cartoons, enthusiastic letters of support, the text of the Covenant[159] and a poem by William Watson celebrating the Covenant.[160]

The paper's correspondents, and indeed its editor, reported from the various venues staging campaign meetings, frequently running out of superlatives as they filed their copy. At the start of the Covenant trail, the *Gazette* noted that 'Ulster has planted her standard and it is for the Government to say whether they will try to uproot [it]'.[161] The following day's editorial stressed the moral righteousness of Ulster loyalists and dismissed their 'lampooners', who had described them as 'a sordid, unimaginative, money-grabbing, self-centred race'. Rather, the

Gazette argued, 'such men could never be prompted to stake their all for the Union unless the issue penetrated to the very roots of their being'.[162]

On the 'eve of Ulster Day', the *Gazette* reviewed the 'great campaign', which they considered to have been 'the most remarkable political pilgrimage' since William Gladstone's historic Midlothian campaign in 1880. The paper's assessment of the campaign was unambiguous. Above all else, the IUP leader's tour had 'done more to unite and coalesce the elements of unionism' in the province than 'any other movement that has taken place during that period'.[163]

In another editorial a few days later, the *Pall Mall Gazette* referred directly to the extensive coverage of Covenant Day in their columns, 'entirely without apology'. In a special article in the same edition of the paper, entitled 'Personal impressions', Garvin wrote at length about the 'amazement' of the last few days. He told his readers:

> Stronger in energy, determination, wealth, resources of every kind than any other city of equal size on earth, Belfast in this business is an Iron City, and those who talk of coercing it have their work cut out ... I have come back as certain of that fact – Belfast would fight, would have universal sympathy and it would dominate Great Britain's politics – as of my own being. Belfast will not have Home Rule and the Nationalists will never have Belfast![164]

Other Conservative journals provided considerable support for the Ulster unionist position, although some, like the *Daily Telegraph* and the *Spectator*, remained anxious that Ulster would detract from other important issues, and also that the Tories would become too closely associated with the increasing paramilitary threat in the province. Yet most of these papers and magazines remained constant in their general condemnation of the government's bill and in their broad sympathy for Irish unionists. Of all the respected, 'quality' newspapers, the *Daily*

Telegraph offered the most reasoned endorsement of Ulster's cause, emphasising the Liberal administration's 'unconstitutional' approach and attacking them for 'clinging to power by means of a coalition which sticks at nothing and regards nothing but its own self-preservation'.[165] The paper also insisted that Ulster had been 'goaded into an attitude which makes Home Rule a certain failure', and praised its leaders for conducting a Covenant campaign which illustrated 'a combination of wisdom, ability and restraint' which was clearly discernible in 'a great movement in defence of civil and religious liberty'.[166]

Like the *Pall Mall Gazette*, the popular daily the *Morning Post* offered unconditional support to the Ulstermen, much of it motivated by fundamental conservatism and love of empire. Its editor, H.A. Gwynne, was a fervent admirer of Sir Edward Carson, regularly writing to the Ulster leader, offering him words of encouragement. One such offer of assistance from Gwynne bordered on the irrational and probably embarrassed Carson. Writing to the IUP leader on 18 February 1914, Gwynne emphasised his 'strong attitude to the Ulster question' and declared:

> if civil war arises or you or your friends think it inevitable, I would wish to place my services at the disposal of the provisional government. I am not unacquainted with war and perhaps may be useful. Would you see that I am sent the proper form to fill up[?] Please don't mention this to anybody. I don't want people to think that I am anxious for a display of cheap notoriety, but I really want you and your friends to rely on my services for whatever they may be worth.[167]

Gwynne reminded Carson of his promise at the height of the Curragh crisis, informing Sir Edward: 'henceforth I am a private soldier and you are the general'.[168]

Gwynne's paper praised the steadfastness, orderliness and

grim resolution of Ulster's Volunteers and condemned the actions of their various opponents, ranging from Asquith's administration to the small parliamentary Labour Party for 'betraying the interests of the industrial population of Ireland'.[169] The *Post* also contrasted Ulster's 'zeal for the Union' with what they regarded as the relative apathy for Irish unity emanating from the ranks of Home Rulers. An editorial in May 1913 argued that Carson's followers would 'freely and joyfully stake everything for their liberty', pointing out that history was 'not made by Act of Parliament or the tramping of the division lobbies, but by the strength of purpose that is in the hearts of men'.[170] The *Post* was also effusive in its support for the formation and active involvement of the British League and the British Covenant movement. Acknowledging the 'plain and urgent need' for such an organisation, the *Post* maintained that English unionists were 'bound to give Ulster their fervent and unflinching support, since they realise not only the justice of their cause, but also the fact that she is in the forefront of a battle for the national strength and security'.[171]

Further support for Ulster came from other right-wing publications. These included weekly journals designed for a more elitist, intellectual audience, like the *Spectator*, and also tabloid papers like the *Daily Express*, which, like its chief competitor the *Daily Mail*, maximised the human-interest factor in several of its Ulster stories. For instance, the *Express* reported the massive Hyde Park meeting in support of Ulster during the spring of 1914 in considerable detail, suggesting that the 'overwhelming great demonstration' would have 'impressed the most cynical Fenian'. Estimating the crowd as being similar in size to that gathered in Glasgow at the same time to watch the Scotland–England football game (around 120,000), the paper's correspondent wrote how, 'for an hour and a half a Niagara of men and women poured through Hyde Park's eight gates'.[172] The paper also led an appeal for likely Ulster 'war refugees'. During the summer of 1913, the *Express*'s front-page headline addressed 'the Women of England', asking them, 'what is to become of the women during the days of terror that threaten Ulster?'[173] This concern was taken up by the Primrose League, forever active for Ulster's cause, and inside a year the association had been promised financial support approaching £17,000 and offers of accommodation for some 8,000 such refugees.

The *Spectator* was edited by another confidant of the Conservative and Irish Unionist Party leadership, John St Loe Strachey, who was an early advocate of Ulster exclusion. This was evident in a *Spectator* editorial that followed within days of Edward Carson proposing an exclusion amendment for the province at the start of 1913. The *Spectator* argued that 'if the Irish Nationalists have a right to Home Rule simply because they want it then Ulster Unionists have an equal right to the form of government which they desire'.[174]

In conclusion, it would be disingenuous to suggest that British right-wing newspapers were dominated on a daily basis by stories relating to the Irish crisis and overflowing with editorials in sympathy with the plight of Ulster loyalists. Blanket coverage was restricted to major events during the Home Rule crisis, including the Covenant campaign, the Curragh crisis and the Ulster gun-running. During these times, the depth of sympathy for the Ulster unionist underdogs was unrestrained. Many newspapers, ranging from the *Morning Post*, the *Daily Mail* and the *Daily Express* to *The Times*, the *Observer* and the *Pall Mall Gazette*, encouraged their readers to empathise with UVF drilling squads and 'ordinary' citizens signing the Ulster Covenant. Most of the Conservative press, along with British mainland-based propaganda teams and pressure groups, used the appeal of a threatened, loyal minority being pressurised by a bellicose majority and bullying government with no electoral mandate on the issue to drum up a patriotic response from the traditionally fair-minded English public. Whilst it was by no means due only to the efforts of the Tory press, British public opinion eventually shifted to a significant extent in its support for Ulster unionists. Levels of apathy towards Irish Home Rule were reduced and the public was increasingly willing to empathise with Ulster unionism (especially during the latter stages of the crisis). To a large extent, this was the result of the 'campaign for Ulster' conducted on a regular basis in many of Britain's most popular and respected newspapers and journals.

Punching its weight

The powerful potential of the political message transmitted in the form of a cartoon was fully appreciated by both Radical and Tory journals during this period. There are several memorable cartoons lampooning the deficiencies of political opponents at crucial points during the Home Rule crisis. Space forbids a detailed analysis of cartoons in the Radical press. However, the central characteristic of such cartoons was their satirical depiction of the 'bluffing' nature of Ulster's opposition to Home Rule. As Gary Peatling has pointed out, much of this coverage was mocking and patronising. Apart from pouring oil on the fires of loyalist anger, it also prevented many Radicals from fully understanding the true nature and scale of Ulster's opposition to Irish unity, at least until the crisis neared its climax in the summer of 1914.[175] Perhaps the most celebrated Radical cartoon was the *Westminster Gazette*'s 'Easter jaunt in Ulster', depicting Edward Carson, Lord Londonderry and Andrew Bonar Law in a jaunting-car at Belfast's Balmoral demonstration in April 1912.[176]

Key themes of pro-Ulster cartoons in newspapers and satirical journals included the mocking of opponents, especially 'Farmer' Redmond and accident-prone premier Asquith, the lauding of their own leaders (Edward Carson was frequently portrayed as a king or conquering knight) and the loyalist predilection for one-upmanship (a consequence, as they saw it, of their superior organisation and intelligence and the moral righteousness of their cause). I would like to concentrate here on the cartoons in that most famous of satirical magazines, *Punch*.

By 1912, *Punch* already had a long and not especially distinguished history of poking fun at all things Irish. As far back as 1841, the editor of *Punch* had described how the chief delight of the Irish 'seems to consist in getting into all manner of scrapes, for the main purpose of displaying their ingenuity by getting out of them again'.[177] Yet the stereotypical images and impressions of Irish people and political movements underwent a noticeable change during the last quarter of the nineteenth century, as the Irish 'street movement' of Daniel O'Connell and the paramilitary campaign of the Fenians were replaced by Parnell's conspicuous parliamentary emphasis throughout the 1880s. The dominant view of cartoonists changed from 'antagonism to amused condescension'.[178] However, the political campaign of Ulster unionists opposing Home Rule, especially that of the Edwardian period, was to prove a more complex subject for English cartoonists, especially those not subject to toeing a particular party line. Some writers have suggested that the *Punch* cartoons during this period depict the lack of a clear consensus, and rather illustrate 'a mixture of apprehension and amusement' in which 'the importance of restraint is repeatedly stressed' in an atmosphere of 'storm clouds and pious hopes'.[179] At times, *Punch* could be cruel in its depiction of Ulster Volunteers as 'toy soldiers', drilling with wooden rifles and without uniforms. Sir Edward Carson's image as the 'king' of Ulster was mocked from time to time. For instance, a cartoon entitled 'The Ulster king at arms' portrayed the Ulster leader in regal clothes but bearing a rifle and with a machine-gun belt around his neck. Carson, depicted as a modern-day version of Henry V preparing for Agincourt, gains the audience's respect because of his obvious power but he is also portrayed as vulnerable and uncertain.[180] At other times, *Punch* could be more sympathetic in its portrayal of Ulster's leader. On the eve of Covenant Day, a *Punch* cartoon entitled 'Ulster will write', depicted Carson on a horse, but this time bearing a pen rather than a sword. The drawing still implied that, if the pen failed, the Ulster 'general' would use his sheathed sword instead.[181] Another cartoon the following month, 'The sincerest flattery', created in the wake of the nationalists' own gun-running exploits in Howth, portrayed 'General' John Redmond asking Carson, 'Ulster King of Arms is it? We'll be afther showin' 'em what the other three Provinces can do!'[182]

The 'policing' role of Mr Punch or John Bull, in negotiating between two irreconcilable Irish factions, was another key feature of *Punch* cartoons. This message, very similar to the 'unreasonable Irish' cartoons of the Victorian period and, indeed, not dissimilar to cartoons from the early phase of the modern conflict, is evident in many *Punch* cartoons of 1914. For instance, in 'The wooing' in March 1914, an ardent lover (Herbert Asquith) is pictured peering through the window of the delectable 'Miss Ulster's' cottage as she receives her suitor's bouquet labelled 'concessions' from an intermediary (Mr Punch). The reluctant colleen explains her position to a baffled *Punch*: 'An' what's the good of him sendin' me flowers when I've told him "No" already?' The conciliatory Mr Punch replies, 'Well now, come, my dear – won't you just take a good look at them before you start turning up your pretty nose?'[183]

What is not in dispute, however, is the level of attention afforded to the Home Rule crisis in general, and the Ulster situation in particular. During the peak period of the crisis, between January and July 1914, 21 cartoons relating to Ulster were printed in the magazine. The popularity of the Irish question in cartoons during this Edwardian period was in sharp contrast with its marginal role in the 20-year period between 1922 and 1942, when only 15 cartoons on Irish themes featured in *Punch* (and only three of these related directly to Northern Ireland). As mentioned above, the positive influence of John Bull, or occasionally Mr Punch, was often required to mediate in depictions of the warring loyalist and nationalist factions in Ulster. In 'The swashbucklers', John Bull takes a clear stand for common sense and the need for English parties to distance themselves from the extreme posturing of the respective Irish political camps. As a 'Tory diehard' and 'Radical extremists' bang their drums, call out their respective war-cries and wave their fists at each other, John Bull informs them that he is far from being amused at their behaviour and that he refuses to consider 'having civil war to please either of you'.[184] In another cartoon, which was published a month before, John Bull rebukes the two Irish leaders for jostling one another over who would hold a 'Peace for Ireland' banner. In a plea for compromise between the two Irish factions, John Bull asks in 'The flight for the banner': 'Why can't you carry it between you? Neither of you can carry it alone.'[185]

Other *Punch* cartoons maximised key moments of the crisis and their demoralising effect upon Liberal fortunes in order to poke fun at Radical politicians. 'There's many a slip …', printed in the 1 April edition, depicts Herbert Asquith attempting to hand over the Home Rule chalice to the outstretched arms of his Irish nationalist colleague John Redmond. However, a 'ghostly' arm bearing a sword with the inscription 'Army Resignations' suggests that such a handover was now unlikely.[186] This cartoon does little to conceal its editor's delight in the obvious thwarting of Liberal and Nationalist Home Rule aspirations. A few weeks before, the magazine had concentrated on the Liberal administration's indecision over the issue of Ulster exclusion, a trait that Tory critics of the prime minister firmly associated with his overall leadership of the country. 'Herbert', the 'premier' parrot, is experiencing difficulty pronouncing the word 'exclusion'. A frustrated John Bull scolds the flustered and confused bird, reminding it: 'if you're going to say "exclusion", for heaven's sake say it and get it over'.[187] This drawing attracts the reader's attention to the prime minister's continuing indecision over Irish Home Rule and especially Ulster's resistance to it, and, in particular, the Liberal government's division and uncertainty over the question of part or all of the province being exempted from the bill's provisions.

Punch's take on the arming of Ireland's respective Volunteer armies on the eve of international war in Europe, 'The triumph of the voluntary system', pictures ex-War Office minister Lord Haldane proudly pointing to the respective camps of unionist and nationalist Volunteers pitched opposite one another. His recognition that such signs of community armies were 'grossly illegal and utterly unconstitutional', yet also 'beautiful', should be seen within the context of growing military concern over the strength and size of the British Army as a European war beckoned.[188]

Sir Edward Carson inspecting UVF ranks

The tide turns

5

Introduction

We have seen how Sir Edward Carson's Ulster unionist resistance movement responded to the political danger posed by imminent Home Rule and how the relative cohesion within Ulster's loyalist community was boosted by a vote of confidence from their British friends in high places. In this chapter, the focus will be on how the tide turned clearly in favour of Ulster unionists during the first half of 1914.

The irreparable damage caused by the government's blundering over the Curragh affair, the boost to unionist morale occasioned by the successful importation of a large arsenal of weaponry, along with the apparent switch in government policy to a point where exclusion for some part of Ulster became an increasingly likely scenario, will be considered in detail below. As international war clouds drew closer to British shores, attention would swing away from the question of Ireland to the more pressing matter of international war. The implementation of the Home Rule legislation would be suspended for the duration of the war.

Clandestine conduits

A major source of support for the plight of Irish unionists was the relationship between leading figures of the right in the political, social, press and military worlds, often driven by shared membership of gentlemen's clubs. The interest and involvement of the military class in the Home Rule crisis of 1912–14 was considerable. What occurred at the Curragh camp near Dublin in 1914 was far from accidental. Many serving army officers at that time were from landed Anglo-Irish families and had an obvious, practical interest in any major political change in the country's relationship with Britain. Others had served abroad in British or Irish regiments and were now enjoying retirement on their Irish estates. These shared experiences – in terms of social background, Irish land interests and military service (either past or present), often in the cause of maintaining British imperial interests – meant that highly charged emotions were prevalent in the officer class during the Edwardian period. This class had ready opportunitues to form relationships with vital contacts in political decision making and, indeed, to influence them. There was no better example of such influence than Lord Roberts, the most celebrated soldier of his generation.

A veteran of imperial service, particularly renowned for his role as commander-in-chief of British forces in South Africa, Lord Roberts of Kandahar was outspoken in denouncing Home Rule for Ireland. Though he had entered his eighties by the time of the Irish crisis, the diminutive military icon, known to his friends as Little Bobs, remained active in championing political and military causes. However, his close involvement in a campaign to introduce compulsory military service had prevented him accepting the leadership of the UVF at the beginning of 1913. The enigmatic Roberts recommended Lieutenant-General George Richardson for the post and maintained a deep interest in political developments affecting Ulster. For instance, he was keen to be identified with Alfred Milner's British Covenant movement and was a regular letter writer to the 'quality' press, especially during the fortnight of the Curragh crisis. Despite his advanced age, he was very active at this time of gloom and uncertainty. Inside one ten-day period, the venerable military leader wrote to the prime minister, visited the king, met with the chief of imperial staff (Sir John French) and delivered a major House of Lords speech on recent events. Counselling Herbert Asquith to avoid a situation where the army would be used to enforce Home Rule, Roberts stressed the 'intolerable strain' that this would impose on military discipline and forecast that it would 'produce a state of demoralisation from which it would ... never recover'.[1] Speaking with authority and considerable passion during a House of Lords debate days after the crisis had subsided, Lord Roberts emphasised the political independence of the soldier and the 'deplorable situation' produced by the government's ultimatum – a 'choice between two terrible alternatives'. He went on the offensive against the government for their 'perversions of the truth' and for ' tarnishing the reputation of the national army':

> My Lords, what of the choice that was put before these officers? ... They were to be ready to operate against the men of Ulster – loyal subjects of the King, flying the Union Jack – or to send in their resignations and be dismissed from

the Army with consequent loss of their careers and pensions ... They are made the subjects of false charges, are accused of wishing to dictate to the Government, and are branded as conspirators. My Lords, it is high time for the sake of the nation – no less than for the sake of the Army – that these perversions of the truth should cease, and that the Army should be allowed to disappear from the political arena into which it has been thrust – much against its own wish or expectation.[2]

Lord Roberts died in November 1914, shortly after visiting troops on the western front, and it was his protégé, County Longford-born Field Marshal Sir Henry Wilson, who would prove to be the most vital cog in the machine that united the military and political establishments during 1912–14.[3] Wilson, who would briefly represent the North Down constituency at Westminster after the war, before being gunned down in a fashionable London street by IRA personnel, acted as a conduit between military officers increasingly uneasy with the prospect of being required to implement the terms of Home Rule in Ulster and a host of leading politicians, especially those on the right. Henry Wilson's support for Ulster's cause was unambiguous, as his diary entries reveal. Though not present, he wrote enthusiastically about the loyalist demonstration at Balmoral in April 1912, declaring that the papers had been 'full of Bonar Law's fine meeting', which 'must have been a wonderful sight'.[4] The following year, he again illustrated his depth of feeling for Ulster in other diary insertions. Following dinner with his old mentor Roberts, Henry Wilson recorded:

> He told me he had been approached to know if he would take command of the Army of Ulster and if he could get me as his Chief of Staff and he wanted to know if I would. I said that if the alternatives were to go and shoot down Ulster or shoot for Ulster I would join him if he took command. Imagine our having come to such a state![5]

Sir Henry Wilson's political antennae were amazingly far reaching and he fully realised the growing significance of the Ulster question in wider national politics. On the last day of 1913, he observed that Ulster was 'rapidly becoming the sole and governing and immediate factor in the national life'.[6] Wilson visited Belfast the following February, ostensibly to inspect the Royal Irish Rifles, but he also reportedly visited UUC headquarters in the city. Following the Curragh incident and the successful UVF gun-running in the early months of 1914, there was a clear need for leading military personnel to be more discreet in their discussions with key politicians. Wilson, who had regularly corresponded or met with people like Andrew Bonar Law and Edward Carson, now resorted to more distant intercourse, employing intermediaries like his friend Sir Charles Hunter, Conservative MP for Bath. In May, Hunter reported the results of a meeting with his party leader:

> I saw Bonar Law this evening and I sounded him on Ulster's probable action on the signing of the Bill. He is most strongly of the opinion that Carson will be propelled to take action ... and told me to tell you so: the pressure of public opinion would be too strong for him not to. He does not want to come into touch with you and would probably prefer to use some channel of communication like myself for any further communication. They watch him closely. Destroy this ...[7]

The following month, Hunter reported back on Edward Carson's response to Wilson's suggestion about 'flooding Ireland with troops' in order to deter street disturbances, expressing the Irish Unionist Party leader's reluctance to adopt this tactic.[8]

Sir Henry Wilson was especially useful in his role as an intermediary during the Curragh episode. He was proficient in keeping opposition leaders informed of up-to-date developments both in the Curragh and at the War Office. He wrote letters or despatched messages to a host of political and media figures –

including Hunter, Lords Milner and Derby, Leo Amery, Geoffrey Robinson (editor of *The Times*), H.A. Gwynne (editor of the *Morning Post*) and F.S. Oliver – and reassured military officers. He corresponded with officers like Major-General Henry Rawlinson and Lieutenant-Colonel C.J. Sackville-West and liaised closely with Brigadier-General Hubert Gough, who was at the centre of the Curragh drama. In their correspondence with Henry Wilson, both Gough and Lord Roberts were scathing about the role played by Sir John French during the crisis and believed that the latter had conspired with the government to assemble troops against Ulster. Gough also despaired at the lack of resolute action taken by the heads of the army against politicians, particularly criticising French's part in the affair. He believed that it would be 'dreadful' if French were to receive command of British forces in Ireland. The Curragh-based officer showed his lack of regard for his military superior by sardonically suggesting that French should be 'sent out as Governor to New South Wales, or some other colony'.[9]

The people and the army

The unenviable position of British forces based in Ireland had been the subject of much discussion long before a series of farcical rumours and blunders in March 1914 had brought them to national attention. One ex-colonial officer, writing to Edward Carson in November 1913, had raised the potential predicament facing officers and men if they had to implement the Home Rule legislation:

> If the worst comes to the worst, which God forbid, would the oath taken by officers and men in the army justify them in taking up arms against those who are NOT the King's enemies? Or, put it another way, would the oath justify them in refusing, and so preclude them from any idea of mutiny?[10]

Certainly, the military were fully aware of the difficult position they might eventually find themselves in. Hubert

Gough, later to become so closely associated with mutiny in the army, had written to the king's private secretary, Lord Stamfordham, in October 1913, forecasting considerable uncertainty in the army if a call to arms against Ulster was sanctioned. He suggested that between 40 and 60 per cent of officers would refuse to participate in such a move.[11] Such a dilemma also concerned the Irish Unionist Party leader. For Edward Carson, the ultimate nightmare scenario would have been one in which his Ulster Volunteer Force would have been required to deploy weapons – the importation of which he had recently sanctioned – against their own national army. Yet he remained bullish about how the army would respond in such unlikely (as he considered them) circumstances. Addressing Orangemen in Belfast the previous summer, Carson had reassured his followers that 'the army are with us':

> The Government know perfectly well that they could not tomorrow rely upon the army to shoot down the people of Ulster ... The other day – I know of it myself – a British officer was asked to send in his papers and resign because he had joined us ... He did not send them in and they did not turn him out, but they ordered him to rejoin his regiment. They did that because they know that if they once commenced that sort of thing, there would be no end.[12]

A typically forthright speech by the first lord of the admiralty on Saturday, 14 March 1914 resulted in increased tension, both in Ulster and within army messes, especially in Ireland. Winston Churchill had suggested that the threats of Carson and his Volunteers would not be tolerated and warned that force would be met with force. On the same day, the general officer commanding Ireland, Lieutenant-General Sir Arthur Paget, received a telegram from the War Office informing him that government sources believed that army stores at depots in several Ulster towns were in danger of being raided by Ulster Volunteers. He was ordered to take measures to increase security at these bases (especially those in Armagh, Omagh, Carrickfergus and Enniskillen). Paget, an officer with considerable experience in imperial campaigns, was unsuited for a situation that demanded diplomacy, tact and decisive action. Pompous, easy-going and close to retirement, he was put under considerable pressure, both by his military and political masters. The War Office minister, the equally limited Colonel John Seely, pressed him again on measures to improve security at the depots the following Monday. When Paget expressed his reluctance to make wholesale troop movements across Ulster in case it would precipitate disturbances, he was summoned to the War Office in London. There he participated in two days of talks with other military chiefs, including Sir John French, the chief of imperial general staff, Major-General Nevil Macready, and key politicians, including the prime minister, Winston Churchill and Seely. At these meetings Paget was overruled on his reluctance to shift troops and Churchill assured him that the Royal Navy would, if necessary, assist in the movement of troops. Reinforcements were promised for the four depots deemed to be most at risk and it was decided that General Macready would be despatched to Belfast to assume responsibility as a military governor for the area. Although it was acknowledged that officers domiciled in Ulster would have the right to opt out of such service, French and Seely told Paget that if his officers refused to obey orders to operate in Ulster, they would be dismissed.

Paget met senior officers in his Dublin office on Friday, 20 March. Smoking a cigar and pacing the room, the senior officer – doubtless ruffled after being 'put through the mangle' at the War Office the previous week – presented them with a melodramatic diatribe featuring a burning and ravaged Irish countryside. (Those present would later accuse him of failing to provide an adequate account of his discussions at the War Office.) Paget then starkly outlined the War Office's ultimatum regarding military service in Ulster. Instructing his colleagues to consult with fellow officers about whether or not they would engage in such service, the meeting ended abruptly and in a mood of confusion.

One of the officers present was Hubert Gough. Gough, in his early forties, was from a respected and highly decorated Irish military family. He had seen service in the Boer War before being appointed commanding officer of the Third Cavalry Brigade in 1911. Dismayed by what he had just heard, Gough discussed the ultimatum with fellow officers from the Sixteenth Lancers, Fourth Hussars and Royal Horse Artillery in the mess at the Curragh's Posonby Barracks later that day. Outlining the two choices facing them in the event of being ordered to serve in Ulster, only two officers of nearly sixty present were prepared to engage. Paget telegrammed the bad news to the War Office that evening and Gough, along with two other cavalry officers, was summoned for talks in Whitehall the following Monday. Fleet Street also got wind of the divisions in military ranks and press coverage of the story increased from the weekend onwards. The *Daily Mail* demanded an immediate dissolution of parliament 'before Ulster is goaded into insurrection or the discipline of the Army is destroyed'.[13]

Before attending his crucial mid-morning meeting at the War Office on Monday, 23 March, Hubert Gough had breakfast with his confidant Henry Wilson. Over this meal they doubtless discussed tactics, confident that they were in a good position. Sir John French initially attempted to reassure Gough and his colleagues that the recent events had been the result of a misunderstanding and that he would ask them to return to their commands. Assuring them that they would not be ordered to intervene in Ulster, French was taken aback when Gough asked for written confirmation of this guarantee. Colonel Seely was then introduced to the group. The government minister, along with French, tried to persuade Hubert Gough to retract his request. Eventually, the offer of written confirmation was agreed and Gough instructed to return later that day to collect it.

The guarantee that the army would not have to impose any Home Rule settlement on Ulster was drafted by another senior officer, General Sir Spencer Ewart, but Seely realised this would fail to satisfy Gough and his colleagues. He therefore added two short paragraphs, the first of which affirmed the right of His Majesty's government to use military force to maintain law and order in Ireland. It was the second paragraph that would prove to be contentious. In this, the war minister had written that the government had 'no intention of [using] this right to crush political opposition to the policy or principles of the Home Rule Bill'.[14] When Hubert Gough returned, he retired to discuss the document with Wilson and the other two cavalry officers. Desiring a distinct guarantee that he and his colleagues would not be intimidated, and unhappy with the ambiguous language used by the war minister in this second paragraph, Gough jotted down an amended version on a sheet of War Office notepaper. This read:

> I understand the reading of the last paragraph to be that the troops under our command will not be called upon to enforce the present Home Rule Bill on Ulster, and that we do what we can to assure our officers.[15]

Signing this, he returned the document to French, standing in for Seely, who had been attempting to reassure an agitated George V at Buckingham Palace. Gough's military superior also signed it. Gough, who, to the chagrin of the War Office, took a copy of the document with him, was one of the few to come out of the Curragh affair with his reputation enhanced. In a press statement the following day, he said that he had received an 'assigned guarantee that in no circumstances shall we be used to force Home Rule on the Ulster people'. His postscript, on top of his bold contributions at the Curragh and in Whitehall, exemplify why he quickly became a loyalist icon. ('Gough' was chosen as the password used by the UVF during the gun-running operation.) Gough told journalists that, if it came to civil war, he 'would fight for Ulster rather than against her'.[16]

Agreement might have been reached, but the storm was far from over. The prime minister, reading the amended agreement later that day, was unhappy with the actions of his political and military subordinates. He repudiated the guarantee the officials had given Gough and Seely had become a political liability for the Liberal administration. Following a storm of abuse both in the pages of national newspapers and in parliament over the next few days, Herbert Asquith was forced to accept the resignations of Field Marshal Sir John French, General Sir Spencer Ewart and Colonel John Seely.

The fiasco at the Curragh proved to be a godsend for anti-Home Rule campaigners and for the Tory press, which covered it in copious detail for a fortnight. Harmsworth, who was in Paris at the time, telegraphed instructions to his editors to expose fully the government's attempts to employ the army to force Home Rule upon Ulster. *The Times* pointed out that the recent 'crisis in the Army' had 'overshadowed and transformed the problem of Home Rule' and argued that the army had been 'saved from complete destruction' by the government's 'timely retreat from a position they should never have assumed'.[17] The key theme of this vituperative press treatment of the Curragh incident was how a 'plot' had been foiled by a combination of steely military resolve and ministerial incompetence. The *Morning Post* labelled it the government's 'hellish plot', while the *Pall Mall Gazette* maintained that 'the plot engineered by Colonel Seely and Mr Churchill' had resulted in 'a fiasco unparalleled in the history of this country'.[18] *The Times* was equally forthright in its criticism of 'these incomprehensible blunderers' who had engaged in 'a deliberate conspiracy to provoke and intimidate Ulster at a moment when the peace of the province was neither broken nor threatened'.[19]

Many unionist papers and journals focused on the government's 'treachery' and 'bullying' of Ulster, especially as details of the planned deployment of gun-boats to Belfast Lough were leaked a few days after the crisis ended. Some of the tabloid papers had few reservations in calling for the resignations of the prime minister and several members of his cabinet. One journal argued that the 'main responsibility attaches to Mr Asquith, not only as the titular head of the Government, but as the author of the new policy towards Ulster'.[20] Although most Conservative-leaning papers believed that the military crisis would soon prove to be a morale booster for unionists and the key factor in defeating the Home Rule legislation, some of the broadsheets endeavoured to focus attention on some of the wider questions and principles that had been raised by the recent events. *The Times*, in a leader entitled 'Soldiers and civic duties', reminded its readers that the 'general question of military obedience and its limits' had been highlighted. The editorial proceeded to dismiss claims of 'law-breaking' on the part of the Curragh officers put forward by Lord Morley and the Radical press. These, *The Times* maintained, were 'absurdly out of place', since they were not ordered to proceed to Ulster but were issued only with a theoretical option. Instead of giving credence to the alleged illegality of the military action, *The Times*, like many other right-of-centre journals, condemned the government's 'intended coup d'etat in Ulster' – which, they claimed, was on 'a larger scale and farther advanced than the public was yet aware'.[21]

When the dust on the whole affair had started to settle, the *Belfast Telegraph*, which had been vehement in its denunciation of the Liberals' handling of the incident, gave a more considered analysis of its true meaning. Describing it as 'a foul and dastardly plot', the paper's editorial dismissed allegations that this had been 'an affair of aristocrats'. It went on:

> The democracy of the Army refused to be led against the democracy of Ulster in civil conflict. This is not a case of the People against the Army. No statement could, in fact, be more untrue. It is democracy and the Army against the Cabinet – a Cabinet of conspirators against the public peace

who have lied by suppression of the truth and by the gross misrepresentation of the actualities of the case.[22]

There was considerable criticism of the officers' actions in Liberal, nationalist and overseas newspapers. The *Manchester Guardian* suggested that the Curragh incident had raised the much wider question of whether the British Army was to be 'a national army or the private army of a class and party',[23] while a French journal described the 'anarchy and disorder within the British Army'.[24]

It would be wrong to dismiss the scale of the impact made by these orders and the allegations of mutiny made against British military personnel. Responses from members of the officer class, especially those with Irish connections, were certainly spontaneous and hot blooded. Many young serving officers were particularly upset about being issued with an apparent ultimatum at relatively short notice. Although many expressed strong feelings about being ordered to take military action in Ulster, they had to consider the impact of such a decision upon their military careers and pensions. At the height of the crisis, one cavalry officer, who had withdrawn his resignation within hours, wrote to his father:

> We all loathed the idea of going to Ulster for the sake of a few dirty Nationalists who loathe the army and are most unloyal to anything to do with Britain, and yet we wondered what on earth we should do if we left ... The disgrace about the whole affair is that the Government want to find out how many officers they will have. So they have made us decide instantaneously whether we would go or not, without stating any facts as to what we might have to do ... You cannot imagine a more trying day, when in a matter of an hour or so we had to decide between shooting down loyalists and starting a fresh day on nothing.[25]

Other officers undoubtedly felt less empathy with Ulster unionists, but were still extremely critical of the stance taken by their military leaders. One officer, 'a home ruler in principle', believed that 'the greatest danger' involved leaving 'a very delicate situation in the hands of a pompous old ass, whom no one respects'.[26] Ordinary soldiers did not experience quite the same angst or depth of feeling over what orders they might be required to execute in Ulster, or indeed elsewhere in Ireland. One later recalled how the ranks were 'so in the dark that there was no variation in their duties or any talk or worry about going to Ulster'. Bandsman F.C. Wynne, of the First East Surrey Regiment, later recalled that 'thoughts of actual bloodshed never occurred to us'. He added that, to his knowledge, 'no one, except the officers perhaps, had any thought of looking at orders through political glasses and there was never any question of disobeying orders in the minds of the rank and file'.[27] Within days, Herbert Asquith introduced a new Army Order in the House of Commons, which forbade any subsequent questioning of any officer or soldier by his superior rank for the purpose of ascertaining his response to specific orders based on hypothetical directives. The fear that 'tarnishing' the army by such political association would mitigate against the effective deployment in the field of the military units involved soon proved to be unjustified. Both the Third Cavalry Brigade and the Royal Horse Artillery were to the fore during the earliest phase of the Great War, displaying exemplary discipline and courage. However, the effects of the Curragh debacle were more profound at the highest levels in the army. Those on opposing sides during the Curragh dispute, including Henry Wilson and John French, went on to hold high-profile military positions during the war. The events in Dublin produced an atmosphere of distrust between the generals and their political overlords, which persisted for years on the battlefields of Belgium and France.

Ulster unionists were buoyed by the turn in events at the Curragh, which, they believed, had left them squarely in the driving seat. Writing to his daughter Aileen back in Kent,

Edward Carson insisted that it was Herbert Asquith who now had the 'jumps'. Rather than contemplate the army moving in on Ulster – which he conceded would have been the 'beginning of the end' – the Liberal government had appeared to have 'climbed down' after making 'a mess of everything'.[28] Speaking to a news reporter at the end of the crisis, Sir Edward Carson's analysis of what had happened focused on the government's 'devious' plans for Ulster and their administration's political weakness and indecision. Castigating the initial decision to question the officers on whether they would obey military orders relating to Ulster, Carson also attacked military chiefs and government ministers for apparent retractions in their statements, and also for subsequently denouncing a few of their own officials who had been treated as convenient scapegoats.[29]

After several tense and uncertain days, Ulster loyalists felt reassured at the outcome of the Curragh affair. It was now evident that, although some sort of coercion would have to be used to implement Home Rule, the British Army 'could not be relied upon to do it'.[30] Loyalist resistance had, it was maintained, resulted in this very public humiliation for the prime minister. Unionists gained an enormous propaganda coup. They maximised the 'plot' thesis. In his pamphlet, 'The plot against Ulster', Leo Amery MP condemned the Liberals for their 'treacherous' and 'clumsy' attempt to 'prostitute the Army for their own sordid political designs'.[31] This episode, placed in the context of several unionist by-election successes, a growing interest in Ulster expressed at recent political meetings in Great Britain, an extremely positive response to the creation of a British Covenant and the imminent, successful gun-running attempt, suggested that the tide was starting to turn in unionists' favour.

Yet the events at the Curragh did not constitute a complete victory for unionists. Although a big embarrassment for the Liberal administration, it did not hinder the relentless parliamentary progress of Asquith's bill. Also, the political indecision and incompetence displayed by Asquith's ministers and key military officers did not galvanise only loyalists in their resistance efforts. The Curragh set off a chorus of alarm bells in nationalist communities across Ireland. John Redmond and his political supporters were dismayed to discover that, when push came to shove, the Liberal administration might prove to be unable to release its military muscle. This reinforced the conviction of some, more extreme, elements within Irish nationalism that an alternative to political campaigning was urgently needed. The Curragh incident, therefore, did not constitute a loyalist breakthrough as such. Huge political obstacles remained; there was also the urgent task of ensuring that their own paramilitary muscle was taken seriously. Whilst helping to reinforce the growing perceptions of key Liberal leaders that some form of exclusion was required for Ulster, and adding to the widespread impression that Herbert Asquith and his colleagues were merely reacting to loyalist resistance tactics, the main result of the Curragh mutiny was a deepening of the Irish quagmire.

'Loyal rebels'

A momentous UUC meeting at the start of 1913 heralded a shift in strategy and in the potential direction to be taken by the unionist movement. After pursuing a mainly political and propaganda campaign, Ulster unionism prepared to combine this effective approach with a new, overt display of virulent paramilitarism. On the evening of 31 January 1913 in Belfast, the UUC declared its plans to establish a provisional government in the eventuality of Home Rule being passed. Also, the formation of a new 'citizen' army, the Ulster Volunteer Force, was officially announced. Utilising the substantial increase in membership of unionist clubs and the Orange Order, as well as the interest expressed by a variety of other associations, the formation of the force added another element to the anti-Home Rule campaign. Some members of existing church and temperance groups, including the Church Lads' Brigade in Londonderry, joined *en masse*. The decision to establish the UVF constituted a considerable gamble for Carson, who was forever conscious of the dangers of his movement imploding. The reasons behind the creation of such a force were clear. It was anticipated that the new paramilitary group would assuage the fears of many political leaders and unionist benefactors in Great Britain that their movement would be shipwrecked in an outbreak of communal violence. It was hoped that a large force of fully trained and armed citizens would bring a steely determination and discipline to the whole loyalist community. In addition, loyalist leaders saw in the establishment of such a force a new opportunity of challenging the will of a Liberal administration which, to them, appeared to be both dithering and stubborn. Timothy Bowman has acknowledged some clear and lasting criticisms of the new organisation.[32] Yet he also stresses the UVF's success in containing the hooligan element within the loyalist community. He writes that 'even in the face of considerable provocation, there is little evidence of UVF personnel causing damage to persons or property in 1913–4'.[33]

The new organisation was given offices in Belfast's Old Town Hall and within a few months had a retired British officer, Lieutenant-General Sir George Richardson, as its commanding officer. Each of the nine Ulster counties was asked to build up a regiment and the city of Belfast was required to recruit a further four regiments (equating with the city's geographically determined parliamentary constituencies). The regiments were further divided into battalions and companies. Perhaps inevitably, given the demographic complexities of the province, there soon emerged considerable disparity between the sizes of these regiments and in the comparative number of battalions in each. For instance, there were eight battalions in the north-Belfast regiment, whilst mainly nationalist west Belfast could only muster two battalions. Also, recruitment was slowest in areas where Presbyterians predominated within the loyalist community. For example, in the west of Ulster, recruitment was initially sluggish because Presbyterians resented the prominent role of Anglican clergy and rural aristocrats within the Covenant movement.[34] These differences in regimental size were especially significant during 1913, when the recruitment campaigns were in their earliest stages. For example, on the edges of the province, numbers enrolling were only a fraction of those in Belfast or in the north and east of Ulster. Monaghan and Cavan Volunteers numbered 1,155 and 1,920 respectively, compared to east Belfast's complement of 8,599 and Tyrone's muster of 4,762.[35] Enthusiasm was also high in Derry, both in the city and across the county, where by March 1914 there were over 9,000 Volunteers.[36]

Yet the numbers of Volunteers would witness sharp increases across Ulster as the crisis deepened. In those areas where numbers were relatively small, enthusiasm was often strongest. In west Belfast, 'daily drills' were reported in the Greater Shankill district from the start of 1914. Training took place in Fernhill House, close to the Shankill Road, at the Glencairn home of businessman James Cunningham on Ballygomartin Road, and at the Forth River soccer ground.[37] Public parks were also used, though in urban areas, where space was often restricted, regiment and battalion leaders had to improvise in their training schedules. Therefore, one company had to undergo drill outside a picture house in east Belfast. It was, of course, easier for such drill activities to take place outside the city. The stately homes of sympathetic peers and wealthy businessmen were ideal for UVF training manoeuvres and many of these sites – including Shane's Castle, Baronscourt, Springhill, Donard Park, Killyleagh Castle, and James Craig's Craigavon estate – proved to be invaluable in such military preparations.

Despite the enthusiasm and increasing numbers of Volunteers, there were a number of inherent weaknesses in the force, relating to discipline, irregular attendance, quality of leadership and availability of arms. The RIC was sceptical of the force's potential fighting strength, which they believed to be a fraction of its stated membership, and the police were also aware that the force was strongest in those counties where potential confrontation, especially against National Volunteers, was least likely. One of these areas was County Antrim, where Volunteers were reluctant to serve outside their own districts. As time went by and there was no sign of any major boost to the force's weaponry stores, Volunteers got increasingly weary of endless drilling, often with wooden rifles. This frustration manifested itself in erratic attendance at such training exercises, and also in occasional instances of ill discipline (this was reported in south Down). Although up to 140 ex-army officers would become involved with the force, there were doubts about their quality and suitability. Apart from Richardson, who had seen service in India and Afghanistan and had led the British force during the Boxer Rising of 1900, there were a number of capable and respected officers including Colonel William Hacket Pain, the force's senior staff officer, and Colonel Oliver Nugent, who would serve with distinction in the Thirty-Sixth Ulster Division during the Great War. However, many of the retired officers training the Volunteers – an estimated 58 by the summer of 1914 – were elderly and their degree of commitment was uncertain. Additionally, their numbers were insufficient to train a fighting force of close to 100,000, a third of whom were fully armed by this time.

The new force instantly started the task of building the paraphernalia of a modern army. Supplementing the infantry and cavalry sections would be a plethora of support groups, consisting of both men and women, who would be prepared to provide essential backup services for any likely confrontation against military opponents (whether these were the National Volunteers or the British Army). Signalling, ambulance and transport corps (the latter included despatch-riding and motor-car sections) were deemed to be vital in the UVF's preparations.

As noted below, women were involved in many of these key support roles, especially in the Ambulance and Signalling Corps. Leaders of the force and the wider movement were far from reticent about the work of these support sections and reports or photographs of training exercises featured heavily in the local press throughout the second half of 1913 and early months of 1914. One interesting photograph in the *Belfast Telegraph* featured a Boer veteran, sitting between two colleagues in the east-Belfast UVF ambulance corps who had fought (on the British side) against him during the South African war just over a decade before.[38]

The main focus in the new force, however, was on drilling and military training. Drilling had been taking place, within the unionist clubs, throughout 1912, though by the summer of the following year the relatively new force had clearly begun to impress outside observers. A report in a leading provincial newspaper described the drilling of Volunteers in County Antrim as being reminiscent of 'the finest class of our National Reserve' and concluded that there was 'certainly nothing of the mock soldier about them'.[39] Opportunities to exhibit this growing military presence were fully exploited by Ulster unionist leaders. The Ulster Volunteers were to be a constant and key feature of loyalist opposition to Home Rule for the next 18 months, frequently parading at political meetings or being reviewed by the movement's main leaders. One especially memorable occasion was the review of the Belfast Volunteers at Balmoral on 27 September 1913, on the first anniversary of the signing of the Covenant. Up to 12,000 men marched through the city centre to the south-Belfast venue, where they were inspected by Lieutenant-General Sir George Richardson and Sir Edward Carson. The *Belfast Telegraph*'s reporter noted that 'as they marched through the streets of the city they were joyously welcomed by the cheering lines of spectators, who by every indication possible showed their approval of the great Loyalist movement'.[40]

From its inception, the force endeavoured to depict itself as a 'citizen's army', which would soon be accepted as a disciplined, strictly defensive paramilitary force. The fact that it managed to maintain this image for close to two years, despite political provocation from its opponents and the constant threat posed by hard-liners within the organisation itself, is perhaps its greatest achievement, and one which is certainly in stark contrast with the UVF during the 1970s and beyond. This was not an accidental situation. Loyalists were constantly reminded of the need to refrain from becoming embroiled in sectarian disturbances and Volunteers were issued with strict rules for their behaviour, as an internal memo of June 1914 illustrates. Warning its members that 'indiscriminate revolver firing is strictly forbidden', the memo reminded Volunteers 'not to mix themselves up in riots or street fights unless to protect themselves or other Protestants, who may be assaulted, or when called on by police to assist them'.[41]

The force was also successful in quickly moulding raw recruits into disciplined fighting men. Although the tone is overtly condescending and typical of the times, the diary account of Lady Lillian Spender, after witnessing a UVF review at Glencairn in west Belfast during May 1914, indicates the positive effects of military training:

> The west Belfast Regiment is the poorest of all, I mean its men are of a lower class than the others, as they are all in Devlin's constituency, which is the slummiest in the city. Many of the men looked just the type you see loafing about public houses, and were no better dressed, but they marched every bit as well as the others, and looked just as keen and determined.[42]

As the crisis deepened, military commanders focused on devising strategies for what was becoming a likely scenario – direct confrontation with the British Army. UVF leaders were far from keen about engaging in Boer War-style warfare. They were more enthusiastic about defensive or positional strategies, such as that adopted by the IRA less than a decade later. In any case, the size of their Volunteer army and the weaponry available mitigated against serious consideration of the first option. Although sufficient in terms of potential encounters with the local police and small army garrison, or indeed in a civil-war situation against the National Volunteers, the UVF would clearly have struggled when faced with additional military and naval personnel.

The political and military leaders of Ulster unionism discussed their likely responses to such a scenario following a special meeting in London on 17 December 1913. James Craig's report of this meeting shows the pivotal role of Ulster's political leaders, confirming that military plans would be 'secondary to and dependent on the political policy settled by the leaders'. Contingency plans were made in the event of British military intervention. If that happened, 'seizure of arms on a large scale' would result in 'organised, if passive, resistance', but crucially, 'no shooting'. In the event of action being taken against political leaders in Britain ('not probable'), Andrew Bonar Law would travel to Belfast, and if action was taken against Ulster unionist leaders in Ulster, Edward Carson would 'come to Ulster at once'. To counter the problem of extra military personnel being drafted in, loyalists were urged to inform the UVF 'beforehand'; then 'action would be considered'. Finally, at local level, in the event of street disturbances breaking out, it was suggested that 'every effort should be used to stop them'.[43]

Towards the end of 1913, the degree of disquiet and concern in the ranks of Ulster Volunteers was reaching an unprecedented level. This was especially the case in that hotbed of Ulster loyalism, County Antrim, where local UVF commanders wrote to Edward Carson and James Craig early in 1914. Describing the 'great disappointment' expressed at a recent committee meeting about the 'inadequate supply of arms even for instructional purposes', the County Antrim UVF chiefs told how their men were 'tiring of drill' and warned that 'if more rifles and ammunition are not forthcoming', then the regiment would have to demand 'a grant of money with which to arm itself'. The author of the same report claimed that there were barely 200 weapons available for the 11,000 complement of County Antrim Volunteers.[44]

As ever, Edward Carson's knowledge and understanding of loyalist fears and wishes was accurate and he fully realised that a swift response to these fears was needed. Although wary that a better-armed Protestant force might disintegrate following a British military intervention or the start of sectarian street violence, Carson was attracted to sanctioning a gun-running mission. To him, it had three main advantages. Firstly, he was aware that the morale of the rank and file of his movement, buffeted by a stumbling but obdurate government and threatened by coercion, needed to be raised. Secondly, a successful arms mission would be another propaganda coup for an increasingly rampant loyalist movement. Finally, Edward Carson realised that, if successful, such a coup would deflate the optimism of Herbert Asquith and push him towards a political compromise on Ulster.

'Crawford, I'll see you through this business ...'

Loyalists had been discussing the possibility of arms importation since the end of 1910, although it was unlikely that any significant quantities of arms had been brought in before the last few months of 1911. Though he had been commissioned to look out for and purchase arms, Major Fred Crawford was by no means a sole agent when it came to gun-running.[45] Small quantities of arms and ammunition – rarely exceeding 500 in number – were brought in by men like Robert Adgey and William Johnston from places in Great Britain, like Glasgow and Manchester. Adgey admitted that both he and Fred Crawford had been importing smaller quantities of arms for a while. They bought the arms from continental arms dealers, who subsequently informed the authorities, leading to the weaponry being confiscated.[46] There were also more unlikely sources of assistance. In 1913 Edward Carson received a letter from Miss Alexa Jameson of Ardwall in Scotland, proposing that 'machine guns in parts, rifles and ammunition should be sent from the Continent to London as grand-pianos, pianolos, orchestricians, or as spare parts of a French or German make of motor packing cases'.[47]

However, it was the intrepid Fred Crawford who had forged the best contacts with arms dealers and the Ulster unionist leadership would again contact him early in 1914. Yet Crawford was far from being an enthusiastic proponent of a large-scale mission. Deterred by the interception of previous smaller arms caches in a Hammersmith pub in west London (Conservative MP William Bull was implicated in this) and in Leith during 1913, Crawford was far from convinced about the sincerity of many of the people urging him to organise such a mission. Consequently, he wrote to UVF chief of staff, Colonel William Hacket Pain, in January 1914, on the conditions required for him to organise a major gun-running operation. Crawford insisted that money for the weapons be organised in advance of the mission and that written instructions, or guarantees, be provided.[48]

Following the annual meeting of the UUC in January 1914, it was agreed that Fred Crawford should be formally approached about procuring arms in Germany and transporting them to Ulster. On the eve of his departure in February, Crawford visited Edward Carson in London to gain reassurance and clear backing for his dangerous venture. He asked Carson, 'Are you willing to back me to the finish in this undertaking? If you are not, I do not go; but if you are, I shall go even if I know I will not return.' In his subsequent account of their meeting, Crawford recalled how Carson stood up and, shaking his fist replied, 'Crawford, I'll see you through this business if I should have to go to prison for it.' This was the reassurance Fred Crawford had been seeking and he told Carson, 'Sir Edward, that is all I want. I leave tonight.'[49]

Aside from the obvious danger, Crawford's need for reassurances from the man he called 'the Leader' was partly due to his clear lack of confidence in the resolve of many of his colleagues in the UUC, the Orange Order and especially among Milner's associates in England. He later recalled how 'difficult' it had been to 'persuade Englishmen to help us to obtain arms'. Invited to address a 'friendly' association in England promising 'practical' support for Ulster, he was informed that they 'could not send arms or ammunition'. Crawford bluntly told them to change their plans or dissolve their group as 'we did not want unarmed men because we had too many already'.[50] Crawford was also far from convinced about promises of practical support coming from home. Referring to the Orange Order, he noted that the leaders of the society would talk 'glibly about fighting and resistance but when I offered them rifles they looked at me askance'. His most serious reservations, however, remained with certain members of the UUC. Shortly before he returned with the weapons he wrote to German arms dealer Bruno Spiro, expressing his disquiet over the resolution of many colleagues. He bemoaned:

> Remember there must be no weakening or compromise by any of the Ulster Unionist Council. Some of them I noticed were getting nervous some time ago. We have no use for this sort now. Our Leader and General are both right and this is enough for us. The others can go on a holiday till this matter is through![51]

Early in February, Fred Crawford commenced negotiations in Hamburg with Bruno 'Benny' Spiro, who provided him with a variety of options for purchasing arms in bulk. For the next few weeks the Ulsterman travelled between Ireland and Europe, using a variety of disguises and false names. His mission was to purchase about 30,000 modern, high-quality European rifles. Much of the finance needed for this came from the contributions of many wealthy benefactors of Carson's movement. A deal was struck around the end of that month, which would result in about £60,000 being handed over for the rifles and their packaging. On account of Crawford's obsessive need for secrecy and concealment, this took longer than expected. The arms consignment would finally consist of a mixture of Austrian and German rifles (some 20,000 of these, plus two million rounds of ammunition), and a smaller number of Italian rifles and bayonets (about 5,000 rifles and a million rounds of ammunition).

The fact that Crawford had purchased this arsenal of weaponry from a German arms dealer based in Hamburg (and also the brief meeting between the kaiser and Edward Carson while the latter was on holiday in Germany during August 1913) have led some to speculate that Germany was actively engaged in sponsoring paramilitarism in British territory at a time when international war between the two countries was imminent. It does appear surprising that the German authorities would have been completely unaware of this large-scale arms transaction and it is possible that they turned a blind eye on the suspicious movements of Spiro and Crawford. Yet, although there is no evidence of direct involvement on the part of the German authorities in sponsoring such an arms mission – especially during a period when both countries were technically still at peace with one another – it is also likely that Germany would have been pleased at Britain's increasing political and military dilemma in Ireland. Indeed, one historian has argued that the Irish crisis was a 'godsend' for the Berlin authorities, who believed that it would lessen British enthusiasm for a major European confrontation.[52]

Fred Crawford's next task was to make arrangements for the transportation of his large cargo. With the assistance of another Ulsterman, Captain Andrew Agnew, he travelled from Hamburg to Bergen in Norway during the middle of March, where they bought a Norwegian coal-boat, SS *Fanny*. Crawford was fully aware of the need to purchase a boat that would be seaworthy and manned by a reliable crew. Satisfied that this would be the case with SS *Fanny*, he returned to Belfast for briefings with the political and UVF leadership. Meanwhile, the rifles were loaded into a steamer and later transferred onto the *Fanny*, which by the end of the month had berthed in the Baltic Sea. The plan was to take the *Fanny* into a Scottish harbour. There the weapons would be transferred to smaller vessels for the final leg of the journey to Ulster.

Fred Crawford rejoined the *Fanny* on 30 March, shortly after the rifles had been loaded onto her. The long journey back to Ulster got off to a potentially fatal start, with Danish customs officials boarding the vessel on 31 March. Not convinced that the *Fanny* was carrying general cargo and coal, they confiscated Crawford's documents. Told that they would return the following morning, Crawford feared the worst. It would be a night of high tension for Fred Crawford and Andrew Agnew. Recalling many years later the 'mental agony' he had suffered that night, Crawford's thoughts turned to the likely reactions and dashed hopes of the rank-and-file Volunteers in Ulster. He wrote:

> Our hopes dashed to pieces at the very start. What would the Ulster Volunteers think when they heard of this naked failure to deliver the guns after all the promises made to them time and again from every Unionist platform in Ulster? Had we been captured by a man-of-war or sunk when resisting capture there might have been some glory in the enterprise, but to be tamely trapped without a blow being struck! To be brought into a naval base and to lie there while the whole Ulster plot was being unravelled and made known to the world as a ghastly failure, the leaders the laughing stock of the world! The thought of it caused the sweat to pour off me in an agony of remorse and disappointment.[53]

Never one to refrain from taking snappy decisions, Crawford's instincts told him to set off at dawn before the return of the Danish customs officials. Helped by a severe gale and fog, the *Fanny* evaded interception by the suspicious Danes and cruised around the safer waters of the Baltic Sea, where the vessel was repainted and given a general makeover. However, news had leaked out about a suspected arms consignment on a vessel heading for Ireland. Unlike the Belfast unionist press, which underplayed the buildup to the arms consignment's arrival a fortnight later, the normally sympathetic *Times* printed the story, which they reckoned to constitute major news importance, on 1 April. This meant that British warships and other vessels would be on the lookout for Crawford's boat.[54] Fred Crawford made a roundabout trip to Ulster, finally arriving there on 18 April.

Aware of the UUC's panic at the news and feared interception of the arms, an angry Crawford rebuked its members at a hastily arranged meeting at Craigavon, dismissing suggestions that he should abort the mission and take the weapons back to Hamburg. He was given permission, largely because of Carson's backing, to purchase another steamer for the transfer of rifles. The SS *Clydevalley*, a Belfast coal-boat, was offered and discussion turned to the best venues for unloading the arms. Fred Crawford's favoured location was Larne, although the merits of Bangor, Donaghadee and Belfast were also discussed.

Crawford made his way to north Wales and, early on the morning of 20 April, the guns were transferred onto the *Clydevalley*. In an amusing twist, a crew member who had been recruited in Belfast turned out to be a nationalist, and had to be locked in a cabin for much of the return journey. As rumours abounded in Belfast that a large consignment of arms would soon arrive in Ulster, Crawford and his colleagues had arranged for a decoy vessel carrying coal, SS *Balmerino*, to steam into Belfast Lough and for its captain to stall a customs search. Meanwhile, the *Clydevalley* (to be renamed *Mountjoy II*) laboured its way into Larne Harbour shortly before 11 p.m.

As the *Clydevalley* made its way past the Copeland Islands, on-the-ground preparations were fully in place. Thousands of Volunteers had been mobilised in Belfast and in several towns, including the coastal ports of Larne, Bangor and Donaghadee in Counties Antrim and Down, where the offloading of weapons had been scheduled. The main focus was in Larne, which had been the scene of much activity throughout the day. Hundreds of Volunteers had been drafted into the area and were in position before mid-evening, manning roadblocks and blocking off access to the town centre. Volunteers had also been responsible for cutting off the telephone lines by mid-evening, and countless drivers were sitting patiently in rows at the quayside. Teams of the fittest Volunteers, who would be engaged in transferring the weapons from the boat to the motor vehicles, were at the edge of the quay, stamping their feet to keep warm in the cold.

Because of the need for utmost secrecy, the vast majority of Volunteers would have had little inkling of the exact nature of their task. All would have realised that something 'big' was afoot, though, with the exception of those at the three quaysides, most would have assumed that it was all part of a mobilisation trial. Yet an inner clique was aware of detailed and precise arrangements for the receiving of weapons. A secret UVF memo, dated 20 April 1914, informed senior personnel in the organisation's County Antrim battalion of the need to follow exact orders. These included the presence of two unarmed Volunteers in a 'fully-stocked' motor vehicle, which was forbidden to overtake or blow its horn and required to stay in file. Above all, it was stressed that 'no trouble should arise'. The prevailing belief of UVF commanders was that 'a determined attitude will overcome any possible show of interference by the police'.[55]

At the Larne docks, Volunteers would have looked into the distance to catch the first glimpse of the approaching vessel, doubtless discussing the true nature of its cargo, at the same time looking over their shoulders to check on any resistance from the RIC or customs officers. Teams of UVF nurses remained discreetly in the background in case of any confrontation with the official agencies of law and order, and other loyalist women would have dispensed welcome cups of tea, sandwiches and even hot food to hundreds of cold and damp Volunteers in the slow-passing hours before the *Clydevalley*'s arrival. Volunteers also contented themselves by smoking cigarettes and pipes, singing patriotic songs and chatting to local residents.

The most conspicuous presence quayside would have been the fleet of motor cars, parked in taxi-rank style close to the quayside. Organised by the UVF's Motor Car Corps, up to 600 vehicles had been commandeered for the evening (this amounted to nearly half of all registered motor cars in Ulster at this time) and a large team of UVF drivers had been assigned responsibility for these vehicles. They had been assembled at a number of convenient vantage points, especially in the estates of sympathetic aristocrats, including Lord Templetown, whose estate at Castle Upton in Templepatrick, halfway between Belfast and Larne, was an ideal meeting-place for many of these vehicles (a smaller number had their *rendez-vous* at the County Antrim mansion of Lady Smiley). Indeed, the homes of the wealthy and aristocratic would prove to be the destination for many of the weapons. In an age when the motor car was a relative rarity, especially in the countryside and rural parts of Antrim and Down, the sight of hundreds of vehicles making their way to the coast during the early evening must have been highly unusual. Indeed, for a young boy living in his father's rectory near Larne, the road outside was busy throughout the night and they constantly 'heard the cars and we [could] see the trees constantly illuminated by the headlamps'.[56] As Jonathan Bardon has noted, the Larne gun-running was 'probably the first time in history [that] motor vehicles had been used on a large scale for a military purpose, and with striking success'.[57]

Although the Volunteers would have jumped into action the

moment the *Clydevalley* was sighted, they would have had a frustrating wait as the coal-boat took quite a while to berth in the 'brilliantly lighted' harbour. Once the *Clydevalley* had been properly secured, the dockside cranes swung into action. The ship crew and eager Volunteers commenced their duties in what was to prove to be a lengthy but relatively smooth operation. Approximately 80 tons of rifles were taken off the vessel, with around 11,000 rifles being transferred immediately to the waiting cars. They were then counted and checked by Volunteer staff and taken straight away to secret arms dumps, as well as to the spacious grounds of aristocrats' homes, from where they were redistributed the following evening. Many of the first batches of cars to leave were destined for far-flung parts of the province, such as Tyrone and Fermanagh. Some of this weaponry would have been used in the 1920s disturbances and a few weapons dating back to this operation were even confiscated by police during raids early in the modern conflict. Inside three hours, the cargo of weapons had been unloaded from the *Clydevalley* and the attention of those remaining on the quayside would turn to preparing the smaller arms consignments for Bangor and Donaghadee.

The unloading and transportation of rifles, obviously aided by the non-intervention of police and customs, was conducted in a highly efficient manner. Fred Crawford later described the scene as Volunteers loaded the boat bound for Belfast:

> Willing, though amateur, hands started to transport the cargo into her. Number 2 hold was opened and the arms were landed on the wharf. As each crane-hold was landed, a motor-car came along quietly, gathered as many bundles as it would hold, and then drove off rapidly in the darkness to its destination.[58]

Claiming that the local police had been 'surrounded by Ulster Volunteers and were compelled to stay in their barracks', Crawford set off (with a new load of fuel and 40 tons of rifles) at around five o'clock in the morning for Bangor, arriving there about 7.30 a.m. He was welcomed by friends, who were 'overjoyed' at his arrival. Other arms consignments were loaded into smaller boats – the *Roma*, which landed 70 bundles of rifles at the Workman, Clark & Co. wharf in the city and the *Innismurray*, which was bound for Donaghadee. An exhausted James Craig met the delayed *Innismurray* as it docked in the small port around seven the following morning. A small number of local police and customs officials witnessed the weapons being transferred to awaiting motor vehicles without attempting to intervene. In one of only two setbacks that evening, an on-duty Donaghadee customs official suffered a fatal heart attack. Another casualty was a crew member, who was injured after falling into the hold of the *Clydevalley*. Elsewhere, customs officials and police searched Crawford's decoy vessel, SS *Balmerino*, but found only coal supplies.

Many of those involved in the dramatic events at home that cold April evening would doubtless have shared their recollections with family and friends in the years ahead. The significance of what was happening would probably not have occurred to them at the time, as they concentrated fully on their own small, but nevertheless vital, tasks. We have more detailed accounts of the involvement of senior figures within the UVF. Lillian Spender, wife of Wilfrid, recalled his arrival home the morning after the gun-running episode:

> Imagine my delight when, about six o'clock next morning my door opened, and in came a muddy, tousled, disreputable Wolf [her per name for her husband], whose shining eyes however told me that all was more than well. Then I learned that he had been sent to the danger point, to Larne itself, and had been up all night, helping to unload the precious goods, and to carry them to the motors waiting by the wharf ... The whole proceedings are almost incredible, and nothing but the most perfect organisation, combined with the most perfect and loyal co-operation on the part of all concerned,

could have carried it through without a single case of bloodshed.[59]

Lady Spender praised her husband for his orchestration of the reception of arms. In subsequent diary entries we learn of Wilfrid's cycle ride back from Larne, including a tumble as he approached Belfast. The next day she went shopping in the city, where she and a friend 'bought our Ambulance Uniform hats', and noted how 'there must have been a good many sleepy people in Ulster that morning'.[60]

In private, the authorities and Liberal government would have been frustrated and rather peeved at the audacious and successful nature of the gun-running operation that weekend. Though it would restore, to some degree, the Liberals' occupancy of the moral high ground in Ulster, this would be at a price. Loyalists had been buoyed by their success and now, fully armed, posed a much bigger threat to the authorities, especially in the wake of military upheaval the previous month. Caught off guard, the Liberal administration took their time in deciding how to respond to an event they instantly described as 'criminal' and 'treacherous'. Four cabinet meetings were devoted to the incident in the first four days of the following week (28 April–1 May) but, persuaded by his key ministers to be non-confrontational in his response, no arrests were made, as had been widely expected.

Winston Churchill made the government's reluctance to adopt a punitive approach clear. He told the House of Commons on Monday, 28 April that the Liberals would 'not use force till force is first used against the representatives of law and order' and stressed that they would 'in no circumstances use more legal force than is necessary to maintain or restore order'.[61] Herbert Asquith's reaction to the weekend's dramatic events was keenly anticipated and a record number of parliamentary questions – 167 – had been placed for the prime minister. He told an expectant House of Commons:

in view of this grave and unprecedented outrage, the House may be assured that His Majesty's Government will take without delay appropriate steps to vindicate the authority of the law and to protect officers and servants of the King and his Majesty's subjects in the exercise of their duties and in the enjoyment of their legal rights.[62]

Asquith's 'appropriate steps' were seen as a classic case of closing the stable door after the horse had bolted and his clumsy attempt to flex muscle after the event won him little favour amongst Ulster loyalists. Belfast's evening newspaper voiced the view that the Liberals were 'thoroughly panic-stricken' and reported 'rumours of the most contradictory character filling the air'.[63] Such fears of government retaliation appeared to be affirmed by the arrival of up to 18 warships in Belfast Lough and Bangor Bay during the morning of Tuesday, 29 April. Day-trippers flocked down to the County Down coast over the next two days to catch a glimpse of Britain's naval might. This display of force, aimed at deterring any more smuggling of arms, covered a wide area, from Rathlin Island in the north to Carlingford Lough in the south, with particular emphasis on the ports where weapons had been landed a few days before. It was estimated that such a display of naval force was costing the taxpayer around £3,500 per day. In an almost surreal situation, the unionist mayor of Belfast was welcomed aboard one of these battleships, HMS *Hecla*, and afterwards invited the captain to the City Hall for afternoon tea.

Despite such chivalry, rumours of arrests persisted until the following day, when the *Belfast Telegraph* suggested that these were now unlikely, and that 'the theatre of operations [had] now transferred to London, where the next developments may be looked for'.[64] The recollections of Augustine Birrell, writing nearly a quarter of a century after the event, are revealing. Conceding that the government were fully aware of the illegality of such an operation and the undoubted culpability of certain leaders, the chief secretary for Ireland recalled that 'after consideration the Cabinet, with my concurrence, decided to leave it alone, although by doing nothing they almost negated their right to be called a government at all'.[65]

The initial reaction of most Ulster unionist supporters, and especially their leaders, to the startling events along the north coast was one of relief, both at the safe arrival of the arms consignment and at the unwillingness of the Liberal administration to initiate any prosecutions as a result of the incident. Following rapidly in the footsteps of the Curragh mutiny, it reinforced the impression that unionists were gaining the upper hand in their struggle, although their actions at Larne and elsewhere were blatantly illegal. The gun-running incident certainly produced an increased buoyancy within the ranks of the Ulster loyalist community, even though some historians have justifiably questioned the claims that it had been 'the decisive coup that it has often been portrayed to be'.[66] Whilst it undoubtedly resulted in a grudging respect for the political, and now paramilitary, might of their opponents, Herbert Asquith and his colleagues were not deterred in their parliamentary campaign for Irish Home Rule, and the gun-running affair certainly did not lead to the demise of his government, as the unionist leadership had desired. However, Sir Edward Carson was satisfied with the night's work. Adopting a moderate tone both in press statements and in parliamentary speeches during the days after the coup, Carson pointed out that what had occurred had been very much on the Ulster unionist agenda for some time. He told a reporter from *The Times* that, although he had not been involved in the 'finer detail' of the operation, he had fully supported it. He went on:

> We have not deviated one iota from the policy laid down two and a half years ago, when we said that if we were driven to it we should resist by force. Guns and ammunition have been coming in for a long time, but the measures taken on Saturday were necessary on a large scale, because we are getting near the crisis, and our men are now drilled and prepared for the arms.[67]

In parliament, Edward Carson accepted full responsibility for what had happened, but in stark contrast with the nature of the weekend incident (namely, bringing in a large and illegal consignment of arms), he continued to be moderate in his tone and use of language. He pointed out that at his age he 'preferred peace to strife' and said that, if Home Rule were to pass, 'much as I detest it', his 'earnest hope' for the rest of Ireland was to 'prove to be a success in the future'.[68] Inside six weeks, however, Edward Carson's old belligerence had returned. Reminding parliamentary colleagues that he had previously had to 'bear many sneers about wooden guns', the current 'reproach' against him was that he 'now possessed Mausers'. He informed his audience that this had 'always' been his intention and that he would, 'if required, have more Mausers'.[69]

The gun-running operation was especially welcomed by loyalist propagandists, who had already started to capitalise on the military dimension of the Ulster unionist campaign. Distribution of postcards, such as 'The great review', which showed Edward Carson inspecting 12,000 Ulster Volunteers at Balmoral in September 1913, had given credence to the impression that this was a serious, disciplined movement. Now, several cartoons depicting the gullibility of the RIC and British government ministers appeared in the pages of Tory newspapers and several types of propaganda postcards depicting the gun-running were published and widely circulated. Some cards, including those in the 'Historical and national events' series, showed policemen searching vainly for guns in motor vehicles, chimneypots and on unarmed civilians. Other postcards celebrating the successful gun-running included 'Ulster is armed to the teeth!' and 'Searching for guns in Ireland'. Because of the late evening and clandestine nature of the gun-running, however, unionist propagandists were unable to use the latest photographic techniques in their propaganda cards. They had to settle for drawings of the 'Fanny' (*sic*) drawing into Larne Harbour, laden with guns and ammunition and bearing the inscription, 'Bravo Ulster, the mystery ship "Fanny" unloading at Larne Harbour'. Alongside are a motor vessel and the *Roma* receiving cargoes for short journeys to other northern ports. Other postcards showed the UVF's successful use of modern transport. These included drawings of motorcycle convoys despatching guns to secret depots across Ulster and their successful unloading of guns at these ports later that morning (one was entitled 'Bravo Ulster! Unloading the guns at Donaghadee!').

Although one historian has suggested that 'the associations between Tory front bench and the illegal smuggling of weapons into Ulster was closer than has generally been allowed', and it is likely that some of them were aware that something was in the offing, it is most unlikely that Andrew Bonar Law and his colleagues were involved in the planning of the gun-running operation.[70] Bonar Law was supportive of Edward Carson in parliament and keen to place the coup in the context of the government's recent alleged 'plot' against Ulster, as illustrated by the events at the Curragh. Perhaps the most effusive praise came from former party leader and prime minister, Arthur James Balfour. Balfour's defence of Ulster centred on the denunciation of Liberal claims that there were 'no circumstances in which it is justifiable for a population to resist the government'. Balfour maintained that in rare cases this was defensible and he believed that 'compelling Ulster to leave a free environment under which she is happy, and put her under a government which she detests, is one of those cases'. He concluded his parliamentary attack upon his Liberal opponents by arguing that what he strongly 'held now' and indeed also 'some 30 years before' was that 'if Home Rule was forced upon Ulster, Ulster would fight and Ulster would be right'.[71] Backbenchers in both chambers were even more outspoken in their support for the gun-runners. Lord St Audries, speaking in Somerset on 27 April, described the coup as the 'most thrilling story in our history'.[72]

Unionist papers, especially those in Ulster itself, provided copious and colourful coverage of the whole incident. Although inevitably dated and inaccurate in terms of exact detail (given the overnight nature of the coup and the resulting restrictions on up-to-date news), their reports of 'quayside activities' lent colour to the dramatic events and were doubtless avidly devoured by readers at breakfast and tea tables across Ulster. The morning paper, the *Belfast News-Letter*, told of the 'successful mobilisation' of Ulster Volunteers overnight and the 'extensive all night operations' that had taken place, and also reported on 'incidents at the Musgrave Channel' as well as the 'rumours of gun-running'.[73] It gave a fuller and clearer picture of what had happened in its edition of two days later. In a detailed report, 'The arming of Ulster', reporters described how the mobilisation scheme had been a 'blind' and it had succeeded in 'diverting the attention of the authorities from the ports at which the rifles were distributed'.[74] Accepting their London correspondent's assessment of the impact of the gun-running 'sensation' and its 'unique' impact on the London public, the *News-Letter*'s leading article that Monday proudly announced that the whole operation had demonstrated the 'thoroughness' in the UVF and the 'readiness among the ranks to serve without question'.[75]

As an evening paper, the *Belfast Telegraph* was better prepared to provide more detailed information on relatively recent news information. Its editorial on Saturday, 25 April described the events as 'an astounding achievement'. The paper marvelled at the accomplishment of 'a well-formed plan, executed as perfectly as it had been preconceived'.[76] Dismissing the response of the authorities, who 'might as well have been in Timbucktoo [sic]', the *Belfast Telegraph* praised the men who had masterminded the operation for the 'sheer audacity' of their enterprise, and described in no uncertain terms the virtual 'proclaiming of martial law' in Larne and how it had been 'gladly obeyed'. The *Telegraph* concluded that 'the months of drudgery of drilling ... were justified to the full; the faith of the men in their leaders has been strengthened beyond conception'.[77] Subsequent editions of this paper contrasted the success of the gun-running operation – the 'Plot that did not fail' – with other 'plots', particularly the government's alleged 'plot' the previous month, and endeavoured to reassure their readers that the threat of confrontation had been removed by the government's reluctance to issue any arrest warrants.[78]

Support in Conservative newspapers in Britain was not as automatically forthcoming as in Ulster but, considering the undoubted illegality of the gun-running and the fact that it had increased the prospect of civil war in Ireland, the tone of coverage in these papers remained generally positive and sympathetic. The story was handled differently by the tabloid papers, which had a less equivocal attitude towards lending support to such a potential revolt. Also, *The Times*, so frequently the supporter of Ulster's cause, had miscalculated in its reading of Crawford's mission, declaring on the eve of the landing of the weapons that such a mission had already failed.[79] Crawford's mission provided the Tory press with further opportunities of satirising Herbert Asquith and the RIC. For instance, the *Daily Express*, whose reporter had already 'scooped' by travelling to Larne with a UVF motor-transport unit, published a cartoon showing Asquith and Churchill as sleeping coastguards whilst the gun-running vessel steamed away on the horizon. Published on the morning of the English cup final, the caption above the cartoon read, 'The coup final'.[80] The 'unquestionably illegal' actions of the Ulstermen, as the *Daily Mail* put it, did concern many papers on the right, but such behaviour was accepted as being morally justifiable, provoked by threats of interception by the navy and army at the time of the Curragh incident a few weeks previously. This, the *Mail* maintained, was 'the cause and justification' of the events along the northern coast that Saturday morning in April.[81]

Unusually, the Liberal press adopted a draconian position to their coverage of the gun-running, with the *Nation* dismissing the whole incident as 'these modest manouevres' and reproaching the government for failing to give 'even a hint to the Ulster anarchists that there was such a thing as an Army and Navy'.[82]

Preparing for the showdown

Fred Crawford's expedition certainly turned out to be an odyssey. Certainly the odds against its success were high and, as illustrated in the unease of many Ulster unionist luminaries, confidence in Major Crawford delivering the arms was far from high. In purely military terms, the gun-running operation was not, as Timothy Bowman has pointed out, a complete success.[83] Although the arms consignment was far in excess of anything smuggled into Ulster before 1914, it still left the Ulster Volunteers bereft of field artillery and their rifles were mainly of the single-shot type. Above all, the weaponry that had been imported would equip less than a third of the force's 100,000-plus membership and posed further logistical problems for the force's leadership. Yet Fred Crawford's mission had proved to be a boost for the Volunteers' morale, as well as being another propaganda coup for Ulster loyalists and a further blow to the government. Herbert Asquith's administration seemed to be chasing the shadows of Ulster politicians and paramilitaries, and the leadership of Sir Edward Carson, so wary of being damaged by too close an association with the threat of actual violence, was significantly boosted by the success of Crawford's expedition. As Russell Rees has argued, the Larne gun-running, 'coming on the heels of the Curragh incident ... appeared to give the Unionists a decisive advantage in their quest to wring further concessions from the government'.[84]

Once the vast collection of arms had been safely distributed to various points across Ulster, attention turned to providing 'proper' weapons training and staging reviews and marches through town centres, at which the newly procured weapons would be displayed in the hands of the paramilitaries. Crucially, this would ensure that the weapons, now so readily available, would not be employed in potentially disastrous exchanges with the RIC. This latter fear was a very real one, especially during the three-month period between the unloading of weapons on the Ulster coast that spring and the start of international war in the summer of 1914. A circular emanating from the UVF's chief of staff, Hacket Pain, provided advice on protecting the arms shipment and on preventing the arrest of political leaders, but it particularly stressed the importance of Volunteers not being drawn into such encounters with the police, recommending psychological deterrents such as 'our force of numbers' to make such stand-offs less likely. The circular read:

> Only if and when the Constabulary commit the first act of aggression by firing will the Volunteers fire in reply. To render effective this system of protection it is most essential that intelligence should be obtained at the earliest possible moment of any concentration or movement of constabulary, and probably such information might be obtained from police constables in sympathy with the movement.[85]

Training in the use of the new weaponry started almost immediately, in Orange halls and in open spaces ranging from city backstreets to the spacious homes of aristocrats and wealthy businessmen. Such drilling even took place when Volunteers were on holiday. One press photograph showed a UVF company drilling on an Isle of Man seafront! Although details of such manoeuvres would not have been publicised in advance, the authorities were doubtless aware of many of these clandestine meetings and conspicuously refrained from initiating interventions that would doubtless have led to bloodshed. It was important to showcase the recently strengthened 'Carson's Army' and this was facilitated by several reviews of Volunteers between mid May and mid-July, as political tension came to a climax with the final stages of the Home Rule legislation at

Westminster and the conference between the various parties at Buckingham Palace. Further visits by Edward Carson and other leading unionist figures lent an air of legitimacy to subversive activities. The Ulster unionist leader was photographed being mobbed by an enthusiastic loyalist crowd at Belfast docks at the start of another tour at the end of May. A few days later, he reviewed an estimated 30,000 Volunteers (including a contingent of Young Citizen Volunteers) at Balmoral and a smaller number of west Belfast UVF men at Glencairn. There he told his men that he was hoping to 'soon see every one of you armed'.[86] (On the same afternoon, Saturday, 6 June 1914, elsewhere in west Belfast, Joe Devlin inspected a gathering of around 15,000 National Volunteers.)

Sir Edward Carson returned to Belfast early in July, when he was again mobbed as he disembarked at Belfast docks. Although assured by the belief that Asquith was unlikely to order imminent military action, Carson was undoubtedly concerned by the constant threat that a sectarian incident would spark off street clashes and, more importantly, bring security forces and Volunteers into direct confrontation. Yet he was lifted by the steely resolve of the people he passed as he motored to a field at Drumbeg, just outside Belfast, to address a huge gathering of Orangemen. He pleaded with them to be resolute and non-provocative, especially now that many of them had access to arms. He pleaded with them to 'take care to understand what the rifle means' and urged the many Volunteers present to use the weapons in 'such a way as may be necessary for the maintenance of our rights'.[87]

Before, during and after this visit, there were several reviews of regiments and battalions of Ulster Volunteers proudly displaying the weapons recently brought in by Fred Crawford. Armed Volunteers quickly became accepted as part of everyday life in Ulster and were used in slick advertisements in the local press. One gent's outfitters in the city's North Street area offered suits for sale from 42 shillings, with the text:

it is now a recognised fact that Ulster will resort to force of arms rather than submit to the present Home Rule Bill. It is also a recognised fact that we [Cornhill Company] give by far and away the best value in Gents' fittings.[88]

There was a review of Volunteers in Belfast on 16 May, and north-Belfast Volunteers featured heavily in two major reviews in the city during July. The first occasion was their parade through the city centre on 4 July. Along with colleagues from east Belfast branches, an estimated 4,000 'fully armed' men paraded in central Belfast on 25 July (the same weekend as the Howth gun-running). Indeed, a growing increase in loyalists' confidence in their own military might was evident in the opinion columns of local papers. Within a few weeks of the Larne gun-running, the *Belfast Telegraph* argued that the government had finally realised that Ulster 'can only be conquered at a terrible sacrifice of life after a bitter struggle' and sardonically denounced Radicals for criticising their own administration for 'having failed to take strong steps against the gun-runners'. This, the *Telegraph* reminded its readers, came from 'the very men who held up their hands in holy horror at the idea of Coercion Acts against moon-lighters and assassins'.[89]

Readiness for the showdown many believed was just around the corner extended beyond drilling and military manoeuvres. Much of this preparation was undertaken by women and there were numerous references in local newspapers to a variety of roles undertaken by female members of the UVF at this time. More traditional contributions came from groups like the Ladies of Knock, who organised a cake fair in May to raise funds for the east-Belfast Volunteers. However, more active involvement was undertaken by women of the force's Signalling Corps, who underwent training at Magilligan Camp in County Londonderry at the end of June. Here, they were taught how to send telegrams and 'passed examinations' in despatch-riding.[90] Also around this period, Tyrone female workers were pictured receiving rifle training. Up to 40 women – 'all fine shots' – were believed to have participated in this training exercise. The caption alongside the *Belfast Telegraph* photos of their field activity read, 'Their objective is to be able to defend their homes and parents if their brothers are called upon to serve with the Ulster Volunteers.'[91] Meanwhile, unionist newspapers contained articles, letters and even poetry from Ulster 'exiles' promising their help. One such case was the news story about a group of County Londonderry men who had formed a branch of the UVF in Toronto and had promised to return to Ulster when needed.[92]

These preparations for an imminent conflagration against an Irish enemy would soon be replaced by foreboding over mobilisation for international hostilities. War against Germany was declared at the start of August and there was much frenetic activity in mobilising forces, as well as setting up a mass recruitment campaign. The declaration of war posed Sir Edward Carson and his Irish followers with a new quandary. Ulstermen's unabashed loyalty of king and country meant that their non-participation in a patriotic war would be unthinkable. Yet the unionist leadership was fully aware of the delicate position they might find themselves in by recommending their Volunteers to enlist to fight in an overseas war. Carson and his colleagues worked behind the scenes in parliament to offset any political deals between Liberals and Irish Nationalists that might have resulted in Irish unity being foisted on Ulster Protestants when their fighting men were engaged in a foreign battle on Britain's behalf. Meanwhile, those responsible for organising recruitment endeavoured to entice the trained fighting men of the UVF into formally joining the British Army.

Like most military men of the time, the new War Office minister, Lord Kitchener, was well aware of the fighting potential of the Ulster Volunteers and declared his desire to have them ready for active service as soon as possible. Within the first few days after the declaration of war, Edward Carson had sent telegrams to the commanders of the UVF battalions, ordering reservists to join their regiments at once. He also contacted the

War Office to commence discussions about how the UVF might be incorporated into the British Army. Carson, who had pledged on the eve of war that his Volunteers would be available for both home defence and for service in the British overseas military forces, had difficult negotiations with Kitchener in London during August. The personal chemistry between a military man like Kitchener and Carson, an obdurate Irish politician, was not good, especially as it soon became clear that unionists would not be able to strike a deal over the Home Rule Bill, which was set to become law on 18 September. At the end of August, Carson and Craig, acknowledging that political uncertainty might backfire on discipline at home, agreed that a distinctive division containing the Ulster Volunteers should be established and Edward Carson offered to help recruit around 35,000 men for the allied war effort. James Craig reportedly went from this meeting in Whitehall to Moss Brothers in the Strand, where he ordered uniforms for this new force.

A few days later Carson was back in Belfast, determined to oversee the transformation of his Volunteers into a proper fighting unit. At a meeting of the UUC in Belfast on 3 September, Carson announced the formation of the Thirty-Sixth Ulster Division. This would recruit and, initially at least, train local men, who would be structured in territorial units comprised of existing Volunteer groups, including twelve battalions and three infantry brigades. Recruitment took place at Belfast's Old Town Hall and at various civic centres across Ulster; Carson and his colleagues spoke at several recruitment meetings. This was far from being an easy task. Although there was considerable patriotic fervour during this early stage of the Great War, Ulster was a different case from the rest of the country. Indeed, it bore testimony to the huge trust Ulster loyalists had in their leader that they swallowed their fears about their long-term political future and joined up in considerable numbers (well over 20,000 Volunteers joined Kitchener's various 'citizens' armies'). Certainly, the veteran Ulster leader needed all his powers of persuasion to reassure those Ulster Volunteers contemplating enlistment that such an offer would not endanger Ulster's position. Addressing a large group at Belfast's Old Town Hall, Carson also rejected any possibility of Ulster adopting an opportunistic position during this time of national danger. He reminded his audience:

> England's difficulty is not Ireland's opportunity. However we are treated, and however others act, let us act rightly. We do not seek to purchase terms by selling our patriotism ... I say to our volunteers without hesitation, go and help save our country.[93]

'To the brink of fratricidal strife'

As the crisis entered its final phase, there would be shifts in political positioning, as both sides braced themselves for one final concerted effort. The attitudes of unionists' opponents would alter as recognition of Ulster's difference from the rest of Ireland became gradually accepted, and even loyalism's leading advocates would reconsider their political options, especially on the proposal of exclusion. Secret, direct meetings between the leaders of the opposing factions were held in late 1913 and early 1914. Although they did not result in a coming together of minds, these discussions did constitute a genuine attempt on the part of Andrew Bonar Law and Herbert Asquith to find an exit route from the ever-deepening morass over Ireland. This feeling of a constantly approaching Armageddon deepened as the Third Home Rule Bill entered the final stage of its parliamentary journey. The extent of the crisis warranted the intervention of the monarch and led to an all-party conference being called at Buckingham Palace in July 1914. The leaders' failure to reach an agreement in these negotiations and the start of an international war resulted not in what most were anticipating – a bloody climax to the turmoil in Ireland – but rather a postponement in any fateful decisions over the island's political destiny. The implementation of the Home Rule Bill would be placed on hold until the war ended and feelings in Ulster would temporarily subside in their intensity as attention switched to unfolding events in Belgium and France.

An important means of influencing government policy at this time was to write letters to prominent national newspapers. This put pressure on ministers to alter existing policy on specific issues. Perhaps the best illustration of such an influential letter, as far as the Home Rule crisis was concerned, was the one written by Lord Loreburn to *The Times* in September 1913. Loreburn, an ex-lord chancellor, had earned a reputation as a strong advocate of Irish Home Rule. But, following discussions with proponents of federalism (including William O'Brien) and acting on his own initiative, he recommended a compromise approach of 'Home Rule within Home Rule' and urged the various parties to meet at a conference that aimed to result in a negotiated settlement of the Irish problem. Loreburn's letter, entitled 'Lord Loreburn's appeal to the nation', highlighted the likelihood of serious civil disturbances in Ulster if the Home Rule Bill were to be passed. He urged Asquith and his former colleagues, who 'assuredly have not taken leave of their senses', to 'consider proposals for accommodation'.[94] Not surprisingly, Loreburn's letter was not warmly received by his Radical colleagues or their nationalist allies. The prime minister was annoyed by 'this typical elder statesman's show of non-partisan wisdom' and dismissed the notion of a conference when there was 'no common ground to meet on'.[95] In proposing an immediate convocation on the Irish question, Lord Loreburn had hoped to draw the sting from the threats of the Irish Unionist Party leader, but his action was not appreciated by the leader of the Irish Nationalist Party. John Redmond believed it exhibited the Radicals' lack of willingness for a fight on the issue and was annoyed by the obvious boost that such an intervention would give Edward Carson in his campaign.

Carson was undoubtedly cheered by the veteran Liberal

politician's suggestion. Though he erroneously believed that the letter actually reflected the fears of the Liberal administration itself and had been merely a ploy to ensure that violence would be avoided in Ulster, the IUP leader correctly spotted the loss of nerve in his opponents' camp. He realised that if he and his colleagues could fully exploit such divisions and concerns, their own campaign would stand a considerably greater chance of success. It was becoming clear that some Liberal politicians, including Lloyd George and Churchill, were combining words of condemnation for threats emanating from the Ulster Volunteers with an acknowledgement that Ulster was different from the rest of Ireland and that a policy of coercion would prove to be fatal. The intervention, along with rumours of Liberal division and uncertainty, also helped clarify Carson's own thinking on the evolving political situation and swung him more in the direction of exclusion. Whilst Lord Loreburn's proposals for an all-party conference and a negotiated settlement of the crisis were rejected, they did result in stimulating discussion within the opposing groups. His appeal bore belated fruit in the Buckingham Palace conference the following summer.

The political leaders realised that some form of direct dialogue between them was required in order to break the stalemate that had surrounded the Home Rule issue. Three meetings, initially brokered by Winston Churchill and involving the prime minister and the leader of the opposition, took place during the period between October and December 1913. They were held in secret (only becoming public knowledge in the middle of January 1914) at Sir Max Aiken's home at Cherkley, near Leatherhead in Surrey, and were followed by shorter meetings involving the prime minister and the leader of the Irish Unionist Party. This clandestine, back-door political diplomacy was in stark contrast with the open, parliamentary nature of previous debate between the key protagonists. The meetings were designed to discover common ground for possible compromise and to clarify the other side's position. Herbert Asquith wanted to know the minimum concession his counterpart was prepared to consider and, although Bonar Law was sceptical of the prime minister's real intentions – he believed that Asquith had few fresh proposals and was really stalling for time – he recognised that his party would suffer electoral damage if they refused to participate in vital discussions on Ireland. His strategy was to appear to be adopting a moderate approach on account of the likely refusal of the Irish Nationalist Party to accept any concessions to unionism.

The atmosphere at the first Surrey meeting on 14 October – the first private meeting between the two party leaders – was edgy and frosty, and by the end of the meeting there was distinct confusion over what the respective sides had offered. Differences on what constituted 'Ulster' were apparent, with Asquith restricting the area to the four counties with Protestant majorities and Bonar Law regarding the term to mean all of its nine counties, irrespective of religious demography. The prime minister claimed later to have mentioned the possibility of exclusion for these four counties (Antrim, Down, Armagh and Londonderry) with plebiscites offered in Fermanagh and Tyrone, though Andrew Bonar Law believed the offer had included all six counties. The Conservative Party leader raised the issue of the dissolution of parliament to facilitate such a radical measure as Home Rule gaining electoral approval. In dismissing this request, the prime minister pointed out, with considerable justification, that it was far from certain that the Ulster loyalists would accept any parliamentary majority backing the dreaded measure. Andrew Bonar Law appeared to be convinced, in private at least, that the exclusion option for Ulster was the most he and his supporters might extricate from the deepening mire surrounding Home Rule. In a private letter to the editor of the *Scotsman*, Bonar Law confided:

> in my view if the questions were left to the electors I think they would decide that Ulster must not be coerced; but I

think also that they are so sick of the whole Irish question that they would vote in favour of trying the experiment [Home Rule] so long as the Ulster difficulty was solved.[96]

Another meeting was arranged at the same location for the following month. On 6 November the two leaders discussed the option put forward by the foreign secretary, Sir Edward Grey, of 'Home Rule within Home Rule'. This proposed limited autonomy for Ulster within the context of an all-Ireland parliament in Dublin, and there was further discussion around the issue of Ulster exclusion. The Conservative leader was under the mistaken impression that the prime minister was willing to accept the principle of such an option being extended to six Ulster counties (the ones which eventually constituted Northern Ireland), and was increasingly frustrated when Asquith failed to respond to his request for further discussions. Eventually a third meeting was arranged, to be held at Cherkley on 10 December. Bonar Law was frustrated by its predictably negative outcome, rejecting outright David Lloyd George's idea of temporary exclusion, which the prime minister had again articulated. Hopes for the meetings had not been high, given the shadowy figures lurking in the background of their respective camps. Herbert Asquith was constrained by the inevitable anger of the Irish Nationalist Party at the very suggestion of 'slicing off' a portion of Ireland from his government's proposals, whilst Andrew Bonar Law was only too aware of the fears and suspicions of his party's diehards, especially over the fate of southern-Irish unionists.

The meetings did, in the end, produce greater clarity in the leaders' understanding of their respective positions. In a sense they helped to confirm Bonar Law's view that the prime minister was in 'a funk about the resistance of Ulster' and also his impression that Herbert Asquith was 'quite at sea' about what to do.[97] The Tory leader was not content with these face-to-face meetings with Asquith and encouraged Sir Edward Carson to meet with the prime minister at Cherkley on 16 December and in London a few weeks later. Although these discussions resulted in little progress – the Irish Unionist Party leader instantly rejected Asquith's suggestion of 'Home Rule within Home Rule' – at least they provided an opportunity for frank exchange of opinions outside of the heat of a parliamentary debate. Andrew Bonar Law also kept the pot boiling by ensuring that the king was fully informed about his concerns and was doubtless reassured by the monarch's own reputed sympathy with the idea of some form of exclusion for Ulster.

After the rejection of Sir Edward Carson's amendment to the Irish Home Rule legislation early in 1913, the bill followed a slow and predictable passage through the respective parliamentary chambers. The terms of the recently passed Parliament Act meant that a measure that enjoyed a successful passage in three successive Commons sessions would become law irrespective of the actions of the upper chamber. Thus, despite the decisions of the House of Lords to reject the bill by a large majority (257) on 30 January 1913 and also in July 1913 (238), it was in the Commons where the ultimate fate of the proposed legislation was sealed. Despite the trundling nature of its parliamentary passage and attempts by unionists to delay its progress, the bill successfully passed through the House of Commons in July 1913 and for the final time in May 1914. This meant that only the royal assent was required before it would become law that September. Although the actions of elected parliamentarians would be of ultimately greater significance, there were several passionate defences and criticisms of the bill during debates in the House of Lords for the second half of 1913. The arch-imperialist Lord Curzon dismissed notions that British electors would consider Ulster loyalists 'rebels' if they continued to oppose a measure narrowly agreed by the lower chamber. Curzon argued that British people would be 'very loth to condemn those whose only disloyalty it will be to have been excessive in their loyalty to the King'.[98]

A few months later, speaking in the same chamber, Lord Crewe moved the final reading of the bill on behalf of the government. Dismissing the importance of a parliamentary majority in favour of the measure and the threat of violence by loyalists, the Liberal peer insisted that the moral obligations of parliamentarians should be of paramount importance in executing their duties. He ended by claiming that if the bill was 'morally wrong in itself, it would remain morally wrong however large the Parliamentary majority that desires it'.[99]

Much of the discussion on Home Rule during its Commons passage in 1913 and early 1914 was on the subject of Ulster's exclusion. Herbert Asquith had anticipated virulent Ulster unionist opposition to the bill prior to its introduction in the Commons during the spring of 1912 and, indeed, had identified 'special treatment' for Ulster if need be. Asquith had promised that the government would be 'ready to recognise the necessity [of exclusion] either by the amending of the Bill, or by not pressing it on under the provisions of the Parliament Act.' However, the prime minister had characteristically qualified this statement of intent by stressing that first 'careful, confident inquiry' was to be undertaken into ascertaining 'the real extent and character of the Ulster resistance'.[100] This raises the larger question of whether some form of Ulster exclusion should have been included in the original bill. There is a strong argument to back up claims that this would have deterred Irish unionist resistance to the proposed measure.

Having abandoned his offer of granting Ulster limited Home Rule under the overall authority of an Irish parliament, the prime minister made the alternative suggestion of granting temporary exclusion to Ulster – initially for three years, but subsequently extended to a six-year period – in February 1914. In the debate that followed, the Irish Unionist Party leader combined his trademark candour and resilience with the somewhat surprising offer of advice to his opponents on appropriate strategies for tempting Ulster into accepting such proposals. In promising to 'go on with these [Ulster] people to the end with their policy of resistance', Edward Carson typically lauded the province for its 'fight for a great principle and a great ideal'.[101] He then proceeded to treat Herbert Asquith and especially John Redmond to a pep talk on the 'two ways to deal with Ulster'. Carson then expanded on his thesis that nationalists had failed to appeal directly to the aspirations of Ulster loyalists:

> You must therefore coerce her if you go on – or you must, in the long run, by showing that good government can come under the Home Rule Bill, try and win her over to the case of the rest of Ireland ... I say this to my nationalist fellow-countrymen, and indeed, also to the government: you have never tried to win over Ulster. You have never tried to understand her position ... I say to the leader of the Nationalist Party, if you want Ulster, go and take her, or go on and win her. You have never wanted her affections; you have wanted her taxes.[102]

Edward Carson rejected Herbert Asquith's emphasis on time restrictions on any offer of exclusion to Ulster and scorned the suggestion of individual county opt-out following a plebiscite. He characteristically dismissed the prime minister's offer of a six-year moratorium on Ulster's position within an Irish national parliament, employing one of his most memorable phrases in doing so. The leader of the Irish Unionist Party told the prime minister in the House of Commons on 9 March that 'we do not want sentence of death with a stay of execution for six years'.[103] Sir Edward Carson's tactic at this late stage was to hold out for exclusion for the whole province of Ulster, rather than settle for a more realistic catch of four or even six counties. The arch-loyalist, Carson still harboured hopes that by holding out for the larger area and the whole provincial unit, the chances of the measure being applied to the rest of Ireland would be at least delayed. *The Times* agreed with Carson's prognosis, claiming it was 'unquestionable that the exclusion of the whole of Ulster holds out far more hope of ultimate unity than the exclusion of a part'.[104]

The Third Home Rule Bill finally received its third reading and was duly passed on 26 May. Tension inevitably heightened in Ulster during the days leading up to the parliamentary climax at Westminster, though as Conservative-leaning newspapers duly pointed out, discipline was maintained within UVF ranks. *The Times* informed its readers that the Ulster Volunteers had placed 'protective cordons across streets' in west Belfast and asserted its opinion that the government would take 'no measures to suppress the supremacy of the Volunteers, who would be 'in full possession of the town'.[105] The following day the same paper pointed out that the Ulster Covenanters 'remain ready for any emergency but are making preparations solely for the preservation of order'.[106] The prime minister had promised that his administration would introduce an Amending Bill in the House of Lords, offering the prospect of an agreed, negotiated settlement to the Irish crisis. However, when this bill was finally introduced in the upper chamber early that summer, it proved to be a disappointment for unionists. It offered little more than the county opt-out scheme and time-limit proposal for Ulster exclusion that had been discussed back in March. However, this eventually passed through the House of Lords on 14 July. Asquith reassessed his original plan to consider this amendment in the Commons and instead announced that a conference would be staged at Buckingham Palace towards the end of July.

There were deep-rooted fears that the monarch, King George V, was in danger of being dragged into an impossible position over the Home Rule legislation. The king had been under considerable pressure from Bonar Law and other Tory leaders to use his royal prerogative to dissolve parliament so that an election could be fought on the issue of Home Rule. George V was naturally reluctant to take a constitutional precedent like this, but was equally concerned about the worsening situation in the north of Ireland, as well as being influenced by wider issues such as the need for imperial unity. Such a strategy was also risky for both the Conservatives and the Irish Unionist Party. It was far from certain that public opinion would look kindly upon such a move and some feared that it would be construed by its opponents as 'a thinly disguised Tory plot to overturn an elected government'.[107] The king's own attitudes, fears and even prejudices, arguably a mirror image of the Edwardian establishment, were an undeniable influence on his approach to the Irish question. George V obviously had strong reservations about Home Rule being imposed upon Ulster and his reservations about the government's Irish policy were undisguised. In September 1913 he had expressed his disquiet over the predicament of the army if it were called on to intervene in Ulster, and two months later he wrote to Herbert Asquith articulating his belief that Ulster would 'never agree to send representatives to an Irish Parliament in Dublin, no matter what safeguards or guarantees you may provide'.[108]

King George V had first raised the idea of an all-party conference on Ireland back in the summer of 1913. Deterred by Asquith's advice to avoid becoming embroiled in the crisis, the king had been persuaded not to proceed with such a meeting. But, as the crisis deepened, and as the constitutional necessity of the king's involvement drew ever closer with the passing of the bill for the third time in the Commons on 25 May 1914, a renewed offer from the king for a 'clear the air' meeting was made and this time accepted by the prime minister. Theoretically the closed conference at Buckingham Palace between 21 and 24 July was to discuss the use of the area in Ulster likely to be exempted from the measure and also the degree of time restrictions for any such exclusion, but the second issue was not raised and much of the time was spent by the various participants reiterating their well-known positions. The king, much as he was to do in that speech that opened the northern parliament in Belfast seven years later, reminded the delegates for the real need to be 'conciliatory' in his opening address. He stressed the magnitude of what was at stake:

> For months we have watched with deep misgivings the cause of events in Ireland ... and today the cry of civil war is on the lips of the most responsible and sober-minded of my people ... We have in the past endeavoured to act as a civilising example to the world, and to me it is unthinkable, as it must be to you, that we should be brought to the brink of fratricidal strife upon issues apparently so capable of adjustment as those you are now asked to consider, if handled in a spirit of generous compromise.[109]

Interest in the crucial meeting involving the king and the leaders of the Liberal, Conservative, Irish Nationalist and Irish Unionist Parties was intense in Ulster during the second half of July. If anything, tension had increased since the bill's passage through the Commons in May and the recent Orange celebrations and demonstrations involving the now-armed Ulster Volunteers. Within two days of the Buckingham Palace conference closing, 1,500 rifles were unloaded at Howth Harbour, near Dublin, and disturbances between British military and local people led to three fatal shootings. Although John Redmond and other Irish nationalists were to complain of different treatment for the National Volunteers compared to their Ulster counterparts three months before, the cases were very different. The unloading of a much smaller and lower-quality arms cache had been publicised in advance and executed in broad daylight. Roy Foster has written that 'the contrast with the Ulster operation could not have been more marked ... the UVF venture had been organised secretly; the National Volunteers were deliberately creating a provocative gesture'.[110] Feelings on Ulster streets and in its countryside reflected the belief that events were leading up to a climax and the meeting in London was given detailed coverage in the Belfast press over the three days of the conference. On its eve, the *Belfast*

Telegraph stressed the epochal significance of the occasion, although it remained doubtful about a clear outcome. The paper's editorial believed that the meeting would 'bring matters to a head' but was 'not very optimistic' about its likely success. Still, the *Telegraph* supported such face-to-face talks, which, they believed, represented 'a final effort to sort out the tariffs which the Government has created by its constant clinging to the Nationalists'.[111]

Supporters of the unionist leadership were deeply concerned about the gravity of the situation and, although optimistic about their prospects, were far from convinced about the integrity of the prime minister's intentions. Alfred Milner wrote to Edward Carson at the start of the Buckingham Palace negotiations, describing Herbert Asquith as an 'eel', and wishing Carson 'well out of the Buckingham Palace trap'. Milner urged Carson to 'stick out for the six counties as a minimum', pointing out the government's 'weak' position: 'they can't fight because they can't rely on the army, and they daren't face an election, because they know they would be beaten'.[112]

If anything, the conference's main result was to expose further the intractable nature of the Irish problem, and clearly the doubts expressed in Belfast papers were well founded. Yet, apart from providing a rare opportunity for the various leaders to express their views in one room (some were privately surprised by the warm relationships that developed between political opponents such as John Redmond and Edward Carson), the conference represented a genuine attempt on the part of George V to stave off an imminent rebellion. The conference also spurred on the various leaders, most particularly Herbert Asquith, to continue to explore various political options, including the permanent exclusion of four Ulster counties (offered on 30 July).

The heir to the Austrian throne, Archduke Franz Ferdinand, was assassinated in Sarajevo on 28 June and war clouds darkened across Europe from this period onwards. Even now, however, Asquith was still trying to come to terms with proposals that might bring about agreement, particularly after the failure of the conference. At a time when the small print of international alliances was being studied fervently by ministers, ambassadors and governmental advisers across Europe, Herbert Asquith was spending much of his time poring over maps of Ireland. He eventually devised a final plan that would abandon the principle that individual counties would be allowed to withdraw from the terms of the legislation, and instead proposed that specific parts of Ulster be carved up, principally along lines of religious dominance. This proposal, which would have resulted in a small nucleus of Ulster counties being exempted from the governance of a Dublin administration and divided others (including Tyrone) along sectarian lines, was instantly dismissed by Edward Carson and Andrew Bonar Law.

The former was a frequent visitor to Ulster during this period (between June and September). Speaking in Larne during the Orange celebrations in July, he exhibited his increasingly pessimistic feeling on the outcome of the crisis. Stressing the need for a disciplined response to the growing threat, Carson warned his followers:

> Remember that we must have no act committed against any individual or any man's property which would sully the great name which you have already attained ... I am bound to tell you that I see no hopes of peace. I see nothing but darkness and shadows.[113]

The first half of September was a hectic period as far as the bill was concerned. Herbert Asquith was accused of reneging on an assurance given to Bonar Law and Edward Carson the previous month that the Amendment Bill would not be considered until the war was over. The prime minister now intended that both measures would be placed on the statute book, but that their implementation would be suspended until the war ended. Unionists were angry as Asquith gave in to

Redmond's demand that the bill should gain the royal assent on 18 September. Disappointed by the king's role in this, some Ulster loyalists uncharacteristically refused to acknowledge the national anthem at public meetings. Edward Carson was annoyed by Asquith's decision and joined Bonar Law in a House of Commons protest on 15 September. Carson believed that the successful parliamentary passage of the bill would precipitate considerable nationalist rejoicing in the province, which would in turn spark off street disturbances. He also believed that once the bill was on the statute book it would be difficult to have it repealed. However, his sense of patriotism combined with his belief in Ulster's strong moral position meant that he reluctantly accepted Herbert Asquith's assurances that Ulster would not be coerced and that the new measure would not be implemented until after the war. With the Irish legislation on the back burner, international issues increasingly dominated the thinking of British and Irish people alike. Winston Churchill recorded in his diary:

> The parishes of Fermanagh and Tyrone faded back into the mists and squalls of Ireland, and a strange light began immediately, but by perceptible gradations, to fall and show upon the map of Europe.[114]

As observed in detail in the next chapter, Ulster was to experience 'militant action' in August and September, though it would not be of the sort that most observers had feared. Local newspapers reported 'busy scenes' outside military recruitment centres in Belfast during mid-August, with the crowds of enthusiastic would-be recruits 'so great' that the 'doors had to be closed'.[115] Despite this obvious determination to support the national war effort, unionist leaders were aware of the potential dilemma they faced by their rally-call for Ulster Volunteers and other loyalists to join up. Edward Carson and James Craig were conscious that the greater part of the UVF's fighting strength would initially be deployed in action across the English Channel and unavailable for any required, instant, intervention at home. Carson appealed for temporary replacements for those Volunteers opting to serve king and country and also insisted that the vast majority of his Ulster Volunteers would stay together as a fighting force. Although this was in any case favoured by the War Office, Carson and his lieutenants were aware that by keeping the UVF together as a unit they would be liable for a speedier redeployment of forces to Ulster if this were needed.

Doubts over joining up were not confined to ordinary soldiers. Wilfrid B. Spender, who had been appointed to the Coastal Defence Staff, wrote from Kent to Edward Carson at the start of August, stressing that if the government 'used the mobilisation as a means of advancing Home Rule, I shall have no hesitation in returning to Belfast with or without leave'.[116]

The mood in the Catholic and Protestant sections of the Ulster community in the summer of 1914 would have been somewhat different from that experienced by other communities across Britain and Ireland. Many in the province, not least the many thousands of young men in the ranks of the Ulster and National Volunteers, would have shared the feelings of uncertainty and foreboding experienced by potential recruits elsewhere in the country. However, there was a unique mood of relief at this time that the ultimate dread of the whole Ulster community – that of a bloody civil war – had been avoided, at least for the time being. Some hoped that the anticipated short duration of the international conflict (the predominant feeling was that the 'boys would be home for Christmas') would provide a timely respite from home trials and tribulations and that the respective sides in Ireland's Home Rule crisis would return to the negotiation table to revisit the key issues in a few months' time, refreshed by a wave of postwar optimism and generosity of spirit. Although the enormity of danger surrounding Home Rule was not understated, most Ulster loyalists accepted that the latest international threat had to be prioritised. Like a bad, recurring illness, Home Rule would remain, ever present and ever threatening, until more immediate, 'life-threatening' problems had been sorted. As Protestants flocked to recruiting stations, so too did many young Catholics in their endeavours to register with other Irish regiments. The irony of potential foes joining forces to fight a common enemy would not have been lost on most citizens, as attention in newspapers, workplaces, church halls and sports clubs turned to denouncing early German military manoeuvres and the 'ransacking' of Belgium, and to training the Ulster Volunteers in preparation for action in France.

The UVF march past Belfast's City Hall, May 1915

Epilogue

6

War against Germany was declared on 1 August and there was much frenetic activity in the mobilisation of forces and the start of a mass recruitment campaign. Reaction to Carson's exhortations to join up was generally enthusiastic and the majority of Ulster Volunteers soon joined the newly created Thirty-Sixth Ulster Division, one of three Irish Volunteer divisions. Training was in full swing by the end of September 1914, with camps established at Ballykinler, Clandeboye (both in

County Down) and at Finner in County Donegal.

Inside nine months the Thirty-Sixth Ulster Division would become a professional fighting machine. An inspection of over 17,000 of its men was carried out by Major-General Sir Hugh McCalmont on 8 May 1915 at Malone in south Belfast. Marching to unrestrained cheering from large crowds and patriotic tunes played by accompanying bands, the division paraded through the streets of central Belfast after this inspection, before making their way to the docks.

'Carson's army', as they were known, started their final training in southern England a few weeks later. They were quartered at Seaford, near Beachy Head on the Sussex coast, and during the summer they could hear the echoes of the big guns on the western front. The Thirty-Sixth Division was inspected by Sir Edward Carson, who received a predictably warm welcome, and also by the secretary of state for war, Lord Kitchener, during September. Also that month, Major-General Sir Oliver Nugent was appointed as officer in charge and the division was paid the ultimate accolade of being inspected by King George V, just a few days before embarking for France. Kitchener later told Carson that 'your Division of Ulstermen is the finest I have yet seen'.[1]

The Thirty-Sixth Division was now a very different 'army' from that which had paraded before Carson some two years previously. Fully trained and professional, the Ulstermen were soon involved in General Haig's 'big push' against the Germans. They were engaged in military operations against the enemy in May and early June 1916. A major offensive – aimed at relieving pressure on the overstretched French forces around Verdun – was planned by the British military leadership to start later in June, but the advance by a British contingent estimated at 200,000 was delayed by bad weather. The Thirty-Sixth Division held the section of the British front line to the north-east of

Thiepval Wood and their mission was to take the heavily fortified German position at Schwaben Redoubt and to move towards the village of Grandcourt.

Most members of the Thirty-Sixth Ulster Division had become accustomed to conditions in Thiepval Wood, which was situated in beautiful French countryside and where, at daybreak, they could hear the plaintive singing of nightingales. Coincidentally, the British offensive started just after dawn on 1 July, the anniversary of the battle of the Boyne, and many in the division wore Orange lilies or even sashes on that fateful morning. Although some would have appreciated the potent symbolism of the date, most of the soldiers' thoughts would have been about their loved ones at home. Standing in this foreign wood on the eve of what they realised would be a major battle, some would have recalled their involvement in previous 'military' events, such as parading at Craigavon or Balmoral or marching through rural towns in Ulster with newly acquired rifles barely two years before. Yet such recollections would have been quickly replaced by their pride in being Ulster Volunteers, and their conviction that their imminent blood sacrifice, as they saw it, would ultimately cleanse their distant homeland from the evils of Home Rule.

The division was led into battle by its commanding officer, Colonel Crozier. With many chanting their old battle-cry, 'For God and Ulster!', the division made some progress, capturing enemy trenches at Schwaben Redoubt. However, the progress of other British units was slower and, with German resistance proving to be considerable, the division had to retreat before nightfall. Losses were great. British losses for the first two days of the Somme offensive were over 21,000, with a further 35,000 soldiers suffering injuries. Over 5,500 officers and men of the Thirty-Sixth Ulster Division were reported killed, wounded or missing during this first day alone. Four Victoria Crosses were posthumously awarded to its members. Some groups and battalions within the division were decimated. Out of an estimated 600 former UVF men in the Armagh, Monaghan and Cavan Battalions (known as 'Blacker's Boys'), only 64 returned to British lines that day, whilst Colonel Crozier mourned the fact that barely one-tenth of his 700 'Shankill Boys' had returned unscathed. News of the huge scale of losses took a few days to reach Ulster, where many families mourned the loss of a loved one (the Twelfth of July celebrations were cancelled that year). Perhaps the most fulsome tribute to the former Ulster Volunteers came from Wilfrid Spender, who had played such an active role in the gun-running operation two years before. He wrote in his diary the following day:

> I am not an Ulsterman, but yesterday, the 1st July, as I followed their amazing attack I felt that I would rather be an Ulsterman than anything else in the world.[2]

A restructured Thirty-Sixth Division (including many non-Ulster personnel) would re-emerge and gain further distinction at places like Messines during the second half of the Great War.

When the majority of Ulster Volunteers made it back to Ulster at the end of the war, many would have recognised that they – and more particularly their political leaders – were returning to unfinished business. Yet their immediate concern, certainly by the summer of 1919, was to find regular employment. Many of the positions that these returning soldiers had once held in Belfast factories and shipyards had been filled during the war years by migrant Catholic workers from across Ireland. Embittered soldiers and loyalists described this trend as 'Shinners [Sinn Féin supporters] getting the boys' jobs!' The situation had been compounded by the inevitable economic depression precipitated by the ending of international hostilities.

It was a combination of this economic tension and political uncertainty over Lloyd George's postwar coalition administration's plans to deal with Ireland's political future that led to sectarian disturbances in east Belfast in July 1920. A few weeks previously, there had been serious disturbances in Derry, and the Anglo-Irish War that had commenced the previous year had already claimed the lives of several Ulster-born police officers. The intimidation of several hundred Catholic shipyard workers and many more in other industrial workplaces, followed by sectarian disorder across the city, led to the emergence of IRA gunmen and bombers and the expulsion of many, mostly Catholic, families from their homes through intimidation. In intermittent, though extremely bloody and vicious, disturbances spanning a period of just over two years, the conflict claimed over 500 lives and resulted in several thousand injuries, as well as causing over £3 million worth of damage to property. The IRA's campaign was an extensive and varied one. Soldiers and policemen were shot in central Belfast streets; industrial workers were victims of bomb attacks on tramcars bound for loyalist areas; unionist politicians were assassinated in broad daylight in busy Belfast shopping areas and fashionable London squares; and republican 'firebugs' targeted dozens of premises in Belfast's commercial sector. The violence was mostly confined to the Greater Belfast area, although there was trouble in several other parts of Ulster.[3]

Despite the virulent nature of the IRA Third Northern Division's campaign, the majority of deaths and injuries inflicted during this short conflict were the consequence of the actions of sinister 'rogue cops' and 'freelance' loyalist paramilitaries, several of whom had connections with the shadowy Belfast Protestant Association. Most of these loyalist attacks on Catholic neighbours or fellow citizens were carried out by opportunistic killers. They were only seriously challenged by the authorities once the IRA's northern campaign petered out after the start of the Irish Civil War in August 1922. It is certainly true that many ex-soldiers, both Catholic and Protestant, were the victims of such disturbances in Belfast. It is equally obvious that some of the arsenal of UVF weapons that had been garnered before the start of the Great War was used by the ill-disciplined gangs to attack Catholics. It is also likely that individual members of the old UVF, perhaps including some recently returned from France, became embroiled in the sectarian clashes on Belfast streets during the early 1920s. However, the UVF was not an operational movement in 1920 and there is no evidence that they were used in an organised capacity for such bloodletting. Many more of Sir Edward Carson's old force would have been persuaded to defend the security of the new state by joining the auxiliary police force devised by Carson and Wilfrid Spender, the Ulster Special Constabulary (USC).

For those who had forecast uncontrollable, widespread sectarian bloodshed back in the days and months leading up to the summer of 1914, the outrages experienced in Belfast between the summer of 1920 and the autumn of 1922 (especially during the particularly vicious first half of 1922) would have come as no great surprise. Sympathisers of Ulster unionism pointed out that the military discipline and unity of purpose of Sir Edward Carson's movement had been chiefly responsible for preventing such disturbances between 1912 and 1914. Whilst there is much credence in this argument, it would be disingenuous to suggest that, given the very different prevailing circumstances existing in the postwar world, the presence of such a unified force would have, in itself, prevented the outbreak of sectarian violence in July 1920.

The end of hostilities in Europe meant that the British government's attention inevitably returned to the future political governance of Ireland. Winston Churchill memorably stated in the House of Commons:

> As the deluge subsides and the waters fall short, we see the dreary steeples of Fermanagh and Tyrone emerging once again. The integrity of their quarrel is one of the few institutions that has been unaltered in the cataclysm which has swept the world.[4]

Yet dealing with Ireland's political and constitutional

nuances, a far from easy task at the best of times, had been further complicated by significant changes, not only in that country's political landscape (especially the Easter Rising of 1916 and the subsequent political dominance of Sinn Féin), but also in the creation of new national boundaries and states following the postwar settlement at Versailles in 1919. The new British prime minister, David Lloyd George, believed he had found a meaningful compromise in tune with the underlying principle of self-determination prevalent at Versailles, and this was enshrined in his Better Government of Ireland Bill, which was introduced at Westminster early in 1920 (it became law just before Christmas).

Many of the features of Herbert Asquith's Home Rule Bill were apparent in this new piece of legislation, which recognised the different status of Ulster (or at least a substantial part of that province) from the rest of Ireland in facilitating its opting-out of a Dublin parliament. This provision was undoubtedly well received by Ulster unionists, but it was the alternative to this southern parliament that most concerned them. Ulster unionists had stubbornly resisted Irish Home Rule before the Great War. What they were now being offered – separate legislative chambers in Belfast and Dublin, both of which were subservient to Westminster, and the retention of Ireland's constitutional status under the monarchy and within the United Kingdom – appeared to be a recognition of the north's difference not only from the rest of Ireland, but also from the remainder of the United Kingdom.

Edward Carson and his colleagues recognised that a new administration in Belfast was the best deal they could achieve under the circumstances and grudgingly, in a mood of obligation, duty and political compromise, accepted the new legislation. Ordinary loyalists were confused by this new parliamentary measure but they sought reassurance in the statements of their trusted leaders and in the editorials of their favoured newspapers. The *Belfast Telegraph* noted that the threat of the Third Home Rule Bill would 'no longer haunt us' and expressed its 'thankfulness that the right of Ulster to separate treatment and to be arbiters of her political testimony is now recognised in fact and by Act of Parliament'.[5]

Despite the willingness of unionists to accept such advice from their leaders, there was a growing feeling that the potential republican threat to Ulster – in the light of the 1916 Easter Rising and the Anglo-Irish War of 1919–21 – was of greater danger to their immediate security than any political change. The elections to the new parliament in Belfast in May 1921 resulted in a predominantly unionist chamber. Of 52 elected representatives, 40 were from the Ulster Unionists. The remainder of seats were equally shared between Devlin's nationalist group and Sinn Féin, which instantly boycotted the assembly. Despite this, the main hope of the British establishment was that the creation of such an assembly would help to defuse sectarian tension and promote reconciliation across the island. This was the theme of King George V's speech when he opened the new Northern Ireland parliament in Belfast's City Hall in June 1921 and appealed to 'all Irishmen to pause, to stretch out the hand of forbearance and conciliation, to forgive and forget, and to join in making for the land they love a new era of peace, contentment and goodwill'.[6]

The disillusionment of Ulster unionists and their reluctance to accept political initiatives and exhortations from Westminster increased after the Anglo-Irish Treaty, which was signed at Downing Street in December 1921. The treaty precipitated a hard-line republican stance of opposition and protest, which would fully manifest itself in the civil war that would break out the following summer. Ulster unionism's old friends in parliament and press supported such moves, urging their erstwhile friends in Belfast to refrain from blocking any solution to the wider Irish problem. Disagreements over the treaty led to Carson having harsh words for his former friends Bonar Law and F.E. Smith (now Lord Birkenhead). In his maiden House of

Lords speech, Lord Carson of Duncairn argued:

> I was fighting with others [Tories] whose friendship and comradeship I hope I will lose from tonight, because I don't value any friendship that is not founded upon confidence and trust. I was in earnest. What a fool I was! I was only a puppet, and so was Ulster, and so was Ireland, in the political game that was to get the Conservative Party into power.[7]

The first prime minister of the new state was James Craig, the organiser of much of Ulster unionism's resistance during the 1912–14 campaign. The job had originally been offered to Carson, but Carson had turned it down due to his ill health and recommended in his place his loyal lieutenant. The new parliament and its government were to be sorely tested in their infancy as the region suffered internal and external attacks from the IRA and from the communal disturbances described above. The legacy of this two-year conflict was lasting and very real for both sections of the community and also for the attitudes of British and Irish administrations. The sense of isolation felt by northern Catholics as a clear minority in a state to which few of their number could claim to hold close allegiance was deepened by their vulnerability to intimidation and attack during the Belfast disturbances of the early 1920s and also by their low level of participation in local politics. They could not claim to suffer from electoral discrimination in parliamentary elections at this time, but Catholics were rarely called upon to take major decisions in the regional parliament. This was because of their representatives decided to boycott the local assembly – even Joe Devlin's Nationalist Party was to adopt a sporadic abstentionist policy to the regional parliament – and also because of unionism's lack of conciliatory gestures to the minority community. Unionists, on the other hand, perceived themselves to be vulnerable and exposed to hostile interventions from across the border and also from inside their own boundary. The paramilitary campaign of the IRA's Third Northern Division, the apparent 'expansionist' policy of the anti-treaty, hard-line former chiefs of the IRA who constituted the political leadership of the Irish Free State during its first three decades, along with the reluctance of the Catholic minority to recognise the existence of the new Northern Irish state, provided Ulster loyalists with what they saw as justification to resist demands for an inclusive style in the governance of their region. Thus, early hopes of liberal political and social reforms prompted by the proportional-representation voting system and proposed educational reforms were soon dashed.

Meanwhile, British politicians, spared the hassle of constant intervention in Irish affairs, were reassured by the low levels of violence during the first four decades in the new state's life and, although ultimately responsible for the province, Westminster adopted a low-profile role. Indeed, the unionist regime was bolstered by Clement Attlee's Ireland Act (1949), which guaranteed the political boundaries of Northern Ireland unless its parliament at Stormont decreed otherwise. This was seen to be a reward for Northern Ireland's contribution to the national war effort. (Indeed, that great scourge of Ulster unionists, Sir Winston Churchill, also praised the province for its war contribution.) Yet the *laissez-faire* approach of Westminster politicians to everyday politics in the region could not forever stifle nationalist allegations of discrimination and one-party government. A new Labour administration came into power in London in 1964 and responded positively to the demands of the civil-rights movement, at the same time putting pressure on the progressive unionist premier, Terence O'Neill, who was further weakened by schisms within his own party.

When the first serious street disturbances erupted in late 1968 in what would mark the start of the modern Northern Ireland conflict, the Ulster Unionist Party (as it was by then known) experienced fissures in its once-undisputed hegemony over the northern state. This was the result of the fact that traditional supporters were deserting the party and moving their support to the Protestant (later Democratic) Unionist and Vanguard Parties. Also, the Ulster Unionist Party was failing to gain meaningful support in Great Britain. Carson's party, which had succeeded in mobilising considerable parliamentary and public sympathy for the plight of Ulster Protestants between 1912 and 1914, struggled to justify its record in government or present its case to an increasingly sceptical British public in the late 1960s and early 1970s.[8] Although the degree of empathy for the Catholic position declined somewhat after the IRA's bombing campaign and onslaught against the British Army from the early 1970s (especially its activities in Great Britain), this did not lead to a direct increase in political support or approval for the position of the leaders of the Ulster Unionist Party.

Why, then, were Ulster Unionist Party leaders apparently unable to garner similar levels of support for their political position as Edward Carson had achieved some 60–70 years before? Obviously the political, social and religious landscape had altered radically over these six decades. Ulster unionists' status as a 'minority' in 1912 contrasted sharply with the unionist administration's far-from-sympathetic treatment of other minorities in the late 1960s. As noted above, political expediency prompted by the lack of a decisive parliamentary majority for either party at Westminster had resulted in Ulster unionists gaining unprecedented political support for their cause. Sixty years after Carson and Craig had been able to rely on religious and aristocratic support in Great Britain, an increasingly secular and classless British society had difficulty in empathising with what they regarded as the outdated nature of Ulster's tribal divisions. The age of empire had long since disappeared and most citizens in the Britain of Harold Wilson and Edward Heath appeared more concerned about entry into Europe than with their imperial heritage. In addition, the scope and nature of media coverage of political affairs had developed considerably since the Edwardian era. No longer reliant on the written word, the general public's perception of politicians increasingly owed more to the image of a party or individual politician. For a host of reasons, the Ulster Unionist Party did not project itself well in this sphere.

However, perhaps the most crucial change was in terms of the unity of the Unionist Party in Ulster and its quality of leadership. As we have seen, there were few apparent divisions within Ulster unionism during the Edwardian period. The movement's key leaders, Edward Carson and James Craig, complemented each other perfectly. The opposite was the case during the late 1960s, when a progressive but remote and aristocratic party leader enjoyed little personal support within his party, which was increasingly divided along class lines as well as on law-and-order policies. Unionism's political hegemony in Ulster – not remotely threatened between 1912 and 1914 – was an early casualty of the modern conflict, with disillusioned unionists deserting the ranks of the traditional pro-union party to find political solace in new groups like the Democratic Unionists and Vanguard. Further fractures within unionism were to occur when Brian Faulkner created the Progressive Unionist Party in 1974.

This book has investigated the perceived dangers facing Ulster's loyalist population between 1912 and 1914 and examined the nature of their anti-Home Rule campaign – most especially, its capacity to maximise the support provided by influential friends in Great Britain. Ulster unionists' response to political events at Westminster did not reflect unnecessary paranoia on their part. They saw a genuine threat to their long-term future in the proposed Home Rule legislation and their opposition to it was far from cosmetic. This opposition was based on what they believed to be their difference from the rest of the island – which, they stressed, was symbolic of 'the two Irelands'. This difference related to the manner in which their economic infrastructure contrasted with that of the rest of Ireland, the fact that a substantial part of the province, most notably in the Greater Belfast area, was non-Catholic, and their differing political allegiance and sense of wider identity.

The threat they encountered from early in 1912 was a very real one. An all-Ireland parliament centred in Dublin was proposed in the Third Home Rule Bill and there were relatively few substantial concessions to the province of Ulster in the bill's numerous clauses. Many Ulstermen had memories of previous threats of Home Rule, but on this occasion the likelihood of it becoming a reality had substantially increased. The new Parliament Act of 1911 had restricted the powers of the House of Lords to delay a measure of which they disapproved; in the House of Commons, a pact between Liberals and the Irish Nationalist Party meant that, without a fresh election and a change in the composition of the lower chamber, the bill could be expected to complete its parliamentary passage. The dismissive tone of the Liberal government and their refusal to take unionist opposition seriously further increased loyalist apprehension within Ulster. This was particularly evident in the period just before and after the bill's introduction in the House of Commons. Winston Churchill's controversial visit to Belfast nearly culminated in a riot and the cabinet minister narrowly escaped serious injury in February 1912. During that summer a series of sectarian incidents indicated the very real danger that this political tension would incite civil disturbances in the province. The dangers associated with Home Rule were not to subside for what must have appeared to unionists to be an eternity. However, they received considerable sustenance during this difficult two-year period from their own growing confidence in the validity of their cause, from the strength of their numbers – reflected in the success of loyalist demonstrations at Craigavon and Balmoral in Belfast in 1911 and 1912 – and from the growing acceptance of Ulster's claims by sympathetic sections of British right-wing opinion. Whether this support manifested itself in parliament or at large meetings – such as the demonstration in the grounds of Blenheim Palace – it would offer imperilled Ulster unionists crucial hope in what appeared to be a time of doom.

Facing such a threat to their everyday way of life and long-term future, the unionist community within Ulster gelled together to an unprecedented degree. The relative lack of division and open dissent amongst their ranks stood their cause in good stead over this period. Considerable preparation for such a crisis had been made in the years leading up to the introduction of the Third Home Rule Bill in 1912. An administrative body overseeing the party's day-to-day running, the Ulster Unionist Council, had been established in 1905, and this group invited participation from all classes and sections of the loyalist community. The UUC coordinated most of the major events and initiatives during this period, including proposing a provisional government, which would have become operational when Home Rule came into effect.

The organisation's close liaison with Sir Edward Carson was also vital. Grassroots unionist supporters would have been reassured by the standing of the man leading their party. Carson's oratorical skills and charisma, influential contacts and willingness to be flexible in his tactics proved to be of inestimable value. Along with the organisational ability of 'local' man James Craig, the Irish Unionist Party was to enjoy a rare combination of riches at the head of their movement. However, despite his eventual success in staving off Ulster's incorporation within an all-Ireland parliament, Carson's calculated gamble, mixing extreme political rhetoric with the formation and drilling of a 'citizen army', would result in a political settlement – Irish partition – that he fundamentally abhorred.

Unionism was also advanced in its skilful use of political propaganda. Using a variety of strategies, including producing and distributing pamphlets, organising political tours of Ulster for British electors, by-election campaigning in Britain, distributing political postcards and stamps and staging political meetings at venues across Great Britain, Ulster unionists were successful in ensuring that their political message was heard and understood by the British public.

Underpinning this cohesion within the broader unionist movement was the unqualified backing of various Protestant organisations, institutions and churches. Political and religious organisations such as the revitalised unionist clubs and the invigorated Orange Order played an important role in ensuring impressive turnouts at loyalist demonstrations and meetings. They also helped to bring together Ulster's rural and industrial workforce, their employers and the region's small but influential group of aristocrats and major landowners. The fusion of Ulster's Protestant society was best illustrated in the cross-class support for the Ulster Volunteers, formed in 1913. This paramilitary force, which openly flirted with lawbreaking, also received the literal blessing of the Protestant churches, which appeared to go out their its way to be directly associated with the political movement opposing Irish Home Rule.

The UVF, especially after being armed in April 1914, served fundamental purposes for different groups. The strength, efficiency and operational capacity of the force reassured ordinary loyalists that they would not be, in the end, lightly dismissed by their opponents, and the presence of such an armed group had a major influence on the way in which Ulster unionists were perceived, both by their political sympathisers and by their opponents in Great Britain. This Protestant unity in Ulster was epitomised by the province's response to the Covenant campaign in September 1912. During this two-week-long outpouring of loyalist fervour, rural and urban Protestants alike made their opposition felt to the proposed change in their status and clearly voiced their rationale for desiring to be governed directly from Westminster. The true significance of Ulster's Solemn League and Covenant was that it illustrated the scale and degree of the province's opposition to Home Rule. By its peculiar mix of historical symbolism and pageantry alongside religious and political certainty of purpose, the Covenant was a unique example of a community taking ownership of its political and constitutional future.

The significance of the fact that Ulster unionists possessed sympathetic supporters in high society across Britain cannot be underestimated. These friends in high places included leading figures within the Conservative Party, the aristocracy, the press and the military. Ulster unionists enjoyed considerable support from the Tories, who represented to them a government in waiting. With a highly sympathetic party leader who had strong family links to Ulster and sustained support in both parliamentary chambers, the Conservative Party also sanctioned and participated in the British extra-parliamentary campaign. Extreme levels of backing were offered from several mavericks on the political right, including Lords Willoughby de Broke and Milner. This was balanced, however, by the natural reluctance of many mainstream Tories to become too closely allied to Ulster at the expense of creating distance between it and unionists in the other Irish provinces, and also by a concern that the party risked being tarnished by its close association with the Ulster Volunteers in the event of a civil war or confrontation with British forces. Ulster unionists were not too inquisitive or sceptical about the reasons for such support from the right and were appreciative of the empathetic response of most sections of Conservatism. Without such fraternal links, they suspected they would be stranded and even more vulnerable to attack from their opponents at Westminster. Certainly, Andrew Bonar Law was taking a calculated gamble on Ulster and it is doubtful that his support would have remained constant if discipline within the loyalist ranks in Ulster had started to crumble.

Ulster unionists also benefited from sympathetic responses in large sections of the British press. Many key press magnates and newspaper editors were responsive to the calls for help emanating from Ulster loyalists. Papers like *The Times*, *Daily Mail*, *Morning Post*, *Pall Mall Gazette* and *Observer* provided copious coverage of key events in Ulster's political campaign, though everyday treatment of the Irish question tended to be less detailed and less constant.

Edward Carson's movement also enjoyed further help from the highest ranks of British society, a trend which was crucial not just on account of the individual and group contributions of aristocrats but also because of the influence of such involvement upon those below them on the social ladder. Practical support came in the form of generous financial donations from the titled, wealthy and celebrated, in the granting of access to their estates in Ulster for military training and storing of weapons, and by their attendance at political meetings across Ulster and Great Britain. In addition, peers could be relied upon to delay the Home Rule legislation in the House of Lords. Some, especially Willoughby de Broke and Alfred Milner, offered the prospect of more physical and practical assistance through their respective groups, the BLSUU and the British Covenant movement. Further support was collected via the web of contacts accessible to those within the highest tiers of Edwardian society. Often leading Conservatives, army officers, members of the judiciary and aristocrats shared membership of the same gentlemen's clubs and doubtless similar political views. Given the chronological and contextual background surrounding the Home Rule crisis – occurring as it did at a time of imperial pride and awareness – the cause of a 'loyal' minority in Ireland being threatened by a 'disloyal' majority appeared to be both just and fashionable for the highest strata of British society. This largely explains the response of sections of the military class to events at the Curragh in March 1914. Though there is little evidence to suggest that the wider national army was at risk of mutiny over the question of Ulster (its rank and file certainly was not), the events near Dublin at this time did indicate the extent of sympathy felt for Irish unionists by large sections of the officer class.

It is natural to ponder whether Ulster's campaign against Home Rule would have been successful without such support emerging from Great Britain. Having friends in high places certainly bolstered the morale of Ulster Protestants and encouraged them to forge ahead with their campaign in a disciplined manner. Yet, although it undoubtedly comforted

Ulster loyalists during a very trying time, this situation would not have continued indefinitely, given the inevitable success of the Home Rule legislation. Clearly, if sufficient support had not been forthcoming from Great Britain, it would have been harder for the unionist leadership to contain its wilder elements and sectarian disturbances would have harder to prevent. Also, the likelihood of the UVF being drawn into military confrontation with John Redmond's Irish Volunteer Force would have been greater. However, the central thrust or drive behind the campaign would not have evaporated in the absence of such support from England and Scotland. Ulster unionists would have maintained their parliamentary and extra-parliamentary resistance to Home Rule without such backing, although the prospect of its preventing Home Rule would have diminished as the possibility of civil disturbances increased.

The two years that immediately preceded the Great War genuinely constituted a period of unimaginable crisis and danger for Ulster's unionist community. Full of numerous memorable moments of defiance, they encompassed feelings of danger, a pride and passion generated by community resistance and a sense of achievement as the tide apparently started to turn in their favour. For many loyalists the events of 1912–14 represented an emotional rollercoaster that would not be repeated in their lifetime. The loyalist population in Ulster had exhibited a grim determination in their resistance, which had resulted less in triumphalism (which would be associated with unionism in subsequent decades) and rather more in producing cohesion across the Protestant community. This class and religious unity, which was sustained through the period, was embodied by the resistance displayed during the Covenant campaign of September 1912.

The unionist campaign of resistance could not, of course, claim to have been a complete success, since the bill was merely suspended and the eventual solution to the problem of the region's governance was only reluctantly accepted by loyalists.

Yet unionist tactics between 1912 and 1914 – those of street and extra-parliamentary protest as well as more formal opposition within parliament – were modern and efficient and would be copied, albeit less successfully, by other unionist leaders during spells of crisis later in the twentieth century. The unique blend of leadership qualities possessed by the leading luminaries of Ulster unionism, Edward Carson and James Craig, meant that unionists were able to capitalise both on their own strengths and on the weaknesses in their opponents' arguments. Though he undoubtedly took considerable risks and was never in complete control of the situation, Sir Edward Carson did display political pragmatism and defiance in his leadership. Whilst strongly influenced by events in Dublin at Easter in 1916, and the mood of optimism and emphasis on the underlying right of self-determination expressed at Versailles in 1919, those contemplating the postwar governance of Ireland would have recalled the events in Ulster prior to the commencement of international hostilities. The inevitability of some form of partition involving a part of the province of Ulster had been acknowledged by the British administration by the early summer of 1914, and there would be no retreat from a position accepted by Edward Carson, albeit reluctantly.

At the start of this book I mentioned a chance encounter with Sir Douglas Savory many years ago. I recently unearthed more information on this man, who was a neighbour of my family many years ago. Although he would not become a public unionist representative until years after Edward Carson's death, Savory did play a role during the Third Home Rule crisis, pressurising the chief secretary for Ireland and the prime minister (he formally met Herbert Asquith at Westminster on 4 July 1912) and liaising closely with the representatives of Dublin University, Edward Carson and J.H. Campbell.[9] It transpires that Douglas Savory's main contribution to Carson's campaign was his orchestration of opposition amongst academics at Trinity College, Dublin and Queen's University, Belfast to the implications of Home Rule on the financial future and autonomy of Irish universities. As this threat loomed larger, Savory returned to Westminster for meetings with leading politicians and the architects of the proposed legislation. His efforts would finally bear fruit as Campbell's amendment to the clause within the bill dealing with the provision of higher education – retaining Westminster's responsibility for these Irish universities – was passed by the end of 1912. Savory noted in his memoir:

> I obtained an interview with Edward Carson at his house in Eaton Place on that same day [as the amendment was presented] and he assured me that the new Clause gave as strong a safeguard as we could make ... I later obtained a seat in the Gallery of the House of Commons, and I was greatly struck by the admirable speeches made by Sir Edward Carson and Mr Campbell, and by the fairness of Mr Birrell's reply.[10]

Therefore, while he was not at the forefront of the unionist campaign, Douglas Savory did make a significant contribution to one particular, specialist sphere of Irish unionist resistance. His story is an excellent illustration of the wide-ranging nature of support received by Ulster unionists. So in a sense my father was correct – Sir Douglas really was 'one of Sir Edward's men'; or, as I have described them here, one of Ulster's friends in high places.

APPENDIX 1
Chronology

1910	28 January	Herbert Asquith and Liberals win election
	21 February	Sir Edward Carson elected as IUP leader
	6 May	George V accedes to throne
	3 December	Asquith wins second election but is still dependent on Irish Nationalist Party support
1911	23 January	UWUC founded in Belfast
	18 August	Parliament Act passed, restricting powers of House of Lords
	23 September	Large anti-Home Rule demonstration takes place at Craigavon in east Belfast
	13 November	Andrew Bonar Law appointed leader of Conservative Party
1912	8 February	Winston Churchill attacked before addressing a Home Rule meeting in west Belfast
	9 April	Bonar Law and Edward Carson address loyalists at Balmoral in south Belfast
	11 April	Third Home Rule Bill introduced in House of Commons
	11 June	Liberal MP Thomas Agar-Robartes introduces amendment proposing exclusion of four Ulster counties
	29 June	Sunday-school party attacked by AOH in Castledawson
	2 July	Start of industrial expulsions in Belfast
	27 July	Large demonstration in support of Ulster at Blenheim Palace, Oxfordshire
	14 September	Riot involving Protestant and Catholic football supporters in west Belfast
	17 September	Ulster's Solemn League and Covenant campaign begins
	28 September	Ulster's Solemn League and Covenant is signed (major ceremony in Belfast)
	29 September	Major meetings in support of Ulster take place in Liverpool
	1 October	Major meetings in support of Ulster take place in Glasgow

1913	1 January	Carson introduces Ulster exclusion amendment
	16 January	Third Home Rule Bill passes first reading in House of Commons (367–257)
	30 January	Third Home Rule Bill defeated in House of Lords (326–69)
	31 January	Formation of UVF announced
	June	Irish unionists' speaking tour of Great Britain takes place
	7 July	House of Commons passes Third Home Rule Bill for second time (352–243)
	15 July	House of Lords rejects Third Home Rule Bill for second time (302–64)
	11 September	Lord Loreburn's compromise letter appears in *The Times*
	24 September	UUC approve plans for provisional government
	14 October	Bonar Law and Asquith begin secret meetings
	16 December	Edward Carson secretly meets Asquith in Surrey
1914	4 March	Formation of British Covenant movement announced
	20–25 March	'Mutiny' involving British Army officers at the Curragh
	4 April	Pro-Ulster demonstration takes place in London's Hyde Park
	24–5 April	UVF gun-running along Antrim and Down coasts
	25 May	House of Commons passes Third Home Rule Bill for third time
	10 July	First business meeting of Ulster's provisional government takes place
	21–4 July	Buckingham Palace conference on Ireland involving political leaders and King George V takes place
	4 August	United Kingdom declares war on Germany
	August	Thirty-Sixth Ulster Division established
	15 September	Suspending Act delays implementation of Home Rule for one year or duration of war
1915	8 May	Thirty-Sixth Ulster Division leaves Ulster for final training in southern England
	30 September	Thirty-Sixth Ulster Division leaves for France

1916	24 April	Easter Rising begins in Dublin
	1 July	Thirty-Sixth Ulster Division go 'over the top' at the Somme
1920	21 July	Sectarian conflict erupts in Belfast's industrial centres
	23 December	Better Government of Ireland Act passed
1921	24 May	Elections to Northern Ireland parliament take place
	22 June	King George V opens Northern Ireland parliament

APPENDIX 2
Dramatis personae

HERBERT HENRY ASQUITH (1852–1928): Liberal MP for East Fife (1886–1918) and Paisley (1920–4); secretary of state for home affairs (1892–5); chancellor of the exchequer (1906–08); prime minister (1908–16); architect of Third Home Rule Bill (1912–14); appointed to House of Lords in 1925.

AUGUSTINE BIRRELL (1850–1933): Liberal MP for West Fife (1889–1900) and North Bristol (1906–18); president of Board of Trade (1906–7); chief secretary for Ireland (1907–16).

ANDREW BONAR LAW (1858–1923): born in Canada of an Ulster father and raised in Glasgow; successful businessman before entering parliament as secretary at Board of Trade (1904); appointed leader of the Conservative Party in 1911; great supporter of Ulster cause between 1912 and 1914; colonial secretary (1915); chancellor of the exchequer and deputy prime minister (1916); prime minister (1922).

EDWARD CARSON (1854–1935): born in Dublin and educated at Portarlington School and Trinity College, Dublin; called to the Irish Bar in 1889 and appointed solicitor general in 1892; Irish Unionist MP for Dublin University (1892–1918) and Belfast Duncairn (1918–21); earned reputation as one of Britain's leading lawyers, especially for his advocacy in controversial cases, including the Oscar Wilde trial (1895) and the 'Winslow boy' case (1909); knighted in 1900 and succeeded Walter Long as IUP leader in 1910; leader of Ulster's resistance to Irish Home Rule (1912–14); served as attorney general (1915) and first lord of the admiralty (1916) during the Great War; resigned as IUP leader, rejecting the offer to become Northern Ireland's first premier, in 1921; created Baron Carson of Duncairn in 1921 and served as lord of appeal (1921–9).

WINSTON CHURCHILL (1874–1965): grandson of the seventh duke of Marlborough and son of Randolph Churchill; educated at Harrow and Sandhurst; worked as a journalist in South Africa during the Boer War; Conservative MP for Oldham (1900) before representing the Liberals in Manchester North West (1906–08) and Dundee (1908–22);

made controversial pro-Home Rule visit to Belfast (February 1912); served in Liberal administrations as president of Board of Trade (1908–10),
home secretary (1910–11) and first lord of the admiralty (1911–15); held wartime posts as minister for munitions, secretary of state for war and colonial secretary; returned to Tory benches as MP for Woodford (1924–64); chancellor of the exchequer (1924–9); returned to front benches as first lord of the admiralty (1939–40); prime minister (1940–5 and 1951–5); knighted in 1953.

JAMES CRAIG (1871–1940): born in Belfast; landowner and director of Dunville's distillery; served as a captain in Royal Irish Rifles during the Boer War; Irish Unionist MP for County Down (1906–18) and Mid Down (1918–21); quarter master general, Thirty-Sixth Ulster Division (1914–16); knighted in 1918; succeeded Carson as leader of the Irish Unionist Party in February 1921; represented County Down in the Northern Ireland parliament (1921–40); Northern Ireland's first prime minister (1921–40); created Viscount Craigavon in 1927.

FRED CRAWFORD (1861–1952): served in Boer War, rising to rank of lieutenant-colonel; Belfast businessman; senior figure in UVF and responsible for gun-running operation to Ulster (April 1914); involved in secret reorganisation of UVF (1920); district commander of B Specials; worked for Northern Ireland Ministry of Home Affairs (1925–36).

JOE DEVLIN (1871–1934): former barman and *Irish News* reporter; secretary of United Irish League (1901); Home Rule MP for Kilkenny (1902–06); general secretary of Home Rule Party (1904–20); president of Ancient Order of Hibernians (1905–34); MP for West Belfast (1906–18); MP in Northern Ireland parliament (1921–34); leader of nationalist opposition party in northern parliament (1925–34).

JAMES LOUIS (J.L.) GARVIN (1868–1947): born in Birkenhead of Irish parentage; worked on *Newcastle Chronicle* and *Daily Telegraph*; editor of the *Observer* (1908–42); editor of the *Pall Mall Gazette* (1912); confidant of Churchill and Lloyd George during World War I, condemning Versailles Treaty; initially pro-appeasement in 1930s but later supported Churchill; worked on *Sunday Express* (1942–5) and *Daily Telegraph* (1945–7).

ALFRED CHARLES WILLIAM HARMSWORTH (1865–1922): part of childhood spent in relative poverty in Dublin; later became a newspaper and publishing magnate, famed for transforming unprofitable newspapers into entertaining, best-selling publications; established Amalgamated Press; pioneer of tabloid journalism; newspapers included *Evening News* and *Edinburgh Daily Record* (1894), *Daily Mail* (1896), *Daily Mirror* (1903), *Observer* (1905) and *The Times* (1908); director of war propaganda (1916); created Viscount Northcliffe in 1918.

JOSEPH RUDYARD KIPLING (1865–1936): born in India; journalist, novelist and poet; works included *The jungle book*, *Kim* and *Plain tales from the hills*; Nobel Prize winner (1907); supporter of Ulster and the empire.

DAVID LLOYD GEORGE (1863–1945): born in Manchester but educated at a Welsh church school before training as a solicitor; Liberal MP at Westminster (1890–1945); supporter of Irish Home Rule (1912–14); chancellor of the exchequer (1908–15), minister of munitions (1915–16) and secretary of war (1916); succeeded Asquith as prime minister (1916–22); architect of Government of Ireland Act (1920) and mastermind behind Anglo-Irish Treaty negotiations (1921); leader of Liberal Party (1926–31); created Earl Lloyd George in 1945.

ALFRED MILNER (1854–1925): educated at Balliol College, Oxford; called to bar in 1881; journalist at *Pall Mall Gazette*; entered politics in 1884; chairman of Inland Revenue (1892); knighted in 1895; high commissioner for South Africa (1897–1905); organiser of British Covenant in support of Ulster (1914); secretary of state for war (1916–18); secretary of state for colonies (1918–21); later created Viscount Milner.

JOHN EDWARD REDMOND (1851–1918): elected nationalist MP for New Ross in 1881; called to Irish bar in 1886; elected MP for Waterford in 1891; chair of Irish Nationalist Party (1900); leader of nationalist movement before World War I; endorsed formation of National Volunteers (1913); condemned Easter Rising (1916); member of Irish Convention (1917–18).

DOUGLAS SAVORY (1878–1969): son of a Suffolk clergyman; educated at Marlborough and Oxford; appointed professor of French at Queen's University, Belfast (1909); supporter of Sir Edward Carson's resistance campaign (1912–14); worked for Admiralty's intelligence division in World War I; elected Ulster Unionist MP for Queen's University (1940), later representing South Antrim at Westminster; led special investigation into Nazi massacre of Polish officers at Katyn Wood (1941); knighted in 1952.

EARL OF SELBORNE (1859–1942): elected to Westminster as Liberal MP for East Hampshire (1886), switching to Liberal Unionists shortly afterwards; elected as MP for Edinburgh West (1895); held political offices including first lord of the admiralty (1900–05), high commissioner for South Africa (1905–10) and president of the Board of Agriculture (1915–16); supporter of Ulster cause in Great Britain.

FREDERICK EDWIN SMITH (1872–1930): educated at Oxford; leading member of the English Bar during the Edwardian era; Merseyside MP and later created Earl Birkenhead; colourful and outspoken champion of Ulster's cause; held a number of government offices including solicitor-general (1915), lord chancellor (1919) and secretary of state for India (1928).

WILFRID SPENDER (1876–1960): educated at Winchester and Camberley Staff College; served in India and on general staff (1911); resigned to join UVF headquarters staff in 1913; signed British Covenant (1914); appointed as lieutenant-colonel in Thirty-Sixth Ulster Division (1916); worked at Ministry of Pensions (1919–20); involved in creation of Ulster Special Constabulary (1920); first secretary to Northern Ireland cabinet (1921–5) and head of Northern Ireland civil service (1925–44); knighted.

HENRY HUGHES WILSON (1864–1922): born in County Longford; director of military operations at War Office (1910–14); acted as a go-between with unionist leadership and army officers at centre of Curragh crisis (1914); chief liaison officer, British Army (1915); commander, Fourth Corps (1916); chief imperial general staff (1918); knighted; elected MP for North Down (1922); assassinated by IRA in London (1922).

RICHARD GREVILLE VERNEY, NINETEENTH EARL WILLOUGHBY DE BROKE (1869–1923): landowner and huntsman; MP for Rugby (1895–1900); entered House of Lords in 1900; adopted extreme stance in support of Ulster; founded BLSUU.

NOTES

CHAPTER 1
1. See biographical summary in Appendix 2.
2. All PRONI source references given were correct at the time of writing.

CHAPTER 2
1. J. Bardon, *A history of Ulster* (Belfast, 1992), p. 387.
2. J. Bardon, *Belfast: an illustrated history* (Belfast, 1982), p. 89.
3. This was the theme of a paper, 'Belfast 1845–1914: economic prosperity and political entrenchment', which I gave at the European Social History Conference at Amsterdam in 1998.
4. M. Tanner, *Ireland's holy wars: the struggle for a nation's soul, 1500–2000* (New Haven and London, 2001), p. 264.
5. T. Gray, *Nationalist and unionist: Ireland before the treaty* (London, 1989), p. 27 (Gladstone made this speech in the House of Commons on 8 April 1886).
6. Gray, *Nationalist and unionist*, p. 26.
7. H.M. Hyde, *Carson: the life of Sir Edward Carson, Lord Carson of Duncairn* (London, 1953, repr. 1987), p. 60.
8. A. Jackson, *Home Rule: an Irish history, 1800–2000* (London, 2003), p. 65.
9. *The Times*, 18 June 1892.
10. R. Kee, *Ireland: a history* (London, 1980), p. 140.
11. Jackson, *Home Rule*, p. 84.
12. See biographical summary in Appendix 2.
13. See N. Blewett, *The peers, the parties and the people: the general elections of 1910* (London, 1972), p. 317.
14. A. Morgan, *Labour and partition: the Belfast working class, 1905–23* (London, 1991), p. 122.
15. C. O'Clery, *Phrases make history here: a century of Irish political quotations, 1886–1986* (Dublin, 1986), p. 35 (Asquith made this speech on 10 December 1909).
16. T. Wilson, *Ulster: conflict and consent* (Oxford, 1989), p. 39.
17. D.G. Boyce, *The Irish question and British politics 1868–1996* (Basingstoke, 1996), p. 56.
18. *Belfast Telegraph*, 11 July 1912.
19. *Morning Post*, 11 July 1912.
20. Jackson, *Home Rule*, p. 113.
21. See biographical summary in Appendix 2.
22. E. O'Halpin, *The decline of the union: British government in Ireland, 1892–1920* (Dublin, 1987), p. 100.
23. See biographical summary in Appendix 2.
24. J. Grigg, *Lloyd George: from peace to war, 1912–1916* (London, 2002), p. 122 (Lloyd George made this speech at Denmark Hill on 20 June 1914; the 'galloper' was F.E. Smith, who had promised 'fighting men' for Ulster's cause and who had tangled with a police horse and its rider in Parliament Square).
25. See biographical summary in Appendix 2.
26. O'Clery, *Phrases make history here*, p. 36 (Winston Churchill made this speech at Dundee on 3 October 1911).
27. O'Clery, *Phrases make history here*, p. 44.
28. D. Gwynn, *The life of John Redmond* (London, 1932), p. 21.
29. J.B. Armour to W.S. Armour, January 1912 (Public Record Office of Northern Ireland (PRONI), Armour papers, D1792/A/3/3/5). See also J.R.B. McMinn, *Against the tide: a calendar of the papers of Rev. J.B. Armour, Irish Presbyterian minister and Home Ruler, 1869–1914* (Belfast, 1985).
30. *Saturday Review*, 27 January 1912, quoted in R. McNeill, *Ulster's stand for union* (London, 1922), p. 70.
31. T. Carnduff, 'Thomas Carnduff: life and writings' (1954), in P. Craig (ed.), *The Belfast anthology* (Belfast, 1999), p. 327.
32. *The Times*, 9 February 1912.
33. Ibid.
34. Ibid.
35. Ibid.
36. *The Times*, 10 February 1912.
37. See biographical summary in Appendix 2.
38. Gwynn, *John Redmond*, p. 232 (John Redmond made this speech on 12 December 1913).
39. O'Clery, *Phrases make history here*, p. 35 (John Redmond wrote this on 27 November 1909).

40 R. Hattersley, *The Edwardians* (London, 2004), p. 186.
41 See biographical summary in Appendix 2.
42 Jackson, *Home Rule*, p. 39.
43 H. Maxwell, *Ulster was right* (London, 1934), p. 60.
44 *Belfast News-Letter*, 25 September 1911.
45 Hyde, *Carson*, p. 291.
46 Annual report, UUC, 1912 (PRONI, Barbour papers, D972/17).
47 PRONI, UUC papers, D1327/3/1.
48 *The Times*, 8 April 1912.
49 *The Times*, 19 April 1912.
50 Ibid.
51 *Northern Whig*, 6 April 1912.
52 Ibid.
53 See biographical summary in Appendix 2.
54 *Northern Whig*, 8 April 1912.
55 *Northern Whig*, 10 April 1912.
56 Rudyard Kipling, 'Ulster 1912', in *Morning Post*, 9 April 1912.
57 *Northern Whig*, 10 April 1912.
58 *Belfast News-Letter*, 10 April 1912.
59 *The Times*, 10 April 1912.
60 *The Times*, 10 April 1912.
61 *Belfast News-Letter*, 6 April 1912.
62 Ibid.
63 *Manchester Guardian*, 10 April 1912.
64 Ibid.
65 Ibid.
66 Ibid.
67 See E. Pearce, *Lines of most resistance: the lords, the Tories and Ireland, 1886–1914* (London, 1999), pp. 399–400.
68 A.T.Q. Stewart, *The Ulster crisis* (London, 1967), p. 54.
69 *The Times*, 10 April 1912.
70 *Daily Telegraph*, 10 April 1912.
71 *Morning Post*, 10 April 1912.
72 *The Times*, 10 April 1912.
73 *Pall Mall Gazette*, 9 April 1912.
74 *Daily Express*, 10 April 1912.
75 *The Times*, 10 April 1912.
76 Ibid.
77 *Belfast News-Letter*, 10 April 1912.
78 *Northern Whig*, 11 April 1912.
79 *Manchester Guardian*, 10 April 1912.
80 *Irish News*, 10 April 1912.
81 Ibid.
82 Hyde, *Carson*, p. 312.
83 Stewart, *Ulster crisis*, p. 56.
84 G. Dangerfield, *The strange death of Liberal England* (London, 1935, repr. 1997), p. 92.
85 Jackson, *Home Rule*, p. 110. See Chapter 3 for a further account of the *Ne temere* decree and the McCann case.
86 See P. Jalland, *The Liberals and Ireland: the Ulster question in British politics to 1914* (Brighton, 1980).
87 M.C. Bromage, *Churchill and Ireland* (Notre Dame, IN, 1964), p. 30.
88 *The parliamentary debates*, fifth series, House of Commons, 1909–42 (vol. xxxvi, London, 25 March–12 April 1912).
89 Gwynn, *John Redmond*, p. 203.
90 Ibid.
91 *Northern Whig*, 12 April 1912.
92 R.J.Q. Adams, *Bonar Law* (London, 1999), p. 105.
93 Adams, *Bonar Law*, p. 104.
94 *Daily Mail*, 12 April 1912.
95 *The Times*, 12 April 1912.
96 *Glasgow Herald*, 12 April 1912.
97 *Spectator*, 13 April 1912.
98 *Northern Whig*, 12 April 1912.
99 *Daily News*, 12 April 1912.
100 *Irish News*, 12 April 1912.
101 J. Beckett, *The making of modern Ireland, 1603–1923* (London, 1966), p. 427.
102 Jackson, *Home Rule*, p. 112.
103 Hyde, *Carson*, p. 313.
104 *The Times*, 12 June 1912.
105 *Northern Whig*, 17 June 1912.
106 *Northern Whig*, 14 June 1912.
107 Hyde, *Carson*, p. 314.
108 Adams, *Bonar Law*, p. 113.
109 Hyde, *Carson*, p. 324.
110 *Belfast News-Letter*, 31 December 1912.
111 Stewart, *Ulster crisis*, p. 167. Interestingly, Ronald McNeill makes no reference to the incident during his classic account of the Home Rule crisis.
112 *Belfast News-Letter*, 30 December 1912.
113 *Northern Whig*, 2 January 1913.
114 Ibid.
115 I.D. Colvin, *The life of Lord Carson* (3 vols, London, 1934), p. 166.
116 *Hansard 5 (Commons)*, xxxix, 1085–7.
117 Hyde, *Carson*, p. 327.
118 *Northern Whig*, 2 January 1913.

119 *Northern Whig*, 15 January 1913.
120 *Standard*, 27 July 1912.
121 *The Times*, 29 July 1912.
122 *Daily Mail*, 29 July 1912.
123 See biographical summary in Appendix 2.
124 *The Times*, 29 July 1912.
125 Ibid.
126 Ibid.
127 Ibid.
128 Ibid.
129 *Morning Post*, 29 July 1912.
130 *Nation*, 3 August 1912.
131 *The Times*, 6 October 1912.
132 Jackson, *Home Rule*, p. 59.
133 G. Lewis, *Carson: the man who divided Ireland* (London, 2005), p. 99.
134 *Belfast Telegraph*, 3 July 1912.
135 *Belfast Telegraph*, 1 August 1912.
136 *Belfast Telegraph*, 3 July 1912.
137 *The Times*, 5 July 1912.
138 *Belfast Telegraph*, 8 July 1912.
139 *Belfast Telegraph*, 31 July 1912.
140 *Daily Chronicle*, 31 July 1912.
141 *Daily Mail*, 12 July 1912.
142 *Belfast Telegraph*, 12 July 1912.
143 F.E. Smith, *Unionist policy and other essays* (London, 1913), pp. 118–19.
144 Smith, *Unionist policy*, p. 124.
145 *Irish News*, 15 July 1912.
146 *Belfast Telegraph*, 16 September 1912.
147 *Pall Mall Gazette*, 16 September 1912.
148 *Daily Telegraph*, 17 September 1912.

CHAPTER 3
1 W.F. Monypenny, *The two Irish nations? An essay on Home Rule* (London, 1913), p. 28.
2 See the 'presbyterianisation' thesis in G. Walker, *A history of the Ulster Unionist Party: protest, pragmatism and pessimism* (Manchester, 2004), p. 33.
3 D.W. Miller, *Queen's rebels: Ulster loyalism in historical perspective* (Dublin, 1978), p. 103.
4 Minute book, UUC, 2 February 1912 (PRONI, D5403/2).
5 Annual report, UUC, 1913 (PRONI, Barbour papers, D972/17).
6 Stewart, *Ulster crisis*, p. 220.
7 Stewart, *Ulster crisis*, p. 142.
8 D. Fitzpatrick, *The two Irelands, 1912–1939* (Oxford, 1998), p. 47.

9 *Belfast Telegraph*, 29 April 1914.
10 See A. Morgan, *Labour and partition: the Belfast working class, 1905–1923* (London, 1991), p. 125.
11 *Daily Mail*, 23 August 1912.
12 F. Neal, *Sectarian violence: the Liverpool experience, 1819–1914* (Manchester, 1988), p. 250.
13 D.N. MacRaild, *Faith, fraternity and fighting: the Orange Order and Irish migrants in northern England, 1850–1920* (Liverpool, 2005), p. 264.
14 *Daily Mail*, 30 April 1912.
15 'A businessmen's protest against the Home Rule Bill', November 1913 (PRONI, IUA papers, D989/C/2/2).
16 R.M. Liddell to Edward Carson, May 1915 (PRONI, Carson papers, D1507/A/12).
17 A.T.Q. Stewart, *Edward Carson* (Dublin, 1981), p. 73.
18 R. Rees, *Ireland 1905–1925* (Newtownards, 1998), i, p. 150.
19 *Irish Worker*, August 1914.
20 For a detailed account of the reciprocal nature of Ulster Protestants' loyalty see Miller, *Queen's rebels*.
21 See biographical summary in Appendix 2.
22 Tanner, *Ireland's holy wars*, p. 273.
23 Bardon, *History of Ulster*, p. 433.
24 *Northern Whig*, 4 January 1913.
25 R.M. Liddell, 'Miscellaneous correspondence relating to the collection of funds for the Sir Edward Carson Unionist Defence Fund', 1913 (PRONI, UUC papers, D1327/14/5/2).
26 A more detailed analysis of these 'Carson tours' across Ulster is given in the section below.
27 *Northern Whig*, 2 October 1913.
28 *Northern Whig*, 1 October 1913.
29 *Northern Whig*, 2 October 1913.
30 *Northern Whig*, 3 October 1913.
31 Ibid.
32 'Notice for meeting of the Standing Committee', 23 April 1911 (PRONI, UUC papers, D1327/7/1).
33 Beckett, *Making of modern Ireland*, pp. 428–9.
34 Fitzpatrick, *Two Irelands*, p. 45 and Jackson, *Home Rule*, p. 118.
35 Fitzpatrick, *Two Irelands*, p. 45.
36 Jackson, *Home Rule*, p. 118.

37 'Notice for meeting of the Standing Committee' (PRONI, UUC papers, D1327/7/1).
38 P. Buckland, *Irish unionism 1885–1923: a documentary history* (Belfast, 1973), p. 298.
39 Minute book, UAI, 1911 (PRONI, UUC papers, D1327/2/1).
40 Ibid.
41 Stewart, *Ulster crisis*, p. 138.
42 N. Mansergh, *The Irish question, 1840–1921: a commentary on Anglo-Irish relations and on social and political forces in Ireland in the age of reform and revolution* (London, 1965), p. 14.
43 'Loughborough working men's report on visit to Ireland', 7 June 1914 (PRONI, IUA papers, D989C/1/20).
44 *Belfast Telegraph*, 29 May 1914.
45 *The Times*, 3 June 1914.
46 *Belfast Telegraph*, 2 June 1914.
47 Linen Hall Library, Belfast (LHL), Northern Ireland Political Collection.
48 'The Irish unionist pocket book: for use of unionist workers in Great Britain', 1911 (PRONI, IUA papers, D989/C/1/11A).
49 Ibid.
50 Ibid.
51 See details in the next chapter.
52 T.G. Houston, 'Ulster's appeal to Scotland', n.d. (probably late 1913) (LHL, Northern Ireland Political Collection).
53 'Messages to English Nonconformists', 1912 (LHL, Northern Ireland Political Collection).
54 J. Craig, 'Home Rule from a Protestant standpoint', n.d. (probably late 1911) (LHL, Northern Ireland Political Collection).
55 'Ulster and home union: unionist policy', n.d. (probably late 1910) (LHL, Northern Ireland Political Collection).
56 See illustration number 11.
57 See John Killen, *John Bull's famous circus: Ulster history through the postcard, 1905–85* (Dublin, 1985).
58 Ibid.
59 See illustration number 8.
60 'Notes from Ireland', January–December 1913 (PRONI, IUA papers, D989/C/3/66).
61 Ibid.
62 Jalland, *The Liberals and Ireland*, p. 267.
63 A. Megahey, '"God will defend the right": the Protestant churches and opposition to Home Rule' in D.G. Boyce and A. O'Day (eds), *Defenders of the union: a survey of British and Irish unionism since 1801* (London, 2001), p. 171.
64 D. Hempton, *Religion and political culture in Britain and Ireland: from the Glorious Revolution to the decline of empire* (Cambridge, 1996), p. 107.
65 Megahey, '"God will defend the right"', p. 170.
66 J. de Wiel, *The Irish factor 1899–1919: Ireland's strategic and diplomatic importance for foreign powers* (Dublin, 2008), p. 102.
67 *Northern Whig*, 2 April 1912.
68 Minute book, 24 January 1911–21 October 1913 (PRONI, UWUC papers, D1098/1/1).
69 Megahey, '"God will defend the right"', p. 160.
70 A. Scholes, *The Church of Ireland and the Third Home Rule Bill* (Dublin, 2009), p. 41.
71 *Irish Churchman*, August 1912, quoted in Megahey, '"God will defend the right"', p. 169.
72 *Belfast Telegraph*, 17 April 1912.
73 Ibid.
74 C.F. D'Arcy to E. Carson, 12 February 1914 (PRONI, Carson papers, D1507/A/5/8).
75 Scholes, *Church of Ireland*, p. 41.
76 R.G.S. King, 'Ulster's protest', n.d. (probably early 1914) (LHL, Northern Ireland Political Collection, MS 158).
77 *Belfast Weekly News*, 8 February 1912.
78 See Graham Walker's chapter on this theme in R. English and G. Walker, *Unionism in modern Ireland* (Basingstoke, 1996), p. 35.
79 *Belfast Weekly News*, 8 February 1912.
80 Annual report, UUC, 1912 (PRONI, Barbour papers, D972/17).
81 Bardon, *History of Ulster*, p. 440.
82 McMinn, *Against the tide*, preface.
83 *Belfast Telegraph*, 14 March 1912.
84 *Belfast Telegraph*, 20 June 1914.
85 *Morning Post*, 26 November 1912.

86 Lewis, *Carson*, p. 102.
87 *Belfast News-Letter*, 19 September 1912.
88 See illustration number 6.
89 Ibid.
90 Ibid.
91 G. Lucy, *The Ulster Covenant: a pictorial history of the 1912 Home Rule crisis* (Belfast, 1989), preface.
92 *Belfast Telegraph*, 14 September 1912.
93 *Belfast Telegraph*, 20 September 1912.
94 *Belfast Telegraph*, 18 September 1912.
95 *Daily Mail*, 13 September 1912.
96 *The Times*, 18 September 1912.
97 *Morning Post*, 18 September 1912.
98 *Belfast Telegraph*, 18 September 1912.
99 *The Times*, 19 September 1912.
100 Ibid.
101 Hyde, *Carson*, p. 319.
102 *Belfast Telegraph*, 19 September 1912.
103 *Daily Telegraph*, 19 September 1912; *Daily Express*, 19 September 1912.
104 *The Times*, 19 September 1912.
105 *Irish News*, 20 September 1912.
106 *Daily Chronicle*, 19 September 1912.
107 *The Times*, 20 September 1912.
108 *Belfast Telegraph*, 20 September 1912.
109 *The Times*, 20 September 1912.
110 Colvin, *Life of Lord Carson*, ii, p. 140.
111 *Belfast News-Letter*, 20 September 1912.
112 *The Times*, 21 September 1912.
113 O'Clery, *Phrases make history here*, p. 39.
114 Lucy, *Ulster Covenant*, p. 20.
115 *Belfast News-Letter*, 25 September 1912.
116 *Pall Mall Gazette*, 26 September 1912.
117 Pearce, *Lines of most resistance*, p. 423.
118 *Daily Express*, 25 September 1912.
119 Hyde, *Carson*, p. 320.
120 Lucy, *Ulster Covenant*, p. 37.
121 *Belfast News-Letter*, 28 September 1912.
122 Hyde, *Carson*, p. 320.
123 *The Times*, 28 September 1912.
124 Hyde, *Carson*, p. 321.
125 *The Times*, 28 September 1912.
126 *Irish News*, 28 September 1912.
127 St J.G. Ervine, *Craigavon, Ulsterman* (London, 1949), p. 235.
128 *Belfast News-Letter*, 30 September 1912.
129 *Standard*, 30 September 1912.
130 *Belfast News-Letter*, 28 September 1912.
131 Ibid.
132 Hyde, *Carson*, p. 321.
133 *Belfast News-Letter*, 30 September 1912.
134 Ervine, *Craigavon*, p. 235.
135 *Standard*, 30 September 1912.
136 Lucy, *Ulster Covenant*, p. 57.
137 *Belfast News-Letter*, 30 September 1912.
138 Tanner, *Ireland's holy wars*, p. 274.
139 *Northern Whig*, 30 September 1912.
140 Ibid.
141 McNeill, *Ulster's stand for union*, p. 122.
142 *Pall Mall Gazette*, 30 September 1912.
143 *Belfast News-Letter*, 8 October 1912.
144 Lucy, *Ulster Covenant*, p. 58.
145 O. Purdue, *The Big House in the north of Ireland: land, power and social elites, 1878–1960* (Dublin, 2009), p. 179.
146 Ibid.
147 'The social side of the Ulster campaign' in *Daily Graphic*, quoted in Purdue, *The Big House*, p. 182.
148 Beckett, *Making of modern Ireland*, p. 428.
149 Hyde, *Carson*, p. 322.
150 *Pall Mall Gazette*, 30 September 1912.
151 *Belfast News-Letter*, 15 October 1912.
152 *Belfast News-Letter*, 1 October 1912.
153 PRONI, UWUC papers, D1098/2/1-9.
154 Neal, *Sectarian violence*.
155 *Liverpool Courier*, 30 September 1912.
156 Ibid.
157 *Belfast News-Letter*, 1 October 1912.
158 Jackson, *Home Rule*, p. 78. Jackson also compared Carson's Liverpool reception with a 'royal coronation' (p. 80).
159 *The Times*, 7 October 1912.
160 *Belfast News-Letter*, 2 October 1912.
161 *Observer*, 29 September 1912.
162 *Pall Mall Gazette*, 28 September 1912.
163 *The Times*, 30 September 1912.
164 *Daily Express*, quoted in Lucy, *Ulster Covenant*, p. 82.
165 *The Times*, 30 September 1912.
166 *The Times*, 22 August 1912.
167 Tanner, *Ireland's holy wars*, p. 274.
168 Walker, *History of the Ulster Unionist Party*, p. 35.

169 Lewis, *Carson*, p. 107.
170 R. Grayson, *Belfast boys: how unionists and nationalists fought and died together in the First World War* (London, 2009), p. 3.
171 Hyde, *Carson*, p. 324.
172 Ibid.

CHAPTER 4
1 This is covered in the next chapter.
2 Dangerfield, *Strange death of Liberal England*, p. 89.
3 *The Times*, 8 December 1911.
4 Adams, *Bonar Law*, p. 101.
5 See R. Blake, *The unknown prime minister: the life and times of Andrew Bonar Law, 1858–1923* (London, 1955).
6 Mansergh, *Irish question*, p. 195.
7 I. McLean and A. McMillan, *State of the union: unionism and the alternatives in the United Kingdom since 1707* (Oxford, 2005), p. 125.
8 Ibid.
9 J. Ramsden, *An appetite for power: a history of the Conservative Party since 1830* (London, 1998), pp. 217–18.
10 Ibid.
11 C.B. Shannon, *Arthur J. Balfour and Ireland, 1874–1922* (Washington D.C., 1988), pp. 167–8.
12 *Northern Whig*, 8 January 1914.
13 O'Clery, *Phrases make history here*, p. 43 (Newman made this speech at a Potters Bar rally on 5 December 1913).
14 J. Kendle, *Walter Long, Ireland and the union, 1905–20* (Montreal, 1992), p. 72.
15 Annual report, UUC, 1912 (PRONI, Barbour papers, D972/17).
16 Annual report, UUC, 1913 (PRONI, Barbour papers, D972/17).
17 Buckland, *Irish unionism*, p. 310.
18 R.R. Smylie to UAI committee, 8 April 1914 (PRONI, UUC papers, D1327/2/1).
19 PRONI, IUA papers, D989/C/1/11B.
20 A.P. Blackburn to UAI committee, n.d. (PRONI, UUC papers, D1327/2/1).
21 *The Times*, February 1914.
22 Minute book, UAI joint committee, 12 November 1913 (PRONI, UUC papers, D1327/2/1A).
23 Report, UAI, 1913 (PRONI, UUC papers, D1327/2/1).
24 Ibid.
25 Ibid.
26 *Northern Whig*, 11 May 1912.
27 *Standard*, 18 March 1914.
28 See A.F. Parkinson, *Ulster loyalism and the British media* (Dublin, 1998).
29 D.M. Jackson, *Popular opposition to Irish Home Rule in Edwardian Britain* (Liverpool, 2009), p. 208–09.
30 *The Times*, 24 January 1912.
31 *Standard*, 12 June 1913.
32 'Irish facts: the Ulster tour', July 1913 (PRONI, additional UUC papers, D4503/3).
33 *The Times*, 13 June 1913.
34 *Belfast News-Letter*, 16 June 1913.
35 'Great west of England' programme, 20 June 1913 (PRONI, UUC papers, D1327/21/10).
36 *Northern Whig*, 8 November 1913.
37 Jackson, *Popular opposition to Irish Home Rule*, p. 172.
38 *Northern Whig*, 9 December 1913.
39 Jackson, *Popular opposition to Irish Home Rule*, pp. 231–2.
40 Jackson, *Popular opposition to Irish Home Rule*, p. 242.
41 Ibid.
42 Dangerfield, *Strange death of Liberal England*, p. 75.
43 This is the argument F. Coetzee makes in *For party or country: nationalism and the dilemma of popular conservatism in Edwardian England* (Oxford, 1990), p. 154.
44 J. Smith, *The Tories and Ireland: Conservative Party politics and the Home Rule crisis, 1910–14* (Dublin, 2000), p. 200.
45 L. Amery to N. Chamberlain, 25 July 1914, quoted in M. Bentley, *Politics without democracy, 1815–1914: perception and preoccupation in British government* (Oxford, 1999), p. 262.
46 Smith, *Tories and Ireland*, p. 200. Another historian has argued that the political crisis of this period was a 'British' rather than an 'Irish' one (C. Fitzgibbon, *Red hand: the Ulster colony* (London, 1971), p. 308).
47 Smith, *Tories and Ireland*, p. 50.
48 Purdue, *The Big House*, p. 177.

49 Minute book, UCC (PRONI, UUC papers, D1327/1/1).
50 Purdue, *The Big House*, p. 179.
51 *Belfast Telegraph*, 10 October 1913.
52 Purdue, *The Big House*, p. 185.
53 D. Urquhart, *The ladies of Londonderry: women and political patronage* (New York, 2007), p. 106.
54 Ibid.
55 Urquhart, *Ladies of Londonderry*, p. 111.
56 M. Hill, *Women in Ireland: a century of change* (Belfast, 2003), p. 61.
57 Ibid.
58 Urquhart, *Ladies of Londonderry*, p. 115.
59 Lady L. Spender, diary entry, 16 April 1914 (PRONI, Lady Spender papers, D1633/2/19/1).
60 Duchess of Somerset to E. Carson, early 1914 (PRONI, Carson papers, D1507/A/6/41).
61 A.V. Dicey, *A fool's paradise: being a constitutionalist's criticism of the Home Rule Bill of 1912* (London 1913), p. 34.
62 Dicey, *Fool's paradise*, p. 50.
63 D.G. Boyce and A. O'Day (eds), *The Ulster crisis, 1885–1921* (Basingstoke, 2006), p. 53.
64 Boyce and O'Day, *Ulster crisis*, p. 60.
65 See biographical summary in Appendix 2.
66 A. Milner to Lord Selborne, February 1914, in D.G. Boyce, *The crisis of British unionism: Lord Selborne's domestic political papers, 1885–1922* (London, 1987).
67 Lord Selborne to Sir Edward Grey, 3 April 1914, in Boyce, *Crisis of British unionism*.
68 Lord Selborne to Thomas Comyn-Platt, 19 September 1912, in Boyce, *Crisis of British unionism*.
69 Lord Selborne to Austen Chamberlain, 12 August 1914, in Boyce, *Crisis of British unionism*.
70 See biographical summary in Appendix 2.
71 R. Kipling to H.A. Gwynne, 26 November 1913, in D. Gilmour, *The long recessional: the imperial life of Rudyard Kipling* (London, 2002), p. 245.
72 Gilmour, *Long recessional*, p. 247.
73 See biographical summary in Appendix 2.
74 Dangerfield, *Strange death of Liberal England*, pp. 47–8.
75 Lord W. de Broke to A. Bonar Law, 11 September 1913 (Parliamentary Archives, Bonar Law papers, HOL BL/30/2/10).
76 *Morning Post*, 11 September 1913.
77 W. de Broke to Conservative peers, 25 January 1914 (Parliamentary Archives, Willoughby de Broke papers, HOL WB/8).
78 4 February 1914 (Parliamentary Archives, Willoughby de Broke papers, HOL WB/8/4).
79 Lord Northumberland to Lord W. de Broke, 7 February 1914 (Parliamentary Archives, Willoughby de Broke papers, HOL WB/8/35 and HOL WB/6/16).
80 Parliamentary Archives, Willoughby de Broke papers, HOL WB/10/13.
81 Lord W. de Broke and Lord Ampthill to Lord Lansdowne, 13 May 1914 (Parliamentary Archives, Willoughby de Broke papers, HOL WB/10/10).
82 Parliamentary debates order paper, 10 February 1914 (Parliamentary Archives, Willoughby de Broke papers, HOL WB/8/4).
83 Ibid.
84 Ibid.
85 *The Times*, March 1913.
86 *Daily Mail*, 11 June 1913.
87 *Morning Post*, quoted in Parliamentary Archives, Willoughby de Broke papers, HOL WB/6/7.
88 *Morning Post*, quoted in Parliamentary Archives, Willoughby de Broke papers, HOL WB/6/1.
89 W.H. Nightingale to E. Carson, 17 October 1913 (PRONI, Carson papers, D1507/A/4/10).
90 Lord W. de Broke to General Richardson, 21 March 1914 (Parliamentary Archives, Willoughby de Broke papers, HOL WB/10/3).
91 Captain F. Hall to Lord W. de Broke, 23 March 1914 (Parliamentary Archives, Willoughby de Broke papers, HOL WB/10/4).
92 Minute book, Headquarters Council, UVF, 6 April 1914 (PRONI, UUC papers, D1327/4/2C).
93 T.C. Kennedy, 'Tory Radicalism and the Home Rule crisis, 1910–1914: the case

of Lord Willoughby de Broke' in *Canadian Journal of History*, xxxvii (April 2002), pp. 23–40.
94 Smith, *Tories and Ireland*, pp. 80–81.
95 See biographical summary in Appendix 2.
96 A. Milner to Colonel Denison, 25 October 1913 (Bodleian Library, Oxford (Bodl.), Milner papers, MS 40).
97 Stewart, *Ulster crisis*, pp. 130–31.
98 A. Milner to Lord Selborne, 18 January 1914, in Boyce, *Crisis of British unionism*, pp. 102–03.
99 T.H. O'Brien, *Milner: Viscount Milner of St James's and Cape Town, 1854–1925* (London, 1979), p. 251.
100 *Morning Post*, 6 March 1914.
101 A. Milner to Lord W. de Broke, 6 March 1914 (Parliamentary Archives, Willoughby de Broke papers, HOL WB/10/1).
102 PRONI, Carson papers, D1507A/1/11.
103 *Covenanter*, 20 May 1914 (Bodl. MS 158).
104 Ibid.
105 Ibid.
106 Ibid.
107 Ibid.
108 Ibid.
109 *Belfast Telegraph*, 11 April 1914.
110 *The Times*, 6 April 1914.
111 *Morning Post*, 6 April 1914.
112 *Daily Mail*, 6 April 1914.
113 *Morning Post*, 6 April 1914.
114 *Belfast Telegraph*, 6 April 1914.
115 Ibid.
116 *Daily Chronicle*, 6 April 1914.
117 G.R. Wilkinson, *Depictions and images of war in Edwardian newspapers, 1899–1914* (Basingstoke, 2003), p. 8.
118 Wilkinson, *Depictions and images of war*, p. 88.
119 See biographical summary in Appendix 2.
120 Quoted in A.J.P. Taylor, *English history, 1914–1945* (Oxford, 1965), p. 57.
121 T. Clarke, *Northcliffe in history: an intimate portrait of press power* (London, 1950), p. 170.
122 J.L. Thompson, *Northcliffe: press baron in politics, 1865–1922* (London, 2000), p. 217.
123 H. Trench in *Nation*, 18 April 1914.
124 *The Times*, 13 August 1912.
125 S.E. Koss, *The rise and fall of the political press in Britain* (2 vols, London, 1981–4), ii, p. 202.
126 *New York Times*, 15 July 1914.
127 Belfast Historical and Educational Society, *Lovat Fraser's tour of Ireland in 1913* (Belfast, 1992), p. 6.
128 Fraser's leading articles at this time included 'The real problem in Ulster' (16 October), 'The governing of Ulster' (25 October), 'Unionists and Ulster' (30 October), 'The growing anxiety about Ulster' (1 November) and 'The business men of Ulster' (5 November).
129 Belfast Historical and Educational Society, *Lovat Fraser's tour of Ireland*, p. 9.
130 Belfast Historical and Educational Society, *Lovat Fraser's tour of Ireland*, p. 12.
131 Ibid.
132 Belfast Historical and Educational Society, *Lovat Fraser's tour of Ireland*, p. 13.
133 Ibid.
134 Belfast Historical and Educational Society, *Lovat Fraser's tour of Ireland*, p. 19.
135 *The Times*, 5 January 1912.
136 *The Times*, 14 July 1913.
137 *The Times*, 28 April 1914.
138 *The Times*, 27 March 1914.
139 *The Times*, 6 April 1914.
140 *The Times*, 19 May 1914.
141 *The Times*, 26 March 1914.
142 Monypenny, *Two Irish nations?*, p. 65.
143 Clarke, *Northcliffe in history*, p. 28.
144 Wilkinson, *Depictions and images of war*, p. 7.
145 These incidents are dealt with more fully in the next chapter.
146 *Daily Mail*, 23 March 1914.
147 Ibid.
148 *Daily Mail*, 28 April 1914.
149 Ibid.
150 Ibid.
151 *Daily Mail*, 7 July 1914.
152 *Daily Mail*, 22 July 1914.
153 See biographical summary in Appendix 2.
154 A.M. Gollin, *The Observer and J.L. Garvin, 1908–1914: a study in a great editorship* (Oxford, 1960).

155 *Observer*, 16 June 1912.
156 *Observer*, 25 August 1912. The three *Observer* issues in which the Ulster question featured heavily were this one and the editions of 22 and 29 September.
157 *Observer*, 29 September 1912.
158 D. Ayerst, *Garvin of the* Observer (London, 1985), pp. 133–4.
159 *Pall Mall Gazette*, 20 September 1912.
160 *Pall Mall Gazette*, 14 September 1912.
161 *Pall Mall Gazette*, 19 September 1912.
162 *Pall Mall Gazette*, 20 September 1912.
163 *Pall Mall Gazette*, 27 September 1912.
164 *Pall Mall Gazette*, 1 October 1912.
165 *Daily Telegraph*, 6 May 1912.
166 *Daily Telegraph*, 3 January 1913; *Daily Telegraph*, 25 September 1912.
167 H.A. Gwynne to E. Carson, 18 February 1914 (PRONI, Carson papers, D1507/A/5/10).
168 H.A. Gwynne to E. Carson, 20 March 1914 (PRONI, Carson papers, D1507/A/5/15).
169 *Morning Post*, 8 January 1913.
170 *Morning Post*, 17 May 1913.
171 *Morning Post*, 29 March 1914.
172 *Daily Express*, 6 April 1914.
173 *Daily Express*, 12 August 1913.
174 *Spectator*, 4 January 1913.
175 G. Peatling, *British opinion and Irish self-government, 1865–1925: from unionism to liberal commonwealth* (Dublin, 2001) p. 74.
176 *Westminster Gazette*, April 1912.
177 J. Darby, *Dressed to kill: cartoonists and the Northern Ireland conflict* (Belfast, 1983), p. 29.
178 Darby, *Dressed to kill*, p. 41.
179 See R. Douglas, L. Harte and J. O'Hara, *Drawing conclusions: a cartoon history of Anglo-Irish relations, 1798–1998* (Belfast, 1998), p. 42.
180 *Punch*, 6 May 1914. See illustration number 12.
181 *Punch*, 25 September 1912.
182 *Punch*, 10 June 1914.
183 *Punch*, 11 March 1914.
184 *Punch*, 13 May 1913.
185 *Punch*, 15 April 1914.
186 *Punch*, 1 April 1914. See illustration number 10.
187 *Punch*, 18 February 1914.
188 *Punch*, 17 June 1914.

CHAPTER 5

1 Lord Roberts, 'Ulster and the army', n.d. (Bodl. MS 158).
2 Lord Roberts, 'In defence of the army' (House of Lords speech), 30 March 1914 (LHL, Northern Ireland Political Collection).
3 See biographical summary in Appendix 2.
4 H.H. Wilson, diary entry, 10 April 1912 (Imperial War Museum (IWM), HHW diaries, 1-1-12-31-12-14).
5 H.H. Wilson, diary entry, 16 March 1913 (IWM, HHW diaries, 1-1-12-31-12-14).
6 K. Jeffrey, *Field Marshal Sir Henry Wilson: a political soldier* (Oxford, 2006), p. 119.
7 C. Hunter to H.H. Wilson, 8 May 1914 (IWM, HW2/73/8).
8 C. Hunter to H.H. Wilson, 24 June 1914 (IWM, HW2/73/19).
9 H. Gough to H.H. Wilson, 24 March 1914 (IWM, HHW2/74/47).
10 T.H. Hatton-Richards Jr to E. Carson, 29 November 1913 (PRONI, Carson papers, D1507/A/4/17).
11 I.F.W. Beckett, *The army and the Curragh incident, 1914* (London, 1986), p. 35.
12 O'Clery, *Phrases make history here*, p. 40 (Carson made this speech on 12 July 1913).
13 *Daily Mail*, 23 March 1914.
14 Stewart, *Ulster crisis*, p. 170.
15 Stewart, *Ulster crisis*, p. 171.
16 *Daily Telegraph*, 25 March 1914.
17 *The Times*, 24 March 1914.
18 *Morning Post*, 25 March 1914; *Pall Mall Gazette*, 25 March 1914.
19 *The Times*, 24 March 1914; *The Times*, 25 March 1914.
20 *Standard*, 26 March 1914.
21 *The Times*, 25 March 1914.
22 *Belfast Telegraph*, 31 March 1914.
23 *Manchester Guardian*, 25 March 1914.
24 *Manchester Guardian*, 27 March 1914.
25 E.G. Miles, 21 March 1914, quoted in Beckett, *The army and the Curragh incident*, pp. 90–91.
26 Major Howell, quoted in Beckett, *The army and the Curragh incident*, pp. 102–03.

27 Beckett, *The army and the Curragh incident*, pp. 102–03.
28 Hyde, *Carson*, p. 355.
29 *Belfast Telegraph*, 27 March 1914.
30 R. Foster, *Modern Ireland, 1600–1972* (London, 1988), p. 469.
31 L. Amery, 'The plot against Ulster', 1914 (Bodl., Milner papers, MS 158).
32 T. Bowman, 'The Ulster Volunteers, 1913–14: force or farce?' in *History Ireland*, x, no. 1 (spring 2002), pp. 43–7.
33 T. Bowman, *Carson's army: the Ulster Volunteer Force, 1910–22* (Manchester, 2007), p. 206.
34 See Bardon, *History of Ulster*, p. 440.
35 PRONI, UUC papers, D1327/4/19.
36 W. Clark, *Guns in Ulster* (Belfast, 1967 (repr. 2002)), p. 20.
37 Grayson, *Belfast boys*, p. 4.
38 *Belfast Telegraph*, 8 April 1913.
39 *Yorkshire Post*, July 1913.
40 *Belfast Telegraph*, 27 September 1913.
41 Captain R. Hall, 'Memorandum from Roger Hall, Commanding 2nd Bn. S. Down Regt. re, how the Ulster Volunteers are to conduct themselves', 14 June 1914 (PRONI, Hall papers, D1540/3/74B).
42 Lady L. Spender, diary entry, 6 May 1914 (PRONI, Lady Spender papers, D1633/2/19).
43 J. Craig, December 1913 (PRONI, UUC papers, D1327/4/21).
44 Col. G. Hacket Pain, circular, 20 January 1914 (PRONI, North Antrim Regt, UVF papers, D1238/108.
45 See biographical summary in Appendix 2.
46 R.J. Adgey, *Arming the Ulster Volunteers* (Belfast, n.d.), pp. 13–14.
47 A. Jameson to E. Carson, 1913 (PRONI, Crawford papers, D1700/5/17/3).
48 F.H. Crawford to G. Hacket Pain, 19 January 1914 (PRONI, UUC papers, D1327/4/21).
49 F.H. Crawford, *Guns for Ulster* (Belfast, 1947), pp. 28–9.
50 Ibid.
51 F.H. Crawford to B. Spiro, 4 April 1914 (PRONI, Crawford papers, D1700).
52 J. de Wiel, 'The "Irish factor" in the outbreak of war in 1914', in *History Ireland*, xix, no. 4 (July/August 2011).
53 Crawford, *Guns for Ulster*, pp. 38–9.
54 *The Times*, 1 April 1914.
55 W.T. Adair to 'Sir', 20 April 1914 (PRONI, North Antrim Regt, UVF papers, D1238/71).
56 The ten-year-old boy was the writer George Buchanan, in K. Haines, *Fred Crawford: Carson's gunrunner* (Donaghadee, 2009), p. 203.
57 Bardon, *History of Ulster*, p. 444.
58 Crawford, *Guns for Ulster*, pp. 56–7.
59 Lady L. Spender, diary entry, 27 April 1914 (PRONI, Lady Spender papers, D1633/2/19).
60 Ibid.
61 *Belfast Telegraph*, 29 April 1914.
62 *Belfast Telegraph*, 28 April 1914.
63 Ibid.
64 *Belfast Telegraph*, 30 April 1914.
65 P. Bew, *Ideology and the Irish question: Ulster unionism and Irish nationalism, 1912–1916* (Oxford, 1994), p. 110 (Birrell wrote this in 1937).
66 Bew, *Ideology and the Irish question*, p. 112.
67 Quoted in *Belfast Telegraph*, 28 April 1914.
68 Stewart, *Ulster crisis*, p. 215 (Carson made this speech on 29 April 1914).
69 *Belfast Telegraph*, 4 June 1914.
70 See Jackson, *Home Rule*.
71 Shannon, *Arthur J. Balfour and Ireland*, p. 205.
72 *Belfast Telegraph*, 28 April 1914.
73 *Belfast News-Letter*, 25 April 1914.
74 *Belfast News-Letter*, 27 April 1914.
75 Ibid.
76 *Belfast Telegraph*, 25 April 1914.
77 Ibid.
78 *Belfast Telegraph*, 30 April 1914.
79 *The Times*, 25 April 1914.
80 *Daily Express*, 28 April 1914.
81 *Daily Mail*, 28 April 1914.
82 *Nation*, 25 April 1914.
83 Bowman, 'The Ulster Volunteers, 1913–14'.
84 R. Rees, *Ireland 1905–1925*, i, p. 175.
85 Colonel G. Hacket Pain, circular memo. re. 'Directions as to the protection of arms and ammunition', 14 May 1914 (PRONI, North Antrim Regt, UVF papers, D1238/139).
86 *Belfast Telegraph*, 8 June 1914.
87 *Belfast Telegraph*, 13 July 1914.

88 *Belfast Telegraph*, 12 June 1914.
89 *Belfast Telegraph*, 9 May 1914.
90 *Belfast Telegraph*, 1 July 1914.
91 *Belfast Telegraph*, 2 July 1914.
92 *Belfast Telegraph*, 12 May 1914.
93 Colvin, *Life of Lord Carson*, ii, p. 35.
94 *The Times*, 11 September 1913.
95 Lewis, *Carson*, p. 122.
96 Bonar Law to J.P. Croal, 18 October 1913 (Parliamentary Archives, Bonar Law papers, HOL BL/33/6/84).
97 Bonar Law to Lord Selborne, quoted in Adams, *Bonar Law*, p. 144.
98 *The Times*, 16 July 1913.
99 Lord Crewe, 'The Third Home Rule Bill and the Parliament Act: a speech', 14 December 1913 (LHL, Northern Ireland Political Collection).
100 Adams, Bonar Law, p. 102.
101 *Belfast Telegraph*, 12 February 1914.
102 R.G. Crawford, *Loyal to King Billy: a portrait of the Ulster Protestants* (Dublin, 1987), p. 137.
103 Colvin, *Life of Lord Carson*, ii, p. 298.
104 *The Times*, 11 March 1914.
105 *The Times*, 25 May 1914.
106 *The Times*, 26 May 1914.
107 Smith, *Tories and Ireland*, p. 96.
108 R. Jenkins, *Asquith* (London, 1964), p. 301.
109 Bardon, *History of Ulster*, p. 446.
110 Foster, *Modern Ireland*, p. 469.
111 *Belfast Telegraph*, 20 July 1914.
112 A. Milner to E. Carson, 21 July 1914 (PRONI, Carson papers, D1507/A/6/40).
113 Lewis, *Carson*, p. 162.
114 W. Churchill, *The world crisis, 1911–1914* (London, 1929), p. 193.
115 *Belfast Telegraph*, 12 August 1914.
116 W.B. Spender to E. Carson, 1 August 1914 (PRONI, Carson papers, D1507/A/7/1).

CHAPTER 6

1 *Belfast Telegraph*, 28 September 1915.
2 W. Spender, diary entry, 2 July 1916 (PRONI, Spender papers, D1295/4/11).
3 See A.F. Parkinson, *Belfast's unholy war: the 1920s 'Troubles'* (Dublin, 2004).
4 Bardon, *History of Ulster*, p. 465.
5 *Belfast Telegraph*, 22 December 1920.
6 Parkinson, *Belfast's unholy war*, p. 133.
7 *The parliamentary debates*, fifth series, *House of Lords, 1909–43* (vols i–cxxix, London, 1909–43), xlviii, cols 44–50, 14 December 1921.
8 See Parkinson, *Ulster loyalism and the British media*.
9 See biographical summary in Appendix 2.
10 D. Savory, memoir, 20 December 1912 (PRONI, Sir Douglas Savory papers, D3015/2/14/A).

INDEX

Abercorn, duke of, 15, 122, 138, 177, 178, 212
Adair, W.T., 329
Adams, John, 97
Adams, R.J.Q., 321, 325, 330
Adgey, Robert, 254, 329
Agar-Robartes, Thomas, 7, 48–9, 50, 52, 160, 313
Agnew, Captain Andrew, 257, 258
Aiken, Sir Max, 279
Amery, Leo, 174, 198, 200, 201, 237, 246, 325, 329
Ampthill, Lord, 191, 192, 326
Ancient Order of Hibernians (AOH), 26, 58, 62, 63, 313, 317
Anglo-Irish Treaty (1921), 300, 301, 318
Anglo-Irish War, 297, 300
Anti-Repeal Union, 13
Antrim, County, 7, 32, 48, 61, 120, 123, 138, 178, 250, 251, 253–4, 260, 261, 280, 314, 319, 329, 330
Apprentice Boys, 35
Armagh, County, 48, 123, 124, 178, 280
Armagh, County Armagh, 212, 239
Armour, Rev. James Brown, 22, 111, 112, 320
Armour, W.S., 320
Arran, Lord, 191, 192
Asquith, Herbert, 16, 17, 18–19, 20, 25, 27, 29, 31, 37, 38, 43, 44, 45, 46–7, 48, 50, 51, 52, 53, 54, 55, 58, 59–60, 63, 65, 79, 85, 87, 95, 98–9, 101, 104, 109, 110, 112, 155, 156, 157, 158, 159, 161, 165, 168, 184, 190, 197, 198, 200, 214, 218, 219, 225, 227, 229, 230, 234, 242, 243, 245, 246, 247, 254, 264–5, 266, 270, 271, 273, 277, 278, 279, 280, 281, 282, 283, 284, 285, 286, 287, 288, 289, 290, 299, 311, 313, 314, 316, 318, 320, 330
Astor, Waldorf, 189, 199, 200
Attlee, Clement, 302
Ayerst, D., 328
Ayr, Ayrshire, 166
Ayrshire, 163

B Specials. *See* Ulster Special Constabulary (USC).
Balfour, Arthur James, 95, 127, 154, 158–9, 161, 174, 268, 325, 329

Ballymoney Town Hall, County Antrim, 112
Ballymoney, County Antrim, 111
Ballynafeigh, Belfast, 34
Ballyroney, County Down, 123
Balmerino, SS, 259, 263
Balmoral demonstration (1912), 3, 7, 9, 10, 29–42, 43, 46, 55, 83, 84, 113, 150, 177, 227, 235, 295, 305, 313
Balmoral, Belfast, 85, 251, 267, 273
Bangor, County Down, 259, 260, 262, 263
Barbour, Milne, 78
Bardon, Jonathan, 111, 261, 320, 322, 324, 329, 330
Baronscourt, County Tyrone, 138, 178, 212, 249
Bates, R. Dawson, 36, 72, 90, 114, 115, 126, 133, 143, 149, 182, 196
Beaverbrook, Lord, 208
Beckett, I.F.W., 328, 329
Beckett, James, 88, 139, 321, 323, 324
Bedford Street, Belfast, 127, 130, 132
Bedford, duke of, 189, 193
Belfast Castle, 183
Belfast Celtic F.C., 66, 141
Belfast Chamber of Commerce, 79
Belfast City Corporation, 134
Belfast Harbour Commissioners, 134
Belfast Lough, 28, 141, 183, 212, 242, 259, 265
Belfast News-Letter, 41, 51, 52, 114, 128, 129, 136, 146, 269, 321, 324, 325, 329
Belfast Poor Law Guardians, 134
Belfast Protestant Association, 297
Belfast Telegraph, 32, 63–4, 65, 92, 97, 119–20, 121, 126, 136, 202, 203, 204, 243–4, 251, 265, 269–70, 274, 275, 287–8, 299–300, 320, 322, 323, 324, 326, 327, 329, 330
Belfast Trades Council, 75
Belfast Weekly News, 323, 324
Bentley, M., 325
Beresford, Admiral Lord Charles, 125, 128, 138, 193
Bergen, Norway, 257
Berlin, Germany, 257
Bethnal Green, London, 163, 164, 168
Bew, P., 329
Birkenhead, Lord. *See* Smith, Frederick Edwin (F.E.)
Birkenhead, Merseyside, 57, 317

Birmingham, 169, 195, 198
Birmingham, George, 111
Birrell, Augustine, 19, 26, 27, 62, 64, 87, 89, 265–6, 311, 312, 316, 329
Blackburn, A.P., 164, 325
Blackburn, Lancashire, 172
Blackpool, Lancashire, 97
Blake, R., 325
Blenheim demonstration (1912), 3, 7, 10, 50, 55–61, 177, 204, 209, 305, 313
Blenheim Palace, Oxfordshire, 3, 7, 50, 55, 313
Blewett, N., 320
Bloomfield, Constance, 200
Boer War, 58, 98, 210, 240, 251, 252, 316, 317
Bolton, Lancashire, 172
Bonar Law, Andrew, 4–5, 6, 9, 20, 32–3, 35, 36, 37–8, 41–2, 45–6, 48, 49–50, 55, 57–9, 60–01, 80, 98–9, 109, 127, 129, 153–8, 159, 160, 165, 168, 171, 173, 174, 188, 189, 191, 196, 198, 207, 209, 201, 220, 221, 227, 235, 236, 253, 268, 277, 279, 280–01, 281–2, 285, 287, 289, 290, 300, 308, 313, 314, 316, 321, 325, 326, 330
Bootle, Merseyside, 155
Bowden, Major H., 164
Bowman, Timothy, 248, 271, 329, 330
Boyce, D. George, 18, 185, 320, 323, 326, 327
Boyne, battle of the (1690), 37, 64, 110, 128, 132, 136, 295
Bradford, West Yorkshire, 21, 74
Bristol, 89, 143, 170, 171, 316
British Covenant movement, 162, 185, 186, 197, 198, 199–202, 203, 204, 205, 225, 234, 246, 256, 309, 314, 318, 319
British League for the Support of Ulster and the Union (BLSUU), 100, 160, 162, 191, 193–7, 198, 199, 202, 203, 204, 205, 225, 309, 319
Bromage, M.C., 321
Buckingham Palace conference, 1914, 200, 273, 277, 279, 285, 286–7, 287–8, 289, 314
Buckingham Palace, London, 241
Buckinghamshire, 163, 164
Buckland, P., 323, 325
Bull, Sir William, 51, 195, 255

Campbell Bannerman, Henry, 16
Campbell, J.H., 311, 312
Canada, 90, 142, 143, 154, 200, 275, 316
Carnduff, Thomas, 320
Carrickfergus, County Antrim, 32, 239
Carson, Aileen, 245
Carson, Annette, 28, 52, 81
Carson, Sir Edward, 1, 2, 4, 6, 7, 8, 10, 15, 20, 21, 23, 27, 28–9, 32, 33, 36, 37, 39, 42, 45, 48, 49–50, 52, 53, 57, 61, 69, 73, 77, 78, 79, 80–03, 84, 85, 86, 91, 94, 98, 107, 108, 109, 110, 111, 113, 114, 117–8, 119, 121, 122–3, 124, 125, 126, 127, 128, 129–30, 131, 132, 133, 134, 135, 136, 137, 140, 141, 143, 144, 146, 147, 148, 149–50, 153, 156, 158, 159, 160, 161, 168, 169, 170, 171, 172, 177, 178, 179, 182, 183, 189, 192, 194, 195, 197, 198, 200, 201, 202, 205, 207, 208, 209, 210, 212, 215, 218, 219, 220, 221, 222, 223, 224, 225, 226, 227, 228–9, 230, 232, 236, 237, 238, 246, 248, 251, 253, 254, 255, 256, 257, 259, 266, 267, 268, 271, 272, 273, 275–6, 276–7, 278–9, 281–2, 284, 287, 288, 289, 290, 291, 293, 294, 298, 299, 300–01, 303, 304, 306, 308, 311, 312, 313, 314, 316, 317, 318, 320, 321, 322, 324, 325, 326, 327, 328, 329, 330
Casement, Roger, 112
Castle Upton, County Antrim, 138, 178, 261
Castledawson, County Londonderry, 61–2, 64, 313
Castlereagh, Viscount, 125, 177, 193
Cater, H.R., 97
Cavan, County, 106, 249
Cave Hill, Belfast, 141, 183
Cecil, Lord Hugh, 125, 138
Celtic Park, Belfast, 23–4, 66
Chamberlain, Austen, 154, 187, 326
Chamberlain, Joseph, 159
Chamberlain, Lord, 161
Chamberlain, Neville, 174, 325
Chartist movement, 113, 134
Cherkley, Surrey, 279, 280, 282
Churchill, Clementine, 22, 23
Churchill, Lord Randolph, 13–14, 20, 21, 316

Churchill, Sir Winston, 16, 19, 20–04, 32, 44, 49, 51–2, 53, 55, 74, 87, 159, 179, 208–9, 238, 239, 242, 264, 270, 279, 290, 298, 302, 305, 313, 316–17, 320, 321, 330
City Hall, Belfast, 68, 100, 131, 132, 133, 134, 135, 136, 150, 221, 265, 293, 300
Clandeboye, County Down, 178, 293
Clare, County, 35, 111
Clark, George S., 78, 79
Clark, W., 329
Clarke, Tom, 216, 327
Clogher, bishop of, 138
Clydeside. *See* Glasgow.
Clydevalley, SS, 259, 261, 262, 263
Coatbridge, North Lanarkshire, 146
Coetzee, F., 325
Coleraine, County Londonderry, 95, 122–3, 154
Colston Hall, Bristol, 171
Colvin, I.D., 322, 324, 330
Comyn-Platt, Thomas, 187, 194, 196, 326
Connolly, James, 81
Cookstown, County Tyrone, 86
Cork, County, 26, 35
Cork, County Cork, 93
Cornhill Company, 274
Cornwall, 48, 172
Corona Publishing Company, 97
County Armagh Women's Unionist Association, 181
Covenant, Ulster. *See* Ulster's Solemn League and Covenant.
Covenanter, 189, 200–01, 327
Cowan, Samuel K., 129
Craig, Charles, 71
Craig, Sir James, 4, 5, 6, 27, 28, 29, 36, 54, 69, 71, 73, 78, 80, 83–4, 95, 96, 98, 100, 114, 115, 117, 125, 127, 129, 130, 134, 168, 169, 176, 178, 181, 249, 253, 263, 276, 290, 301, 303, 304, 306, 311, 317, 323, 324, 329
Craigavon demonstration (1911), 7, 10, 27–9, 33, 36, 73, 80, 83, 113, 150, 177, 295, 305, 313
Craigavon, County Armagh, 117, 118, 183, 249, 259
Craigavon, Viscount. *See* Craig, Sir James.
Crawford, Major Fred, 4, 5, 133, 135, 196, 199, 254, 255–9, 262–3, 270, 271, 273, 317, 329

Crewe, Cheshire, 49
Crewe, Lord, 283, 330
Croal, J.P., 330
Crom Castle, County Fermanagh, 178
Crozier, Colonel, 295, 296
Crozier, Dr John Baptist, 107
Crumlin, County Antrim, 123
Cunningham, James, 249
Curragh crisis (1914), 3–4, 7, 74, 101, 186, 195, 201, 202, 214–15, 218, 224, 226, 233, 234–5, 236–47, 266, 268, 270, 271, 309, 314, 319, 328, 329
Curragh, County Kildare. *See* Curragh crisis (1914).
Currie, G.W., 165
Curzon, Lord, 160, 282
Cushendun, Lord. *See* McNeill, Ronald.

D'Arcy, Rev. Dr Charles Frederick, 106, 107, 132, 323
Daily Chronicle, 64, 120, 204, 322, 324, 327
Daily Express, 40, 87, 120, 124, 147, 218, 225–6, 270, 321, 324, 325, 328, 329
Daily Graphic, 324
Daily Mail, 46, 56–7, 59, 64, 78, 87, 118, 204, 208, 216–20, 225, 226, 240, 270, 308, 318, 321, 322, 324, 326, 327, 328, 329
Daily Mirror, 207, 318
Daily News, 47, 208, 321
Daily Telegraph, 39–40, 67, 120, 223–4, 317, 321, 322, 324, 328
Dangerfield, George, 42, 173–4, 190, 321, 325, 326
Darby, J., 328
Darlington Star, 93
Darlington, Durham, 93
Davidson, Archbishop Randall, 107, 109
de Broke, earl Willoughby. *See* Willoughby de Broke, earl.
de Wiel, J., 323, 329
Denison, Colonel, 327
Denmark Hill, London, 20, 320
Derby, Lord, 45, 237
Derbyshire, 164, 168
Derry, County Londonderry, 54, 62, 110, 122, 123, 249, 296, 326
Devlin, Joe, 26, 31, 62–3, 252, 273, 300, 301, 317
Dicey, Professor A.V., 115, 184–6, 199, 326

Donaghadee, County Down, 259, 260, 262, 263, 268
Donard Park, Newcastle, County Down, 249
Donegal, County, 86, 119, 294
Donegall Pass, Belfast, 34
Donegall Place, Belfast, 133
Donegall Road, Belfast, 66
Donegall Square, Belfast, 133, 141
Douglas, R., 328
Down, County, 7, 33, 48, 123, 139, 178, 179, 235, 250, 260, 261, 265, 280, 294, 314, 317, 319, 329
Downing Street, London, 17
Dromore, County Tyrone, 123
Drumbeg, County Down, 273
Dublin, 13, 15, 17, 26, 30, 42, 68, 70, 74, 79, 80, 82, 88, 90, 93, 96, 104, 105, 110, 131, 142, 143, 150, 162, 184, 185, 209, 214, 218, 233, 239, 245, 281, 286, 287, 289, 299, 304, 305, 309, 311, 315, 316, 317
Dublin Castle, 19
Dublin University, 80, 311, 316
Dufferin, Lady, 142
Dumfries, Dumfries and Galloway, 166
Duncairn, Baron Carson of. *See* Carson, Sir Edward.
Duncairn, Belfast, 316
Dundee, 20, 171, 316, 320
Dunleath, Lady, 181
Dunmurry, Belfast, 34
Dunville's Whiskey Company, 78, 317
Durham, County, 179

Eastbourne, East Sussex, 172, 203
Easter Rising (1916), 14, 150, 299, 300, 311, 315, 318
Eaton Place, London, 218, 312
Edinburgh, 95, 143, 319
Edinburgh Daily Record, 318
Elgar, Sir Edward, 188, 199
English Channel, 290
English, R., 323
Enniskillen, County Fermanagh, 118, 119–20, 137, 150, 239
Erne, earl of, 119, 177
Erne, Lady, 181
Ervine, St J.G., 324
Evening News, 318
Ewart, General Sir Spencer, 241, 242

Falls Road, Belfast, 23, 54, 66, 130
Fanny, SS, 257–8, 259, 267–8

Faulkner, Brian, 304
Fenian Brotherhood, 224, 228
Fermanagh, County, 111, 119, 178, 262, 280, 290, 298
Finner, County Donegal, 294
First East Surrey Regiment, 245
Fitzgibbon, C., 326
Fitzpatrick, David, 74, 88, 322, 323
Fleet Street, London, 188, 205, 208, 210, 220, 240
Foster, Roy, 287, 329, 330
Fourth Hussars, 240
France, 244, 245, 277, 292, 294–5, 298, 314
Franckenstein, Baron von, 103
Franz Ferdinand, Archduke, 288
Fraser, Lovat, 211–13, 327
Freeman's Journal, 94
French, Sir John, 234, 237, 239, 240, 241, 242, 245
Fyfe, H. Hamilton, 204, 217, 218–19

Gardiner, A., 208
Garvin, James Louis (J.L.), 5, 135, 140–01, 147, 160, 208, 220, 221–2, 223, 317, 328
George V, 4, 103, 109, 116, 218, 237, 238, 241, 265, 282, 285–7, 288, 290, 294, 300, 313, 314, 315
Germany, 98, 195, 199, 255, 256, 257, 275, 292, 293, 294, 295, 314
Gilmour, D., 326
Gladstone, William, 12, 13, 14, 15, 43, 168, 169, 184, 193, 223, 320
Glasgow, 50, 87, 90, 97, 143, 146, 154, 167, 169, 170, 172, 222, 225, 254, 313, 316
Glasgow Herald, 46, 321
Glencairn, Belfast, 249, 252, 273
Gollin, A.M., 328
Gough, Brigadier-General Hubert, 237–8, 240, 241–2, 328
Grand Central Hotel, Belfast, 22, 24, 212
Gray, T., 320
Grayson, Richard, 149, 325, 329
Greenisland, County Antrim, 32
Grey, Sir Edward, 187, 192–3, 281, 326
Grigg, J., 320
Guildford, Surrey, 84
Guildhall, Derry, 122
Gwynn, D., 320, 321
Gwynne, H.A., 179, 188, 208, 224, 237, 326, 328

INDEX 335

Hacket Pain, Colonel G. William, 250, 255, 272, 329, 330
Hackney, London, 163
Haig, General, 294
Haines, K., 329
Haldane, Lord, 231
Halifax, Viscount, 199
Hall, Captain Frank, 126, 196, 327
Hall, Captain Roger, 177–8, 329
Hamburg, Germany, 256, 257, 259
Hammersmith, London, 51, 255
Hands, Charles E., 76, 217
Harland and Wolff, 78
Harmsworth, Alfred Charles William, 5, 56, 59, 208–10, 213, 216, 217, 218, 219, 242, 317–18, 327
Hattersley, Roy, 26, 321
Hatton-Richards Jr, T.H., 328
Healy, John, 211
Heath, Edward, 303
Hecla, HMS, 265
Hempton, D., 323
Hesse, J.W., 78
Hickman, Colonel T.E., 194, 195
Hone, J.M., 211
Horne, W.E., 84
Houston, Rev. T.G., 95–6, 323
Howth gun-running, 1914, 229, 274, 287
Howth, County Dublin, 229, 287
Hunter, Sir Charles, 236, 237, 328
Hyde Park demonstration (1914), 172, 199, 201, 202–4, 215, 225, 314
Hyde, Douglas, 111
Hyde, H.M., 320, 321, 322, 324, 325, 329

Innismurray, 263
IRA, 235, 252, 297, 301, 302, 303, 319
Irish Churchman, 323
Irish Civil War, 297
Irish News, 41, 47, 66, 120, 128, 317, 321, 322, 324
Irish Times, 211
Irish Unionist Alliance, 88–9, 91, 162
Irish Volunteer Force. *See* National Volunteers.
Irish Worker, 81, 322
Isle of Man, 272
Iveagh, Lord, 200

Jackson, Alvin, 19, 88, 320, 321, 322, 323, 324, 329
Jackson, Daniel M., 5, 60, 145, 168, 173, 325
Jalland, Patricia, 44, 101, 321, 323
Jameson, Alexa, 255, 329
Jeffrey, K., 328
Jenkins, R., 330
Johnston, William, 254
Jordan, Jeremiah, 111

Katyn Wood, Russia, 319
Kee, R., 320
Kendle, J., 325
Kennedy, Thomas C., 196, 327
Kent, 52, 57, 146, 203, 245, 291
Kerry, County, 35
Kidd, James, 165
Kilkeel, County Down, 178
Kilkenny, County, 317
Killen, John, 323
Killyleagh Castle, County Down, 178, 249
Kilmorey, countess of, 139, 181
Kilmorey, earl of, 139, 177
King, Rev. R.G.S., 108, 323
Kipling, Carrie, 190
Kipling, Joseph Rudyard, 5, 33, 161, 188–90, 199, 200, 201, 318, 321, 326
Kitchener, Lord, 275, 276, 294
Koss, S.E., 327

Lagan Valley, 10, 11–12, 115, 144, 176
Lake Champlain, SS, 143
Lane-Poole, Professor Stanley, 201
Lansdowne, Lord, 56, 157, 160, 161, 326
Largs, North Ayrshire, 166
Larkin, James, 74
Larne gun-running (1914). *See* UVF gun-running (1914).
Larne, County Antrim, 22, 24, 32, 42, 259, 260, 261–2, 263, 264, 266, 267–8, 269, 270, 289
Leatherhead, Surrey, 279
Leeds, West Yorkshire, 57, 161, 169, 170, 172
Leicestershire, 92
Leinster, 98, 160
Leith, Edinburgh, 165, 168, 255
Leitrim, County, 119
Lewis, Geoffrey, 61, 149, 322, 324, 325, 330
Liddell, R.M., 78, 79, 85, 322
Limavady, County Londonderry, 108
Limerick, County Limerick, 25, 213
Lindsay, Rev. Herbert, 142
Linfield F.C., 66
Lisburn Road, Belfast, 34, 35

Lisburn, County Antrim, 120–01, 150
'Little Bobs'. *See* Roberts, Lord, of Kandahar.
Liverpool Courier, 324
Liverpool, Merseyside, 50, 57, 77, 90, 140, 141, 143–6, 159, 169, 194, 202, 222, 313, 322, 324
Lloyd George, David, 16, 19, 20, 21, 53, 87, 179, 279, 281, 296, 299, 317, 318, 320
London, 2, 4, 5, 18, 20, 32, 42, 43, 56, 63–4, 78, 80, 97, 103, 119, 125, 129, 143, 155, 161, 162, 163, 164, 168, 172, 179, 180, 194, 195, 196, 199, 200, 201, 202–4, 209, 215, 218, 222, 235, 239, 253, 255, 265, 269, 282, 287, 297, 302, 314, 319, 320
Londonderry House, London, 179
Londonderry, County, 48, 248, 249, 274, 275, 280
Londonderry, marquis of, 23, 36, 56, 125, 126, 127, 134, 146, 177, 179, 227
Londonderry, Theresa, marchioness of, 5, 42, 179, 180, 181, 182, 198
Long, Walter, 36–7, 80, 154, 157, 160–01, 162, 169, 179, 202, 316, 325
Longford, County, 235, 319
Lonsdale, J.B., 71, 176
Loreburn, Lord, 216, 278, 279, 314
Loughborough Working Men's Group, 92, 323
Lucy, G., 324, 325
Lundy, Robert, 38, 122

MacNeill, Swift, 111
MacRaild, D.N., 322
Macready, Major-General Nevil, 239
Maghera, County Londonderry, 62
Magilligan Camp, County Londonderry, 274
Malone, Belfast, 294
Manchester, 49, 143, 169, 171, 254, 316, 318
Manchester Guardian, 41, 208, 244, 321, 329
Manitoba, Canada, 90
Mansergh, Nicholas, 91, 157, 323, 325
Markets, Belfast, 54
Marlborough, duke of, 55–6, 316
Martin, Joseph, 188
Masterman, C.F.G., 164

Maxwell, H., 321
McCalmont, Major-General Sir Hugh, 294
McCammon, T.V.P., 126
McCann, Agnes, 43, 104–5, 321
McCann, Alexander, 43, 104–5, 321
McCaughey, Sir Samuel, 91
McKean, Rev. Dr William, 131
McKee, Thomas, 143
McLean, I., 325
McMillan, A., 325
McMinn, J.R.B., 320, 324
McMordie, Sir William, 134
McNeill, Ronald, 51–2, 125, 134–5, 320, 321, 324
Megahey, Alan, 102, 323
Merseyside, 50, 77, 87, 141, 143, 145, 146, 155, 159, 167, 202, 319
Messines, battle of (1917), 296
Midlothian, 49, 165, 169, 223
Miles, E.G., 329
Millar and Lang, 97
Miller, David W., 70, 322
Millport, North Ayrshire, 166
Milner, Viscount Alfred, 4, 161, 162, 186, 189, 197–9, 200, 201–2, 203, 215, 234, 237, 256, 288, 308, 309, 318, 326, 327, 329, 330
Monaghan, County, 119, 138, 249
Montgomery, B.W.D., 114
Monypenny, William Flavelle, 70, 216, 322, 327
Moore, William, 71, 176
Morgan, A., 320, 322
Morley, Lord, 25, 243
Morning Post, 33, 40, 59–60, 112, 118, 179, 188, 189, 191, 194, 199, 204, 208, 224–5, 226, 237, 242, 308, 320, 321, 322, 324, 326, 327, 328
Mount Stewart, County Down, 33, 179
Mountjoy II, SS. See *Clydevalley*, SS.
Munro, Mr, 165
Munster, 98, 160
Musgrave Channel, Belfast, 269

Narrow Water Castle, County Down, 152, 177
Nation, 60, 209, 271, 322, 327, 330
National Unionist Association, 171
National Volunteers, 230, 250, 252, 273, 287, 291, 310, 318
Neal, Frank, 77, 322, 324
New Brunswick, Canada, 154
New Ross, County Wexford, 318

New South Wales, Australia, 91, 237
New York Times, 210, 327
New York, USA, 34
New Zealand, 90
Newcastle Chronicle, 317
Newcastle upon Tyne, Tyne and Wear, 169
Newman, Lieutenant-Colonel P., 159, 325
Newry and Mourne, Viscount, 139, 178
Newtownards, County Down, 33
Nightingale, W.H., 195, 326
Norfolk, duke of, 56
North Queen Street, Belfast, 54
Northcliffe, Viscount. *See* Harmsworth, Alfred Charles William.
Northern Whig, 31, 32, 41, 46–7, 49, 53–4, 86, 104, 132, 133, 136, 166–7, 171, 172, 321, 322, 323, 324, 325
Northumberland, Lord, 192, 326
Norwich, Norfolk, 161, 170
Nottingham, Nottinghamshire, 158
Nova Scotia, Canada, 142
Nugent, Major-General Sir Oliver, 250, 294

O'Brien, T.H., 327
O'Brien, William, 26–7, 278
Observer, 147, 208, 220–01, 226, 308, 317, 318, 324, 328
O'Clery, C., 320, 321, 324, 325, 328
O'Connell, Daniel, 11, 113, 228
O'Day, A., 323, 326
O'Halpin, E., 320
O'Hara, J., 328
Old Town Hall, Belfast, 117, 124, 125, 142, 248, 276, 277
Oldham, Manchester, 316
Oliver, F.S., 159–60, 216, 220, 237
Omagh, County Tyrone, 239
O'Neill, Terence, 302, 304
Orange Association of Manitoba, 90
Orange Order, 7, 14, 15, 21, 27, 29, 31, 34, 41, 54, 64, 66, 69, 71, 72, 74, 75, 76–8, 86, 90, 101, 119, 122, 123, 127, 130, 131, 135, 136, 137, 141, 144, 145, 171, 181, 200, 218, 219, 238, 247, 256, 272, 273, 287, 289, 295, 307, 322
Ormeau Park, Belfast, 29
Ormeau, Belfast, 1
Oxford, Oxfordshire, 4, 161, 194
Oxfordshire, 3, 10, 55, 56, 59, 60, 313

'Pacificus'. *See* Oliver, F.S.
Paget, Lieutenant-General Sir Arthur, 238–40

Paisley, Renfrewshire, 316
Pakenham, Colonel, 178
Pall Mall Gazette, 40, 66–7, 140–01, 147, 208, 220, 221, 222–3, 224, 226, 242, 308, 317, 318, 321, 322, 324, 328
Paris, France, 218, 242
Parliament Square, London, 320
Parnell, Charles Stewart, 11, 12, 24, 49, 81, 82, 193, 228
Patriotic, 141, 143
Pearce, Edward, 39, 124, 321, 324
Peatling, Gary, 227, 328
Perth, Perth and Kinross, 171
Photocrom Company, 97
Piccadilly, London, 215
Picture Stamp Company, 95
Pirrie, Lord, 21, 22, 78, 111
Pitt the Younger, William, 39
Plymouth, Devon, 172
Portadown, County Armagh, 124
Portora Hill, Enniskillen, 119, 150
Presbyterian Assembly Hall, Belfast, 131
Primrose League, 55, 202, 203, 226
Punch, 4, 97, 100, 227–31, 328
Purdue, Olwen, 176, 177, 178, 324, 326

Queen's University, Belfast, 311, 318–19

Ramsden, John, 157, 325
Raphoe, County Donegal, 86
Rawlinson, Major-General Henry, 237
Redmond, John Edward, 17, 21, 24–6, 27, 31, 45, 47, 49, 53, 86, 100, 111, 155, 173, 188, 195, 213, 227, 229, 231, 247, 278, 284, 287, 288, 290, 310, 320, 321
Redmond, Willie, 25
Rees, Russell, 81, 271, 322, 330
Reform Club, Belfast, 23, 32, 136, 140
Richardson, Lieutenant-General Sir George, 76, 195, 196, 211, 234, 248, 250, 251, 256, 326
RMA Sandhurst, Surrey, 316
Roberts, Lord, of Kandahar, 199, 233–5, 237, 328
Robinson, Geoffrey, 179, 210–11, 212, 213, 237
Roma, 263, 268
Roscommon, County, 104
Rothesay, Argyll and Bute, 166
Rothschild, Lord, 189, 199, 200
Rottingdean, Kent, 146
Royal Albert Hall, London, 50, 155
Royal Avenue, Belfast, 22, 32, 97, 133

Royal Horse Artillery, 240
Royal Irish Constabulary (RIC), 24, 28, 43, 105, 249, 261, 262, 267, 270, 271
Royal Irish Rifles, 236, 317

Sackville-West, Lieutenant-Colonel C.J., 237
Salisbury, Lord, 138, 186
Salisbury, Wiltshire, 169
Salvidge, Archibald, 144, 145, 146
Sarajevo, Bosnia and Herzegovina, 288
Saskatchewan, Canada, 90
Saturday Review, 22, 320
Saunderson, Colonel Edward, 13
Savory, Sir Douglas, 1, 311–12, 318, 330
Scholes, Andrew, 5, 105, 107, 323
Schwaben Redoubt, France, 295
Scotland, 32, 75, 112, 155, 162, 163, 164–6, 169, 171, 201, 225, 255, 258, 310, 323
Scotsman, 280
Scott, C.P., 207
Scottish Covenant (1638), 114, 201, 222
Seaford, Sussex, 294
Seely, Colonel John, 239, 240, 241, 242
Selborne, earl of, 184, 186–8, 198, 319, 326, 327, 330
Serpentine, London, 203
Sevenoaks, Kent, 203
Seymour, Sir E., 199
Shane's Castle, County Antrim, 178, 249
Shankill Road, Belfast, 54, 97, 130, 249
Shannon, C.B., 325, 329
Sheffield, South Yorkshire, 171
Sheil Park, Liverpool, 144, 146
Short Strand, Belfast, 54
Sinclair, Mrs, 181
Sinclair, Thomas, 15, 110, 114
Sixteenth Lancers, 240
Sligo, County, 119
Smiley, Lady, 261
Smith, Frederick Edwin (F.E.), 54, 57, 65, 66, 122, 125, 140, 143, 146, 159, 179, 215, 300, 320, 322
Smith, Jeremy, 174, 175, 197, 325, 326, 327, 330
Smylie, R.R., 163, 325
Somerset, 163
Somerset, duchess of, 183, 326
Somme, battle of the (1916), 25, 295–6, 315
South Africa, 39, 58, 197, 210, 216, 234, 251, 316, 318, 319. *See also* Boer War.
Spectator, 46, 223, 225, 226, 321, 328
Spender, Lady Lillian, 183, 252, 263–4, 326, 329

Spender, Wilfrid B., 183, 263, 264, 291, 296, 298, 319, 330
Spiro, Bruno 'Benny', 256, 257, 329
Springhill, County Tyrone, 178, 249
St Anne's Cathedral, Belfast, 107, 131
St Audries, Lord, 268
St Thomas's Parochial Hall, Belfast, 35
Stamfordham, Lord, 238
Standard, 56, 131, 167, 322, 324, 325, 328
Stanhope, Lord, 191, 192
Stead, W.T., 208
Stewart, A.T.Q., 2, 4, 39, 42, 321, 322, 323, 327, 328, 329
Strabane, County Tyrone, 96, 181
Strachey, John St Loe, 226
Stranraer, Dumfries and Galloway, 32
Stronge, Lady, 181
Suffolk, 318
Sunday Express, 317
Surrey, 279, 280, 314
Sussex, 148, 203, 294
Sydenham, Belfast, 29, 129

Tanner, Marcus, 148–9, 320, 322, 324, 325
Taylor, A.J.P., 327
Templemore Avenue, Belfast, 34
Templepatrick, County Antrim, 138, 261
Templetown, Viscount, 27, 75, 138, 146, 161, 177, 178, 261
Thiepval Wood, France, 295–6
Third Cavalry Brigade, 240, 245
Thirty-Sixth Ulster Division, 250, 276, 293–6, 314, 315, 317, 319
Thompson, J.L., 327
Thompson, Rev. J. Radford, 112
Times of India, 211
Times, The, 15, 23, 27, 30–01, 35, 39, 40–01, 46, 56, 59, 63, 118, 119, 120–01, 147, 148, 160, 165, 169, 170, 184, 194, 208, 209–10, 211–16, 226, 237, 242, 243, 259, 266, 270, 278, 284–5, 308, 314, 318, 320, 321, 322, 323, 324, 325, 326, 327, 328, 329, 330
Titanic, 34, 208, 217
Toronto, Canada, 275
Trench, H., 327
Trinity College, Dublin. *See* Dublin University.
Troon, South Ayrshire, 166
Troubles, the (modern), 3, 5, 206, 229, 252, 262, 302, 304
Truro, Cornwall, 172, 173

INDEX 339

Tunbridge Wells, Kent, 97, 161, 189
Tyrone, County, 86, 119, 123, 138, 178, 213, 249, 262, 274, 280, 289, 290, 298

Ulster Athletic Club, 195. *See also* British League for the Support of Ulster and the Union (BLSUU).
Ulster Club, Belfast, 42, 140
Ulster Defence Fund, 33, 78, 79, 84, 85, 91, 322
Ulster Division (Thirty-Sixth). *See* Thirty-Sixth Ulster Division.
Ulster Hall, Belfast, 13, 21, 22, 72, 75, 96, 126, 127, 130, 131, 132, 142
Ulster Liberal Association, 21, 23, 24, 62
Ulster Publishing Company, 97
Ulster Special Constabulary (USC), 298, 317, 319
Ulster Unionist Council (UUC), 4, 22, 29, 30, 52, 69, 71–3, 77, 80, 92, 96, 100, 124–6, 138, 161, 162, 170, 176, 180, 182, 196, 236, 247, 255, 256, 259, 276, 306, 314, 321, 322, 323, 324, 325, 326, 327, 329
Ulster Volunteer Force (UVF), 4, 7, 8, 21, 75, 76, 79, 85, 86, 93, 102, 103, 107, 108, 111, 137, 148, 156, 160, 176, 177–8, 180, 181, 183, 192, 194, 195, 196, 200, 209, 210, 211, 212, 218, 219, 220, 221, 225, 226, 228, 231, 232, 234, 238, 241, 247, 248–64, 267, 268, 269, 270, 271, 272–4, 275–7, 279, 285, 287, 290–01, 292, 293–6, 297, 298, 306, 307, 308, 310, 314, 317, 319, 327, 329, 330
Ulster Women's Unionist Council (UWUC), 105, 142, 180, 181–2, 313, 323, 324
Ulster's Solemn League and Covenant, 3, 7, 8, 15, 50, 68, 69, 70, 77, 84, 85, 105, 107, 108, 109, 112, 113–43, 147, 148–51, 159, 177, 181, 185, 188, 197, 198, 201, 203, 215, 221, 222, 223, 224, 226, 228, 249, 285, 307, 310, 313, 324, 325
Union Defence League (UDL), 100, 162, 198, 199, 202, 204
Unionist Associations of Ireland (UAI), 87, 88–9, 90, 93, 97, 101, 143, 162–6, 322, 323, 325
unionist clubs, 7, 14, 27, 30, 34, 41, 69, 74, 75–6, 114, 119, 120, 122, 126, 130, 132, 135, 137, 138, 143, 144, 145, 177, 247, 251, 307
Unionist Clubs Council (UCC), 177, 326

United Irish League, 317
Urquhart, Diane, 179, 180, 326
USA, 34, 91
UVF gun-running (1914), 4, 7, 78, 79, 101, 103, 108, 178, 179, 186, 195, 199, 206, 214, 218, 226, 233, 236, 241, 254, 255–72, 273, 274, 287, 296, 297, 307, 314, 317

Vancouver, Canada, 90
Vanity Fair, 97
Verdun, France, 294
Verney, Richard Greville. *See* Willoughby de Broke, earl.
Versailles, treaty of (1919), 299, 311, 317
Victoria Street, London, 199

Wales, 112, 155, 194, 199, 259, 318
Walker, Graham, 149, 322, 323, 325
Wallace, Colonel R.H., 77, 127, 128
Wallsend, Tyne and Wear, 171
War Office, London, 218, 231, 236, 238, 239, 240, 241, 275, 276, 291, 319
Ward, V.E., 219–20
Waterford, County, 318
Watkinson, Rev. Dr W.L., 112, 201
Watson, William, 222
West Lothian, 165
Westminster Gazette, 227, 328
Westminster, London, 7, 9, 15, 18, 27, 43, 54, 71, 72, 73, 79, 83, 105, 150, 160, 161, 176, 184, 185, 212, 235, 273, 285, 299, 300, 302, 303, 304, 307, 308, 311, 312, 318, 319
Weyman, S., 216
White, Arnold, 40
Whitehall, London, 54, 240, 241, 276
Whitehouse, County Antrim, 61
Whitla, Sir William, 96
Wick, Highland, 164–5
Wicklow, County, 11
Wilhelm II, 257
Wilkins, Vernon, 163–4
Wilkinson, G.R., 327
Wilkinson, James, 93
William III (of Orange), 119, 128, 133, 136, 146
Willoughby de Broke, earl, 4, 123–4, 138, 160, 162, 186, 190–03, 194–7, 198, 200, 205, 308, 309, 319, 326, 327
Wilson, Field Marshal Sir Henry Hughes, 4, 5, 235–7, 240, 241, 245, 319, 328
Wilson, Harold, 303

Wilson, Tom, 17, 320
Wiltshire, 203
Winchester, Hampshire, 319
Winnipeg, Canada, 90, 143
Wise, Pastor George, 77, 146
Wolverhampton, 161
Women's Covenant, 85, 181
Woodford, London, 317
Woodstock, Oxfordshire, 56
Workman, Clark & Co., 78, 263
World War I, 2, 4, 5, 8, 69, 87, 99, 101, 145, 173, 190, 207, 210, 231, 233, 245, 250, 272, 275–6, 277–8, 288, 289, 290, 291–2, 293, 294–6, 297, 298, 299, 302, 310, 311, 314, 316, 317, 318, 319, 325

World War II, 319
Wynne, F.C., 245

York Road, Belfast, 32
York, North Yorkshire, 143
Yorkshire, 57
Yorkshire Post, 329
Young Citizen Volunteers, 272